Graham Balfour

The Educational Systems of Great Britain and Ireland

Graham Balfour

The Educational Systems of Great Britain and Ireland

ISBN/EAN: 9783337323806

Printed in Europe, USA, Canada, Australia, Japan

Cover: Foto ©Paul-Georg Meister /pixelio.de

More available books at **www.hansebooks.com**

The
Educational Systems
of
Great Britain and Ireland

BY

GRAHAM BALFOUR, M.A.

OXFORD
AT THE CLARENDON PRESS
1898

PREFACE

IN this book I have tried to give a brief and fairly comprehensive account of general education in the United Kingdom during the nineteenth century. An impartial and even tedious catalogue of existing agencies seemed likely to be more effectual in indicating the present deficiencies and requirements of these islands than any more impassioned advocacy of my own or anybody else's views. The Introductory chapter was written last as a review of the sections, so that there has been no temptation to distort or even to emphasize any of the facts in order to illustrate the general views there suggested. On the other hand, the explanation of any passages or allusions in the Introduction which seem obscure will be found in the corresponding chapter of the book by reference to the Index.

My materials have been drawn largely from the many and lengthy series of Departmental reports which deal with so much of the education of the country, but more especially from the blue-books of the numerous Commissions and Committees which from time to time have examined the abuses or summed up the progress of schools, colleges, and universities—the outcome of what Bagehot called 'the modern stock-taking habit: the habit of asking each man, thing, or institution, "Well, what have you done since I saw you last?"' There are many subjects into which no investigation has recently been made, or on which no relevant report exists; in such cases I have tried to present the best information obtainable, and can only regret that there is no more definite judgment on record, or no more complete evidence to sum up.

Other books I have used rather as guides than as independent authorities; but no author, so far as I know, has ever before attempted to cover the whole field and describe the three grades of education in the four countries. Of those who have written monographs on separate departments of the subject, I should like to record my special debt to Sir Henry Craik for his admirable sketch of elementary education in England and Scotland [1], and to Dr. Karl Breul for his excellent account of the secondary schools of Great Britain and Ireland in Baumeister's *Handbuch* [2]. I have been at pains to give as many references as possible for my statements, and hope that the footnotes will form a sufficient guide to direct any one commencing investigations for himself.

---

[1] *The State in its relation to Education*, Sir Henry Craik, K.C.B.: The English Citizen Series, Macmillan, 2nd edition, 1896, 2s. 6d. I did not have the advantage of reading Mr. Holman's *English National Education* or the proof-sheets of Mr. Sadler's article in the second volume of *Special Reports* in time to make use of them.

[2] Baumeister, *Handbuch der Erziehungs- und Unterrichtslehre für höhere Schulen*, i. 2: Einrichtung u. Verwaltung des höheren Schulwesens: Grossbritannien, von Karl Breul, Ph.D.: Beck, Munich, 1897. It contains a good bibliography of our secondary school literature.

For the sake of clearness I have had to confine myself almost entirely to the central authorities which have controlled and the statutes which have regulated the development of our education. The origin and history of each department and each class of institutions have been described just so far as seemed necessary for the understanding of their present condition.

The very attempt, however, to describe our education as a set of systems at once draws attention to the defects with which it is most often reproached—its want of uniformity and its incompleteness. It has variety, it has elasticity, it has vigour ; there have been great energy, great generosity, and much power of practical administration shown in its service : but these qualities have varied widely in their application to individual circumstances, and a complete tribute to them would involve a description of almost every separate institution in the country. I have been unable to give any account of individual schools or institutions, and it was not until the region of higher education was reached that any notice of separate foundations became either feasible or desirable.

Professional education was at once too wide and too detailed a subject to be treated within any reasonable compass, and much else has been omitted which in itself it would have been desirable to include. As it stands, this is not a history of education but an account of the framework of which education is the life and spirit. I have had to deal only with the dry bones, for the first and most pressing need was a picture of the existing skeleton. Little allusion has been made to the general tendencies of the time, which have affected education as they have affected other departments of our activity[1]; no account has been taken of the theories[2] and hopes, and aims of those who have changed the schools and universities of 18co into the schools and universities of to-day; no reference has been made to foreign influence, philosophic or practical, and no comparison between this kingdom and other countries. I have recorded little but accomplished facts, and taken small notice of Bills which were never passed, recommendations which fell to the ground, or agitations before they issued in tangible success. I have been able to take no cognizance of private and individual or local enterprises, especially in the case of persons working for private emolument, although from such exertions many improvements in education have resulted[3]; and my references to the subjects taught and the differences of curricula are necessarily of the slightest.

In most instances I have given the latest figures obtainable. I have added a few tables of statistics as an Appendix, but the returns of different countries are very seldom closely comparable. The decrease of the population in Ireland is in such contrast to the increase in the rest of the kingdom, that any comparisons in that direction must be inseparable from the census returns, which I have accordingly included.

For convenience of description, Royal Commissions and Committees have been quoted in most cases under the name of the chairman, but a more exact reference

[1] Cf. M. E. Sadler, *Handbook of the Victorian Era Exhibition*, 1897, p. 39; Right Hon. A. H. D. Acland and H. Ll. Smith, *Studies in Secondary Education*, p. 2.
[2] Cf. Sir H. Craik, *The State in its relation to Education*, p. 41.
[3] Bryce Commission Report, v. p. 14.

will generally be found on the first mention of each report, and in all cases in the Index.

I have touched on many points, of which a specialized knowledge alone could secure immunity from error ; and though all possible care has been given, it cannot but be that in so widespread a net-work I have occasionally missed a connexion or made some mistake of detail. I should be greatly obliged to any one who would kindly send me any corrections to the Clarendon Press, Oxford.

I am indebted for information to many persons whom I have thanked elsewhere, but must here acknowledge my special obligations to Mr. G. W. Alexander, the Clerk of the Glasgow School Board, who bestows on the work of strangers an amount of labour and interest which many men fail to give to their own books; to Mr. T. W. Rolleston of Dublin ; to Mr. M. E. Sadler, who suggested this book ; and here in Oxford, to Mr. H. T. Gerrans and Mr. W. H. Hadow, Fellows of Worcester College.

September 1, 1898.

TABLE OF CONTENTS

C. Ireland.

D. Scotland.

III. HIGHER EDUCATION.

A. England.

B. Wales.

C. Ireland.

D. Scotland.

APPENDIX.

ABBREVIATIONS.

P. P. stands for the Parliamentary Papers of this country.

Roman figures following a date indicate the number of the bound volume in the official set for that year; occasionally a recent paper is quoted by its individual reference number.

Q. denotes the Question asked of a witness in evidence before a Commission or Committee.

Hansard, T.S. and F.S. denote the Third and Fourth Series of Hansard's *Parliamentary Debates.*

THE
EDUCATIONAL SYSTEMS
OF
GREAT BRITAIN AND IRELAND

INTRODUCTION

In these pages will be found side by side the systems in which education has developed itself during the nineteenth century in England, Ireland, Scotland, and Wales [1]. England has held the purse and called the councils in her capital, but the development of each system has progressed according to the nature and circumstances of the country. On the whole, the results are much what might have been predicted; at any rate it is not very difficult now to discern the national characteristics and conditions which have directed the course followed by each of the four countries. We can see England, businesslike and unphilosophical, slowly realizing first the commercial advantages of education, and then the possibility of applying scientific methods to the process: great in self-government, yet delegating to the localities only those powers which she intends them to use; making a working compromise at every step, and triumphantly disregarding consistency in details: strong in her sense of duty, greatly proud of her ancient institutions,

---

[1] The order is alphabetical, but in later chapters I have placed Wales next to England, as it is identified with it in elementary education.

b

liberal in grants once her hand is opened. There are Wales and Scotland, to whom education is far more dear: Wales, in a newly born fervour for knowledge, producing, as it were by magic, order out of chaos ; Scotland, equally thrifty with her little property and wise ; with an ecclesiastical history 'the most perverse and melancholy in man's annals,' yet without a religious difficulty in her schools ; having taught her children for centuries past to mind their book and get on in the world, and to be independent and upright—a lesson well learned at home and practised with great success abroad. Last comes Ireland, poor and in subjection ; passionately attached to her faith ; lovable and unreliable and helpless, the child among nations : the Celtic genius, mysterious and unpractical, 'always bound nowhere under full sail,' abandoned to obsolete methods and inadequate instruction, because reform means the calling up of many quarrels.

At the beginning of the nineteenth century many elementary schools were maintained in England by the clergy and devout laity, both within and without the Established Church. Indeed, very little elementary instruction given in this country was of any value which was not given in schools directly or indirectly connected with religious denominations or societies—unless the Lancasterian schools [1] be considered an exception. Consequently, when the State began to encourage education, it could not possibly do better than pay its grants over to the two leading educational societies [1] ; and when it began to direct education, its only hope of success was to conciliate the Established Church, and at the same time foster the efforts of those denominations which enjoyed a less splendid position.

So the new department began with a compromise, and utilized the conflicting materials with great patience and tact. The almost unconstitutional [2] device by which the Ministry avoided the veto of the Upper House was a

---

[1] *Vide* p. 3.
[2] *Vide* p. 5 ; cf. Hansard, T. S., xlviii. 1,335, *vide* p. 6.

triumph of political management, for if the country had not been in sympathy with the Ministers, they would have had to give way on this point, just as in fact they had to retreat in the matter of an undenominational Normal School. When the various elements of the system had been sufficiently developed, there followed the application of a searching business test prescribed by the Revised Code [1]. Educational monstrosity as that Code was, yet in its intolerance of shams and abuses it was in sympathy with the general refurbishing of endowed institutions (seen in the appointment of the permanent Charity Commission), with the creation of Civil Service Commissioners, with the first reform of the Universities from outside, and with the legislation for the Public Schools and Endowed Schools which immediately ensued.

When examinations had shown, as far as examinations could show, that the rudimentary teaching was reasonably efficient, the compromise was readjusted and elevated into a national system [2] from which the method of payment by result was gradually withdrawn, as the evil it was doing was revealed.

The whole attitude of the Education Department towards the schools has changed in the last quarter of a century, and though 'Lord John Russell's Bashaws' (as the early Inspectors were called) were grossly misrepresented, there can be no doubt that the tone of some of the earlier officials was far more departmental than educational.

The germ of the religious difficulty has lain in the elementary system from the beginning. The denominational schools which smoothed the early progress of the Education Department have brought their drawbacks with them. As ideals of education have improved, the cost of maintaining them has increased to such an extent, that it is hard for the poorest denominational schools to extract the requisite subscriptions from districts which either are heavily rated or have many calls made upon their generosity and their

----

[1] *Vide* p. 17.   [2] *Vide* p. 20.

attachment to their particular creed. Unfortunately it is just the denominational schools with the most limited means which are most in need of improvement[1].

The services of the Churches to Education have been many and splendid, and the Church of England has been pre-eminent in its self-sacrifice and devotion as in its privileges. It is a real misfortune that the policy of keeping out School Boards arises not only within the Church from a sincere and honourable desire to secure definite religious instruction, but outside it also from a penurious anxiety to reduce rates to the lowest possible minimum. It is a fact that Voluntary schools receive subscriptions from corporations and individuals who have no direct interest whatever in education, but pay them as a sort of blackmail to secure themselves against the heavier charges which a really

---

[1] This must not be taken as a depreciation of Church schools in general. Often in the country they are better than they would be under a small School Board. No deliberate verdict of any public authority has, so far as I know, been pronounced in the matter, for the Cross Commission of 1888 was divided into two strong parties from the outset. But the speech of Sir John Gorst in the House of Commons on April 19. 1898, seems to me to give a reasonable version of the present merits of the two systems; and if not a decision, it is at any rate the *obiter dictum* of a well-informed and dispassionate judge :—

' I have never concealed from the House my opinion that Board schools in towns and great urban districts are—with some significant exceptions—eminently successful. They have far better buildings than Voluntary schools. They have a far better staff—not that there are not in Voluntary schools individual teachers quite equal to Board school teachers, but they have more of them. If you compare the staffs of the general Board school with those of the Voluntary school, you find far more certificated teachers, far fewer child-teachers and uncertificated " women over eighteen." And besides that they have, as might very naturally be supposed from these advantages, very much better results. If you look at the county scholarship examinations, for instance, in any district, you will find that a far larger percentage of county scholarships is won by children in the Board schools of the large towns of London, Liverpool, Manchester, and so on, than by the children in Voluntary schools . . . .

' In rural schools the case is absolutely reversed. The country clergyman is a far better and more competent school manager than the parsimonious farmer or the ignorant village tradesman, and the exception to the general inferiority of the village Board schools are those cases in which a clever and energetic clergyman himself manages the Board and carries on the schools.' (*The Times*, April 20, 1898; *vide* also June 18, 1898.)

efficient system of schools within the district would demand. As Lord Salisbury has said, nothing is eternal in this world, not even a compromise, and it may be that the future has further modifications in store. In the meantime the enormous majority of School Boards throughout the country have declined to abandon religious teaching to other agencies [1], and our religious instruction, if somewhat deficient in dogma according to Anglican ideas, is probably as complete and thorough as that of any Protestant national system. The problem is likely to solve itself, and if no interruption comes from the platform and the hustings, little difficulty will arise within the schoolroom. It is inefficiency arising from lack of means rather than denominational intolerance which is likely ever to precipitate a crisis, and the most immediate need seems to be the provision of ampler opportunities of training for Nonconformists who desire to become elementary teachers [2].

It seems probable that the areas of local administration will some day be readjusted, perhaps in connexion with a scheme for regulating secondary as well as elementary schools. In the meantime the demands of reformers are chiefly for improvements within our existing system [3].

Let us turn for a moment to the minor departments of education which fell earliest under the care of the State.

As England was first in industries, so she was first in showing tenderness to the children engaged in her factories, mines, and workshops; and if her solicitude showed itself chiefly in preventing physical overwork, at any rate she was less negligent of these children than of her other boys and girls.

---

[1] *Vide* p. 26.

[2] In 1897, 1,146 male and 2,698 female candidates passed the examination and wished to enter Training Colleges, but there were only 880 vacancies for men and 1,300 for women. P. P., 1898, C. 8,781, p. 4.

[3] These requirements may be briefly summed up : more teachers, all fully qualified, well paid and well pensioned; raising of school age; no half-time; better attendance; better buildings; provision for transference to higher education.

Our prison management is not even yet characterized by extraordinary sympathy or enlightenment, but at any rate our reformatories were modelled on the best Continental example [1] ; and so far as we have failed. to obtain the best results in reformatories and industrial schools, our failure has been chiefly in consistent development of industrial training, and is common to the education of the whole country.

Poor Law education remains one of the most difficult of our social problems; if considered from the school point of view alone, the Scotch practice of boarding out all children and dispensing altogether with Poor Law schools seems preferable. Workhouse schools run occasional risks of inefficiency in their administration : large institutions are manifestly unsuitable for the training of children who, unless they return to the workhouse, will have to live the rest of their lives in little houses, where they will forget most of the lessons they have learned.

Our military and naval systems especially are the natural outcome of their conditions. Given a paid army and fleet which must spend a large portion of their service at foreign stations, it becomes necessary to provide interchangeable schools, and schools adapted for men as well as for children, and to ensure the power to improvise instruction on the smallest scale in the most remote places.

An urgent problem of the day in England is to decide where elementary education ceases and where secondary education begins, and this difficulty is due to the extreme confusion in which secondary teaching in this country is involved. No adequate system of intermediate schools exists to receive, as a matter of routine, those elementary pupils who are fitted for further education, and consequently the higher primary schools have pushed on into the secondary region, in some 'cases without possessing any satisfactory organization for definitely advanced instruction. Training of elementary teachers has long been

[1] Mettray.

regarded as indispensable, while training of secondary teachers, or at any rate of secondary masters, has been treated as a crotchet of wrong-headed and revolutionary theorists. The result is that elementary teachers have become a separate caste, whose qualities and preparation fit them admirably for their professional duties, and the defects of whose qualities fit them, it may be, less admirably for taking any wide view of education as a whole. At any rate, their excellent organization increases their power beyond its natural limits, and it would undoubtedly be for the benefit of secondary education if the division between the staffs of the two systems were somewhat less abrupt.

At the beginning of the century secondary education was given only in grammar schools [1], according to classical, or rather medieval ideals, and little was taught except the dead languages. Slowly the movement for reforming the abuse of charitable endowments made its way, and equally slow was the progress of public opinion. But even in the worst days there was much to be learned at the English Public Schools which was not written in the books and was hardly taught elsewhere. Many of the masters were men of great ability and force of character before ever Arnold came from Laleham in 1828 to make the name of Rugby famous and to change the face of education all through the public schools of England. They may not have been great in didactic; they may not have realized to the full their opportunities or their duties; the scholastic instruction may have been narrow, the school life rough and almost squalid; but the discipline of intercourse and common training enabled the schoolboys of these islands to become as well fitted to conduct their own affairs and the affairs of the State with honour and success as nations of far greater learning and far profounder theories. It was in these schools that there grew up spontaneously that system of games which has done so much for the physical development of the upper classes, and is too valuable to be

[1] Including, of course, the Public Schools.

allowed to degenerate into 'the tyranny and the idolatry of athletics.' The struggle between nations is becoming more intense, and the accomplishments necessary for success are more numerous and more elaborate than they were. We cannot afford to neglect the cultivation of any faculty of our minds, but in developing intellectual qualities we must beware lest we lose, for the few to whom it is open, that discipline of character which, being infinitely rarer and harder of attainment, is the admiration of foreign critics, who anxiously seek for the causes of the success of our ruling classes and the subtle reasons that underlie the superiority of the Anglo-Saxons.

The rival and supplement to this ancient[1] and distinguished system appeared in 1836 in the form of a trade designing school founded by the State. It developed into an Art Department, and in 1853 received the arbitrary addition of a Department for Science[2]. With this organization the first International Exhibition in London in the year 1851 had much to do, and the subsequent opportunities for comparing our industrial products with the work of other nations led with progressive force to a conviction that technical education was necessary, if we were to retain our position as the manufacturers and merchants of the world. The new department gradually trained teachers in Science and Art, and was the only channel of State aid to those who gave or received instruction in the new studies which were so necessary to our commerce. Unfortunately we needed two distinct things which are easily confused—secondary education and technical education[3]; the former is the necessary basis of the latter, but we tried to build without regard to the security of our foundations.

In the meantime the reform which had begun in the

---

[1] Bryce Report, v. 57 ; A. F. Leach, *English Schools at the Reformation*, p. 7 : Constable, 1896.

[2] *Vide* p. 169.

[3] Cf. *Secondary Education Legislation: Considerations worth weighing*, by Dr. R. P. Scott. Incorporated Association of Headmasters. London, 1898 : 8 pp.

old schools improved and greatly widened their work. Endowments were revised and made effective; not swept away or confiscated wholesale, but gradually and with much pains applied to new uses. In some cases there was a fusion between the two systems, and schools of old foundations, devoting themselves to the new studies, earned the new grants, and were fed from both sources. Secondary teachers began to organize themselves, to work for a higher standard, and to demand a guarantee of competence. Examinations were introduced and various tests of efficiency were applied to those who chose to submit to them, but unfortunately no organization of schools took place, and no measures were taken to supply the deficiencies which existed.

It was largely because local interests had not been represented in any active and practical way, and because it was nobody's business to see to the administration of the endowments, that so many school foundations had sunk into uselessness. The Taunton Commission[1] in 1867 assigned the provision of the necessary secondary schools to local authorities, but no such authorities with powers for this purpose were in existence, and none were created by the resulting measure. It was not until 1888 that County Councils were created by the Local Government Act, but being created they immediately received permission to raise a rate for technical education, and then, almost before they had time to use this power, they were given a well-filled pocket from which they might draw for the same purpose[2]. In one grant they received the power to employ for technical instruction an annual sum equal to the income of all the endowed schools of England, and the Science and Art Department was constituted arbiter of the meaning of 'technical instruction,' which it proceeded to interpret by the light of a hastily drawn statute as including all secondary education except the dead languages.

The need for technical education was recognized and to

[1] *Vide* p. 159.   [2] *Vide* p. 182.

a certain extent met by the Technical Instruction Act of 1889. The need for secondary education met with no formal recognition, but was so urgent that the administration of the Statute was twisted in order to satisfy it. Two chief evils resulted from this. First, the Science and Art Department, which has always had a thoroughly bad educational tradition, became to a considerable extent the State authority for secondary education, and the confusion between technical and secondary education became worse confounded. In the second place, the endowed schools, the original provision made for secondary education, were in many instances either neglected, or injured by competition, or were compelled in self-defence to join in the universal grant-hunt.

South Kensington in 1892 discontinued its payments for the most elementary science teaching, and practically transferred most of this burden to the local authorities. In 1895 it made literary instruction compulsory in all organized Science schools. In 1898 it transferred elementary drawing and manual training to the Education Department. In 1897 it offered to delegate—without losing its control as a central authority—its powers over 'technical instruction' to those local authorities which apply to it for recognition.

After many years the voice crying for organization has made itself heard, and a measure setting up some central authority in secondary education is only a matter of time. Political prediction lies outside the scope of this book, and how that authority will be constituted or what powers it will possess it is not for me to say. No proposal will satisfy the friends of secondary education in this country, which does not create at least an Advisory Council and a genuine Minister of Education [1], and require inspection

---

[1] For the history of proposals to create a Minister of Education *vide* Hansard, T. S., ccxix. 685 sqq.; cclxxx. 1,933 sqq.; P. P., 1884, No. 312, Report of the Select Committee of the House of Commons in 1883-84, over which the Right Hon. H. C. E. Childers, then Chancellor of the Exchequer, presided, appointed to consider how the Ministerial Responsibility under which the Votes for Education, Science, and Art were administered might best be secured; Taunton Report, i. 633; Bryce Report, i. 257.

and registration of schools, and registration and training of teachers [1].

England began the century with two Universities, and seems likely to end it with six, and the nuclei of more [2]. Tests and restrictions have been abolished; new studies have been freely introduced. The merely examining university has had a trial; colleges in separate cities have been federated; the Universities, old and new, have sent out lecturers in all directions, they have provided instruction and examinations wherever and in whatever subjects they were demanded, and they have even taken measures for the professional training of the secondary teachers whom they educate [3].

The creation of the university colleges and the introduction of university teaching into manufacturing towns have changed the face of higher education as it can hardly be changed again in England at any future time. Endow-

[1] Since these words were written the Duke of Devonshire has introduced the 'Board of Education Bill,' which is to be brought forward by the Government early next session. A Board of Education (practically the old Committee of Council, with one extra member) is to take the place of the Education Department and the Science and Art Department. Its President is to be appointed by the Queen, and if he be also Lord President of the Council, there is to be a Vice-President. The Charity Commission is to retain its powers, but some of them are to be exerciseable by the new body. Schemes under the Endowed Schools Acts are to be framed by the Charity Commission in consultation with the Board, and must be framed, if the Board so request. The Board may by its officers visit, inspect, and examine any endowed school, but these powers may be exercised in the case of any other school only with the consent of its governing body. Provision is made for the appointment of a consultative committee by the Queen in Council, to advise the Board on any question referred to it by the Board.

The Duke, in introducing the Bill in the House of Lords on August 1, 1898, stated that there was to be one Permanent Secretary to the Board, and that it might be found advisable to assign the work of the Board to Elementary, Secondary, and Technical Departments. The general establishment of local authorities for education is to be deferred for the present, and registration of teachers is to be provided by another Bill.

The whole scheme is in the barest outline, and if the measure is passed, everything will depend on the development of its suggestions and the spirit in which it is administered.

[2] *Vide* pp. 238-266.

[3] Cf. Bryce Report, i. 238.

ments may be increased; fresh foundations, fresh extensions, and fresh alliances may be made; but the difference between the eighteenth and nineteenth centuries, between the century of stagnation and the century of progress, will always be the most striking contrast in the history of English Universities. Further funds will be needed to enable the new institutions to develop and the old Universities to keep abreast of these developments. Already Cambridge has had to appeal to the generosity of its members and of the public, and Oxford wonders whether she can much longer wait for the coming of the millionaire.

It will probably be some time before the new conquests are consolidated and the best work found for each type of university; but although their minimum of requirements may be raised, and although the undue worship of athleticism in Oxford and Cambridge may be discouraged, it must always be borne in mind that the Universities are not merely the home of learning or the seat of research, but a school for the youth of the whole nation.

Fifty years ago education in Wales was at least as bad as any to be found in the whole kingdom, and the only sign of better things seemed to be a desire for knowledge, which manifested itself, however, chiefly in the somewhat unintelligent study of the Scriptures by Sunday School pupils of all ages [1]. The people really cared, they welcomed the opportunities offered them, and created new ones for themselves. Largely out of their weekly wages they paid for a training college and they paid for a university college. They pressed for an Intermediate Education Act and were fortunate 'enough to obtain it; they have systematized and extended their secondary schools, and they have devoted the whole of their Customs and Excise money, without exception, to education. They have attended their university colleges and made them efficient; finally, they have procured their federation in a national University. Wales, long yoked to England as it has been,

-----

[1] *Vide* p. 13.

has out of its limited material produced the most complete organization in the country within quarter of a century. Education elsewhere may rise to greater heights or have a longer tradition, but no other division of the kingdom has so definite an achievement to present as the intermediate and higher education of Wales.

In Ireland we have a poverty-stricken Catholic country governed by a bureaucracy mainly Protestant. It is characteristic of the difference between England and Ireland that when the National Board of Education was appointed in 1831, the outcry that was made was raised against the disendowment of Protestant missionary societies, and not, as in the case of the Committee of Council, against anything arbitrary or unconstitutional in the decree of the Castle. The system has been worked with constantly increasing forbearance and liberality, but it is impossible to regard Irish education as a whole with any degree of satisfaction. The principle of united secular education has failed. After half a century of refusal Government consented to subsidise and encourage denominational training colleges, and fewer and fewer children go to schools which are attended by any but members of their own faith. The attempt to introduce obligatory attendance has, with few exceptions, failed ; the attempt to encourage local rates has failed even more completely.

A large part of the elementary grant is still paid for the results of bare examination, and no alternative to individual examination (except in the case of infants) is allowed. Singing is taught only in one school in every seven, and this in a country which has some of the best Celtic melodies in the world. Drawing has not been introduced generally into the schools ; manual training has been grievously neglected by a people with a natural gift for decorative art, whose crying need is to develop manufactures and industrial pursuits. The study of agriculture, the one practical subject which has received attention, has fluctuated between ruinous extravagance and the mechanical study of text-books.

The few small secondary endowments have been reformed, but there is no secondary education which derives any benefit from Government except the Board of Intermediate Education with its large money payments and prizes[1]. Nowhere has the scramble for money.. among children and among rival institutions been set up so entirely to the exclusion of other systems, and nowhere has there been more complete disregard of the wholesome maxim that the school should not follow the examination, but examination should follow the school[2]. The great windfall of two and a third millions from the funds of the disestablished Church, and Ireland's share of the Customs and Excise money, have resulted only in this miserable mechanical scheme, and an Elementary Teachers' Pension fund pronounced bankrupt in 1897.

Partly from this system, partly from the decline in Irish industries[3] arises the monstrous disproportion of students of 15 and upwards to the rest of the population in Ireland.

STUDENTS OVER FIFTEEN IN 1891.

	Numbers.	Rate per Million.
England and Wales	147,489	5,085
Scotland	29,215	7,257
Ireland	95,766	20,356
United Kingdom	272,470	7,221

Between 1881 and 1891 this class increased in Ireland by 15,040 persons.

In higher education Sir Robert Peel's measure has provided at any rate two adequate University Colleges; but the attempt to require the condition of residence which was made by the Queen's University failed, and as a means to provide university education for Catholics the attempt proved unsuccessful. On the other hand, the Catholics resort to the examinations of the Royal University of Ireland as they resort to those of the Intermediate Board.

---

[1] A Vice-Regal Commission has been appointed to examine and report upon the system; it is not desirable to discount the verdict before it appears, but it is quite certain that in no other State of the Empire would such a body be composed solely of the persons who are responsible for the administration of the Act in question.

[2] Taunton Report, Q. 17,870.

[3] *Journal of the Statistical Society*, May, 1886. Mr. Charles Booth.

I. ELEMENTARY EDUCATION [1].

A. In England and Wales.

1. UNDER THE PRIVY COUNCIL.

i. *The Education Department.*

IN the beginning of the nineteenth century there was no system whatever of elementary education existing in England and Wales. Many endowments had been created, various societies raised considerable sums annually for the purpose, the clergy and ministers in many parts of the country were zealously promoting schools according to their different ideals, but there was no relation between the different bodies, no independent test of their work, and no control over them if they failed in the performance of it.

It was known that the elementary instruction given was very defective, and that the foundations of pious benefactors were in many cases badly administered; and in 1816 Henry Brougham moved for a Select Committee of the House of Commons to inquire into the former of these subjects [2], and himself sat as chairman until the report was presented in 1818. In that year he introduced a Bill for the appointment of a Royal Commission to inquire into

---

[1] I have not thought it necessary to look beyond the generally recognized division of education into elementary, secondary, and higher, nor do I offer any definition more subtle than that elementary education is the education given in public elementary schools, that higher education is that general training which is given in Universities and University Colleges, and that secondary education is that mass of instruction which lies between the elementary schools on the one hand and the Universities on the other, whether it ends in itself or leads to higher instruction.

[2] 'The Education of the Lower Orders.'

educational charities existing in England and Wales ; and these Commissioners were appointed and re-appointed until 1837 [1]. The scope of the first inquiry was confined to the metropolis, and that of the second was much restricted by the House of Lords' amendments to the enabling Act, but the results showed that neither needs nor abuses had been exaggerated.

Education was in the air, but it was some time before Parliament proceeded to deal with it as a practical question.

A Bill had been introduced by Mr. Whitbread in 1807 to found a school in every parish, as in Scotland, with power to employ local rates ; and this first measure dealing with English elementary education as a whole was passed by the House of Commons but rejected by the House of Lords. In 1820 Brougham brought in an Education Bill based on his investigations, but religious jealousy and dislike of change rendered all attempts at legislation abortive, and it was not until 1833 [2] that the House of Commons voted a sum of £20,000 ' for the purposes of education.' It was passed late in the session, and carried by a majority of twenty-four, only seventy-six members being present. Joseph Hume voted against it on the ground that Brougham's reports had shown that there was a sum of half a million applicable to these purposes. Cobbett declared that the sole result of the movement was ' to increase the number of schoolmasters and mistresses, that new race of idlers ' ; and that this was nothing but an attempt ' to force education on the country— a French, a Doctrinaire plan,' to which he should always be opposed [3]. As it was a vote in Supply, it needed no confirmation from the House of Lords, and the money was given to the Treasury to be administered in the erection of school-houses in Great Britain [4].

---

[1] 58 Geo. III, c. 91 ; 59 Geo. III, c. 81 ; 10 Geo. IV, c. 57 : 1 & 2 Will. IV, c. 34 ; 5 & 6 Will. IV, c. 71 ; *vide* p. 155, The Charity Commission ; Parliamentary Papers, 1877, lxvi. p. 21.

[2] August 17, 1833.

[3] Hansard's Parliamentary Debates, Third Series, xx. 734.

[4] Appropriation Act, 1833, 3 & 4 Will. IV, c. 96. In the following

In 1833 two voluntary societies shared between them the main part of such weekday teaching as was given to the poor in England and Wales. The larger of these, the National Society for Promoting the Education of the Poor in the Principles of the Established Church [1], had been founded in 1811 to take up the educational part of the work of the Society for Promoting Christian Knowledge, founded in 1698 [2], and its schools were carried on in accordance with the ideas of Dr. Bell [3]. The pupils were all obliged to receive instruction in the Liturgy and Catechism of the Established Church of England, and were required to attend its prayers and services. If the Society ever consented to admit the children of other denominations to its teaching, it was only for missionary purposes and on its own terms, but it never sought nor desired their attendance [4].

The British and Foreign School Society was founded in 1808 to carry on the work of Joseph Lancaster, and received its present name in 1814. The Bible was read in its schools, but no denominational religious teaching was given; children of Church folk, Dissenters, Roman Catholics, and Unitarians were all received and taught. It naturally derived its chief support from Dissenters, and was regarded as the society representative of them.

As there was no State machinery in existence for the administration of the new grant, the Treasury Board employed the best means ready to their hand, and relied solely on the recommendations of these two Societies [5] to

years the same sum was voted for 'school-houses in England' only (4 & 5 Will. IV, c. 84).

[1] English National Schools, i. e. schools in connexion with this Society, must not be confused with the Irish National Schools under the Commissioners of National Education, p. 88.

[2] *Account of the Efforts of the Society for Promoting Christian Knowledge on behalf of National Education:* T. B. Murray, 1848.

[3] *An Old Educational Reformer: Dr. A. Bell*, by Prof. J. M. D. Meiklejohn: Blackwood, 1881.

[4] Archdeacon Denison, *Notes of my Life*, pp. 105, 137: Oxford, 1878. Dean Gregory, *Elementary Education*, p. 70, 1895: National Society.

[5] The National Society in fact allotted £69,710 in grants in the next five years, while the British and Foreign Society only found use for

make grants in aid of building new school-houses, subject only to the condition of half the cost being met by voluntary contributions, actually received, expended, and accounted for, while preference was given to applications from large cities and towns [1], and therein to schools intended to accommodate four hundred scholars and upward [2]. Some useful work was begun by Parliament in the way of facilitating the provision of sites for schools [3].

During the sessions of 1834 and 1835 a Select Committee of the House of Commons took evidence on the state of public instruction, but made no recommendations. In 1838 another Select Committee [4], reporting on the best means for providing useful education in large towns in England and Wales, considered it desirable that provision should be made for not less than one-eighth of the population, but 'under existing circumstances and under the difficulties which beset the question,' they were 'not prepared to propose any means for meeting the deficiency beyond the continuance and extension of the grants at present made by the Treasury for the promotion of education through the medium of the two Societies [5].' The proposal to create a Board or Office of Education under the control of Parliament was negatived without a division. Mr. Wyse [6] fought stoutly for tolerance and enterprise, but to no apparent purpose [7].

Nevertheless in 1839 a further step was taken. From the attitude of the House of Lords it was evident that no popular educational measure had any chance of passing into law. What, however, could not be done with the aid of

£34,145, and granted only about a third as many applications as their more popular coadjutor (P. P., 1837–38, xxxviii. pp. 327, 354; vii. p. 166). Successful applicants must submit to an audit, and to making periodical reports on the state of their schools (Minute, August 30, 1833; P. P., 1834, xlii. p. 525). 'But the matter was left to the superintendence of the two Societies (P. P., 1837–38, xxxviii. p. 365).

[1] Minute, August 30, 1833.
[2] Minute, March 7, 1834; P. P., 1834, xlii. p. 529.
[3] School Sites Acts, 1836, 1841, 1844, 1849, 1851.
[4] Of which Mr. Slaney was chairman and Mr. Gladstone a member.
[5] Report, p. xi.   [6] *Vide* p. 102.   [7] P. P., 1837–38, vii. 157.

the Upper Chamber was dexterously carried into effect by
a method for which its consent was not needed [1].

The Queen published an Order in Council appointing a
Special Committee of the Privy Council to administer the
money voted by the Commons. The Lord President of the
Council, Lord Lansdowne, was chairman, and the other
members were the Lord Privy Seal, the Chancellor of the
Exchequer, the Home Secretary, and the Master of the Mint.

It is perhaps worth quoting part of the letter from Lord
John Russell to Lord Lansdowne, requesting him to act on
this Committee ' for the consideration of all matters affecting
the education of the people,' as this clearly expresses the
views with which the Committee was formed and the needs
which it was intended to supply.

'Whitehall, *Feb.* 4, 1839.

' MY LORD,

'I have received Her Majesty's Commands to make
a communication to your Lordship on a subject of the
greatest importance. Her Majesty has observed with deep
concern the want of instruction which is still observable
among the poorer classes of Her subjects. All the inquiries
which have been made show a deficiency in the general
Education of the People which is not in accordance with
the character of a Civilized and Christian nation.

' The reports of the chaplains of gaols show that to a large
number of unfortunate prisoners a knowledge of the fundamental truths of natural and revealed Religion has never
been imparted.

' It is some consolation to Her Majesty to perceive that
of late years the zeal for popular education has increased,
that the Established Church has made great efforts to promote the building of schools, and that the National and the

---

[1] The Upper Chamber, by 229 to 118, presented an address to the
Queen, which was practically a protest against the new Committee
(Hansard, T. S., xlviii. p. 1255). The Queen replied, ' I cannot help
expressing my regret that you should have thought it necessary to take
such a step on the present occasion ' (ibid. vol. xlix. p. 128).

British and Foreign School Societies have actively endeavoured to stimulate the liberality of the benevolent and enlightened friends of general Education.

'Still much remains to be done; and among the chief defects yet subsisting may be reckoned the insufficient number of qualified schoolmasters, the imperfect mode of teaching which prevails in perhaps the greater number of the schools, the absence of any sufficient inspection of the schools and examination of the nature of the instruction given, the want of a Model School which might serve for the example of those societies and committees which anxiously seek to improve their own methods of teaching, and finally the neglect of this great subject among the enactments of our own voluminous Legislature[1].'

The Committee was appointed on April 10, and first met on April 13.

In 1835 a sum of £10,000 had been voted by the House of Commons for the erection of Model Schools, and the creation of a State Training College was the scheme which the Ministry now had most at heart to carry out. It was proposed to divide the religious instruction given in this school into special and general, and to entrust the former, the denominational instruction, to licensed religious ministers belonging to the various communities[2]. This arrangement, which had already been carried out at Dublin in a more extreme degree, raised such a storm of indignation that all idea of the school had to be dropped, and the annual vote was only carried in the House of Commons by 275 against 273 votes. It was assumed that the system proposed for the Normal School would be adopted in all schools, and there was a strong opposition to any weakening of denominational instruction[3].

[1] P. P., 1839, xli. p. 255.   [2] Newcastle Commission Report, vi. 300.
[3] The vote this year was taken for Great Britain as in 1833, and became £30,000 by the inclusion of the ten thousand pounds which in 1834 and 1836 and the following years had been voted separately for Scotland (4 & 5 Will. IV, c. 84; 6 & 7 Will. IV, c. 98; 7 Will. IV, c. 79; 1 & 2 Vict. c. 111). *Vide* p. 132.

However, the money was voted, a permanent staff of officials was appointed [1], and Dr. Kay (afterwards Sir James Kay-Shuttleworth), an Assistant Commissioner of Poor Laws, well known for his interest in the education of the poor, was made the secretary of the new Committee. 'A born educator,' Matthew Arnold called him, 'an earnest student of methods and problems of education [2].'

By an early Minute [3] of the Committee (June 3, 1839), the money which had been voted in 1835, and was to have been spent in creating the State School, was directed to be divided equally between the two Societies in order to establish Training Colleges, and it was readily met by corresponding contributions on their part. The Committee decided that the annual Government Grant was still to be spent chiefly in granting aid to the building of school-houses, and only exceptionally of school-houses unconnected with the two Societies. But the continuous right of inspection by Government was to be a condition of assistance to any school, and the principle of requiring a corresponding local contribution in all cases was observed. Later Minutes of the same year laid down that in helping schools other than those connected with the two Societies, two conditions were to be observed—that the Bible at least should be read as part of the regular instruction, and that there should be a conscience clause to the effect that children whose parents objected might be withdrawn from the religious instruction [4].

The Education Establishment was thus fairly instituted,

---

[1] The appointment of the first two Inspectors, Rev. W. Allen and Mr. Tremenheere, was sanctioned Dec. 9, 1839. *London Gazette*, p. 2608.

[2] T. H. Ward's *Reign of Queen Victoria*, ii. p. 265 : Smith, Elder & Co., 1887. The subsequent secretaries have been Mr. (afterwards Lord) Lingen, 1849-69, promoted to be Permanent Secretary to the Treasury; Mr. (afterwards Lord) Sandford, 1870-84, subsequently first Under-Secretary for Scotland; Mr. Cumin, 1884-d. 1890; Sir George Kekewich, 1890.

[3] The Minutes of the Committee in chronological order will be found in P. P., 1854-55, vol. xli.

[4] These applied to Church schools, unless recommended by the National Society (Report of Select Committee of House of Commons, 1866, Lingen, Q. 3,461, 3465).

and proceeded to do the best work that lay in its power; but it had to feel its way cautiously, for there was much jealousy between the various religious bodies, and great suspicion of the new creation of the State[1].

The opposition of the Established Church to the new Inspectors was settled in 1840[2] by a concordat by which the Archbishops of Canterbury and York were to approve of the Inspectors appointed to inspect Church schools in their provinces. In practice none but clergymen were appointed for this branch of the work, and no objection was ever raised to any nomination, but the Church attached great importance to the point, and the adhesion of their schools was at that time of the most critical importance to the new scheme.

The British and Foreign School Society received in 1843[3] a similar privilege as to the approval of the Inspectors examining their schools, and the principle was afterwards extended to other Nonconformists.

In 1843 Sir James Graham introduced a Government Bill for the Regulation of Factories, to which he had tacked on a number of educational clauses[4]. A distinct preponderance was to be given to the established clergy in the management of the proposed schools for factory children, and the Dissenters were up in arms at once. Their opposition was not to be appeased; it was calculated that twenty-five thousand petitions were presented against the Bill, containing not less than four millions of signatures[5]. No concessions were of any avail; the Bill was dropped, and did not reappear as a measure of educational reform.

In 1843 grants in aid were extended to teachers' houses, and to furniture and apparatus for schools; and in the following year the Inspectors were directed to offer to visit and advise schools which had received building grants before 1839, but which the Government had acquired no

---

[1] Taunton Report, Q. 17,429.   [2] Minute, August 10.
[3] Ibid. Nov. 30, 1843.
[4] *Life of Lord Shaftesbury*, E. Hodder, vol. i. p. 461 : London, 1886.
[5] F. Adams, *The Elementary School Contest*, p. 122 : London, 1882.

right to inspect. The results of these early inspections showed that the general quality of the education given was almost worthless : even of the children who came to school only one half learned to read at all, and one quarter to write [1]. The system of teaching by means of monitors, common to both Lancaster and Bell, stood hopelessly condemned [2], while it was impossible to expect any general improvement in the schools as long as the mass of teachers was alike incapable and untrained. In 1847 in the House of Commons Macaulay described the schoolmasters of the poor. 'How many of these men are now the refuse of other callings—discarded servants or ruined tradesmen ; who cannot do a sum of three ; who would not be able to write a common letter ; who do not know whether the earth is a cube or a sphere, and cannot tell whether Jerusalem is in Asia or America ; whom no gentleman would trust with the key of his cellar, and no tradesman would send of a message.' As for the dames, let one who was quoted the same evening speak for herself. 'It's little they pays us, and it's little we teaches them [3].'

Progress, however, was being made, and on sure ground. The grant of £10,000 for Normal Schools to the Societies had resulted in the opening of St. Mark's Training College at Chelsea in connexion with the National Society in 1841, and of the new buildings of the British and Foreign School Society in the Borough Road in 1842 [4]. Messrs. Kay and Tufnell had been experimenting, largely at their own expense, with the school at Battersea [5], which was handed over

---

[1] In the Midlands: Sir Henry Craik, *The State in its relation to Education*, p. 32 ; Sir J. Kay-Shuttleworth, *Four Periods*, 1862, p. 473.

[2] Horace Mann, of Boston, wrote after his visit to England in 1844 (where he had seen on one occasion a thousand pupils in one Lancasterian schoolroom): 'One must rise to some comprehension of the vast import and significance of the phrase "to educate" before he can regard with a sufficiently energetic contempt that boast of Dr. Bell, "Give me twenty-four pupils to-day, and I will give you twenty-four teachers to-morrow"' (*Report of an Educational Tour*, p. 58: Simpkin, Marshall & Co., 1846).

[3] Hansard, T. S., xci. pp. 1016, 1060.   [4] Newcastle Report, i. p. 111.

[5] Kay-Shuttleworth, *Four Periods of Public Education*, p. 293.

in 1844 to the National Society[1]. There were already nine of these training establishments, the want of which the Government had felt so keenly in 1839, but the quality of the students desiring to become elementary schoolmasters was as yet very inferior, and the supply inadequate. .

To remedy these defects the Committee published a Minute and Regulations (August 25, Dec. 21, 1846) which established new principles and marked a new departure. The double purpose of improving the instruction given in the elementary schools and of providing a succession of pupils for the training colleges was to be served[2]. The grants were no longer to be confined to the starting of schools. Monitors were to be replaced by pupil teachers, from whom greater progress and higher qualifications were required; training and Training Colleges were to be encouraged by grants; teachers and pupil teachers were to receive grants direct from the State. Before pupil teachers were authorized in any school, the Inspector was to report on the teacher, the school, and the local resources. Pupil teachers, not less than thirteen years of age, were to be apprenticed for five years, during which they received annual grants, and were then eligible for the 'Queen's Scholarships' of £20 to £25 a year during their course at some Training College under inspection[3]. Teachers who had undergone this preparation and obtained certificates received an annual grant in augmentation of their salary proportionate to the length of their training and subject to the annual report on their school, and provision was made for pensions on their retirement[4]. Voluntary contributions, however, must provide teachers with a house rent free, and a further salary equal

[1] M. Arnold, T. H. Ward's *Reign of Queen Victoria*, vol. ii. p. 247.
[2] Newcastle Commission, i. 22; *Four Periods*, p. 481.
[3] The system has lasted to the present day, and its continuance was recommended by a Departmental Committee, which reported in 1898 (P. P., C. 8,761). The age was raised in 1897 from fourteen to fifteen; but a further rise was recommended, together with increased opportunities and qualifications.
[4] All grants to teachers were made by Post Office Orders, payable personally to them.

to not less than twice the amount of their augmentation grant.   Mistresses received two-thirds of the grant which was paid to masters' of the same class.

Teachers received an annual payment for the pupil teachers under their charge. The Training Colleges received grants of £20 to £30 for Queen's Scholars for each year of their training.

This extension of the Government Grants apparently marks the decision of the State department to accept as permanent the denominational system of education in England and Wales in the form which had been gradually developed.   In the first instance the whole scheme of education was regarded as a temporary and provisional expedient, but as the system became consolidated and assumed larger proportions than had seemed possible, it was thought unfeasible to change it[1].

In July, 1847[2], teachers who had not been at any Training College received permission to enter for certificates which carried with them the new augmentation of salary, and it is these certificates which have become the indispensable qualification for teachers in public elementary schools, and not as yet the professional training at a College[3].

In 1847 and the following years difficulties arising as to clerical supremacy and monopoly were chiefly fought out over the 'management clauses' of the Committee of Council, who endeavoured gradually to introduce such safeguards of·conscience clause as they could induce the denominations to adopt.   When the Department was first created, it was found that the trust deeds of schools were often very loosely and inadequately drawn, and that it was necessary to insist on seeing the deeds of new schools and ascertaining that

---

[1] Newcastle Commission, vol. vi, evidence of Sir James Kay-Shuttleworth, Questions 2,345, 2,351, 2,360; Mr. Chester, Q. 704; vol. i. p. 20. Mr. Lowe once compared it to a man who went to call on a friend and stayed thirty years (Hansard, T. S., clxv. 197).

[2] Minute, July 23, 1852.

[3] The first examinations were held in 1848 : for Church of England candidates in April; for Scotland in May and June; and for English Dissenters in the autumn (P. P., 1847–48, vol. l. pp. 55, 61).

sufficient provision was made that the buildings should be permanently devoted to school purposes[1]. Four specimen forms, with clauses varied to suit circumstances of population, had been recommended by the Commissioners as models, and in 1847 the adoption of these was declared compulsory. Certain of the clergy objected to a clause securing a share in the management to lay subscribers, but it was retained ; and into these deeds in 1853 a conscience clause, which the Wesleyans had adopted in 1847, was introduced, permitting children to be withdrawn during religious instruction in Church schools if their parents objected. Against this there was a more vigorous struggle, but a few years later it was generally adopted, subject to the right of the school to repay the grant and repeal the obnoxious clause, though such a right was never actually exercised[2].

In 1847 grants of school books and maps were made on greatly reduced terms to schools by arrangement with publishers and with assistance from Government, but no publication of books was ever undertaken by the Department as in Ireland, nor have recognized Government text-books ever been imposed on the schools. Arrangements were also made by which Roman Catholics found it possible to submit to the conditions necessary to earn a grant[3]. No Inspector was allowed to examine in religious knowledge where the managers objected on religious grounds[4].

In 1846 the Home Secretary undertook in the House of Commons that there should be an inquiry under the authority of the Committee of Council into the state of education and the provision for teaching English to the labouring classes in Wales. Three Commissioners were

---

[1] Temple, *Oxford Essays*, p. 226, 1856.

[2] Gregory, *Elementary Education*, p. 72 ; Hansard, T. S., clxxvi. p. 519 ; Newcastle Report, vi. 100. The clause, however, was not invariably insisted upon till 1864 (Adams, *The Elementary School Contest*, p. 189). No Minute was ever issued on the conscience clause in National Schools, owing to the difficulties of negotiation (Report of Select Committee of House of Commons, 1865 ; Q. 452, Lingen).

[3] Minute, December 18, 1847.   [4] Minute, July 10, 1847.

appointed, and reported in the next year[1] that in Wales and Monmouthshire, with a population (in 1841) of 1,046,000, there were 1,657 weekday schools with 78,846 pupils on the books. The Sunday Schools, numbering 2,664 and receiving 256,270 scholars of all ages, had hitherto been almost the sole, as they were still the most congenial, centres of education[2]. The ordinary accommodation was unspeakably bad[3]; the teaching was most inefficient[4]; the ignorance appalling[5]; the Bible was used as a mere spelling-book[6]; and such endowments as there were, were grievously abused or neglected[7]. The Commissioners were not instructed to go beyond a report and make any recommendation.

By 1853 the great want at first existing of proper school buildings and trained teachers had been supplied to a sufficient extent to allow the attention of those interested in education to be turned to the shortness and irregularity of the attendance of the pupils in England and Wales[8].

In this year Lord John Russell introduced a Bill which gave a power of rating to towns of over 5,000 inhabitants, in order to supplement the local income of elementary schools. As the rural districts were supposed to be too poor to pay an additional rate, the Bill did not apply to them, and they received from the Central Government[9] a capitation grant of four to six shillings a head for boys' schools, and three to five shillings a head for girls' schools, paid to the managers on all children making a certain specified attendance, provided that the teacher in charge had the certificate of the Government examination (or at first of mere registration), and that at least three quarters of the children were present at the inspection.

---

[1] P. P., 1847, xxvii.   [2] Report, i. 7.
[3] Ibid. i. 20; ii. 28, 348.
[4] Ibid. i. 37; ii. 29, 281, 354. ' The Welsh workman never becomes a clerk or agent; he may be an overseer or subcontractor' (ibid. i. 7).
[5] Ibid. i. 32; ii. 47, 385.   [6] Ibid. i. 33; ii. 39, 389.
[7] Ibid. i. 45; ii. 21, 393.   [8] Newcastle Report, i. 24.
[9] Minute, April 2, 1853.

The grant was conditional on the income from endowment, subscriptions, collections, and school pence having amounted in the preceding year to fourteen shillings per scholar in boys' schools and twelve shillings a head in girls' schools. The principle was thus abandoned of making the Government Grant proportionate to local effort; only a certain previous effort was required to give a certain amount of instruction to a certain number of children, but the capitation grant was not required to be met by any sum in relation to it[1].

The Borough Bill, however, did not pass, and for three years there existed an anomaly between country schools and borough schools, until in 1856 another Minute of the Department extended the attendance grant to the non-rural schools.

This grant was intended to encourage attendance, which there was no prospect of making compulsory; but there were no adequate means of checking the returns, and there is no doubt but that these Minutes led to a very exaggerated estimate of the number of children receiving a regular education.

In 1856 the first measure relating to English elementary education successfully passed through Parliament, but it was very limited in its aim. By an Order in Council of February 25, 1856, the Education Department was founded under this title, and the two existing bodies, 'The Educational Establishment of the Privy Council Office' and 'The Establishment for the Encouragement of Science and Art[2],'

---

[1] This had also been the case with grants to pupil teachers (Newcastle Report, vi. Q. 652). The Minute was also a new departure and an exception, both from what came before and what followed after, in that it established a distinction between grants to boys and girls. Otherwise the State has always made grants to both sexes on the same scale in elementary education, and the only subsequent difference has lain in the encouragement of different subjects suited to the respective occupations of the sexes, e.g. agriculture and laundry-work. Boys and girls are taught in the same classes to some extent, especially in the smaller country schools, but there is much more co-education in Scotland. Cf. Bryce Report, i. 159.

[2] *Vide* p. 168.

hitherto under the direction of the Board of Trade, were included in it under the chairmanship of the Lord President of the Privy Council. By the new statute (19 & 20 Vict. c. 116) the office of Vice-President of the Committee of Privy Council on Education was created to provide the Department with a responsible representative in the House of Commons, from which it derives its annual grant. Before this the Committee had as its only official representative the Lord President of Council, its chairman, who was always a member of the House of Lords. Most of the members of the Cabinet who constituted the Committee were members of the House of Commons, but they were not individually responsible for the proceedings of the Committee, and although consulted on important steps they were seldom in fact closely identified with it[1].

A general supervision of the education under Government control seems to have been contemplated at this time for the Department[2]. The Order in Council of February 25 this year sanctioned inspection by H. M. Inspectors of the Army schools and of the Naval land schools as part of their duties, and directed the Department to advise the Charity Commissioners. In 1857 the grants to Reformatories and Industrial Schools were greatly extended. But the tide turned, and of these projects hardly anything survived. Even the inspection of the Poor Law Schools was withdrawn from the Department in 1863, and the Inspector, to whom was assigned the naval work, was transferred to the Navy in 1863.

In 1858 a Royal Commission was appointed, with the Duke of Newcastle as chairman, to inquire into 'the state of popular education in England, and as to the measures required for the extension of sound and cheap elementary

---

[1] The Vice-President is selected by the Premier on the same grounds as any other Minister, and changes with the Administration, but he has seldom been included in the Cabinet. Lord Sandon in 1874, and Mr. Acland in 1892, were the exceptions and not the rule.

[2] On this basis the Committee of Council was constituted at this time (Sandford: Childers Committee, 1884, Q. 249).

instruction to all classes of the people.' Their most exhaustive and able report was published in six volumes in 1861, and although optimistic in tone, disclosed a state of things very far from satisfactory.

Less than two-thirds of the estimated number of children in England and Wales were returned as attending school at all, though even their attendance must often have been merely nominal[1].

Of these two-thirds, only two-thirds were attending any public school, and of these again little more than half the children were at public schools receiving any grant subject to a Government inspection. Of inspected schools only the upper classes were reasonably efficient, and only one quarter of the pupils remained at school to an age sufficient to get into these classes[2]. Thus only one-seventeenth part of the children of the poor in this country were receiving an education which could be definitely declared to be satisfactory[3].

The Commission reported that a county rate also should be levied, to be administered by a County Board of Education with county examiners (in addition to H.M. Inspectors) to examine individual scholars and apportion the share of the local rate; a like arrangement was to hold good in the boroughs; there was to be a searching examination of every child in elementary subjects in every school receiving

---

[1] The total estimated population of England and Wales in 1858 was 19,523,103, and by modern calculations one-fifth of these would be children of school age belonging to the class usually found in public elementary schools (Cross Commission Final Report, p. 53, last paragraph), i. e. 3,904,600. The children attending weekday schools were returned at 2,535,462, of which number 1,675,158 were in public schools, but only 917,255 in schools in receipt of an annual grant (Newcastle Report, i. 573–574, 591), i. e. 917,255 out of 3,904,600 children.

[2] Craik, p. 55; Newcastle Report, vol. i. 171, 242, 245.

[3] The majority report of the Cross Commission in 1886 (Final, p. 14) quotes the opinion of three Inspectors at the time to show that the proportion of good education was greater. The minority, however, did not accept this view (p. 240), and Mr. Cumin considered the numbers overstated. The Newcastle Commission thought that three-fifths of the children made sufficient attendance to obtain a fair elementary education as then understood, if they were properly taught. I. 225.

grants : the religious arrangements were not to be altered, and compulsory attendance was not to be introduced [1].

No legislation was attempted at the time, but in the same year, 1861, the Rt. Hon. Robert Lowe, afterwards Lord Sherbrooke, and then Vice-President of the Committee, published a Revised Code of all the Minutes issued by the Education Department which had been codified for the first time in the preceding year.

It may here be noticed that it was definitely laid down in this first code and repeated in the Revised Code that the object of the Government Grant was 'to promote the education of children belonging to the classes who support themselves by manual labour.'

There was no attempt at a new system [2], but the revision amounted to a revolution in existing arrangements. 'Payment by results' was now the ruling principle. The grant [3] to schools was to depend entirely on the results of an individual examination by H.M. Inspector passed by each child in reading, writing, and arithmetic, subject to the conditions that the children must have made a certain number of attendances, that the school must be held in approved premises and under the charge of a certificated teacher, and that the girls must be taught plain needlework as part of the ordinary course of instruction. The backward children were no longer to be neglected for the sake of the more promising scholars, but every child was actually to receive at least his minimum of education. Payments were to be made, not personally to teachers any longer, but to the managers of schools. Thus the teacher ceased to be in any degree the employé of the State, and became merely the servant of the managers, who were no longer bound to

[1] It was for this Commission that Matthew Arnold reported on the elementary school systems of France, Holland, and Switzerland, and first raised the cry, 'Organize your Secondary Education.'

[2] There had even been a Minute in 1853 providing for individual examination, but not carried out by the Department. Royal Commission on Scientific Instruction, 1872, Q. 8084. The Minute is printed at p. 246, P. P., xli. 1854–55.

[3] Calculated on the attendance.

observe any proportion between the salary they paid him and the amount of the grant he earned from Government, but might drive with him the best bargain they could conclude. The State required the teacher to possess certain qualifications before his pupils could earn grants for the school, but that was the extent of its recognition of him as an individual : the grants in augmentation of his salary were discontinued, and, subject to the rights of teachers already retired, the pension system was withdrawn. The principle of proportionate local contribution was again enforced, as the total Government Grant to any school was not to exceed the amount of school fees and subscriptions, and it was limited to fifteen shillings per head for each scholar in average attendance.

Economy, to which Mr. Gladstone, then Chancellor of the Exchequer, was pledged, and reality, which was his own study, were the ends at which Mr. Lowe aimed. 'If the new system will not be cheap, it will be efficient, and if it will not be efficient, it will be cheap [1],' and whether the education imparted was good or not, at any rate the system was one which imposed a very exact test.

The grants which were formerly paid in full or else withheld for the whole of a school, were now almost always diminished to some extent by the failure of individual children to pass their examinations in whole or part. Private contracts no doubt reduced the amount of teachers' salaries which had before come out of the Government Grant.

The new plan excited great hostility on all sides, if only as involving retrenchment. As Bagehot said of the House of Commons, 'If you want to raise a certain cheer, make a general panegyric on economy; if you want to invite a sure defeat, propose a particular saving.'

Already in 1862, before the new Code had come into actual work, a fresh Minute (May 9, 1862) was issued fixing the grant for each child at twelve shillings, of which only two-thirds were to depend on the result of the examinations [2]

---

[1] Hansard, clxvi. p. 223.	[2] Of children making 2c6 attendances.

in the three elementary subjects—two shillings and eight pence being withheld for a failure in any one subject—while the other four shillings were to be given for average attendance.   Children under six were not to be examined individually, and the six standards under which all children were to be examined were to be fixed by the capacity and consequent position in the school, and not by the respective ages of the pupils.   No child was to be presented for examination a second time in the same or a lower standard, whether it had passed or whether it had failed the first time, but there was no limit of age beyond which grants might not be given.

Economy was effected, and genuine tests were imposed, but still the unpopularity remained.   The parliamentary grant decreased steadily year by year, although the average attendance of children increased [1], and to this day the champions of the voluntary system attribute their deficiencies in 1870 to the discouragement they received during the ten preceding years [2].

The Revised Code was accused on all hands of reducing education to the narrowest limits and the meanest aims;. and the tone assumed by the authorities was said to be disheartening and unsympathetic.   Mr. Lowe will probably go down to posterity as the Education Minister who denied the possibility of a science of education [3]; the examinations, though searching, were necessarily mechanical, and there settled on the elementary schools a monotonous and lifeless uniformity, to have avoided which is the chief justification of the irregular development of the English system.

Examination became a touchstone indeed, but only in the sense that if a subject could not be tested by examination, it was considered not fit to be taught [4].

---

[1] From £842,119 in 1861 to £636,806 in 1865. Cross Report, i. 1842.
[2] Gregory, *Elementary Education*, p. 102.
[3] Donaldson, *Lectures on Education*, p. 184: Edinburgh, 1874.
[4] One of H.M. Inspectors wrote in 1867: 'The studies of the class-room must be those wherein progress can be definitely measured by examination.   For examination is to the student what the target is to the rifle-

In 1864 it was found that the Queen's Scholars were using the Training Colleges, especially in Scotland, for purposes of general education, and were not carrying out the original design of supplying teachers for the schools. Accordingly measures were taken to prevent this, the chief being the limitation of the Government Grant to 75 per cent. of the actual cost of each scholar, and this rule continues to the present day [1].

In 1867 when Mr. Corry was Vice-President, a Minute was issued to promote the teaching of more subjects, to encourage pupil teachers, and to increase the staff of schools beyond the bare minimum. Children who had passed the Sixth Standard might earn the Grant by passing in certain 'Specific Subjects,' but one-fifth of the elder children in average attendance must pass in them.

But the times were ripening fast for a more complete change, a change of principle and not of detail. It was evident by this time that the deficiencies in the existing school system could never be overtaken by voluntary effort, and that some more certain basis of support and more responsible means were needed than subscriptions which might cease at any time, or schools which might sever their connexion with the State. Up to this time if a school were wanted in any place, the State would help to build it and help to maintain it on certain terms, but the initiative and the payments supplementary to the Government Grant must come from the locality itself and could only be voluntary, while the body managing the school was also voluntary and not necessarily representative of the locality. Education was only offered to those who cared to come, and in many cases only conditionally on their coming to denominational as well as to general instruction. Except in the cases of factory or military children and those in workhouse, industrial, and criminal schools, no child in

man ; there can be no definite aim, no real training without it.' Taunton Report, iv. p. 60*.
[1] Report of Argyll Commission on Scotch Education, 1865, p. 326.

England or Wales need receive any education at all, or even have its name entered on the books of any school.

At last in 1870, in the first Ministry of Mr. Gladstone, a Government Bill was introduced in the House of Commons by the Rt. Hon. W. E. Forster, and after numerous modifications was passed by both Houses of Parliament. Although considerable additions have been made, only five or six sections of the 'Elementary Education Act, 1870,' have been repealed, and it remains the basis of English public elementary education to-day.

The Elementary Education Act, 1870
(33 *and* 34 *Vict. c.* 75).

The Act laid down that there should 'be provided for every school district a sufficient amount of accommodation in public elementary schools available for all the children resident in such district, for whose elementary education efficient and suitable provision is not otherwise made'; and that when there was an insufficient amount of such accommodation, the deficiency should be supplied in manner provided by this Act.

An elementary school was defined as 'a school or department of a school at which elementary education is the principal part of the education there given, and not including any school or department of a school at which the ordinary payments in respect of the instruction from each scholar exceed ninepence a week.' This restriction of fees was substituted for the limitation in 1860 of the schools to the children of those supporting themselves by manual labour.

An elementary school to be public must fulfil the following conditions. No attendance at any place of worship or Sunday School nor any religious instruction is to be imposed on any child in attendance, if his parents or guardians object. Any religious teaching or observance at a school meeting must be either at the beginning or end of the meeting, and any scholar may be withdrawn from these by his parent or guardian without forfeiting any benefits[1]. The school must be open at all times to H.M. Inspector, but it shall be no part of his duties to inquire into or examine on religious teaching. The school must conform to the conditions laid down for earning the Parliamentary Grant in the code of the Education Department for the time being.

School Boards. After due investigation the Education Department

---

[1] This is known as 'the time-table conscience clause.'

were to publish a notice of the public school accommodation which they considered necessary in each district[1] in England and Wales, and a direction that it should be supplied.

If this were not done within a reasonable time, or if the voluntary schools were not likely to be maintained, or if application were made by the electors, the Department might order a School Board to be formed in any district, in which case it was to be elected triennially, in a borough by the burgesses, and in a parish by the ratepayers. The election of a School Board for the whole of London was directed by the Act. The voting was cumulative, every voter had as many votes as there were seats on the Board, but might give them all to one candidate or distribute them as he chose.

School Board. Each Board was to consist of not less than five or more than fifteen members, as determined in the first instance by the Department, and subsequently by the Board itself. No qualification for candidates was required by the Act itself, or by the regulations issued by the Department, other than that any member must be of full age and subject to no penal disqualification. Thus any one may be elected, whether male or female, lodger or householder, resident or non-resident[2]. In the electorate women are entitled to vote equally with men, subject to their being independent ratepayers[3].

In default. If a School Board within a year after their election did not supply the accommodation required by the Department, or if subsequently they failed in their duties in maintaining or conducting their schools, and did not respond to the requirements of the Department, they were to be declared in default, and in all cases of default the Department had power to appoint a School Board of their own, paid if necessary, and with full power to act for as long as was needed.

Duties. School Boards were bound to maintain and keep efficient every school provided by them, and from time to time to provide such additional school accommodation as they deemed necessary. They had powers to provide school houses properly fitted; to improve, enlarge, and fit up any school provided by them; to take over existing schools; to contribute to or to build and maintain industrial schools. Power was given to School Boards and also to voluntary managers to acquire land for school purposes under the Land Clauses Consolidation Act, 1845[4], and its amending Acts: but the power of compulsory acquisition of such sites was limited to the Boards, and granted to them only by order of the Education Department, confirmed in each case by a special Act of Parliament.

---

[1] Consisting of a borough, or parish, or, by order of the Department, of any combination of these.

[2] Owen, *Education Acts Manual*, 17th ed., p. 125.

[3] 45 & 46 Vict. c. 50, s. 55. [4] 8 Vict. c. 18.

Any Board might from time to time delegate their powers—except that of raising money—to not less than three managers appointed by them.

Fees at Board Schools. Every child attending a Board School was bound to pay a weekly fee prescribed by the Board with the consent of the Department, but the Board might in case of poverty remit the whole or part payment. A School Board might similarly pay the whole or part of the school fees payable at any public elementary school by any child resident in the district, whose parent was in their opinion unable from poverty to pay it : but this power was in 1876 transferred to the Poor Law Guardians.

In neither case of payment were the parents to be disfranchised on the ground of receiving parochial relief.

Religious Teaching. Every School Board school was to be conducted under the conditions required for public elementary schools, and no religious catechism or religious formulary distinctive of any particular denomination was to be taught therein[1].

Subject to this a School Board might cause such religious instruction to be given as they thought fit, but the schools do not suffer in respect of grants if no religious instruction is given.

Any voluntary school in order to receive a grant had, of course, to fulfil the conditions of being a " public elementary school " within the meaning of the Act, but the exception was granted that an inspection or examination might be made by an inspector other than H.M. Inspector, and a day or not more than two days in any year might be devoted to such inspection. On such days any religious observance might be practised, and any religious instruction given in the school, but notice was to be given, and no child whose parents objected need attend[2].

Attendance. Any School Board with the consent of the Department might make by-laws requiring the compulsory attendance of all children between the ages of five and thirteen, subject to the conscience clause, and providing for the total or partial exemption of children under the Factory Acts or on the inspector's certificate that a child between ten and thirteen had passed a Standard specified in the by-law[3]. (§ 74.)

Efficient instruction in some other manner, sickness, or more than

---

[1] This clause was an amendment introduced by Mr. Cowper Temple, and is known by his name.

[2] This regulation was intended chiefly for the benefit of the diocesan inspectors, clergymen appointed in nearly all dioceses of the Established Church to inspect the religious teaching in the school. These were already numerous in 1858 (Newcastle Report, i. 19), but of course have become of far greater importance to Church schools since 1870.

[3] The Standard for total exemption was and is in some cases as low as the Third, and for partial exemption the First (Sadler, Special Reports, 1897, pp. 18, 21).

three miles' distance from a public elementary school were regarded as reasonable excuses for non-attendance.

The by-laws might impose penalties on parents and guardians, but no fine imposed was with costs included to exceed five shillings.

No provision for compulsory attendance was made in districts where no School Board existed.

Power of raising money. The expenses of a School Board were to be paid out of the 'school fund,' into which was paid all the money received in scholars' fees, Parliamentary Grant, loans and otherwise, and any deficiency was supplemented by money raised by local rates, to the amount of which there was no limit fixed. The local rating authority, i.e. the Council in Boroughs and the Overseers in parishes, were required at the request of the School Board to pay the money needed out of any money in their hands, or to levy it by a fresh rate. If the local authority was in default, the School Board had power to levy a rate on their own authority. Powers of borrowing money for building or enlarging schools were given to School Boards contingently on the consent of the Department.

The Parliamentary Grant. After March 31, 1871, the Parliamentary Grant was strictly limited to schools which fulfilled the conditions of being 'public' and 'elementary.' It was not for any year to exceed the income of the school for that year derived from voluntary contributions, school fees, and any source other than the Parliamentary Grant. This included the local rate levied for Board Schools, and this regulation was thus a distinct advantage to them. It was provided that no future Minute of the Education Department should be deemed to be in force until it had lain for a month on the table of both the Houses of Parliament. After that it took its place as controlling 'the conditions required to be fulfilled by an elementary school,' and any new requirements thus acquiesced in by Parliament have the force of a law in controlling the Parliamentary Grant.

If a local rate of 3*d.* in the pound failed to produce £20 in any district, or the amount of 7*s.* 6*d.* per child, an additional Government Grant was to be given to bring it up to the larger of those amounts[1].

Voluntary schools might apply for building grants up to the end of the year, but after that no applications were entertained, and the grants ceased. If a School Board wanted to build, they did not apply for a building grant, but employed the rates or availed themselves of their powers of borrowing money. It was in the discretion of the Department to withhold the Government Grant from any voluntary school established after this date, if they considered such school unnecessary.

A report of the proceedings of the Department was to be laid before both Houses of Parliament every year.

[1] *Vide* p. 34.

The measure aroused feelings not only of active hostility in the Opposition but of sore disappointment in the advanced section of the Government party. For the Conservatives it went too far, while for the Radicals it did not go nearly far enough. Mr. Miall, for example, as the champion of the Dissenters, spoke of being 'once bit, twice shy,' and of passing through 'the Valley of Humiliation[1].' The voluntary schools which now became synonymous with denominational schools were still subsidised, but on the other hand the Concordat of 1840 was broken[2], and the alleged guarantees of 1846; rivals with unlimited means were set on foot, who neither withheld religious instruction nor satisfied those who desired dogmatic teaching.

It will be seen that three principles were carried into effect for the first time in English public education—a compulsory local rate, a representative local authority, and the compulsory attendance of children at school.

The Local Rate. The new local rate was to be applied for the benefit of Board schools alone, and not of voluntary schools, but the Board schools were bound to charge fees[3].

In the Bill as first introduced, it was proposed to allow a School Board to give grants to all the voluntary schools in their district out of the rates, but this form of patronage was not favourably regarded, and in place of this schools were enabled to earn larger grants from Government than before.

'Speaking roughly,' said Mr. Gladstone in the House of Commons[4], 'it is said that the expense of educating a child in an efficient secular school is thirty shillings, of which it may be said one-third is now provided by the Privy Council, one-third from voluntary sources, and one-third by payments from the children. We think that if

---

[1] Hansard, T. S., cciii. p. 745.

[2] After 1869 no clergymen were appointed H. M. Inspectors (Annual Registers).

[3] Mr. Forster anticipated that the rate would not amount to anything like threepence in the pound in the vast majority of cases (Hansard, T. S., cxcix. p. 445).　　　　[4] Hansard, T. S., ccii. p. 280.

to the one-third which is now dispensed, the half of the second third were added, the voluntary schools would have no reason to complain.'

In the voluntary schools there was no obligation on the managers to charge fees if they could raise the money in another way, but that was seldom the case.

The Local Authority. As to the new local authority, School Boards were only to be elected in those districts where they were needed in order to supply more school accommodation, or where the electors desired them, and it was only in School Board districts that attendance could be declared compulsory, and then only if the School Board so determined.

Compulsory Attendance.   As for the compulsory attendance, its sphere was at first very narrow, and it was limited to the districts of such School Boards as chose to pass by-laws and to enforce them.   But until there were schools to go to, it was useless to make it an offence not to attend them.

Religious Teaching. The recognition of denominational teaching adopted in 1846 was withdrawn; no cognizance of religious instruction was now taken by the State either in inspection or grant, and all denominational schools which wished to earn a grant from Government must admit any child who came for secular teaching whether he remained to receive religious instruction or not

Until 1870 no public elementary school which did not include the daily reading of the Bible among its subjects could earn a Government Grant; but now, although this is the customary practice in the Board Schools, a purely secular school may earn the grant without any question arising.

In practice almost the only exceptions to the rule of giving religious instruction in public elementary day schools occur in four counties in Wales, where Sunday schools form an important part of the life of the whole people[1].

---

[1] In 1894 there were only fifty-seven School Board districts in England and Wales in which no provision was made for religious teaching.

To the Act in general there was naturally strong opposition from the supporters of denominational schools, who
did not like to see an undenominational rival created with
power to levy compulsory rates against their voluntary
subscriptions. There was, however, no time to waste in
vain regrets, and they put forth a great effort, availing
themselves to the utmost of the last opportunity of obtaining building grants from the Government, and raising
money on a heroic scale. Of the 1,600,000 school places
added between 1869 and 1876, about two-thirds were due
to voluntary agencies; only about one-fifteenth of the cost
of these was met by the building grant of the State, and
the total of voluntary subscriptions in these few years
amounted to not less than three million pounds [1].

On the other hand the supporters of School Boards were
very active. Some towns elected them forthwith, without
waiting for the Department, although they needed no additional school accommodation, in order that they might pass
by-laws and secure the only possible means of compelling
attendance. Boards were at once voluntarily adopted by
all but one of the boroughs with a population of 50,000 or
more inhabitants [2].

Further Elementary Education Acts were passed in 1872
and 1873, chiefly to amend and strengthen the original
Act. An amendment to introduce the Ballot at School
Board elections had been lost in 1870, but the Ballot Act
for parliamentary and municipal elections [3] having been
passed in 1872, the Elementary Education Act of the
following year declared that in any School Board election
the poll should be as far as possible conducted as at a
municipal election under the new Act.

reading, or observances. Of these forty-three were in the counties of
Cardigan, Carmarthen, Pembroke, and Glamorgan, seven in the rest
of Wales, and seven in England (House of Lords, paper No. 2, 1895).

[1] Craik, p. 109.

[2] Mr. E. M. Hance in J. Samuelson's *Subjects of the Day*, i. p. 33:
Routledge, 1890.

[3] 35 & 36 Vict. c. 33.

In 1876, Mr. Disraeli being in power, a new measure[1] of greater importance was brought in by Lord Sandon, the Vice-President of the Committee, which ultimately created local authorities with powers to secure compulsory attendance in districts where no School Boards existed, and greatly increased the effectiveness of compulsion. At first the Bill contained only a provision for indirect compulsion: the labour of children was to be limited, but there was no security that the leisure thus obtained must be spent at school. At the second reading an amendment of Mr. Mundella proposing compulsory attendance was rejected; but in Committee, to the surprise of the Opposition, stringent judicial compulsion was introduced by the Government[2].

The Act as passed declared that 'it shall be the duty of the parent of every child to cause such child to receive efficient elementary instruction in reading, writing, and arithmetic, and if such parent fail to perform such duty he shall be liable to such orders and penalties as are provided by the Act.' A child was now defined as ' between the ages of five and fourteen years.'

Attendance. In case of habitual neglect on the part of the parent to provide efficient elementary instruction, or of habitual truancy on part of the child, the School Board or School Attendance Committee had to apply to a Court of Summary Jurisdiction to issue an Attendance Order, requiring the child to make an invariable or a specified attendance at a specified school. If this Order were disobeyed, the parent could be summoned and fined a sum not exceeding 5*s.* including costs, or the child, if quite unmanageable, could be sent to a certified industrial school or a certified day industrial school, and the parent compelled to contribute to his maintenance. On every subsequent offence both these punishments could be inflicted.

Remission of school fees for poverty was transferred from the School Boards to the Poor Law Guardians. As to employment, except as then laid down by the Factory Acts, no child might be *employed* at all below the age of ten, and no child might be employed between the ages of ten and fourteen without a certificate from H.M. Inspector of having passed the Fourth Standard in reading, writing, and elementary arithmetic, or of having made a certain[3] attendance at any elementary school certified as efficient by H.M. Inspector.

---

[1] 39 & 40 Vict. c. 79.   [2] Adams, *El. School Contest*, p. 316.
[3] 250 attendances for each of five years.

The age of the compulsory attendance of backward and truant children was thus raised from thirteen to fourteen, and a minimum not wholly formal was imposed on all before exemption was granted.

By-laws previously made by School Boards held good, though many of them were much easier to satisfy: with leave of the Education Department by-laws of greater stringency than the Statute might now be made, but they could not hereafter go below its standard.

Any employer (including a parent employing his child in any labour exercised by way of trade or for purposes of gain) who was found employing children under age was to be liable to a fine not exceeding 40*s.*

School Attendance Committees. To enforce attendance a new set of bodies was called into existence to supplement the School Boards. In all districts in England and Wales which had no School Board, School Attendance Committees were to be appointed in parishes by the Guardians of the Poor Law Union, and in boroughs by the Council: each Committee was to consist of from six to twelve members of the body appointing it. An urban sanitary district might with consent of the Department have a Committee appointed by its Local Board. These Attendance Committees were thus practically Attendance Sub-committees of the body appointing them. Their expenses were to be met out of the borough rate, or in parishes out of the poor rate.

It was the duty of School Boards and Attendance Committees to enforce this law as regards the parent and the child: as regards employers it was to be carried out by the inspectors under the Factory Acts[1]. Any person might inform the Committee or School Board of any breach of the Act, and they were bound to proceed upon it.

Attendance Committees in boroughs if they thought fit might make by-laws: an Attendance Committee in a parish, if it received a requisition from the ratepayers, was bound to make them. It was also their duty to report to the Education Department any infringement of the conscience clauses or any complaints of the same within their district. They might if they chose delegate their powers to local committees. In case of default the Department had power to appoint a School Attendance Committee for a period not exceeding two years.

Parliamentary Grants. The annual Parliamentary Grant was not to be reduced by reason of its excess above the income of the school from other sources, provided that it did not exceed 17*s.* 6*d.* per child in average attendance, but it might only exceed that sum by the same amount as the income of the school from all other sources exceeded it. Thus, for instance, if the general income from fees, rates, and contribu-

---

[1] Not the by-laws (Owen, *Education Acts Manual*, p. 307), and only of course for factory children, v. p. 47.

tions averaged 18*s*., the annual grant might amount to 18*s.* a head and no more, even though more were earned.

Extra grants were also given in districts with a scanty population.

Certified Efficient Schools. To escape from penalties for non-attendance under this Act, a child must have a certificate of proficiency or of due attendance at some certified efficient school, of the efficiency of which H.M. Inspector had to be satisfied. Such schools need not be 'public,' but must not be conducted for private profit, must be open to inspection, must require the same attendance as a public elementary school, and keep registers as prescribed by the Department. A child was exempt from the action of by-laws made under the Act of 1870 if it were shown to be under efficient instruction in some other manner, but certificates of efficiency for non-public schools were now first instituted, and definite inspection introduced of a new class of school[1].

Provision was made for the establishment of Industrial and Day Industrial schools and for their certification by the Home Secretary, under certain conditions, the latter being now for the first time introduced and being defined as schools in which industrial training, elementary education, and one or more meals a day, but not lodging, are provided for the children [2].

Elementary Education Act, 1880. In 1880, Mr. Mundella being Vice-President, the provisions for compulsory attendance were still further strengthened by a new Act[3].

It became obligatory on all School Boards and School Attendance Committees to pass by-laws under the Act of 1870, § 74, and the Committees had no longer to wait for the requisition of their parish. If the by-laws were not made, the Education Department might treat the locality as in default under the law of 1870, or might themselves make the by-laws for the district: these by-laws being needed to define the new provisions for attendance, and at the same time to allow for the varying needs and desires of different parts of the country.

---

[1] These voluntary schools did not apply for a grant, mostly because their managers were unwilling to submit to the conscience clause, but they needed to be returned as efficient in order to secure their pupils from being compelled to attend some other school which satisfied the definition of the Act. A child attending a private school—private in the ordinary sense of the word of being conducted for the schoolmaster's profit—could not obtain exemption as a whole or half-timer until he or she was beyond school age.

[2] *Vide* p. 57 sqq.   [3] 43 & 44 Vict. c. 23.

No child between ten and thirteen was allowed by these by-laws to be absent from school, even for half-time, without obtaining a certificate of having reached a standard of education fixed by the local by-law. A certificate of previous attendance was of no use unless the child were thirteen, when by the law of 1876 he or she was still obliged to attend school for another year, but could claim exemption on a certificate of attendance only.

Children actually employed under the Factory Acts at the time of the passing of this Act were specifically exempted from it, and therefore—by inference—it was to override the Factory Acts in the future, and impose an educational qualification for half-timers between the ages of ten and thirteen, while no child under ten could now escape the obligation to make full-time attendance at school. The various by-laws made before 1880 remained in force, and the difference between them in different places is considerable. One-fifth of the population obtains total exemption at the Fourth Standard; the children of over a million persons obtain partial exemption at the Second[1].

The effects of the three successive Acts may be thus summed up :—

After 1870, by-laws enforcing attendance at school might be made by School Boards.

After 1876, they might be made by School Attendance Committees.

By the 1876 Act, complete abstinence from employment was enforced under ten.

By the Act of 1880, complete attendance at school was enforced under ten.

In 1886 a Royal Commission was appointed, with Lord Cross as Chairman, to inquire into the working of the Elementary Education Acts in England and Wales. They sat for two years, and issued ten volumes of reports, but the final report ended in five reservations and a minority

---

[1] 1895, Sadler, Special Reports, 1897, p. 21.

report of eight out of a total of twenty-three Commissioners. The chief of their recommendations which have as yet been carried out are raising the school age to eleven, improving evening schools, making drawing compulsory for boys, starting undenominational Day Training Colleges, and giving special help to necessitous rural schools.

It may be here recorded that in 1888 County Councils were established by the Local Government Act [1], bodies which are in the future likely to be prominent in the representation of localities in education. In 1889 and 1890 followed the Technical Instruction Act and the Local Taxation (Customs and Excise) Act [2].

In 1889 Scotland had to a large extent obtained free elementary education, but England and Wales devoted to other purposes the Probate and Licence Duties, of which Scotland had expended her share in relief of School fees. To bring them into line, a fresh Elementary Education Act [3] was passed in 1891, granting ten shillings a year to the day public elementary schools in England and Wales for each child between three and fifteen in average attendance, on condition that no fee should be charged for children above three and under fifteen, except where the average rate of fees had exceeded ten shillings a year, and in that case then the new fee and the fee grant together should not exceed the former rate [4].

If the Education Department were satisfied that the amount of elementary public school accommodation without payment of fees was insufficient in any district, they might direct the deficiency to be supplied as under the Act of 1870, and thus, if necessary, proceed to order the election of a School Board.

In 1893 the age of total or partial exemption from attendance was raised by a short Elementary Education

---

[1] 51 & 52 Vict. c. 41.　　[2] *Vide* p. 181.　　[3] 54 & 55 Vict. c. 56.
[4] In 1896–7 there were 735,142 fee-paying scholars out of a total of 5,507,039 pupils in the public elementary schools, and only 101 of these schools not receiving the fee grant, out of a total of 19,958 schools (E. D. Report, p. 22).

(School Attendance) Act to eleven[1]. In the same year the Elementary Education (Blind and Deaf Children) Act, 1893[2], was passed. Children too blind to be able to read the ordinary school books or too deaf to be taught in a class of hearing children in an elementary school must be sent to schools suitable for them, and due provision of these has to be made by School Boards and District Councils. The Department may declare the local authority or their committee in default, or order them to pay a sum for any child attending such school. The Act does not extend to idiots, imbeciles, or pauper children. Blindness and deafness are no longer an excuse for absence from school except for deaf children under seven, and attendance in all these cases of infirmity is compulsory up to the age of sixteen[3].

A Committee of the Education Department, appointed in the end of 1896 to consider the case of defective and epileptic children, reported in January, 1898, in favour of a similar measure on their behalf, with special provisions for ascertaining what children actually came under those headings[4]. X

In 1897 two separate Acts were passed by Parliament to assist the poorer elementary schools. By the first[5] an aid grant was given to elementary day schools not provided by a School Board. ⁄ Voluntary schools might form themselves into associations within such areas and with such governing bodies as the Education Department approved. Each association was to receive 5s. per scholar in average attendance, or the grant might be apportioned at a different rate for town and country, but the total aggregate amount of the grant was limited to an average of 5s. for the whole number of scholars in average attendance in England and

---

[1] 56 & 57 Vict. c. 51. [2] 56 & 57 Vict. c. 42.
[3] In 1896 there were 91 certified schools with 1,208 blind boarders and 268 day pupils, and 1,699 deaf boarders and 1,305 day pupils (Ed. Dep. Report, published 1897, C. 8,608, p. 18).
[4] P. P., 1898, C. 8,746.
[5] The Voluntary Schools Act, 1897. 60 Vict. c. 5.

Wales. The governing body of each association was to be consulted by the Department as to the distribution. A distribution is also made to unassociated voluntary schools, if they do not unreasonably refuse to join an association, but no such school is deprived of the aid grant for declining to join an association of which the majority of the schools belong to a different religious denomination. After this distribution a corresponding share of any sum which may be available may be further allotted to the associated schools.

The 17*s*. 6*d*. limit [1] was abolished for all day schools in England and Wales, and voluntary elementary schools are henceforth exempt from rates.

The Education Department may require any voluntary school claiming the aid grant to submit to an annual audit under its regulations.

The measure has resulted in the formation of a number of associations, but there have been several sharp struggles between the counties and the dioceses for the right to constitute the recognized area. The grant to country schools has been fixed at 3*s*. 3*d*., while voluntary schools in towns will receive 5*s*. 9*d*.

The Elementary Education Act, 1897. The second Act is intended to show similar generosity to poor Board Schools [2], and amends section 97 of the Elementary Education Act of 1870, by which, where a rate of threepence in the pound produces less than 7*s*. 6*d*. per child in average attendance at the Board Schools in any district, a Government Grant is made to bring it up to that sum [3]. The 7*s*. 6*d*. is 'now increased by the sum of fourpence for every complete penny by which the School Board rate for the year exceeds threepence.' Thus if only 6*s*. 6*d*. per child is realized, and the rate is sixpence in the pound, in future the Parliamentary Grant will bring up the average not to 7*s*. 6*d*., but to 8*s*. 6*d*. per child, and if the rate be one shilling,

---

[1] *Vide* p. 29.   [2] 60 Vict. c. 16.   [3] *Vide* p. 24.

to 10*s*. 6*d*. ; but the total amount is not to exceed 16*s*. 6*d*., which would require at least a rate of 2*s*. 6*d*. in the pound.

The first results of the Act have been that for 1896–97, 710 School Boards received £200 each, being £19 10*s*. apiece more than had been anticipated : and the general Government Grant for each child in the public elementary schools was increased by 3½*d*., chiefly owing to the abolition of the 17*s*. 6*d*. limit[1].

The accounts of all voluntary schools have now to be audited by a professional auditor, banker, or bank manager, or an auditor specially approved by the Department[2].

In 1898, the administration of the grants to elementary schools for drawing and manual instruction has been handed over to the Education Department by the Science and Art Department. Both grants are continued on the same general lines, but manual instruction is only for the three highest standards, and must be in direct connexion with the drawing. This concentration of elementary instruction is, however, less important in view of the amalgamation of the Department of Science and Art with this Department under the promised Board of Education[3].

Under the Voluntary Schools Act seventy-five associations have been formed. Forty-six are composed mainly of Church of England schools, and in all but two cases are coextensive with a diocese or archdeaconry. Eleven are Catholic, eleven Nonconformist : six are Wesleyan and one is Jewish. The Catholic associations are diocesan : the Wesleyan and ' British ' are grouped according to counties. There were in all only 267 voluntary schools which did not join any association : of these, thirty-five received the grant, but twenty-five were refused as ' unreasonable ' and six as ' non-necessitous.'

The success of the Department in securing for the people an efficient education may be traced on p. 306, where the numbers of schools, teachers, and pupils in average atten-

[1] P. P., 1897–98, No. 56, p. 5.   [2] 1898 Code, Art. 85 d.
[3] *Vide* p. xxvii.

D 2

dance will be found [1]. But figures alone can give little idea of the progress made, especially of recent years, in the introduction of improved methods and of truly educational subjects, and least of all can they do justice to the interest and sympathy which has gradually animated the Department. Much, however, remains to be done by the more backward local authorities, and attendance falls far short of what it should be. In 1897 the average attendance in England and Wales was only 81·8 per cent. of the whole number of children on the rolls, and only 82·7 of a sixth of the estimated population of the country [2]. There is evidently still wanting that popular zeal for education which alone can ensure its efficiency.

Codes. The regulation of Education by statute has but slightly diminished the importance of the Code of the Department, which, as we have seen, is submitted annually to Parliament and acquires the force of law [3]. In the Codes is to be traced the gradual abolition of payment by results.

In 1875 'class subjects' were introduced, which, if taught at all, must be taught throughout the whole school, and judged by the proficiency of the classes as a whole.

In 1890 in elementary subjects a fixed grant on the average attendance was introduced, examination was to be by sample, and not less than one-third of the scholars were to be individually examined. The grant might be at the rate of 14*s.* or 12*s.* 6*d.*, according to the Inspector's Report.

[1] For full details refer to the two articles by Messrs. M. E. Sadler and J. W. Edwards in the first and second volumes of Special Reports on Educational Subjects issued by the Education Department in 1897 and 1898. These are the first official publications of the Director of Special Inquiries and Reports, an office created in 1896 for which the Department were fortunate to secure Mr. Sadler's services.

[2] In Scotland the average attendance in 1897 was 84·45 per cent. of children on the rolls: in Wales (included in the English figures) it was no more than 76·69.

[3] In 1872 the attendance of children under three and over eighteen received no recognition; in 1884 the grant was restricted to children who had not passed the Seventh Standard in the three elementary subjects, unless re-examined by permission of the Inspector; but in 1890 an age limit of fourteen was added.

In 1897 the last trace of payment by results vanished. In specific subjects, the last stronghold of the Revised Code, payment was to be at the rate of one shilling for each twenty-four hours devoted to the subject, and payment by examination ceased [1].

Since 1895 Inspectors have been allowed (with leave from headquarters) to omit the regular annual visit, and to pay two visits instead without notice.

Evening Continuation Schools. Night schools were a department from which much was hoped at first. We read of great zeal and earnestness shown in the early days, when few of the labouring classes had received much education and most had deficiencies to supply. At Wells the Bishop himself was found teaching a class of navvies to read and cypher; at Bristol any interruption to the school was greatly resented; at Rochdale the Inspector was told at the end of the school hour, 'Go thou on: we want as much as we can for the money [2].'

By 1855 they were in receipt of capitation grants and payments to teachers, though only in the case of schools in connexion with a day school in receipt of annual grants; until 1861 teachers in day elementary schools were forbidden to teach in night schools also, and from 1839–60 only £2,916 was paid to night schools out of the public grants [3].

The Revised Code withdrew the aid given to teachers, but also withdrew the restriction on day teachers, and made capitation grants on the average attendance and payment for the results of examination in reading, writing, and arithmetic.

In 1871 grants were restricted to persons not over eighteen and (as since 1860) not under twelve, but in 1876 the upper limit was raised to twenty-one.

The average attendance steadily decreased. In 1870 it

---

[1] A table showing the alterations in the successive Codes, 1871–95, has been published by Mr. Sadler in his first volume of Special Reports on Educational Subjects, 1897, pp. 33–44.

[2] Newcastle Report, i. 39.

[3] Sadler, Special Reports, p. 54.

was 73,375, in 1886 it had fallen to 26,009[1]. Since 1890[2] the education given in these schools need no longer be 'principally elementary,' as required by the Education Act of 1870, and in 1893 a special Code for Evening Continuation Schools was published.

The chief changes are as follows. The attendances of persons over twenty-one are recognized; no scholar is compelled to take the elementary subjects. Grants are paid as in day schools for the instruction of the school as a whole, instead of as formerly for the attainments of the individual scholar. The fixed grant is no longer paid on the average attendance, but on the aggregate number of hours received by the scholar at the rate of one shilling for every twelve hours, depending, however, on some other grant being earned[3]. Variable grants are earned on the Inspector's report and according to the hours given to the subjects. Surprise visits are, as a rule, substituted for examinations on a fixed day.

Now that persons of any age over fourteen-may earn grants and need not do elementary work, these schools have become secondary in large measure[4]. From 115,582 scholars on the registers of 1,977 schools in 1893, the number rose to 266,683 scholars attending 3,742 schools in 1894, and 358,268 attending 4,226 schools in 1897.

Canal Boat Acts. Two Acts were passed in 1877 and 1884[5] which require every canal boat used as a residence to be registered in some sanitary district, the children living on board having to attend school at the place of registration, unless receiving instruction elsewhere.

The authority of the Sanitary District has to enforce the Act under the Local Government Board as a sanitary measure; the school authority has to enforce attendance under the Education Acts[6].

[1] Cross Commission Final Report, p. 162. Special Reports, p. 55.
[2] 53 & 54 Vict. c. 22.   [3] The 17*s.* 6*d.* limit still exists, pp. 29, 34.
[4] Bryce Commission Report, i. 290.
[5] 40 & 41 Vict. c. 60, and 47 & 48 Vict. c. 75.
[6] *Vide* Education Department Report for 1896-97, Appendix, p. 200.

Technical Instruction. Genuine technical instruction lies outside the limits of elementary education, but besides the technical teaching given in schools which are still called elementary, the whole tendency of the education of young children in England of late years has been in the direction of sense training, object-lessons, and manual employment.

The Technical Instruction Act of 1889[1] especially excludes pupils in elementary schools from its grants, 'the purpose of this restriction not being to imply that such children should not receive technical instruction, but that sufficient provision is supposed to be already made by grants from the Education Department or the Science and Art Department[2].'

The chief subjects for girls encouraged by the Department in elementary schools are (besides needlework and cutting out)—cookery, domestic economy, laundry work, dairy work, practical housewifery, and domestic science.

Boys are encouraged to take shorthand, bookkeeping, agriculture, and cottage gardening.

The Science and Art Department also, until 1898, paid grants for drawing and manual training, but these subjects in elementary schools have now been transferred to the Education Department.

Inspection. The inspecting staff of the Education Department consists of a Senior Chief Inspector[3], twelve Chief Inspectors (two for the Training Colleges and ten in charge of school divisions, each comprising ten districts), and ninety Inspectors. Until 1882 young men who had taken high honours at the Universities, but had no special knowledge of elementary education, were appointed as Inspectors, but since that date the appointments have been made on grounds of special qualification or experience. There are over fifty first-class Sub-Inspectors, a class insti-

---

[1] 52 & 53 Vict. c. 76.
[2] *Technical, Commercial, and Industrial Education in Great Britain and Ireland*, M. E. Sadler, 1895, p. 3. Bordeaux Conference, 1896.
[3] First appointed, 1889.

tuted in 1882, appointed from the second-class Inspectors (known until 1896 as Inspector's Assistants), of whom there were 161 in 1897 appointed from the head teachers of public elementary schools. In 1896 two mistresses were promoted to be Sub-Inspectors, and a third in 1897.

The staff of more than twenty 'examiners' in the Education Office who examine the Inspectors' reports, assess the grants, and revise the examination papers for Certificates, Queen's Scholarships, &c., is appointed from the class which formerly supplied Inspectors[1].

Training of Elementary Teachers. The growth of arrangements for training teachers has been noticed in the early history of the Committee of Council[2]. The nation preferred voluntary institutions to a State normal school, and the system has continued until the present day. The Revised Code made the profession unpopular, and reduced the numbers and consequently the quality of the teachers supplied, and the Training Colleges passed through a most critical and anxious period[3]; but with 1870 came an enormously increased demand, and an improvement of the position and remuneration of the masters and mistresses.

The only important change of principle that has taken place was the introduction of Day Training Colleges, recommended by Lord Cross' Commission in 1888[4], and finally embodied in the Code of 1890. These Colleges must be attached to some University or College of University rank, and must be under a local Committee responsible for the discipline and moral supervision of their students, and for their regular attendance at professional or other lectures. The usual practising school is of course necessary, and the idea is to enable teachers to obtain during their training some of the benefits of a University course, even if they are not able to take a degree. In the same

---

[1] Cross Report, i. p. 71.   [2] *Vide* p. 9.
[3] Report on Admiralty Schools, 1883, p. 141; P. P., 1867, xxii. 11, 528; 1868, xxv. p. xliii; 1872, xxv. 14.
[4] Final Report, p. 100.

year the resident Training Colleges were also first allowed to admit a small proportion of day students. Day Training Colleges have been established in every town in England and Wales which possesses a University or University College, and secondary training is also attempted in connexion with some of these institutions.

In 1897 there were fourteen Day Training Colleges and forty-five Residential Colleges, and eight of the latter took day students.

The average salary of certificated masters in 1860–70 was £94; it then rose to £121 in 1880, and remains almost unaltered. In 1860 mistresses with certificates averaged £62, but sank by 1870 to £57, and only recovered by 1895 those two-thirds which the Committee of Council in 1846 considered to be their due proportion to the men's earnings [1].

The pension system introduced in 1846 and suspended in 1862 was revived to a limited extent in 1875 for the benefit of the teachers formerly under them. In 1895 a departmental Committee reported in favour of the establishment of a Teachers' Superannuation Fund, and in August, 1898, an Elementary Teachers' Superannuation Act was passed.

'A woman over eighteen years of age, approved by the Inspector' as a teacher, was first recognized in infants', girls', and mixed schools in 1875 and 1876 in place of two monitors, then as an assistant, and latterly as an additional female teacher in these schools, and also for boys in the first three standards [2].

ii. *Science and Art Department.*

The whole of the work now conducted by this Department belongs to secondary and higher education, and an

---

[1] Newcastle Report, i. 641; Special Reports, 1897, p. 47. Cf. p. 11.
[2] This is 'Article 68' of the Code since 1890. As such a woman need not have passed any examination nor received any training, she is regarded with much disfavour by experts and by more fully qualified teachers.

account of the origin and aims of the Department will be found at p. 168.

Grants in aid of the establishment of Schools of Art in 1852 were offered only on condition of special instruction being provided for artisans and in elementary schools; prizes to children, rewards to their masters followed, and augmentation grants to elementary teachers who passed in drawing and taught it satisfactorily.

In 1885 elementary drawing was made a class subject under the Code of the Education Department, but two years later the vote for instruction in drawing was again taken in the estimates of the Science and Art Department, and administered by it until 1898, when it was handed over to the Education Department, both in elementary day schools and evening continuation schools. Manual training was introduced in 1890, and in 1898 was also transferred to the Education Department.

Since 1890 drawing has been compulsory for all boys in public elementary schools (except in infant schools), and grants are given for it on the average attendance according to the report of the Inspector. Girls cannot earn the grant, unless provision is also made for teaching cooking.

2. THE CHARITY COMMISSION.

The history of this department will be found at p. 238 under Secondary Education, with which it is chiefly concerned. The Taunton Commission found that in 1865 or 1866 out of a total of 820 endowed grammar schools with a net educational income of £195,184 (exclusive of exhibitions to the annual value of £14,264), only 198 were elementary schools or departments of schools, and that their income was but £8,762, with exhibitions worth £17 [1]. The Commissioners have the same powers under the Charitable Trusts Acts and the Endowed Schools Acts over foundations for elementary education as over any other endowed schools,

---

[1] Report, i. App. p. (150).

except that by the Endowed Schools Act, 1873 [1], elementary schools with an income of less than £100 from their endowment were excepted from this control.

The income of elementary schools from endowments amounted in 1871 to £50,516; by 1876 it was £102,237; by 1881 £148,000, and the increase of capital between 1871 and 1895 amounted to about three and a half millions [2].

3. The Home Office.

The Home Office touches the system of elementary education in several places: on the one hand it controls children employed in factories and mines, and on the other it deals with the penal organization and the children sent to reformatories and industrial schools.

i. *The Factory Acts.*

The first Act for the benefit of the young who were employed in factories was passed in 1802 [3] at the instance of Sir Robert Peel, father of the Prime Minister, and himself a large mill owner, but its action was limited to apprentices; in 1819 a more general measure was passed, and the employment of children under nine in cotton mills and factories was prohibited, but there was no provision for education in it or any succeeding statute before 1833. In that year a Factories Act [4] was passed, which in respect of education was immensely in advance of all provisions for the working classes at the time [5]. 1833 was the year which first saw £20,000 voted for building schools for the people, but Lord Althorp's Act not only attempted in a rough way to provide schools and have them inspected, but it made the attendance of children at them compulsory.

As originally passed by the House of Commons, the Bill

---

[1] 36 & 37 Vict. c. 87.
[2] Sadler, Special Reports, 1897, p. 27.
[3] 42 Geo. III, c. 73.   [4] 3 & 4 Will. IV, c. 103.
[5] The Inspectors, however, took a low estimate of its value (Newcastle Report, i. 207).

required any of the four Government Inspectors appointed to enforce its provisions to establish a new school, if he thought desirable, out of the poor rate. The employers were to pay a penny in the shilling from the wages of the children, and if this were not enough they were to advance the remainder and deduct the amount from their next poor rates when they fell due ; if that were insufficient, the over-seers were to reimburse them from the local poor rates. But the clause was struck out by the Lords, who merely authorized the Inspector to establish or procure the establish-ment of a new or additional school, wherever he thought it necessary or desirable, and provided no means to that end. This part of the Act consequently remained inoperative, and in any case, even though the Factory Inspectors were able men who took great interest in the schools, technical inspectors could not possibly single-handed start a system of education, the supervision of which formed a very small part of their duties.

Under this Act children between nine and thirteen might only be employed if they had a voucher of having attended school two hours on six days in each preceding week. The Inspector might require the employer to make a deduction of one penny in the shilling from a child's wages, and pay the same for the schooling of the child according to his direction.

Parental responsibility was not expressly declared until 1844 [1], but employers and parents might be fined in case of wilful default. The former were liable to a penalty not under £1 nor over £20, and the latter to a fine not exceed-ing 20s. This Act applied only to textile factories.

There was no reference to religious education in this Act, nor in any of the subsequent Bills which passed into law, and in practice no difficulty seems ever to have arisen on this point.

If the Inspector thought any schoolmaster or mistress

---

[1] § 38.

incompetent or in any way unfit, he might disallow and withhold the order for any payment of salary due. That this provision was by no means unneeded may be seen by the report of the three Inspectors of Factories in England in 1839 [1]. 'It is not at all an unusual thing,' remarks Mr. Horner [2], 'to have certificates presented to me subscribed by the teachers with his or her *mark*; this generally happens in the case of female teachers; but they are held to be equal in quality to the majority of those who keep dame schools.' ... 'I have had to reject the school voucher of the fireman, the children having been schooled in the coal-hole (in one case I actually found them there), and having been made to say a lesson from books nearly as black as the fuel, in the interval between his feeding and stirring the fire of the engine and boiler. It may be supposed that such a thing could only happen at the mill of some poor and ignorant man; but that, I am sorry to say, was not the case, for it occurred at factories where a large capital must be embarked.'

On the other hand, in some cases excellent schools had already been established, and some employers at first refused to give information about their schools, on the ground that it might lead people to say that further educational measures were unnecessary [3].

In 1843 Sir James Graham's Factory Bill, containing a large educational scheme, fell through, as we have seen [4], but a new Act was passed in the next year with more simple regulations [5].

Children might be employed for half-time at eight instead of nine years of age, but the hours of labour were reduced.

The parent or person having direct benefit from the wages of any child employed on alternate days had to cause the child to attend school for at least five hours between eight

---

[1] P. P. Eng., 1839, vol. xlii. p. 358.
[2] A Factory Inspector, and a keen friend of education, brother of the Right Hon. Francis Horner.
[3] P. P. Eng., 1839, vol. xlii. p. 381.　　　　[4] *Vide* p. 8.
[5] 7 & 8 Vict. c. 15.

in the morning and six in the evening on each week-day
preceding each day of employment[1]. Children employed
otherwise than on alternate days were to attend school for
three hours on each working day of the week during any
part of which it was employed, or two and a half on winter
afternoons[2].

The arrangements as to the schoolmaster's certificate and
the schoolmaster's fees remained, but the fee to be paid by
the employer when required by the Inspector was not to
exceed twopence a week, and the amount deducted from
the child's wages was (as in 1833) not to exceed a penny in
the shilling. The powers of the Factory Inspector as to
annulling certificates and disqualifying schoolmasters for
inefficiency, immorality or neglect were increased[3].

In 1864 and 1867 Acts were passed extending the law to
non-textile factories, and in the latter year another Act[4]
applied analogous but less stringent regulations to workshops.

These were defined as 'any room or place whatever,
whether in the open air or under cover, in which any
handicraft is carried on by any child, young person or
woman, and to which and over which the person by whom
the child, young person or woman is employed has the
right of access or control': handicraft being 'manual labour
exercised by way of trade or for purposes of gain in or
incidental to the making of any article or part of an article,
or in or incidental to the altering, repairing, ornamenting,
finishing or otherwise adapting for sale any article.'

No child might be employed under eight; the parents
had to cause every child employed to attend school ten
hours every week, under a penalty of not more than twenty
shillings for each offence; the weekly certificate was required;
the principal teacher of the school might apply to the employer in writing for a weekly fee not exceeding twopence
and not exceeding one-twelfth of the child's wages, such fee

---

[1] § 31.   [2] § 38.   [3] § 39.   [4] 30 & 31 Vict. c. 146.

was to be paid thenceforth as long as the child was at the school, under a penalty of 10*s.*; the Inspector might disqualify the teacher as under the Act of 1844, but the substituted school must be within *one* mile, and notice served on all other employers receiving certificates from such teacher.

In 1874 another Factory Act[1] was passed which took into recognition the new conditions created by the Elementary Education Acts. It dealt only with textile factories, but raised the age of employment in them from the 'eight' of 1844 to ten, and the age of a 'child' from thirteen to fourteen; children of thirteen could now only obtain total exemption by showing a certificate of proficiency, subsequently[2] fixed at the Fourth Standard. In districts where there was sufficient school accommodation within reach, schools attended by half-timers must be recognized as efficient by the Education Department, and thus the principal need for inspection of schools by Factory Inspectors came to an end.

The Elementary Education Act of 1876 applied these new regulations to the non-textile factories, and also placed workshops on the same footing in respect of education[3].

The enforcement of the Factory Acts towards parents and employer and of the Education Act as regards the employer remained with the Factory Inspectors: towards the parent in respect of the Education Act and in respect of any by-law it rested with the School Boards and School Attendance Committees and their officers.

In 1878 the Factory and Workshop Acts were consolidated by a new measure[4]. The latest educational provisions remained substantially the same, although there were several changes of detail. All factories and workshops were subject to this Act, but the employment of fifty persons no longer

---

[1] 37 & 38 Vict. c. 44.

[2] Minute of Education Department, June 23, 1875.

[3] Sections 31, 38 and 39 of the Factory Act of 1844 were now applied to them, as well as the new regulations.

[4] 41 Vict. c. 16.

constituted an establishment a factory as in the Act of 1867. A child failing to make in any week all its required attendances had now to make up the deficient hours before it could be again admitted to employment in the next week. As in the Workshop Regulation Act, 1867, the employer was bound to continue to pay a school fee, not exceeding in this instance *three* pence, and not exceeding one-twelfth of the child's wages (from which it might be deducted as long as the child remained at the school); the application was now to be made not by the Inspector, but by the board authority or persons managing the school.

The standards of proficiency and due attendance were to be fixed from time to time for the purpose of the Act by the Home Secretary with the consent of the Education Department, and were to be published in the *London Gazette*, but not to take effect until the expiration of at least six months from publication. By the *London Gazette*, Feb. 25, 1879, proficiency was fixed at the Fourth Standard[1]; the attendances must be 250 a year, at not more than two schools for five years after five years of age.

The maximum fine of a parent for a breach of the Factory Acts remains twenty shillings, while in the case of the English Education Acts it is only[2] five shillings.

The Elementary Education Act of 1880 made local by-laws for attendance compulsory everywhere, and, while saving existing engagements, implied that in future by-laws should override the Factory Acts. Children of thirteen, however, were allowed to obtain exemption on a certificate of mere attendance as well as on a certificate of proficiency.

The Factory and Workshop Act of 1891[3] directs that after January 1, 1893, no child under the age of eleven years should be employed in a factory or workshop, and so far anticipated the provision of the Elementary Education

---

[1] After 1893, by Orders of March 4, August 16, 1892: the Fourth or any higher Standard required by the by-laws of the locality.
[2] Including costs.   [3] 54 & 55 Vict. c. 75.

(School Attendance) Act of 1893 [1], which raised the age of indispensable attendance at school to the same extent.

From being in advance of their times the Factory Acts fell behind them, and between 1870 and 1880 served to exclude children from the benefits of the Education Acts. To these they are now subordinate, and are consequently of no educational effect at all, except in the degree in which Factory Inspectors enforce upon employers the non-employment of unlicensed children, and in the fact that whole-time employment is forbidden to children between eleven and thirteen who are employed in factories.

Even the question of half-time employment is losing its importance [2], for the number of half-timers is rapidly and steadily dwindling [3].

It must be remembered that this legislation applies only to children employed in factories of a certain class, and that a more real evil is the amount of work that children of poor parents have to do every day in addition to the school work, which is supposed to demand their full energies.

ii. *Mines Acts.*

The first Collieries Act was passed in 1842, and Inspectors were appointed in 1850. Education, however, was not touched until the general Mines Act of 1860 [4] was passed, which required a certificate of proficiency or attendance from boys between ten and twelve, girls not being allowed to work.

As far as metalliferous mines were concerned this Act was repealed in 1872, and the new Act, which prohibited the

---

[1] 56 & 57 Vict. c. 51.

[2] In London in 1893 there were less than 700 half-timers, and in Birmingham and Sheffield together less than 400 (Report on Child Labour, 1893; P. P., 1893, No. 311, p. 24).

[3]
1876	201,284.	
1890 *	175,437	52·46 per cent. of whom were in Lancashire.
1897	110,654	54·27 per cent. of whom were in Lancashire.

 * (Of these only 98,888 were employed in factories. Report on Child Labour, 1893, p. 21.)

[4] 23 & 24 Vict. c. 151.

employment underground of boys below twelve, contained no educational provisions. The Coal Mines Regulation Act of the same year[1] required attendance of boys between ten and twelve. The Coal Mines Regulation Act, 1887[2], consolidated previous Acts, but prohibited all employment of boys under twelve. The employer is still bound to pay over to the teacher of any public elementary school twopence a week, or one-twelfth of the wages of any boy or girl in his employment attending that school, boy or girl being defined as persons under the age of sixteen.

As for above-ground employment, 'pitbanks' are, by the Factory and Workshop Act of 1878, included among non-textile factories or workshops, alike for coal and metalliferous mines.

Agricultural Children Act. In this connexion the Agricultural Children Act, 1873[3], may be mentioned. It forbade agricultural labour under eight and ordered attendance at school ; but no machinery was provided to enforce the Act, and it was placed under the charge of no Department. Consequently it remained a dead letter, and was repealed and superseded by the Education Act of 1876.

iii. *Prison Schools.*

By the Prisons Act, 1865[4], it was directed that provision should be made in every prison in England and Wales for the instruction of prisoners in reading, writing, and arithmetic during such hours and to such an extent as to the Visiting Justices might seem expedient, provided that such hours should not be deducted from the hours prescribed for hard labour.

By the Prisons Act, 1877[5], all these powers previously exercised by the Visiting Justices were vested in the Prison Commissioners appointed by the Act.

In 1878 over fifty officers were employed as teachers in

[1] 35 & 36 Vict. c. 76.　　[2] 50 & 51 Vict. c. 58.
[3] 36 & 37 Vict. c. 67.　　[4] 28 & 29 Vict. c. 126.
[5] 39 & 40 Vict. c. 21.

113 prisons at a cost of £4,300, but were not engaged exclusively in teaching[1].

In 1879 a special Committee reported on a system of education suitable to the conditions peculiar to prison life, and the present regulations were adopted.

In local prisons schoolmaster-warders are specially selected by the Governors and Chaplains and recommended to the Commissioners for engagement: they are tested by one of Her Majesty's Inspectors of the Education Department[2].

No prisoner sentenced for less than four months receives instruction, which only extends to Standard III of the Public Elementary Code[3].

In convict prisons all the schoolmasters have certificates of the Education Department. Instruction is given up to the 'Sixth Standard,' which, however, only corresponds to the public Fourth Standard. It is given in classes, whereas in local prisons it is given in separate cells[4].

In 1896 a Departmental Committee reported on the Education and Moral Instruction of Prisoners in Local and Convict Prisons in England and Wales, and in 1897 the Commissioners of Prisons and Directors of Convict Prisons reported that they had submitted a scheme for carrying out the recommendations. Persons imprisoned for three months might receive instruction; the first three standards of the Day School Code were adopted, and the systems in convict and local prisons were assimilated. The convict's education was to be 'completed' in the nine months before he was transferred to public works prisons[5].

iv. *Reformatory and Industrial Schools.*

These schools, so far as they are recognized by Government, are under the control of the Home Secretary. 'Reformatories are schools to which are sent juveniles up to

---

[1] 1896 Committee Report, p. 5.
[2] Ibid. p. 9.
[3] Ibid. Q. 4,551.
[4] Ibid. p. 10.
[5] Report for 1896–97, p. 18.

the age of sixteen, convicted of an offence punishable with penal servitude and imprisonment. Industrial Schools are for children up to the age of fourteen, who may not have committed an offence, but whose circumstances are such that if left in their surroundings they are likely to join the delinquent population. Thus Reformatories are for actual, Industrial Schools for potential delinquents, and the former contain children some three years older or more than the latter. Both are voluntarily maintained by private associations or local authorities, aided by a Government contribution towards their expenses, and are subject to Government inspection [1].'

Reformatory Schools. Schools which subsequently became Reformatories were founded in the last century, and received recognition from Government prior to 1838, when the Crown exercised its prerogative through the Home Secretary by granting pardons to boys sentenced to transportation on condition that they should submit to the training of some specified school of this class [2].

The Treasury contributed to their support a sum that was intended to cover the expense of these offenders [3].

In 1846 the Committee of Council on Education offered grants for industrial training [4], and schools of the reformatory class availed themselves of these privileges until the end of 1857, when those institutions which had begun to receive aid and inspection from the Home Office were handed over altogether to its consideration [5]. In 1846 the Committee also recommended that £5,000, out of £20,000 voted by

[1] Inspector's Report for 1895, p. 8, slightly abridged.

[2] 1 & 2 Vict. c. 82, s. 11.   This is a recital in an Act by which, in the first year of the Queen's reign, a prison was established for young offenders only at Parkhurst in the Isle of Wight. It was a step in reform, but even at Parkhurst the prisoners at first all wore irons (Lushington Committee Report, i. 182), and in the fields were superintended by sentries with loaded weapons (Aberdare Report, ii. 736).

[3] Minutes of Committee of Council on Education, 1852–53, P. P., lxxix. p. 537.

[4] Minute, December 21.

[5] Minute, Dec. 31, 1857; P. P., 1859, xxi a. xxxiv; Lushington Report, 1896, i. p. 318.

Parliament, should be expended on a Model Penal School ; but this was never done [1].

In 1854 [2] the first Statute dealing directly with Reformatories was passed—'The Youthful Offenders Act [3].' By it the Home Secretary was empowered to certify Reformatory Schools, if on the report of an Inspector of Prisons they appeared useful and efficient for their purpose. Any person under sixteen convicted of any offence punishable by law on an indictment or a summary conviction before a magistrate or two or more justices of the peace might, on the direction of the Court, be sent at the expiration of his sentence to a Reformatory School for an additional period of not less than two or more than five years. The Treasury might defray the cost out of funds to be provided by Parliament for the purpose, and parents or step-parents might be compelled to support such offender while in the school. An Inspector of Prisons visited the institutions and made an annual report.

The Reformatory and Industrial Schools Act [4] passed in 1856 provided that young persons should not be sent to a school to which the parents objected, if they named another school duly certified.

In 1857 the Quarter Sessions or Council of any Quarter Sessions Borough were allowed to grant money in aid of a Reformatory School [5].

In the same year the Rev. Sydney Turner was appointed as a Prison Inspector by the Home Secretary especially to inspect and report on Reformatory and Industrial Schools [6].

---

[1] P. P., 1854–55, p. 394.

[2] In the same year Feltham Industrial School was established for Middlesex by a private Act (17 & 18 Vict. c. clxix), receiving only convicted children between the ages of seven and fourteen, being thus a Reformatory in point of character, and an Industrial School in respect of age.

[3] 17 & 18 Vict. c. 86.   [4] 19 & 20 Vict. c. 109.

[5] 20 & 21 Vict. c. 55 ; now by 51 & 52 Vict. c. 41, ss. 3, 38, transferred to County Councils and councils of larger municipal boroughs.

[6] 5 & 6 Will. IV. c. 38, s. 7; P. P. Eng., 1876, C. 1534; Mr. Turner's last report and review of the system.

During the four years 1854–57 forty-four of these schools were certified in England [1].

By the Reformatory Schools Act, 1866 [2], the previous Acts were repealed, consolidated, and amended. Offences for which persons could be sent to Reformatories must be such as were punishable with penal servitude or imprisonment. No child under ten might be sent to a Reformatory, unless sentenced by a Judge of Assize or Court of General or Quarter Sessions, or previously charged with an offence punishable with penal servitude or imprisonment. The parents might apply within thirty days to have an offender removed to a Reformatory conducted in accordance with the religious persuasion of the offender.

The Prison Authorities [3] were given power to defray the cost as current expenditure, while the Treasury might contribute out of monies provided by Parliament for the purpose a sum recommended by the Home Secretary. A special Inspector was appointed for the Reformatories and Industrial Schools for Great Britain.

The Prison Authority was given power to contract with a Reformatory to receive and maintain offenders, or to contribute to the establishment of such a school, or subsequently (in 1872) to build and maintain such a school themselves.

By Lord Leigh's Act [4], passed in 1893, new provisions were substituted for those of 1866 for sending offenders to Reformatories. The age was raised from ten to twelve, unless the child had been previously convicted, the minimum term raised from two to three years, and the imprisonment previous to being sent to the school might be dispensed with. In no case were offenders to be kept at the school after attaining the age of nineteen.

Industrial Schools. The early history of Industrial Schools is the outcome of two different purposes. On the one hand

---

[1] Newcastle Report, i. 408.   [2] 29 & 30 Vict. c. 117.
[3] As defined by 28 & 29 Vict. c. 126, s. 5.
[4] 56 & 57 Vict. c. 48.

there was the anxiety to prevent boys from falling into bad company, which has latterly been the controlling influence in these schools; and on the other there was that desire to give an industrial training which has recently found its expression rather in technical and manual instruction.

In the early days Ragged Schools were frequently mentioned in the same connexion with Industrial Schools[1]. They were provided by charity free of charge, and made no requirements as to the dress of the pupils; consequently they were used chiefly by the children of outdoor paupers, of the dissolute, and of those unwilling to pay fees[2]. The secular part of their educational work has naturally been absorbed by the Board Schools[3].

The Education Department in 1846 offered Grants to day schools of industry for rent of field gardens, and help to hire or build workshops, washhouses, or kitchens, and to provide tools. It specially referred to schools situated in the denser parts of great cities, intended to attract from the streets vagrant youths who are there trained in criminal pursuits, or accustomed to beggary and vagrancy[4].

By Minutes in 1856[5] and 1857[6] the Committee of Council considerably extended their industrial grants to schools, confining them, however, to schools which were industrial in character, and educated scholars taken exclusively from the criminal and abandoned classes; but by 23 & 24 Vict. c. 108, Industrial Schools were transferred to the charge of the Home Secretary in 1860, and all connexion with the Education Department ceased.

Meanwhile the first Industrial Schools Act for England and Wales had been passed in 1857[7]. Children above seven and under fourteen, convicted of vagrancy, might be com-

---

[1] Education Department Minute, Dec. 31, 1857; Newcastle Report, i. 388, 397.
[2] Newcastle Report, i. 391.
[3] Cross Report, iii. p. 438.
[4] Minute, Dec. 21, 1846; P. P. Eng., 1854–55, xli. p. 209.
[5] June 2.   [6] December 31.
[7] 20 and 21 Vict. c. 48, and an amending Act in 1860, 23 & 24 Vict. c. 108.

mitted to a school certified by the Committee of Council on Education and examined by their Inspector (after 1860 by the Inspector of the Home Department), but only if the parents would not give an assurance in writing for the child's good behaviour or find a security for the same. The parents might be made liable for the support of the child up to 3*s.* a week; the child could not be detained beyond the age of fifteen against his or her will.

In 1861 24 & 25 Vict. c. 113 consolidated the previous Acts and enlarged their scope.

A distinction was introduced between children under twelve and those under fourteen. The latter, if destitute, vagrant, mendicant, or frequenting the company of reputed thieves, might be committed to an Industrial School; under twelve, they could also be sent if they had committed an offence punishable by imprisonment or some less punishment. Children need no longer be *convicted* in order to be sent to an Industrial School, but if convicted previously of felony they were not admissible. Parents might present their children under fourteen before the justices as unmanageable, and obtain an order committing them to school; but in this case the parents had to defray the whole expense. For the maintenance of the others the Treasury was empowered to contribute any sum that the Home Secretary might recommend, and the extent of their parents' possible contribution was raised to 5*s.* a week. Children convicted on a previous charge of felony were not admitted to these schools.

This Act was only temporary, but in 1866 29 & 30 Vict. c. 118 was passed, which embodied most of its provisions, and remains the controlling Act till the present time. Under the new regulations a child under fourteen, being a destitute orphan or with a surviving parent undergoing penal servitude or imprisonment, was added to the list of those liable to be sent to these schools, and the limit of detention without consent was raised from fifteen to sixteen.

The Inspector of Industrial Schools and the Inspector of

Reformatories must be necessarily one and the same person appointed by the Home Secretary. Refractory children might be sent from workhouses and pauper schools, and the Guardians had power to contribute. The same school might not be certified both as a Reformatory and an Industrial School [1]. The Prison Authority might contract for the reception of children at these schools, and contribute to the capital or current expenditure; and in 1872 these bodies received power to establish and maintain schools themselves, if necessary [2].

Children under fourteen of a woman twice convicted of crime, or children living with prostitutes, may be sent to these schools [3].

In 1870, by the Elementary Education Act, School Boards received powers of contributing to the establishment and maintenance of Industrial Schools, and—with consent of the Education Department [4]—of establishing such schools themselves [5]. They also received power to enforce the Industrial Schools Act—if they thought fit [6].

By the 1876 Act, School Boards and School Attendance Committees were compelled to enforce the Act—unless they thought it inexpedient [7].

In the case of offences against the Act, if no Day Industrial School were available, a child might be committed to any certified Industrial School. Children so sent might be released on licence at the end of one month, instead of eighteen months as in 1866.

Industrial Schools established after March, 1872, receive only 3s. 6d. for each child from Government instead of 5s.

Day Industrial Schools. These were a further development introduced by the Elementary Education Act of 1876,

---

[1] Feltham in Middlesex is a partial exception to this, being under a special Act of Parliament, 17 & 18 Vict. c. clxix.

[2] 35 & 36 Vict. c. 21 ; power to borrow, 37 & 38 Vict. c. 47.

[3] 34 & 35 Vict. c. 112 ; 43 & 44 Vict. c. 15.

[4] Since 1876, of the Home Secretary.

[5] c. 75, ss. 27, 28. There were nine Industrial Schools under School Boards in 1896.

[6] c. 75, s. 36.   [7] c. 79, s. 13.

and are schools where children are compelled to attend daily and receive industrial training, elementary education, and one or more meals a day. The Act directs that in the case of children for whom their parents habitually and without reasonable excuse neglect to provide efficient elementary education, or who are habitually found wandering or not under proper control, or in the company of rogues, vagabonds, disorderly persons, or reputed criminals, it shall be the duty of the local authority to apply to a court of summary jurisdiction for an Attendance Order[1], on breach of which the Court may order the child to be sent to a certified Day Industrial School, if the parent be not in default, or the order be disobeyed a second time.

Prison Authorities and School Boards have the same powers of establishing them or contributing to them as in the case of Industrial Schools. They are regulated, in addition to the Act, by the Orders issued by the Home Secretary and Orders in Council. The expense is met by a Treasury contribution of 1*s.* a week per child, being the maximum allowed by law; the parent cannot be made to contribute more than 2*s.* a week, the guardians being bound to pay if he cannot, and the residue (if any) is made up by the managers. There were only twenty of these schools in England in 1896, accommodating over 3,000 children, but the Departmental Committee had 'nothing but praise to give these institutions.' 'The system is non-punitive, and the object is to make the children as happy as possible[2].' They exercise strict control over the children without destroying the bond of family life. The School, though not under the Education Department, resembles in most respects any ordinary public elementary school, with exceptionally regular attendance, as the children are sent for at once every morning, if they do not come. They are all mixed schools for boys and girls. The attendance is usually continued for about two years[3].

---

[1] *Vide* p. 28.   [2] Lushington Report, p. 125.   [3] Ibid. p. 126.

Truant Schools. There are fifteen so-called Truant Schools, established by twelve School Boards, which are ordinary certified Industrial Schools adopting a system of short detention and severe discipline for truant children. They were described in 1882 as practically 'prisons and schools of mere detention[1],' and were unfavourably regarded by the Committee of 1896.

In England and Wales there were on December 31, 1896, 39 Reformatories with 4,026 young offenders actually in the schools, and 109 Industrial Schools with 12,872 scholars[2]. In 20 Day Industrial Schools there were 2,616 children, and 1,220 in 15 Truant Schools[3].

Investigations. The Newcastle Commission reported in 1861 that, on the whole, none of the institutions connected with education appeared to be in a more satisfactory condition than the Reformatories[4]; but, on the other hand, they recommended that Industrial Schools should be gradually replaced by declaring District and separate Union Schools available for the reception of suitable children[5].

In 1882 a Commission under Lord Aberdare was appointed to inquire into Reformatories and Industrial Schools, and their report was presented in 1884. They recommended that the inspection of all Reformatory and Industrial Schools should be transferred to the Education Department, who should make the same grants to them as to Public Elementary Schools, and that contributions from Boards of Guardians on a fixed scale should be substituted for all other grants to Industrial Schools from Councils and School Boards.

In 1893 there was a strong representation made to the Home Office as to the narrowness and insufficiency of the education given in the Metropolitan Schools, and the Home Secretary promised that there should be an improvement[6].

---

[1] Aberdare Report, Q. 1,016.
[2] 40th Report of Inspector, P. P., 1897, C. 8,566, pp. 464, 523. The figures are different on p. 15. For former years *vide* pp. 11, 12 ibidem.
[3] Ibid. pp. 591, 600.   [4] Report, i. 413.   [5] Ibid. p. 405.
[6] Letter, June 2, 1893; Lushington Report, i. 38.

In 1895 a Departmental Committee under Sir Godfrey Lushington was appointed to report on Reformatory and Industrial Schools, and the report was presented in 1896. They recommended that Truant and Day Industrial Schools should be placed under the Education Department, but decided by a narrow majority that this was inadvisable for Reformatories and ordinary Industrial Schools. Children at Industrial Schools should be enabled to attend public elementary schools, if the authorities of both schools agreed.

Education. Reformatories and ordinary Industrial Schools may conveniently be considered together in respect of the education given, as they are under the one Inspector, and their teachers practically belong to the same class. The Act for Industrial Schools directs that industrial training shall be given, while that for Reformatories does not specify this requirement, but the Model Rules issued by the Home Secretary exact it in both cases, for Reformatories for not more than six or less than four hours a day, for Industrial Schools for four hours without alternative.

For the elementary instruction teachers are engaged by each separate establishment, and the only check on their efficiency is the report of the Inspector on the state of education in the school. In Industrial Schools (but not in Reformatories) £20 a year is paid by the Treasury towards the salary of a schoolmaster if he have a certificate, and £15 for a mistress on similar terms[1]. No part of the general grant to the school depends upon the quality of the education. Originally there was a rule that if this were unsatisfactory there should be a reduction of 1s. 6d. from the general grant, but this was never enforced[2].

The standards of the Education Department have been introduced into the schools, but till recently there was no official encouragement to proceed beyond Standard Five[3].

In December, 1895, the standards in elementary subjects were exactly assimilated to the Code of the Education

---

[1] Lushington Report, p. 41, Q. 30,172.
[2] Ibid. Q. 1,543.   [3] Ibid. p. 36.

Department, and the teaching of class subjects, such as
geography and history, was encouraged[1].

The schools are necessarily all half-time schools, three
hours secular instruction being given daily. The children
are more backward on admission into the Reformatories
than into Industrial Schools, even considering the greater
age, the percentage being as follows:—

		Ref.	*Ind. S.*
Below Standard	I.	15	24
„	III.	74	46
„	V.	11	30 [2]

On the whole, progress has been made in the last twenty
years, and apparently the schools are now as good as half-
time schools elsewhere [3], apart from the fact that the pupils
in public elementary schools are, on the average, several
years younger than these 'children with a history[4].'

The industrial training is elementary in most of these
schools, but there is a very wide difference in the equip-
ment of the different establishments, which all, nevertheless,
receive grants on the same scale.

Only the rudiments of a few trades are taught in most
cases, and the Inspectors agree that the majority of boys
leaving Reformatories do not follow the trades they were
taught there. Labour is considered as reformatory in itself,
and the training is not sufficiently directed to educating
a boy to maintain himself[5]. Nevertheless the Factory Acts
are not enforced in these schools[6].

Conscience Clause. Provision is made in both Reformatories and Industrial Schools for children, as far as possible,
being sent to schools of their own denomination ; if this be
not possible, ministers of their own denomination have
access to them for instruction[7], and they are not compelled

---

[1] Lushington, p. 39.   [2] Ibid. p. 36.
[3] The late Inspector pronounced them in 1882 'quite fit to teach as
far as we want them to go' (Aberdare, Q. 582).
[4] Departmental Report, 1896, pp. 37–39.
[5] Lushington Report, p. 50.   [6] Ibid. 53.
[7] 29 & 30 Vict. c. 117, ss. 14–16; c. 118, ss. 18, 19, 25.

to attend other religious services. But in the case of Roman Catholics, at any rate, these safeguards were not regarded as adequate by the Committee of 1896, as the local authorities often refuse to contribute, if the children are moved [1] away to one of their own schools [2].

4. THE LOCAL GOVERNMENT BOARD.

This Board was created in 1871 [3] to take over the functions of the Poor Law Board and the supervision of the laws relating to the public health and local government.

i. *The Poor Law.*

In 1834 the Poor Law system of England and Wales was placed on a new footing [4] and administered by Commissioners until 1847, when a Ministerial Department called the Poor Law Board was formed, consisting of several Cabinet Ministers and a new Minister called the President of the Poor Law Board [5].

Under the old Poor Law there was seldom any education in the workhouses except such as was given by some chance pauper who acted as schoolmaster to the children, who were not often separated from the adult paupers [6].

By the first set of regulations published by the new Poor Law Commissioners in 1835 the boys and girls in every

[1] Lushington, p. 130.

[2] There is probably some danger of high-handed dealings, as appears from the answer of a Secretary of a Reformatory in 1882 (Aberdare Report, Q. 4,046) : 'Yes; we teach the Catechism whatever the denomination may be of the child's parents. We never heard of any parents having a denomination. I fancy that if they got as far as that, we should not have their children.' In which also there is much truth ; in that instance it fortunately could be added, 'They have never raised such a thing as the shadow of a religious difficulty.'

[3] 34 & 35 Vict. c. 70.   [4] 4 & 5 Will. IV. c. 76.

[5] 10 & 11 Vict. c. 109.

[6] *Children under the Poor Law,* by W. Chance, M.A. (Swan Sonnenschein & Co., 1897, 7s. 6d.), p. 2. A most valuable book, with abundant quotations from and references to the original sources. Reports of Poor Law Inspectors on the Education of Pauper Children, P. P. Eng., 1862, xlix. p. 567; Mr. Andrew Doyle's Report ; also G. T. C. Bartley, *The Schools for the People,* p. 269: Bell & Daldy, 1871.

workhouse were to be instructed in reading, writing, and the principles of the Christian religion[1] for at least three of the working hours in every day, and a schoolmaster and mistress and any assistants necessary might be engaged by the Guardians.

At the time this was the only systematic and compulsory education recognized by the Government, except in the case of the Services and the factories. It is the less surprising to find the Bedford Guardians requesting that reading only might be taught in their workhouse, in order that the inmates of the workhouse might not receive greater advantages than the children of the self-supporting poor[2].

A good many Unions even at this date sent their children to the outside village schools[3].

In 1844 power was given to the Commissioners by 7 and 8 Vict. c. 101 to combine poor law unions[4] or parishes not in union into Districts for school purposes, but the consent of the Guardians in writing was necessary for the combination, and the consent of pauper parents was required before their children could be sent to such district school.

No district might be more than fifteen miles in length, nor might more than one-fifth of the average annual rates be expended on such district school[5]. Such a school district was to be governed by a board of qualified ratepayers elected by the Guardians, and the Chairman of each Board of Guardians was, with his own consent, to be an *ex officio* member.

The Acts of 1834 and 1844 both provided that no regulation should authorize the education of any child in any religious creed other than that professed by the parent, and that the licensed minister of the corresponding religious

---

[1] In 1847 arithmetic was added (Chance, p. 12).

[2] Chance, p. 5.

[3] Report on the Training of Pauper Children, E. C. Tufnell, 1841.

[4] The unit of administration was the parish or a combination of parishes directed by the Commissioners and called a Union (Rev. T. W. Fowle, *Poor Law*, p. 25 : Macmillan, 1881).

[5] The last two restrictions, however, were removed or amended by 11 & 12 Vict. c. 82 and 14 & 15 Vict. c. 105.

persuasion might visit the school or asylum for the purpose of instructing a child in the principles of his religion [1].

In 1846 the House of Commons voted a sum of £20,000 to be spent on a normal school for training teachers for workhouse and for penal schools. On the matter being referred to the Committee of Council for Education for their advice, it was recommended by them that half the sum should be spent on the normal school, and two sums of £5,000 each on a pauper and a penal model school.

As a result Kneller Hall was opened near Hounslow in 1850 under the present Archbishop of Canterbury and the late Mr. F. T. Palgrave as a training college for Poor Law schoolmasters, but it was found that the prospects of subsequent employment were not such as to attract suitable candidates. The Model School was never built, and the scheme if not ill-devised [2] was at all events not effectively carried out, and was discontinued at the end of 1855 [3].

In 1846 £15,000 was voted by the Commons towards the salaries of masters and mistresses of workhouse schools, of which there were by this time some 700. These salaries had hitherto been fixed and paid by the separate boards of guardians out of the rates. The distribution of this grant also was referred to the Committee of Council, and they determined to award salaries according to teachers' qualifications [4]. The vote was increased next year to £30,000 [5], and the Committee then made arrangements for the gradual examination of teachers, and fixed their salaries in proportion to the certificates which they obtained and to the extent of their duties. Grants were also made to masters for scholars apprenticed to them (as far as was possible) for five years as pupil teachers, part of the pupil-teacher grant being retained for the apprentice's future

---

[1] 4 & 5 Will. IV. c. 76, s. 19; 7 & 8 Vict. c. 101, s. 43. By another Act of 1844 (c. 101) masters could no longer be compelled to receive apprentices.

[2] Mr. Andrew Doyle's Report, P. P., 1862, xlix. 595.

[3] P. P., 1854-55, xli. p. 394.   [4] Minute, Dec. 21, 1846.

[5] P. P., 1847, xxxv. p. 264.

benefit. Salaries of industrial instructors might also be charged on the grant [1].

In order to proportion the salary more exactly to the work actually done, a circular of the Poor Law Board was issued on May 6, 1850, by which Guardians or Managers guarantee a minimum salary to each teacher, and if the Government Grant to them, based on the class of certificate and the number of children instructed by each teacher, exceeds that minimum, the surplus—up to a certain maximum total for each class of certificate—is paid over to the teacher by the Guardians or Managers. Any such surplus must depend in the last resort upon the capitation grant, and consequently it is to the teacher's interest to keep as many children in his class as possible. For a long time this was said to have a harmful effect on the schools [2], but of late years there seems to have been no abuse of the system, and in the highest class it can only be beneficial [3].

The control over the teachers' salaries was a great power in the hands of the Poor Law Board, as they could withhold the grant and throw the payment of salary on the rates, if the Guardians refused reform.

In 1847 the Committee of Council appointed four Inspectors of Poor Law schools, of the same class as their own Inspectors and with similar duties, and these continued to report to the Education Department until March 31, 1863, when they were transferred to the service of the Poor Law Board at the request of the Department [4]. The reason seems to have been, in addition to 'unnecessary trouble,' 'a certain friction caused by the different ideas which prevailed in the Departments as to how these

[1] Minute, Dec. 18, 1847.

[2] Newcastle Report, i. p. 363; G. T. C. Bartley, *The Schools for the People*, p. 280.

[3] Circular of P. L. B., May 6, 1850; the amount of capitation grant has since been raised slightly. I am indebted for some of this information to the kindness of Mr. J. R. Mozley, the Senior Inspector, who is not in any way responsible for my version of the facts.

[4] 16th Report of Poor Law Board, 1864, p. 19.

schools should be conducted [1].' The Poor Law Board thenceforth issued its own certificates to its teachers, but the principles of inspection and examination were in no way changed [2].

Provision for the education of refractory pauper children in Industrial Schools and of afflicted pauper children in certified special schools was made in 1861 and 1862 respectively [3]. Boarding out children is, as we shall see, the invariable practice in Scotland, and though not officially recognized had been employed in England in some cases, but only within the limits of the same Union. In 1870 an Order of the Poor Law Board first permitted its extension to boarding beyond these limits [4].

In 1878 the Board directed that the Standards of Examination in Poor Law Schools should be those of the Education Department, and that time-tables should be prepared and Attendance Registers kept [5].

The result of all these laws and regulations has been that District Schools have made but little way, only eight school districts having been formed by 1868, and only two having been permanently added since [6]. Some Boards of Guardians have started large schools for their children at a distance from the workhouse, but the really important movement has been in the direction of educating pauper children along with the rest of the population. Mr. Holgate, an Inspector of Schools under the Local Government Board, said, in 1887, that in a short time we should see the last workhouse school pure and simple abolished, unless it happened that there was no public elementary school

---

[1] Childers Select Committee, 1884, Q. 158, 159, 286.

[2] In 1890 the Education Department consented to issue their parchment certificates to Poor Law teachers, on examination by the Education Department Inspectors. Since 1889 salaries to teachers have no longer been paid direct by Government, but by the County Councils out of the sums ceded from the Imperial revenues under the Local Government Act, 1888, the Local Government Board annually certifying the amount.

[3] 24 & 25 Vict. c. 113, replaced by 29 & 30 Vict. c. 118; 25 & 26 Vict. c. 43.

[4] Chance, pp. 28, 29.   [5] Ibid. p. 40.   [6] Ibid. p. 30.

within reach [1]. The progress of this has no doubt been greatly accelerated by the Education Act of 1891, which pays a fee grant of 10*s*. out of the National Exchequer to the school managers for every child in average attendance at public elementary schools, and thus relieves the Guardians to that extent [2]. The rapidity of the process is best illustrated by the following figures :—

Number of Unions in which children attend	1890.	1896.
Workhouse Schools	200	84
Schools detached from Workhouse . .	68	58
District Schools	28	30
Schools of other Unions	26	28
Public Elementary Schools	325	449
	647	649

In 1896 the average daily number of children in District Schools in England and Wales was 7,880, and the children in other Poor Law Schools numbered 15,503 [3].

There has not been a great deal of direct official investigation into the education given to children under the Poor Law. The Newcastle Commission on Elementary Education reported on it in 1861, and the Cross Commissioners referred to it in 1888 [4]. In 1894 a Departmental Committee, with Mr. Mundella as Chairman, inquired into the existing systems of Poor Law Schools in the Metropolis, and reported in 1896.

The first of these authorities laid great stress on the evil of mixing the children with adult paupers in the workhouses, and recommended that the Poor Law Board should have power to order the creation of District Schools. They found the state of the children of those receiving out-relief was morally, intellectually, and physically as low as possible [5],

---

[1] Cross Commission Report, iii. p. 49, Q. 49,865.

[2] The case of each school is judged on its own merits for the fee grant, which may be withdrawn under sec. 4, sub-sec. (3), but in point of fact this never seems to have been done.

[3] 26th Report, Local Government Board, p. xci.

[4] Mrs. Nassau Senior's inquiry in 1874 was confined almost exclusively to physical, moral, and domestic training (Chance, p. 35).

[5] Newcastle Report, i. 381.

and that probably there were a hundred thousand of them receiving no education at all.   They recommended that the Guardians should be required to enable any child (between four and fifteen) of any person receiving out-relief to receive education at any school approved by the Poor Law Board, and that attendance at school should be a condition of the continuance of out-relief[1].

In 1862 the Poor Law Board requested their Inspectors to report on the possibility of improving pauper education[2], and Mr. Andrew Doyle especially showed that the inquiry of the Commission was unfairly restricted, their evidence partial and much of it quite out of date, and abundant data were quoted in contradiction.   A trenchant criticism of Kneller Hall is to be found in the same pages[3].

The Commission of 1888 recommended that the educational inspection should be transferred to the Education Department[4], and in 1896 the Mundella Committee repeated the recommendation.

As to literary efficiency, the Education Department Standards were introduced in 1878[5], but even in 1886 in many District Schools only the three elementary subjects were taught[6].   The inspection does not seem yet to have followed the improvement of H. M. Inspectors of the 'Education Department[7].

In the Metropolitan Poor Law Schools the Committee of 1896 found that the curriculum remained where it was in 1847[8].   But this statement does not seem to be borne out by the actual practice in the schools, although official requirements apparently extended no further[9].   The Committee, however, considered the schools far below the standard usually attained by the children in public elementary

---

[1] Newcastle Report, i. p. 383.   [2] P. P. Eng., 1862, xlix. 513.
[3] Ibid. p. 595.   [4] Final Report, i. pp. 162, 239.
[5] General Order, April 3, 1878; Chance, p. 97.
[6] Cross Evidence, Q. 49,836.   [7] Chance, p. 352.
[8] When arithmetic was added to the subjects taught (General Order, July 24, 1847).
[9] Chance, p. 98; a great number of contrary instances are given.

schools, and had seen no school which would be classed as excellent [1]—statements which admit less of direct disproof.

The industrial training in 1888 seemed hardly what it ought to be, and eight years later it was very unsatisfactory [2], a verdict which Mr. Chance applies to the whole country [3]. Until the General Order of January 30, 1897, Poor Law children of ten were in some cases treated as half-timers, contrary to the Education Act of 1893 [4]. The training of boys as musicians and sailors appears the most satisfactory department [5], otherwise boys do not seem to keep to the employment in which they have been instructed [6]. Special efforts are made to train girls for domestic service [7] in ordinary houses. The chief difficulty where workhouse children attend public schools is to provide for adequate supervision out of school time [8]. Occasionally there seems to be reluctance to mix with the other children—on the part of the clean workhouse child [9].

The Mundella Committee recommended that all Poor Law children should be educated as far as possible in the ordinary public elementary schools, or at all events in schools sufficiently detached from the buildings in which the children are maintained; that the schools should be considered public elementary schools, and receive grants and inspection from the Education Department, the former according to attendance and to efficiency. The standard of teachers should be that of ordinary public elementary schools, and teachers should be allowed to pass into the service of other managers. The use of such 'class' and 'specific' subjects as are deemed suitable should be optional in these schools, and religious knowledge should be tested by the chaplain, subject of course to the conscience clause.

Payment of School Fees by Guardians. Denison's Act [10] enabled Board of Guardians, if they deemed proper, to

---

[1] Report, p. 39.   [2] Ibid. p. 46.   [3] Chance, p. 377.
[4] Ibid. p. 379.   [5] Ibid. p. 86.
[6] p. 25.   [7] p. 92.   [8] p. 173.
[9] Ibid. p. 172; Mundella Report, Q. 15,511.
[10] 18 & 19 Vict. c. 34.

grant further relief to parents receiving out-relief to enable them to provide schooling for any child between four and sixteen in any school approved of by the Guardians. Attendance at school was not to be made a condition of out-relief. But out-paupers were not eager for education, nor were Boards anxious to spend money. So the Act remained nearly a dead letter[1], until it was repealed in 1873 by 36 & 37 Vict. c. 86, under which the power remained with the Guardians. Attendance for children between five and thirteen became a necessary condition for the continuance of out-relief, but the parents were to have the choice of the school, and the fee paid was not to be more than a farthing for each attendance.

In 1876 this in turn was repealed[2]; out-relief remained contingent on school attendance, and the parent still had choice of the school. By the new Act, School Attendance Committees were not allowed to pay or remit fees; the power of School Boards under the Act of 1870 to pay fees not exceeding 3*d*. a week for children of indigent parents not in receipt of relief at any public elementary school was transferred to the Guardians, though the School Boards retained the power of remission. But since the payment of fees was abolished in 1891, the question has lost its importance.

ii. *Control of Local Authorities.*

School Attendance Committees and School Boards. Under the Education Act of 1876, School Attendance Committees appointed in country parishes by Boards of Guardians are strictly controlled by the Local Government Board. In fact, they may not incur any expense or appoint or employ any officer without consent of the Guardians and of the Local Government Board. School Attendance Committees appointed by District Councils have to keep their accounts as directed for those Councils. Under the Education Act, 1870, the accounts of School Boards have to be kept on

---

[1] Newcastle Report, i. 380.　　　　[2] 39 & 40 Vict. c. 79.

forms prescribed by the Local Government Board and audited by Poor Law auditors, subject to the direction of the same authority.

The School Attendance Committees of Borough Councils are responsible only to their respective Councils, who each appoint their own auditor.

5. THE COMMANDER-IN-CHIEF.

The Elementary Education provided for the Army falls under the two heads of soldiers and of their children, but it is administered by the one department and imparted chiefly by the same teachers. It must be borne in mind that the system has to be adapted not only to the United Kingdom, but also to soldiers and their families on foreign service.

Regimental schools were introduced in 1811, the schoolmaster being appointed by the colonel of each regiment.

In 1846 there was a reorganization : a Normal School was started at Chelsea for training Army schoolmasters, and the Royal Military Asylum, which had been opened in 1803 for the sons of soldiers, was used as a model school in connexion with it.

Schoolmistresses, regularly trained at some training college, were engaged for the 'infant' and 'industrial' schools, and these were allowed pupil teachers and two monitresses apiece if necessary. The industrial training was confined to girls and consisted of sewing, materials for which were provided by a small capitation grant.

By the Order in Council of February 25, 1856[1], it was recommended that the Education Department should for the future inspect the regimental schools in the United Kingdom and the training school at Chelsea, and report on them to the Secretary of State for War. But this does not appear ever to have been done[2].

In 1888, as the result of an Inquiry, regimental schools

---

[1] *Vide* p. 15.   [2] Bartley, *The Schools for the People*, p. 42.

were abolished, as being too small for efficiency, and the schools were consolidated in each garrison.

The Normal School was discontinued, and schoolmasters are now selected by competition from the Army, and from pupil teachers at the Asylum and Royal Hibernian School, any remaining vacancies being filled by certificated civilian schoolmasters of the second class without examination. All candidates are posted to a garrison school for a year on trial, and if satisfactory are then regularly enlisted in the Corps of Army Schoolmasters.

Trained schoolmistresses were considered too expensive, and the small children were in future to be entrusted to wives of non-commissioned officers and soldiers acting as schoolmistresses for a small salary. This last arrangement fortunately broke down at once, and competent trained mistresses were appointed as before when needed [1].

In 1875 the Royal Military Asylum was made a half-time school with a view to teaching the boys trades, but the effect on their general literary education was so disastrous that the full elementary course was restored in 1889 [2].

Compulsory Education and Abolition of Fees. Compulsory attendance of the men was always rather a difficult question, as in 1811 Sir James Mansfield had laid down that it was no part of military discipline to attend school [3], and in 1858 the law officers of the Crown had supported this opinion [4].

In 1849, however, the Commander-in-Chief published an Order requiring recruits to attend school for two hours daily; in spite of which attendance remained voluntary [4], and in 1872 all recruits were compelled to attend until they got a fourth-class certificate.

In 1888 the fourth class was abolished as worthless, being only equal to the Second Standard in elementary

[1] 1889 Report, paragraphs 24–26.   [2] Ibid. p. 18.
[3] Taunton's Common Pleas Reports, iv. 88.   *Warden* v. *Bailey.*
[4] Newcastle Report, p. 417.

schools, and compulsory education was abandoned, as it was a waste of time to teach soldiers who were unable or unwilling to pass out of the lowest class [1].

An educational standard has been required of every man for promotion to corporal or higher rank, at any rate since June, 1857.

In 1872 non-commissioned officers had to attend until they got third-class certificates, and since 1888 second and even first class certificates have been necessary for promotion to the higher non-commissioned ranks.

Fees were first remitted in the lowest class [2], and then gradually abolished altogether between 1860 and 1870.

Attendance of the children of soldiers is compulsory [3]: a small payment had formerly to be made by them. If there is no military school, and at depôts where the barracks are near enough, the children attend some certified efficient or inspected school approved of by the Secretary of State for War; provision was formerly made for the payment of their fees.

By the Army Schools Act of 1891 [4] all Army Schools are reckoned as public elementary schools for the purpose of any provision for like benefit of children in such schools in the case of any endowed charity.

The Education given. In 1886 the curriculum in Army Schools was for the first time assimilated to that in public elementary schools as approved by the Committee of Privy Council on Education.

A. To the Men. The object of these schools as declared by the Queen's Regulations is to afford men the opportunity of acquiring a sound and useful education.

The curriculum is elementary, the second class being equal only to the Fifth Standard [5], but any European or

---

[1] Suggested as probable by the Newcastle Commission, i. 427.

[2] Newcastle Report, i. 420; Second Report, Council of Military Education, p. 13.

[3] Second Report of Council, 1865, p. 15; Report, 1872, App. i; Queen's Regulations, 1892; Circular, July 5, 1892.

[4] 54 Vict. c. 16.   [5] 1893 Report, p. 7.

Oriental modern language, field fortification, military topography and tactics, may be taken up as optional subjects.

B. To the Children. In 1893 the subjects of the instruction given were identical in scope with those of the Civil Code, but were fewer in number.

Kindergarten teaching was adopted for the infants, but only in such greatly modified form as was compatible with the teaching obtainable and the expense possible in Army Schools; its introduction is proceeding very slowly[1].

Lessons begin with a prayer and a Bible lesson, but attendance at this is optional.

On the general education given in the older children's schools the Director-General wrote in 1893 :—

'It is evident that the elastic system by which the Code allows to managers of civil schools a wide choice of subjects is only possible in schools where both masters and scholars are stationary, and where the bulk of the civil population not being migratory, many children pass the whole of their school life in the same school. But in Army Schools such a system would not be suitable and would prove very costly.

' Besides periodical and " surprise " visits, there is a very strict system of annual examinations in Army Schools. At these annual examinations the tests in the " elementary subjects " are individual throughout, and in the " class subjects " the tests are collectively oral in the lower standards, but in Standards VI and VII they are partly written and partly oral.

' In Army Schools every child on the register must be examined. If presented for examination in a standard below that proper for its age, due inquiry is made to fix responsibility, and an Army School is held to be efficient only when soundness of attainments in the standard proper for their years is found in the majority of the children[2].'

---

[1] 1896 Report, p. 16.   [2] 1893 Report, p. 11, abridged.

The average daily attendance of children in the schools
at home and abroad in 1895 was—

Infants	6,801
Older children	5,998

Twenty years before, under the long-service system,
there was nearly double the number of children.

Soldiers with certificates.	1873.	1892.	1895.
1st Class . . .	1,257	2,906	4,305
2nd „ . . .	13,855	41,122	45,588
3rd „ . . .	18,942	31,575	31,004

The percentage of certificates to total strength was 36.51
in 1892, and 37.69 in 1895.

In 1895 there were 265 schoolmasters and 285 schoolmistresses. There has been a reduction of about 70 in
the latter since 1871, as they are employed for children alone; the masters remain nearly the same. 123
masters and 133 mistresses were serving in Great Britain,
while the remainder are on foreign service or in Ireland.

The organization of the Department has been changed
several times. In 1860 it was transferred from the Secretary of State for War and placed under the Commander-in-
Chief; it was till 1898 under the charge of an officer,
styled the Director-General of Military Education, who had
the general superintendence of everything connected with
Army Schools and the appointment of teachers. A field
officer, as Director of Army Schools, takes charge of the
necessary inspection; and there is a body of men selected
from the most efficient schoolmasters, known since 1892 as
Inspectors, ten of whom are serving in the United Kingdom,
and each of whom is in charge of a separate district [1].

The new organization is still uncertain (Aug. 1898), but
General Officers commanding districts will now be largely
responsible for the Army Schools in their command—
a new force in education.

[1] Reports, Council of Military Education, on Army Schools, 1862,
1865, 1868–69; Reports of the Director-General of Military Education,
1872, 1874, 1877, 1889, 1893, 1896; Report of Royal Commissioners
on the Present State of Military Education, 1870, ii.

6. The Lords of the Admiralty.

The Elementary Education of the Navy is a complex subject, owing to the numerous classes of those who receive it and the varied conditions of their lives.

The main divisions of the instructed are these :—

A. *Persons* employed or in training.

1. (a) Boys in training ships.

(b) Boys serving in the Navy in seagoing ships, or harbour ships.

2. (a) Men serving in seagoing ships or harbour ships, being either bluejackets or marines.

(b) Marines on shore.

(c) Bluejackets or marines in the Naval Prison.

B. *Children*—

(a) of marines;

(b) of sailors (at Greenwich Hospital School);

(c) of persons in Admiralty employment [1].

A. (1) Formerly there was a class of 'seamen's school-masters' who taught only reading, writing, and arithmetic as far as the 'rule of three.'

By the Order in Council of February 25, 1856 [2], the Education Department was empowered to inspect the Greenwich Hospital Schools, the Royal Dockyard Schools, and the Schools of the Royal Marines, and to report thereon to the Lords Commissioners of the Admiralty. This was not neglected, as in the case of the Army; an Inspector was directed to carry out the Order, and in the end was appointed Director of Education for the Navy in 1864.

In 1862 the elementary education of the Navy was

---

[1] The only official report on this department, except a short chapter by the Newcastle Commission, is the 'Report by the Inspector of Naval Schools on the educational condition of seamen and marines, and the working of elementary schools under the Admiralty,' 1883 (P. P., 1883, C. 3,569), but the present Chaplain of the Fleet has most kindly furnished me with full information relating to the present time. The arrangement of the facts is mine, and the entire responsibility for any mistakes which may have crept into the text.

[2] *Vide* p. 15.

systematized.   Existing teachers had to obtain Education
Department certificates or to resign, and pupil teachers
were introduced.   From 1875 to 1883 there was a system
of training teachers at Greenwich[1], but vacancies are now
filled by ordinary certificated teachers.

There are twelve Head Schoolmasters, one in each
Gunnery and Torpedo Ship and in each of the Training
Ships, and sixty-eight Naval Schoolmasters.   Candidates
must have passed through a recognized Training College,
have obtained at least a Third-Class certificate, and be of
good character and able to swim.   Schoolmasters are
examined and recommended for promotion by the Chaplain
of the Fleet, who is the Inspector of Naval Schools, and
may on his recommendation continue to serve to the age
of fifty-five.

There are seven Home Training Ships educating about
2,500 Boys, who attend school about nine hours a week for
seven months, and are divided into four 'Instructions,' the
highest corresponding to a good Standard VI of the Education Department.   There is an Advanced Class in each of
these Ships for Algebra, Trigonometry, and Navigation.
There are also three Seagoing Training Ships, on board
which Boys recruited at a later age are trained, and, if
backward, receive as much education as circumstances will
permit.

In 1880 there were thirty-one regular schoolmasters in seagoing vessels, but none are now carried except in the case of
the three Training Ships ; the instruction is left to volunteer
schoolmasters ; these receive additional pay and hold a night
school open to men and boys who wish to improve their
education or qualify for higher ratings.   The qualifications
for the various petty officers differ with their ratings, and
are given in somewhat general terms in the Queen's Regulations.

In ships which carry midshipmen their education is
under the charge of a Naval Instructor, who is generally

---

[1] As recommended by the Newcastle Commission in 1861, i. 452.

the Chaplain.   His instruction is mostly professional, and at least secondary, if not higher, but his presence is to be noticed as an educational influence in the Navy.

(2) Marines on shore have their own schools, in five places.   There are four certificated masters at the Depôt at Walmer and two at Eastney, and these schools are attended by recruits.   There is also a certificated master at each of the other stations, and help is given by soldier assistants.   In all the schools men attend voluntarily to qualify for promotion as non-commissioned officers.

(3) There is a schoolmaster at the Naval Prison at Lewes and another at Bodmin, men in the fourth stage attending every evening, and men in the third stage on three evenings of the week.

B. (1) *Schools for Children.*   There are schools for children of the Royal Marines at each of their five stations in England. The boys are taught by the men's schoolmasters, the girls and infants by trained mistresses assisted by pupil teachers. At Walmer there is a Mixed School for boys and girls and an infants' department.   Attendance is compulsory, but all fees were abolished as long ago as 1871.   Since 1876 the Standards of the Education Department have been adopted ; since 1880 the Lords of the Admiralty have issued certificates of exemption under the Education Acts on the report of the Inspector of Naval Schools.

In 1895 these schools were recognized as public elementary schools receiving grants and inspection from the Education Department, the commandants or persons appointed by the Admiralty acting as local managers [1].

Religious instruction is given by the teachers at the beginning or end of the morning lesson, and sometimes by the Chaplain, simultaneously with the ministers of other denominations.

In 1881 there were 444 boys, 417 girls, and 629 infants in the schools, and 113 infants were sent to board and

Local Government Board Departmental Committee Report on Metropolitan Poor Law Schools, 1896, p. 43 (Mundella).

parochial schools, for which the Admiralty paid the fees. In 1898 there were about 698 boys, 672 girls, and 935 infants in attendance at the schools.

(2) There is also Greenwich Hospital School, where 1,000 boys, sons of men in the Royal Navy or Marines, are boarded and educated. This is divided into the Nautical or higher school, containing 120 boys, and the General School with 880, which is now under the Education Department.

The first of the two classes of the Nautical School learns specific subjects, Mathematics, French, and Navigation, and corresponds generally to a higher elementary school. The second class and the General School are half-time schools; the three classes of the General School correspond to Standards V, IV, and III respectively. Religious instruction is given every forenoon at the commencement of school, and due provision is made for the worship and teaching of various denominations.

(3) Besides these schools the Admiralty also pays for the schooling of a number of girls, not exceeding 200, the orphans of seamen, who are educated in schools approved of by the Lords of the Admiralty. It also contributes to voluntary schools in Dockyard towns and other places where it employs many people or holds much property. Thus in 1881 £882 was paid to 54 schools at which 24,275 children were being educated, of whom 9,565 were the children of persons in the Admiralty employment; in 1897 £702 was granted to 54 schools at which 30,395 children were in attendance, of whom 11,728 were the children of persons employed by the Admiralty. Grants are also made to voluntary schools in the United Kingdom, which are attended by the children of coast-guard men.

I. ELEMENTARY[1] EDUCATION.

B. Ireland.

1. THE COMMISSIONERS OF NATIONAL EDUCATION.

IF the problem of public education was difficult in England and Wales at the beginning of this century, in Ireland it seemed almost hopeless.

In that distressful country the vast majority of the people were of a different race from the class who governed them; they belonged to a religious body, which was under political disabilities, and the head of which was a foreign potentate. For centuries they had hated their rulers, who had repressed them without mercy and without intelligence; the trade and manufactures of the country had been persistently discouraged or destroyed; many of the landlords were absentees, and those who remained were remarkable as a body neither for their devotion to learning nor their zeal for reform: everywhere was a squalid poverty almost unknown across St. George's Channel.

Education was naturally at a low ebb. It was only in 1781 and 1792 that the Statutes of William III and Anne[2] were repealed[3], which forbade any Catholic to teach in Ireland or to send his children abroad for their education. The public money had been lavished on societies and schools during the eighteenth century in a fashion unknown to England, but these efforts had been so identified with proselytism that every fresh scheme seemed only to arouse the dislike and suspicion of the Irish people and of their spiritual leaders.

---

[1] 'Primary' is the word generally used in Ireland for the first stage of education.

[2] Irish Statutes, 7 Will. III. c. 4, ss. 1. 9; 8 Anne, c. 38, s. 16.

[3] Ibid. 21 & 22 Geo. III. c. 62; 32 Geo. III. c. 21.

Parliamentary investigations began earlier than at Westminster. In 1788 Commissioners were appointed by the Lord Lieutenant to inquire into all schools on public or charitable foundations and all grants or funds for the purpose of education in Ireland [1]. In 1791 they reported an income of £45,000 available for education, of which £15,000 proceeded from annual grants [2], and over £8,000 fell to the share of grammar schools or Trinity College, thus leaving a yearly sum of more than £20,000 of endowments available for elementary education [3].

In 1806, after the Union, the Commission was revived [4] and sat from 1806 to 1812. They estimated that there were 4,600 schools for the lower orders in Ireland, attended by upwards of 200,000 children [5], 72 per cent. of whom were Catholics ; 44 of these were public establishments, in which upwards of 4,200 children were maintained and educated at an annual cost of £70,000 [6].

Again, in 1824 another Royal Commission was appointed to inquire into schools in Ireland and advise as to the best means of extending education to all classes. They reported in 1825, 1826, and 1827, and found that in 1824 there were 11,823 elementary schools in Ireland, attended by 560,549 pupils and taught by 12,530 masters and mistresses [7].

The population of Ireland in 1824 was 7,091,500 [8], and the children of school age numbered 1,418,000 [9]. Thus two-fifths of the children were on the books of some school or other, but the extent of their attendance and the quality of their instruction may have amounted to anything or nothing.

Irish elementary education, as it exists to-day, dates

---

[1] Irish Statutes, 28 Geo. III. c. 15 ; 30 Geo. III. c. 34.
[2] Kildare Commission Report, 1858, i. 18.
[3] 1791 Report, first printed in Kildare Report, iii. 370, 378.
[4] 46 Geo. III. c. 122.
[5] Fourteenth Report, p. 4.   [6] Ibid.
[7] Second Report, p. 4 ; Ninth Report, p. 60, Appendix.
[8] *Vide* Appendix, p. 305.   [9] *Vide* p. 16.

from 1831, but it was based on previous failures, and can only be understood by noting the attempts which had preceded it, and tracing in their deficiencies the reasons of its development.

In 1824 the numbers were distributed as follows [1] :—

	Schools.	Pupils on the Books.
Kildare Place Society .	919	58,205
London Hibernian Society .	618	37,507
Association for Discountenancing Vice . . .	226	12,769
Erasmus Smith Fonndation	113	8,882
Baptist Society . . .	88	4,377
Charter Schools . . .	32	2,210
Schools of other Societies, &c.	123	7,155
	2,119	131,105
Less Schools included under two headings . . .	392	25,093
	1,727	106,012
Catholic Schools.		
Catholic Day Schools .	352	33,529
Nunnery (Girls') Schools .	46	7,136
The Christian Brothers .	24	5,454
	422	46,119
Maintained by individuals	322	13,686
" *Pay Schools* " . . .	9,352	394,732
	11,823	560,549

Scattered under these headings were many of the *Parish Schools* [2], which were more or less directly the results of an attempt of Henry VIII to establish 'a school to learn English' in every parish in Ireland, to be kept or provided by the incumbent under ultimate penalty of forfeiture of the benefice [3]. But although his Act [4] was reinforced by 7 Will. c. 4 [5], the results were very imperfect, and the Act was generally evaded by the vicar granting £2 a

---

[1] The figures given are from the returns of the Established Clergy as supplemented by the Catholic returns. The Catholic returns supplemented by those of the Established Church give 568,964 scholars. Second Report, P. P., 1826-27, xii. pp. 6-18; xiii. 1058.

[2] Eleventh Report, 1810.   [3] 1825 First Report, p. 3.

[4] Irish Act, 28 Henry VIII. c. 15.   [5] *Vide* p. 79.

year to some school in his parish [1]. In 1825 in the 1242 benefices of Ireland there were 782 schools in receipt of pecuniary aid from the clergy, amounting in all to £3,300 [2], and these were attended by 12,195 Protestants and 15,303 Catholic children [3].

As the Select Committee reported in 1838, 'their establishment, conduct and continuance depended exclusively on individuals. It is a matter therefore of no surprise that Parish Schools "were never established in any great numbers in Ireland [4]," nor calculated at any time to answer fully the purposes for which they were instituted [5].'

Some of them were included in the *Pay Schools*, which accommodated seventy per cent. of the children ; but these must have been in most cases the old Catholic 'Hedge Schools [6],' where, under the penal laws—

'Still crouching 'neath the sheltering hedge or stretched on mountain fern,
  The teacher and his pupils met feloniously to learn [7].'

Several masters of the Hedge Schools in the South of Ireland at this period enjoyed considerable local reputation as classical and mathematical scholars [8], but on the whole there can be no doubt that a very scanty stock of reading, writing, and ciphering was the utmost that was taught in them [9]. They did not profess to give any religious teaching, but left it entirely to the clergy of each denomination [10].

Of the specifically Catholic Schools the *Day Schools* were supported by the collections and subscriptions of the Roman Catholic inhabitants of certain parishes, and were under the superintendence of the Roman Catholic Priests [11].

---

[1] 1825 First Report, p. 37.   [2] Ibid. p. 37.
[3] Ibid. App. p. 15.   [4] Report, Q. 837.   [5] Ibid. p. 6.
[6] J. A. Froude, *The English in Ireland*, i. 570.
[7] John O'Hagan (1822–1890: afterwards Judge of the Land Court); vide *The New Spirit of the Nation*, p. 16 : Fisher Unwin, 1894.
[8] Report of the Royal Commission under Lord Powis on Irish Primary Education, 1870, vi. p. xxiv.
[9] Ibid. ii. 358.
[10] J. H. Bridges, *Two Centuries of Irish History*, p. 295 : Kegan Paul, Trench, & Co., 1888.
[11] 1827 Second Report, p. 17.

The Institute of the *Christian Brothers* was a 'congregation' founded in 1802 and confirmed by a Papal Bull of 1820. The members took vows of poverty, chastity, and obedience, and also a vow to teach children gratuitously during their lives. In 1825 they had eleven schools taught by forty brothers [1], but have since become the most important Catholic educational body in Ireland [2].

The *Nuns' Schools* for girls belonged chiefly to the Order of the Presentation, which is devoted to giving instruction [3]. In 1825 they were reported as conducted with great order and regularity, and well provided with every school requisite [4].

The Protestant educational societies were the chief distinctive feature of Irish education at this time, and in wealth, if not in numbers, they far outstripped all rivals.

The Incorporated Society, owning the notorious Charter Schools and founded in 1733; The Association for Discountenancing Vice, incorporated 1800; The London Hibernian Society, founded in 1805; and The Baptist Society, formed in 1814, were all more or less avowedly proselytising bodies, supported largely by public subscriptions, and in the case of the first two by a Government Grant [5].

The Erasmus Smith elementary schools were founded [6] from the surplus of an endowment given in 1657 by a London citizen to found grammar schools, in which the only restrictions were that the masters were to be Protestants and read the Bible every day, and the pupils were to be taught Ussher's Catechism [7].

---

[1] 1825 First Report, p. 85; Sadler, Special Reports, 1897, p. 213.

[2] Powis, viii. 83–94, 1003; Ellis, *Irish Education Directory*, 1887, gives 275 of these schools with 27,490 pupils.

[3] 1825 Report, p. 86.   [4] Ibid. p. 88.

[5] *Vide* generally Royal Commission First Report, 1825. The Incorporated Society between 1733 and 1824 spent £1,027,715 of the public money, and £584,423 from private sources (ibid. p. 30), only with the effect of creating grave scandals. It has, however, during the last sixty years had a most useful and honourable career in the education of Protestant children (Kildare Report, i. 14–90; Endowed Commissioners' Reports, 1885–86, App. 2; 1889–90, p. vi).

[6] Sixty-nine were founded, 1808–15. *Vide* also p. 204.

[7] Powis Report, i. 481.

As an outcome of the feeling in favour of a system which should not attempt to proselytise, the Kildare Place Society[1] was founded in 1811 to promote and support schools in which the Bible should be read without note or comment, but no Catechisms or controversial books should be used, and in consequence of the Report of 1812 it began to receive subsidies from Government in 1814. It seems to have been honestly worked, but it allowed itself to aid schools connected with some of the denominational societies, the priesthood declared against it, and its doom was sealed. But the fact was, as Mr. Stanley said in 1831, the rule of reading the Bible without comment was one to which no conscientious Catholic could submit[2].

In addition to the Societies and to the grants which they received, Parliament in 1819 empowered the Lord Lieutenant to make grants from the Consolidated Fund in aid of schools established by voluntary subscriptions. These grants were administered by three unpaid Commissioners, and were free from denominational restrictions, but although the annual amount had risen to £10,833 by 1824, only 12 out of 431 grants made up to 1825 were assigned to Roman Catholics[3], and in 1826 the fund was discontinued[4].

The interesting feature about these various schemes is that into their management every feature but one had been introduced which we shall afterwards find in the Government system.

State grants in aid of building schools, salaries and gratuities to teachers, requirement of local effort, normal schools, adult evening schools, competent inspectors, mixed Boards, publication and free issue of school books, combined secular instruction, and even a conscience clause

---

[1] 'The Society for promoting the Education of the Poor in Ireland ;' its offices were in Kildare Place, Kildare Street, Dublin. 1825 Report, p. 50; Kildare Report, i. 126.
[2] Hansard, T. S., vi. p. 1253.   [3] 1825 Report, p. 58.
[4] Select Committee on Foundation Schools, 1838, p. 11.

as far as Catechetical instruction was concerned—separately
or in combination all these were in actual use. There
only remained one thing—a guarantee for religious inde-
pendence, and this was pointed out·from the first by every
independent body which inquired into the problem.

In 1791 the Commissioners recommended that no distinction should be made between scholars of different
religious persuasions [1].

In 1812 the Commissioners unanimously reported that
'no plan of education . . . can be carried into effectual
execution in Ireland, unless it be explicitly avowed and
clearly understood as its leading principle that no attempt
shall be made to influence or disturb the peculiar religious
tenets of any sect or description of Christians [2].'

The Kildare Place Society was founded, and nothing
else was done, apparently in the hope that the new undertaking might supply the want.

In 1825 the third Commission recommended that, in
a country where marked divisions exist between different
classes of the people, 'schools should be established for the
purpose of giving to children of all religious persuasions
such useful instruction as they may severally be capable
and desirous of receiving, without having any ground to
apprehend any interference with their religious principles [3].'

In 1828 these reports were referred [4] to a Select Committee of the House of Commons, who adopted most of
the recommendations, and stated that in their opinion it
was 'of the utmost importance to bring together children
of the different religious persuasions in Ireland for the
purpose of instructing them in the general subjects of
moral and literary knowledge, and providing facilities for
their religious instruction *separately* when differences of
creed render it impracticable for them to receive religious
instruction together.' They recommended the establish-

---

[1] Kildare Report, iii. p. 364.   [2] Fourteenth Report, 1812, p. 2.
[3] 1825 Report, p. 89.
[4] On March 11, 1828 (Hansard, Second Series, xviii. 1120).

ment of a fixed authority for the control and management
of State-aided schools ; that two days a week should be
set apart for religious instruction by the various clergy,
Protestants and Catholics each to have one day.

The entire body of the Roman Catholic hierarchy in
Ireland presented petitions to both Houses of Parliament [1],
entreating that the recommendations of this Committee
should be adopted, and the same course was urged by
another Select Committee of the House of Commons
which inquired, in 1830, into the State of the Poorer
Classes in Ireland, and recommended education as one of
their remedial measures [2].

Catholic Emancipation was passed in 1829, and in 1830
Earl Grey came into power, but it was not until September 9,
1831, the year before the Reform Bill was passed, that any
steps were taken to carry out these recommendations.   On
that date the House of Commons voted a sum of £30,000
'to enable the Lord Lieutenant of Ireland to assist in the
education of the people.'   The scheme was explained by
the Hon. E. G. Stanley [3], the Chief Secretary for Ireland,
who seconded the vote ; it was received with welcome by
O'Connell, and with great bitterness by some of the Irish
Tories [4].   The general lines were those recommended by
the Select Committee of 1828 ; the system adopted was
afterwards described as a denominational system with a
conscience clause, in which there was to be separate
religious and combined literary and moral instruction [5].
It may be noted that this was no fresh grant to Ireland,
but simply £30,000 withdrawn from the Kildare Place
Society and the Society for Discountenancing Vice, and
paid instead to a new agency for public education.   The
machinery was provided by the Lord Lieutenant, who
appointed an unpaid Board of seven members, including

[1] Hansard, Second Series, xvi. 1259 ; P. P., 1830, vii. p. 50.
[2] Ibid.
[3] Afterwards Prime Minister and fourteenth Earl of Derby.
[4] Hansard, T. S., vi. p. 1249 sqq.
[5] Powis, i. 38; J. Williams, *Education*, p. 332: A. and C. Black, 1892.

the Duke of Leinster, 'a distinguished Protestant in whom the Catholics had much confidence[1],' as Chairman, and Dr. Whately and Dr. Murray, the Protestant and Catholic Archbishops of Dublin. Three of the Board belonged to the Established Church, two were Roman Catholics, and the remaining two a Presbyterian and a Unitarian. Mr. Stanley in his speech hinted that if this body failed, the next expedient of the Government would be a Board of paid members. The scheme, after its exposition by Mr. Stanley in the House, was sketched by him in a letter to the Chairman[2], and then gradually developed in an explanatory document[3] and Rules and Regulations[4], as it was moulded by actual experience and under pressure from the different religious bodies. It is not necessary here to record in detail the numerous differences which existed in these various pronouncements, especially as in the beginning the practice was evidently far from uniform[5], and after the first few years there were for a long time no great modifications. I propose to describe the system as it existed during the first forty years of its existence, and then to draw attention to the most important additions made by statute or otherwise during the last quarter of a century.

(1) *The Central Government.* The Board of Commissioners of National Education in Ireland. The members have always been 'men of high personal character, including individuals of exalted station in the Church and persons professing different religious opinions.' They were (and are) appointed by the Lord Lieutenant at his sole discretion, and may be (but never have been) removed by him at pleasure[6]. Their number was gradually increased, until by their Charter of 1860 it was fixed at not more than twenty members, half of whom were to be Catholics and

---

[1] *Fifty Years of Concessions to Ireland*, 1831–81, O'Brien, i. 120.
[2] Powis Report, i. p. 22, two versions.   [3] Ibid. i. 27.
[4] Ibid. i. 607, reprinted up to 1869.
[5] Ibid. i. 36, 59, 117, 165.
[6] Cross Commission, Report on English Elementary Education, Q. 53,176, Q. 53,186, Q. 53,233.

half Protestants. In a short time after establishment of the Board it was found that a permanent administrative officer was necessary, and the Rev. James Carlile, the Presbyterian member, was appointed Resident Commissioner with a fixed salary[1]. The other members have always been unpaid. The Commissioners are independent of Government, except in so far as they rely upon the House of Commons for their annual grant, and there is a regulation that no fundamental rule may be altered without the express permission of the Lord Lieutenant[2]. Bills and Votes in the House of Commons are introduced by the Chief Secretary for Ireland.

A staff of paid inspectors and clerks was at once appointed. Grants were made for various purposes as far as the gradually increasing Parliamentary Grant allowed.

The right of Inspection of schools was reserved from the first by the Board, who were thus wiser than the English Committee of Council. In 1837 they divided Ireland into twenty-five districts, increased to thirty-two in 1843. Each of these was under its Superintendent, as those officers were called, until the title of Inspector was restored in 1847[3]. In that year a few Sub-Inspectors were selected from the best teachers, and employed chiefly in organizing new schools and improving old ones, which were imperfectly conducted. In later years this duty has been performed by organizing teachers[4].

---

[1] He resigned in 1838, and was presently succeeded by Mr. Macdonnell, who remained in service until 1872. He was succeeded by Sir P. Keenan, who died in 1894, and was in turn succeeded by the Rt. Hon. C. T. Redington.

[2] Cross, Q. 53,189, Q. 53,207 ; Childers, Q. 861.

[3] Powis, i. 110.

[4] The Inspection staff consists of six Head Inspectors (introduced in 1846, ibid.), nearly seventy district Inspectors, and a few Inspectors' assistants, all selected by Civil Service competitive examination, National Schoolmasters being eligible for appointment (*vide* article by Rt. Hon. C. T. Redington, the present Resident Commissioner, in the Special Reports on Educational Subjects, 1897, p. 254). Half the leading officers are Catholics and half Protestants (Childers Report, 1884, Q. 866).

All grants to teachers and monitors are paid to them individually from headquarters by Post Office Orders[1], on a system similar to that in force in England between 1846 and 1862, which was complicated and entailed very much correspondence[2].

(2) *The Local Management.* A 'patron' was recognized in every school receiving assistance from the Board. Unless otherwise specified in the application, he was the person applying in the first instance to place the school in connexion with the Board[3]. He was invested with the local government of the school, and might appoint a fit person as local manager. He (or the manager) had the right of engaging and dismissing the masters, subject to the regulations of the Board[4], but the Commissioners retained the right of dismissing unsuitable persons, although upheld by the patron[5]. The Committee of a school might be its patron, but among the Catholics the patron is almost universally an individual[6].

The manager arranged the time-table of the school, subject to the regulations of the Board[7].

(3) *Religious Instruction.* The one thing necessary for the success of the new system was to procure the indiscriminate attendance of children of all denominations. It was left to the schools to fix their own fees and make regulations as to hours, but the one point on which everything manifestly depended was the entire separation of the denominations during religious instruction.

At first one or two week-days were set apart in every week entirely for religious teaching in schools receiving

---

[1] Powis Report, Q. 3,025.

[2] Lord Lingen before House of Commons Committee, 1865, Q. 561, Q. 576, and Q. 582; Hansard, T. S., clxv. p. 200; Redington, p. 248.

[3] He must be a person of some position and responsibility, preferably a clergyman (Report for 1885, Art. 99 (e); Powis, i. 150).

[4] There seems no protection against arbitrary dismissal (*Journal of Ed.*, 1898, p. 378).

[5] Powis, i. 27.   [6] Cross, iii. Q. 53,150.

[7] The manager is not removable unless after a public inquiry (Childers Report, 1884, Q. 864).

grants from the Board, and opportunity was also afforded for it on the other days before or after ordinary school hours[1]. This time was reduced to a day or part of a day in 1838[2], and in 1840, at the instance of the Presbyterians, the 'fifty-two Popish holidays' were abolished, and the principle of assigning a separate day was abandoned[3].

Religious teaching on ordinary days was given at times set apart for it. After 1838 such times might be during ordinary school hours, if arrangements were made for separating the children who received it, in case of objection being raised by the parents[4].

In 1855 it was laid down that religious instruction or exercises might take place before or after ordinary school hours, *and at one intermediate time only*, except where it appeared that this permission would prevent children of any religious denomination availing themselves of the advantages of a school[5].

In 1865 leave was granted to withdraw children to a limited extent from ordinary instruction for separate religious teaching, provided that the secular education was not materially impeded[6].

Notice had to be published of the hours when religious instruction was to be given, and until 1837 children were *not allowed* to remain for the religious lessons of denominations other than their own[7]. After that year they might remain if they chose, but in 1866 the original rule was restored[8], and now no Protestant may remain for religious instruction given by a Catholic, and no Catholic may remain for that given by the member of any other denomination, unless the parent has requested it in writing[9].

After many small changes and rearrangements the principle of the Board took the following shape in 1866. 'Religious instruction must be so arranged that each school shall be

---

[1] Rules, 1831, iii.
[2] Rules, 1838, ii. 2.
[3] Powis, i. 90. Correen School.
[4] Ibid. i. 90, 138.
[5] Rules, 1855, i. iv. 2.
[6] Powis, i. 185.
[7] Ibid. i. 59, 87.
[8] Ibid. i. 117, 188.
[9] Rules for 1891, Art. 90.

open to children of all communions ; that due regard be had to parental right and authority; that accordingly no child shall receive, or be present at, any religious instruction of which his parents or guardians disapprove ; and that the time for giving it be so fixed that no child shall be thereby, in effect, excluded, directly or indirectly, from the other advantages which the school affords[1].'

Prayers or reading the Bible either in the Authorized or Douay Versions are reserved for the times of separate instruction[2].

Religious instruction was given by the Clergy of the denomination[3], or by laymen approved by the parent : they were not employed or remunerated by the Board.

(4) *School Houses.* As in England the first grants given were in aid of building schools, and out of these building grants there soon arose an important division of the schools into Vested and Non-Vested, which exists to the present day.

The chief conditions laid down by the Board were that the site and not less than one-third[4] of the expense of any school receiving a building grant should be locally contributed, and that the buildings should be *vested* in trustees chosen by the applicants and approved by the Commissioners[5].

From these schools the Board has always required a more permanent and complete submission to their rules than from the non-vested schools, which receive only occasional or annual grants easily discontinued[6].

In 1844 the Board received a Charter enabling it to hold land to the yearly value of £40,000[7], and this they proceeded to utilize by requiring that from that date all schools receiving building grants should be vested, not in trustees, but in the Board themselves, who then became

---

[1] 1866 Rules, i. iv. 2.
[2] *Vide* also under School Houses, and School Books, p. 95.
[3] As in the Pay Schools, p. 83.
[4] In England and Scotland one-half was required.
[5] Powis, i. 27.　　　　　　[6] Ibid.　　　　　　[7] Ibid. i. 106.

responsible for their proper maintenance of the buildings. Their reason for this course was that trustees frequently allowed the school houses to become dilapidated, and could only be compelled to do their duty by a suit in Chancery[1]. There was great opposition to the new rule, which was considered, especially among the Catholics, to imply all sorts of sinister designs on the part of the Commissioners. In 1861 applicants were allowed either to vest their school in the Board, who then undertook all repairs, or to vest it in their own trustees and remain liable for the expense of maintaining it themselves[2]. Finally, in 1866, the managers of any vested school, by repaying the money received, without interest, might have the school reconveyed to themselves[3].

Mr. Stanley in his letter had directed that a fund sufficient for the annual repairs of the school house and furniture should be required before any grant was made, but anything in the nature of invariable permanent endowment was found to be impracticable in a country so poor as Ireland[4].

It was at first announced that peculiar favour would be shown to joint applications from Protestants and Catholics, but this pressure to unite denominations was abandoned on demand of the Presbyterians[5].

Grants for teachers' residences were not in these days made by the Board for their ordinary schools.

Free access to the schoolroom during secular instruction was always allowed to the public in vested schools[6].

Originally the religious teachers approved by the parents must be allowed access to the children for the purposes of religious instruction in any of the schools subsidised by the Board, but the Presbyterians raised the greatest objections to this rule, and after 1840 it was decided that the

---

[1] Powis, i. 107.   [2] Ibid. i. 174.
[3] Ibid. i. 189.   The same right was granted in England, but not exercised.   Cf. p. 12.
[4] Powis, i. 115.   [5] Ibid. i. 48, 74, 90.   [6] Ibid. i. 151.

managers of non-vested schools need not at any time admit religious teachers of any other denomination[1]. In vested schools such teachers still retained the right of access, but, as a matter of practice, it is not generally demanded[2].

No school house may be used for political meetings or converted into a place of religious worship. Subject to these regulations the managers of non-vested schools have entire control of them on Sundays.

No denominational emblems may be exhibited inside a school during united instruction, nor outside in the case of schools built after 1855; nor might political emblems be exhibited inside or affixed to the exterior of schools at any time.

District Model Schools. One of the early schemes of the Board was the establishment of a model school in each of the thirty-two school districts into which Ireland was divided[3]. The first of them, however, were only opened in 1849, and the full number was never completed[4]. The schools were to cost no more than £800 apiece, but they enormously exceeded their estimates, and varied greatly in their size and accommodation[5].

The aim, as afterwards defined[6], was to promote 'united education,' to exhibit the most improved methods of literary and scientific instruction to the surrounding schools, and to train young persons for the office of teacher.

They were to be utilized for supplying teachers for National Schools. Each school was to have a residence for the master and a dormitory for three candidate teachers, afterwards called pupil teachers[7]; a residence near the school was to be provided for the mistress and one female candidate teacher.

[1] Powis, i. 90, 99.
[2] Ibid. Q. 27,062-5, Cardinal Cullen; Report of Childers Select Committee of House of Commons on Administration, 1884, Q. 970.
[3] 1835 Report, p. 40; Powis, i. 77.
[4] Powis, i. 115, 208.   [5] Ibid. i. 210.
[6] In 1867, ibid. i. 426.   [7] Ibid. i. 429.

Six Minor Model Schools were also erected, which did not receive candidate teachers.

In 1861 the Chief Secretary undertook in the House of Commons that no more Model Schools should be erected without reference to the House [1].

These schools were managed by the Commissioners and subject to the same regulations as ordinary National Schools, but there were two important differences in principle. No local contributions were required, and the locality had not the right of appointing the teachers [2].

The Model Schools, after a time, almost more than any part of the work of the Commissioners, aroused the hatred of the Catholics [3], and Catholic children were in many cases forbidden to attend them.

They give a higher education than the ordinary schools [4], and their teachers receive special rates of remuneration. In all, only twenty-six District and Minor Model Schools have been created, exclusive of the four Model Schools in Dublin [5].

(5) *Books.* Nowhere was a supply of good school books more wanted than in Ireland. In the old days instruction was almost entirely individual, and every child used to bring with it to school whatever book it could get in which to learn reading. 'It has occurred to a member of the Commission' of 1824 'to see in a School in the County of Sligo a child holding the New Testament in its Hands, sitting between Two others, one of whom was supplied with *The Forty Thieves* and the other with *The Pleasant Art of Money Catching*, while another, at a little Distance, was perusing the *Mutiny Act*, and all reading aloud their respective Volumes at the same Moment [6].'

A list of the books actually used in four counties is given in the same report, and ranges through Milton and Locke,

<hr>

[1] Hansard, T. S., clxiv. p. 917.
[2] Powis, i. 210.
[3] Ibid. i. 445.
[4] Ibid. i. 213, 436.
[5] National Education Report for 1895, p. 15.
[6] First Report, 1825, p. 44.

and Dusseldorf on *Fratricide, Lydia* (a loose Novel), the *Academy of Compliments*, and the *History of Philander Flashaway* [1].

The Kildare Place Society did much to supply the want and published a number of suitable works, which the new Board at first adopted. The Catholic Book Society's publications were also edited for the use of the National Schools [2]. But these were only temporary and provisional steps, and the Resident Commissioner and his Assistants set themselves to produce a graduated series of lesson books, which was brought out with as little delay as possible. This was the foundation of the classes corresponding to the English standards, which came into prominence in 1872, when payment by results was introduced.

Their merits were well pointed out by Lord Powis' Commission. 'They brought with them uniformity, and rendered class teaching possible; they were graduated to suit the growing capacities of children; they were distributed gratis or sold cheaply; they were generally accepted as containing nothing inimical to Christian faith or morality, and they accomplished beneficial results of national importance [3].'

A book of extracts from the Scriptures for joint use in the schools was also produced with the help of Dr. Arnold of Rugby [4]. It was published with the sanction of the Board and largely used at first [5]. But public feeling ran strongly against it; the Catholics objected to using it at all, while the Protestants, especially the Presbyterians, resented it as a mutilation of the Scriptures. Already, in 1838, a Superintendent was reproved for directing its employment, and it gradually went out of use, though never actually withdrawn [6].

Another book for joint use led to one of the bitterest controversies in the history of the Board. A work on *Christian Evidences*, written by Archbishop Whately, was

---

[1] First Report, 1825, App. p. 553.   [2] Powis, i. 28.
[3] Ibid. i. 119.   [4] Ibid. i. 40.   [5] Ibid. i. 41.
[6] Ibid. i. 96; Cross, Q. 53,426.

prohibited by the Commissioners in 1853. The author demanded that *all* books published by the Board should be read in *all* the Model Schools[1], and being defeated retired from the Board, accompanied by Mr. Blackburne, the ex-Lord Chancellor of Ireland, and Baron Greene.

No books might be used in the schools other than those sanctioned by the Commissioners, but none were prohibited except as containing matter objectionable in itself, or objectionable as belonging to some religious denomination[2]. There never was any compulsion to use the books issued by the Board, although there was great temptation, inasmuch as these alone were supplied gratuitously or on special terms by the Commissioners.

One of the chief Catholic grievances has been the omission of the histories of Ireland and of the Church of Rome from the reading-books[3]. So far was the exclusion of national spirit carried in the early days, that in 1838 Dr. Whately struck out 'Breathes there a man with soul so dead,' and would not allow the children to hear that 'Freedom shriek'd as Kosciusko fell[4].' In Music the indictment is almost incredible, but in the whole music manual in use in 1868 there *was not a single Irish air*[5].

Grants of Books. A first stock of the Board's school books was furnished to their schools from 1833 onwards, and renewed at intervals, and additional copies were supplied at special rates[6]. Between 1843 and 1850 books were sold also at very low prices to poor schools in Ireland not connected with the Board, but on a protest from the leading publishers this was discontinued[7]. The books had at one time a considerable circulation outside Ireland[8], but probably all need for a Government series has now ceased.

Teachers. A large part of the Government Grant was expended on the training and payment of teachers, and,

---

[1] Powis, i. 129.　　　[2] Ibid. p. 120.　　　[3] Ibid. p. 351.
[4] O'Brien, i. p. 194.　　　[5] Powis Report, Q. 2,032.
[6] Ibid. i. 38.　　　[7] Ibid. 120.
[8] Childers Committee Report, 1884, Q. 858.

bad as the state of school books was at first, it is doubtful
whether the teachers were not, if possible, worse.   Dr. J. F.
Murray, one of the first Inspectors, wrote in February, 1833,
'The ignorance of the teachers, generally speaking, is
another barrier to improvement.   To an arrogance and
self-conceitedness peculiarly their own, many of the country
schoolmasters and mistresses unite an innocence of everything except reading and writing, with occasionally a
smattering of mathematics.   I found few who knew anything of English grammar; fewer still who were acquainted
with geography.   However I might lament the limited
extent of their information, I could not but regret the
wretched judgment displayed in communicating the little
they knew[1].'

Conditions—Training.   In Mr. Stanley's letter it was laid
down that every teacher appointed in the future must have
received previous instruction in 'the Model School' to be
established in Dublin, and to be sanctioned by the Board[2].
This was repeated in the Rules and Regulations, but in
practice the Board had to content itself for a long time
with giving a short course to a few teachers selected by the
Inspectors from those already in their service.

Temporary arrangements for training were made in 1832,
and in 1838 the regular Normal establishment 'for training
teachers and educating persons destined to undertake the
charge of schools' was opened in Marlborough Street,
Dublin, at the headquarters of the Board, though it was
not until 1845 that the female training establishment was
completed[3].   The ordinary course, however, lasted only
five months, and even so the proportion of teachers who
ever passed through it was very small.   Religious teaching
was entirely omitted from the curriculum and left to the
voluntary efforts of the different denominations[4].

---

[1] Powis, i. p. 76.   [2] Drafts A and B, ibid. p. 22.
[3] At first it was not proposed to train schoolmistresses at all, nor
indeed to employ them except for sewing and the like (Powis Report,
i. 802).
[4] Powis, i. pp. 88, 409; Cross Report, Q. 53,429.

In 1862 many of the Catholic bishops issued a prohibition against the Training College on account of its secular character [1], and the proportion of Catholics greatly declined. It was not until denominational institutions received recognition that the Catholics were trained in adequate numbers.

In 1855 it was laid down that no clergyman of any denomination nor (except in the case of convent schools) member of any religious order could be recognized as the teacher of a National School [2].

Teachers have been discouraged, and, since 1843, absolutely prohibited, from attending political meetings, except for the purpose of voting, unless officially employed.

Monitors. One of the chief sources of supply to the teaching body and the principal means of assistance in its work were the Monitors in the National Schools. A few were employed in the Dublin Model School from the first [3], but in 1845, the year before the corresponding class of pupil teachers was introduced in England, the system was extended to the provinces in Ireland, and greatly developed during the next ten years [4].

In 1862 the Board secured the co-operation of some of the best convent schools in training pupil teachers, who were introduced under the title of first class monitors into a few very large and highly efficient schools [5].

In 1864 the District Model Schools were supplying about 130 new teachers out of the 700 then annually needed [6].

In 1873 all monitors were placed in three classes [7], and junior monitors abolished.

Teachers' Remuneration. Another condition of assistance required by Mr. Stanley's letter was that 'a permanent salary for the master' was to be 'locally provided for,' no

[1] Cross, Q. 53,328.   [2] Rules and Regulations, I. vii. 2.
[3] Powis, i. 109.
[4] At first (1850) they must be not under fourteen nor over sixteen on engagement; afterwards (in 1855) a junior class might be taken at eleven, and 300 were at once appointed, but these were discontinued in 1873 (Powis, i. 155).
[5] Powis, i. 176–78, 401.   [6] Ibid. i. 182.
[7] Report, p. 25.

amount being stated ; gratuities (also of undefined amount) to teachers of schools conducted under the rules laid down would then be granted by the Board.

But owing to the poverty of the country, all that could be done in this direction was to require that there should be a sufficient number of children to augment by their weekly pence the Government salary[1]. No guarantee was taken that the fees would continue to be paid, and in practice when the people found that the Government provided the salary, in a great many cases they relaxed their efforts[2].

At first the teachers of schools received grants at the rate of £1 for every ten children *expected* to attend their school[3].

In 1841 a new principle of payment was introduced. All the teachers employed were divided into three classes[4], and in the future no teacher was to be recognized or paid except as probationary, until he had been classed after examination either by the Inspector, or, if attending the Normal School, by the Professors[5]. Promotion depended partly on examination and partly on the report of the Inspector. The master or mistress was then paid according to the class of his or her certificate, and not by a capitation grant on the pupils.

The original mode of payment by capitation grant was continued in convent schools conducted by religious bodies, who were unwilling to have their teachers classed by outside examiners. The grant, however, was paid on the daily average attendance[6], and this differed so widely from the old estimates that the amount was raised first to £15 and then to £20 per hundred children.

Various grants were made for good service, for order, for training teachers, pupil teachers and unpaid monitors, but

[1] Powis, i. 115; Cross, Q. 53,144.
[2] Powis, i. 46, 329; ii. 293.
[3] House of Commons Committee Report, 1835, Q. 1,266; Powis, i. 181.
[4] Completed in the case of the masters in 1849 (Powis, i. 114).
[5] Ibid. i. 98, 617.
[6] Ibid. i. 623.

most of these have been discontinued since payment by results was introduced[1].

There has been a steady rise in the amount of State grants to teachers, as may be seen by a comparison between the tables in force in 1841 and 1898. Local contributions are not included; they were uncertain, and now at any rate are very insignificant, as school fees are represented in the Government Grant.

| | *Males.* | | *Females.* | |
Class.	Code 1841.	Code 1891.	Code 1841.	Code 1891.
I. i.	£20	£140	£15	£118
ii.		£109		£93
II.	£15	£91	£12	£77
III.	£12	£73	£10	£62

Into the controversial history of the Board during these forty years it is unnecessary to go into any detail. For some time the Commissioners led an uneasy life, and their only relief seems to have been an occasional change of assailants.

At first the Catholics received the new system with readiness, and even eagerness[2]. The Established Church never liked it in their hearts, though some of its members were influenced by Archbishop Whately and acquiesced in the change. For the first nine years it was the Presbyterians and the Orangemen who resisted every restriction and clamoured for a return to the old state of things. In 1832 the Synod of Ulster[3] raised the cry of 'the Bible unabridged and unmutilated,' and held back from the Board's Schools. Between 1832–35 four school houses were wrecked and burned in Ulster, and five more were closed on account of intimidation[4].

In 1837 Select Committees of the House of Lords and of the House of Commons were appointed to inquire into the new system; the evidence given before both Com-

---

[1] *Vide* p. 106.   [2] Powis, i. 70.   [3] Ibid. 48–66.
[4] House of Lords Report, 1837, p. 94.

mittees was printed, but neither body came to any definite decision nor issued any but a formal report.

In 1835 and 1836 a Select Committee of the House of Commons, with Mr. (afterwards Sir Thomas) Wyse as Chairman[1], took evidence on the Schools of Public Foundation in Ireland, and, being reappointed, published a most striking report in 1838[2]. Its recommendations were far in advance of the times—too far in advance to have had any chance of success if they had been adopted. It proposed for elementary education to retain the Commissioners of National Education as a Central Board co-operating with local bodies in every parish or district, which, subject to the Grand Jury, were to fix a rate to be levied[3]. The education proposed was not less remarkable than the scheme of administration. 'Lessons on objects' was the first item in the curriculum. Manual and physical training were recommended, and agricultural teaching as far as possible. Singing was to form a portion of general elementary education, but even more striking is this sentence, which Ireland after sixty years still requires to take to heart: 'There does not seem to exist any valid reason why the elements of at least linear drawing should not be taught as universally as writing[4].' A Bill for the National Board and School Meetings of ratepayers was introduced in 1835 by Mr. Wyse, and dropped after a second reading.

As the Board began slowly to make concessions to the ultra-Protestant party, the Catholics became dissatisfied.

---

[1] Thomas Wyse, junior, of the Manor of St. John's, Waterford, born 1791, was educated at Stonyhurst and Trinity College, Dublin, and spent some time abroad, chiefly in Italy. He sat as M.P. for Tipperary, 1830–33, and for Waterford City, 1835–47. In 1849 he was made a Privy Councillor, and sent as Minister Plenipotentiary to Greece, where he remained for a number of years. He became a K.C.B. in 1857, and died in 1862. In 1836 he published *Education Reform, or the Necessity of a National System of Education* (1 vol.), a most enlightened book, showing a wide knowledge of foreign educational literature. He was also the author of *Walks in Rome* and *Oriental Rambles*.

[2] P. P., 1837–38, vii. 345.   [3] Report, p. 26.   [4] p. 36.

The Rev. John MacHale, Catholic Archbishop of Tuam [1], had successfully led the attack on the Kildare Place Society in 1820, and in 1838 he began to assail the new Board, on the ground that nothing but Catholic endowed schools would satisfy Catholic Ireland [2].

Archbishop Murray supported his colleagues on the Board, and in 1839 the dispute was referred to the Pope.

In 1840 the Commissioners practically ceded the last of the eight points demanded by the Presbyterians [3], who thereupon withdrew from all opposition and became the staunchest supporters of the Board.

In 1841 the Pope decided that the schools were to have a fair trial and forbade further controversy, directing the pastors of his flock to maintain watchful care and take every precaution [4]. This for a time silenced the Catholics.

In 1845 nine of the Bishops of the Established Church declared decidedly and publicly against any plan of education established and maintained by the State. They tried to press the claims of the Church Education Society, which had established its schools in opposition to the new system in 1839 [5], but the Government turned a deaf ear [6].

In August, 1844, the Board received its first Charter, and the controversy about vesting new schools in the Commissioners began [7].

After this came the Potato Famine, and dissensions were stayed for a time.

In 1850 the Archbishop of Tuam made his next move, and at the Synod of Thurles the Roman Catholic Bishops presented a claim for separate education. Failing that, the vesting of schools in the Board was condemned ; Catholic teachers for Catholic schools were demanded, and the

---

[1] Vide *Dictionary of National Biography*, and *Maynooth College : a Centenary History*, by Bishop Healy, p. 452 : Dublin. 1895.

[2] R. Barry O'Brien, *Fifty Years of Concession to Ireland*, vol. ii. p. 176. A clear and fair account of this controversy from the Catholic point of view.

[3] Powis, i. p. 90.　　[4] Ibid. i. 124.　　[5] Ibid. viii. 29.

[6] Ibid. i. 102.　　[7] *Vide* p. 93 ; Powis, i. 106 ; O'Brien, ii. 188.

censorship of Catholic religious books ; a creed register was prescribed, and a rule forbidding Catholic children to attend Protestant instruction. More representation of Catholics on the Board was especially demanded. These claims were refused at the time, though most of them have since been conceded[1].

In 1854 another Select Committee of the House of Lords was appointed, but, like its predecessor of 1837, failed to make any joint report.

In 1859 the Catholic Archbishops and Bishops of Ireland presented a memorial praying for a participation in educational grants for the separate instruction of Catholic children. This was refused. In 1866 it was repeated, with the same result[2]. In 1860 the supplemental Charter was granted to the Board, which was henceforth to consist of twenty members, Protestants and Catholics in equal numbers.

In 1869 the Irish Protestant Episcopal Church was dis-established, and from its revenues, which were vested in 'the Commissioners of Church Temporalities in Ireland[3],' the various branches of Irish education subsequently received or are receiving either the capital or interest of two and one-third millions sterling[4].

In 1868 a Royal Commission, composed of seven Protestants and seven Catholics, with Lord Powis as Chairman, was appointed to inquire into the whole system of Irish Primary Education, and in 1870 they presented a most elaborate report in nine volumes.

The general conclusion at which they arrived was that the progress of the children in the National Schools was very much less than it ought to be[5], and that it was much the same in the chief denominational schools.

To improve this state of things the Commissioners re-

---

[1] Powis, i. pp. 125–26.   [2] Ibid. i. 185.
[3] 32 & 33 Vict. c. 42. The Irish Church Act.   [4] *Vide* pp. 108, 216.
[5] Report, vol. i. p. 293. 'We know very well that forty-five per cent. of the attendance in the National Schools are in the First Book' (Powis Report, Q. 23,826).

commended the increase of teachers' salaries by an additional payment on results [1], residences for principal teachers at the cost of the locality [2], and written engagements between managers and teachers with three months' notice on either side [3].

Local management was declared absolutely necessary [4]; the principle of local contribution to meet State grants was to be enforced [5], and the local authority was to have power to erect schools [6] and levy a rate not exceeding threepence in the pound [7].

Training of teachers [8] was to be encouraged by aiding other training schools under the management of committees, voluntary societies or religious bodies; the course at Marlborough Street should be extended to twelve instead of six months, and scholars attending it might live in approved boarding-houses or lodgings, and be under the care of pastors of their own religion.

But there was a further breach proposed in the system of combined education. It was recommended that in any school district or within any city or town where for three years there had been two or more schools, of which one was under Protestant and one under Roman Catholic management, having an average attendance of not less than twenty-five children, the National Board might, on application from the Patron or Manager, adopt any such school and award aid subject only to the exclusion of Protestants from religious instruction given by Catholics and of Catholics from religious instruction given by non-Catholics, and of children in general from any religious observances to which their parents objected. Such recognition was to be terminable on twelve months' notice [9].

The distinction between convent and other schools was to cease, and their teachers to be classed and examined.

---

[1] Report, vol. i. pp. 348, 379.   [2] p. 310.   [3] p. 383.
[4] P. 311.   [5] P. 342.   [6] P. 322.   [7] P. 343.
[8] p. 421. Cf. Mr. Chichester Fortescue's letter (ibid. p. 189); *vide* p. 109.
[9] p. 371.

Monks' schools also should be admitted to aid on the usual conditions [1].

The provincial model schools should be gradually discontinued [2], and the provincial and district model agricultural schools should be revised and reduced in numbers [3]; junior monitors should be discontinued, and the lowest standard for teachers raised [4].

It was not considered expedient to introduce compulsory attendance in the rural districts [5].

There were three Commissioners who refused to sign the report, and three more who objected to the opening of endowments to all denominations, but no subsequent inquiry into the system has been held, nearly every important change since introduced was recommended by the Commission, and their list of recommendations has not yet been exhausted.

The further improvement of teachers' salaries by means of a system of partial payment by results was first carried out in 1872, and more completely in the following year.

The scheme was suggested by Mr. (afterwards Sir Patrick) Keenan [6], and was devised to avoid the worst faults of the English machine. Six classes of children were recognized besides infants under seven. Reading, Spelling, Writing, and Arithmetic received grants in all classes, but the scale was graduated, the respective grants being higher in the upper classes than in the lower. Grammar, Geography, Needlework, and (since 1873) Agriculture were taught in the upper classes, and extra subjects, which had been introduced in 1855, continued to receive encouragement.

Thus the system differed from its English prototype in that the whole of the teacher's income did not depend on the results of the examination; the teacher maintained his individual relation to the Board as before, though he had always been the servant of the manager and not of the

---

[1] Report, vol. i. pp. 392, 395.   [2] p. 459.   [3] p. 465.
[4] pp. 405, 424.   [5] p. 325.   [6] Ibid. vol. iii. p. 89.

Government; the upper classes of the school were more remunerative than the lower, though each individual scholar was as valuable as any one else in his class.

The whole of the fees were divided among the teachers in addition to their salaries.   Model and Convent Schools received results fees like any other National School, in spite of the differences existing with regard to the payment of their respective teachers[1].

In return for this fresh grant, Parliament directed the Board to require all managers to enter into a specified form of agreement with their teachers, terminable only on three months' notice on either side[2].

In 1873 the Rules and Regulations were largely revised. Junior and unpaid monitors were abolished[3].   Individual examination of infants might be dispensed with in cases where there was a bonâ fide provision for their systematic training with a separate staff and separate room[4], but even by 1898 there has been no relaxation of the rule in the case of older children[5].

If Public Elementary Education was long in appearing on the Statute book in England, it was longer still in Ireland, where it had been longer in existence.   But in 1875 two Acts were passed in the same session.

The National School Teachers' Residences Act[6] authorized public loans for erecting houses for teachers of non-vested schools, while in the case of vested schools the Commissioners began to make grants for the same purpose.   But the more important Act of the two was the National School Teachers (Ireland) Act, 1875[7].   Government had provided an additional method for the schools to earn grants for the

---

[1] Capitation grants after 1885 have been paid not on the average daily attendance (p. 100), but at the rate of 10*s*. or 12*s*. a head, according to the Results Examinations.

[2] Report for 1872, p. 21.   [3] Ibid. p. 26.

[4] Individual examination is not now required in any case for infants, but for other pupils there is as yet no permission to relax it.

[5] Two surprise visits, however, must also be paid every year, in addition to the inspection; Articles, 116–118.

[6] 38 & 39 Vict. c. 82.   [7] Ibid. c. 96.

teachers; it now remained to provide the additional money with which those grants might be paid, and local rates were to be enabled to help the Imperial Treasury.

Any Board of Guardians was by the Act allowed to become contributory to the extent of one-third of the results fees in the National Schools in its Union, and Parliament provided the remaining two-thirds, while non-contributory unions were to receive only one-third from the Imperial Treasury.

It may be said at once that the Act has proved a failure, as one of the Powis Commissioners predicted of any attempt to levy an education rate[1]. Not more than 73 unions out of 163 ever became contributory at any time[2], and in 1896–97 there were only 25 which continued their payments.

From 1876 to 1880 Government offered to pay two-thirds of the amount of results fees in non-contributory unions if the local contributions amounted to one-third and averaged 3s. 4d. in the year on each child in average attendance. During the great distress in 1880 they offered to find one-third, and then to pay a sum equal to the local subscriptions, whether these amounted to a third of the entire results fees or not; and in 1881 this was made the permanent rule[3]. Thus Government paid one-third of the results fees in these unions, and the remaining two-thirds, as far as they were paid at all, were paid equally by Government and by local contributions.

In 1879 a Teachers Act[4] provided for the building of Residences for teachers of Vested Schools, and also set apart a sum of £1,300,000 from the property of the Disestablished Church as the nucleus of a fund for teachers' pensions[5]. Male teachers were to retire at sixty-five, and mistresses at sixty.

---

[1] Powis, i. 535.　　　　　　　[2] Childers Report, 1884, Q. 903.
[3] *Vide* Annual Reports.　　　　[4] 42 & 43 Vict. c. 74.
[5] In 1897 the Fund was reported by a Committee of investigation to be insolvent to the extent of £1,200,000 at the end of 1895, owing chiefly to the inadequate rate of contributions, although teachers had complained of the length of life for which payment of premiums was

In 1883 a motion was agreed to in the House of Commons without a division, that it was expedient to introduce into Ireland the principle of compulsory education with such modifications as the social and religious conditions of the country required[1].

Nothing, however, was done at the time to carry this unanimous resolution into effect, and the very moderate measure passed nine years later has been met with great coldness. But in 1883 a step far more important for Irish schools was taken with respect to the training of elementary teachers.

We have seen[2] that it was originally intended that all National teachers should receive a preliminary training, but the Board, which relied solely on its own training institution, never really faced the question nor attempted to place that establishment in a position to prepare, even after their appointment, the total number of teachers needed[3]. In 1883 there were 7,907 Roman Catholic teachers in the National Schools, and of these only 2,142 or 27 per cent. had been trained; there were 2,714 Protestant teachers, of whom only 1,412 or 52 per cent. had been trained: thus only one-third of the total number had received the training which more than fifty years before had been declared an indispensable preliminary to employment[4].

In this year the Right Hon. Sir George Trevelyan, then Chief Secretary for Ireland, wrote to the Board declaring the need to be 'no longer one of speculation or expediency, but one of absolute urgency[5].'

calculated (*Subjects of the Day*, p. 64, J. Samuelson, Education, 1890; Parliamentary Paper, 1897, R. 8,471).

[1] Hansard, T. S., cclxxvi. p. 1,299.   [2] *Vide* p. 98.

[3] *Training Colleges*, 1882.

	Numbers.	Teachers in Training.	Annual Cost.	Population, 1881.
England	42	3,150	£110,000	26 millions.
Scotland	7	851	£27,000	3·7 ,,
Ireland	1	220	£7,755	5·1 ,,

(50th Report, Nat. Ed., P. P., 1884, xxv. p. 17).

[4] Report for 1883, p. 17.
[5] Ibid. p. 18.

Accordingly the recommendations of the Powis Commission [1] were at last carried into effect, and the British system of voluntary denominational Training Colleges was introduced in addition to the Board's own College in Marlborough Street. Grants were offered to approved institutions on a credit system by which every student attaining his diploma brought his college £50 for one or £100 for two years of training (£35 or £70 in the case of women). St. Patrick's Training College for Catholic Male Students at Drumcondra, and Our Lady of Mercy Training College for Females in Dublin, were opened within the year, and in 1884 the Church of Ireland placed its Training College for Male and Female Students in Kildare Place, Dublin, in similar connexion with the Board. The De La Salle College at Waterford was added in 1891.

Teachers attending the Marlborough Street College might lodge in any denominational establishment approved of by the Commissioners as a Boarding House, and were allowed at the rate of £26 a year for board. The College in Kildare Place belonging to the Church of Ireland was approved in 1883 [2], and in that year sent 18 students, but this arrangement was superseded as we have seen in 1884.

The period of training was extended to two years [3], and the old rule of paying teachers' salaries during their training, on condition of their providing efficient substitutes, was maintained [4].

As in Great Britain, the grant to voluntary establishments was not to exceed 75 per cent. of the total annual expenditure [5].

In 1884 it was rendered possible [6] to obtain public loans for starting non-vested Schools or Training Colleges, with the approval of the Commissioners of National Education.

In December, 1890, the system of payments in these colleges was revised with a view to place the denominational training colleges on an equal footing with Marlborough

[1] *Vide* p. 105.   [2] Report for 1883, p. 22; Samuelson, p. 69.
[3] Or one year in the case of a certificated teacher.
[4] Samuelson, p. 69.   [5] *Vide* p. 20.   [6] 47 & 48 Vict. c. 22.

Street: and payments were made quarterly at a capitation rate, with an extra grant on obtaining a diploma. The Board also undertook to repay gradually to the managers the value of their buildings [1].

In 1890 the Local Taxation (Customs and Excise) Act [2] was passed, and £78,000 was paid yearly to the Commissioners of National Education in Ireland, to be distributed by them in proportion to the average number of pupils in daily attendance at the National Schools.

(1) In Contributory Unions the money was to be paid to the guardians in relief of local rates as a whole or partial reimbursement of results fees.

(2) In non-Contributory Unions it was to be paid for the benefit of the National Schools as an addition to the local contributions to the schools.

These payments were more valuable even than their amounts seem to show, for being reckoned as voluntary contributions they enabled many schools to claim full payment of the last third of their results fees under the concession first made in 1880 [3]. Thus in 1889–90 576 schools failed to get such payment; in the next year under this new system all but 14 succeeded .

In 1892 came the Irish Education Act [5], which followed the lead of Scotland in 1889 and England in 1891 and freed elementary education, and which also in a half-hearted way provided for compulsory attendance in the larger towns.

£210,000, or any other sum determined by Parliament, proportionate to the English fee grant, was to be paid annually by the Treasury, and in future no fees were to be charged for children over three and under fifteen in any State-aided elementary day school, or only fees to the amount by which the average scale of fees in the school had exceeded 6s. in 1891, unless the Commissioners assented

---

[1] Cf. *The Irish University Question: The Catholic Case*, Archbishop Walsh: Browne and Nolan, Dublin, 1897, p 519.
[2] 53 & 54 Vict. c. 60.   [3] *Vide* p. 108.
[4] Report for 1890, p. 22.   [5] 55 & 56 Vict. c. 42.

to any other arrangement.   Teachers received a bonus, and the salaries were augmented 20 per cent. ; where the capitation grant was still paid, it was increased by 3*s*. 6*d*. a head.   A bonus of £9 was given to each male assistant, and £7 10*s*. to each female classed above the third class.

The attempt at compulsory education was limited to municipal boroughs and towns or townships under Commissioners.   The discretion of extending it to the counties , or any part of them was entrusted to the County Councils, which were not created by Parliament until 1898.

Where the Act applied, School Attendance Committees were to be formed, half of the members being appointed by the Town Council or Commissioners, and half nominated by the National Board.   Parents must cause every child between six and fourteen to make seventy-five attendances each half-year at some National or other efficient school. A certificate of having passed the fourth class procured exemption, and the list of other valid excuses was unusually liberal, even for a plausible people.   Employment of children under eleven, or without a certificate over eleven but under fourteen, was forbidden, unless permitted by the Factory and Workshop Acts.   The Attendance Order is prescribed, unless the School Attendance Committee think it inexpedient to make an application, and the penalty on parents for disobedience is fixed at 5*s*., costs included.   The Commissioners of National Education have power to take action in case of default, and also to extend the powers of the Act to the suburbs of any place where it is in force.

But in point of fact the measure, lenient as it is, has only been steadily put into force in 42 out of the 118 places to which it applied. In many places no Committee was appointed. In more there were no attendance officers. In the 42 places where it has been continuously enforced, the average attendance distinctly improved.

1893	... ...	60,459
1896	... ...	69,914
1897	... ...	68,678.

Upwards of twenty local authorities refused to put the Act in force as long as a certain class of schools[1] were excluded from participation in public grants. It will be remembered that the Powis Commission had recommended that in places where there were both a Catholic and a Protestant school of a certain size, the restrictions as to religious teaching might be to a certain extent relaxed, as long as a compulsory time-table conscience clause was retained. Negotiations to this end between the Chief Secretary and the National Board were entered upon in 1892, and have since been renewed, but the Board has not as yet been sufficiently unanimous or sufficiently circumscribed in its proposals to admit of any result being reached either under a Liberal or a Conservative Government.

Evening Schools. In 1846 the Board reported that a considerable number of evening schools had been opened. 'No experiment that we have made has been more thoroughly successful. . . . We have never witnessed amongst persons in any class greater eagerness or aptitude for knowledge[2].'

Salaries, grants of books, and inspection were afterwards extended to them[3], and after 1872 they received results fees.

But in 1896 only 35 evening schools were in operation, attended only by 1,147 scholars. Since 1883 every school of this kind is restricted to pupils of one sex.

	Number.	Average attendance.
1880 . . .	119	—
1890 . . .	52	1747
1897 . . .	36	1255

Industrial Training and Agriculture. The Commissioners were from the beginning very anxious to encourage industrial training in Ireland, and for a time made grants to schools of industry as a separate class. These chiefly resulted in encouragement of needlework and embroidery, and are still continued, while ordinary sewing and knitting have been compulsory since 1850.

---

[1] *scilicet* denominational.   [2] Powis, i. 109.   [3] 1855 : 1863.

The Sixth Class literary and industrial programme was adopted for girls in 1889 to prepare them for the practical duties of home life, or enable them to pursue suitable industrial employments.

In 1883 a course of handicraft was introduced for the training of masters at Marlborough Street[1].

The really important department was Agriculture, and that has been fostered by the Board with an interest as real as it was unpractical.

In 1837 two agricultural schools were established under local management, and in 1838 the Model Farm and Garden of seventeen acres at Glasnevin near Dublin were opened, which has subsequently expanded into the Albert National Agricultural Training Institute of 180 acres[2]. Glasnevin has served both for higher and intermediate agricultural teaching, and also for training of National School teachers[3], as well as for experiments and for practical dairy work. The Munster Model Farm near Cork was opened in 1853, and it remains in most respects a smaller Glasnevin[4].

In 1849 the Commissioners began to lease and manage farms, of which by 1856 they had 20 of first-class character; but the expense was so excessive that no more were added[5]. They also encouraged smaller farms in connexion with schools, and in 1875 there were 228 of all kinds, of which 19 were first-class farms. The latter were, however, soon after discontinued, with the two exceptions already mentioned.

In 1897 there were only 48 ordinary farms under local management, but gardens in connexion with schools had risen to 101.

In 1873 the theory of Agriculture was introduced as an obligatory subject for boys in results fees examinations in

---

[1] Cross Report, Q. 53,260 ; Belmore Report, p. 24.
[2] Powis Report, i. 462.   [3] Ibid. i. 854.   [4] Ibid. i. 869.
[5] The buildings were of cut stone—even the byres, so that a peasant would say, 'Cowhouses, indeed ; bedad, it's parlours he has them in ! Where would the likes of me be looking for grandeur like them?' (ibid. i. p. 842).

the three upper classes in ordinary country National Schools. For boys in city schools and for girls, it is voluntary.

> In 1880, 32,111 were examined and 14,857 passed.
> In 1890, 80,971 　　　,,　　　,,　　　49,124　,,
> In 1897, 85,044 　　　,,　　　,,　　　58,075　,,

The subject, however, is taught almost exclusively from a text-book, unaccompanied by practical demonstration, and this teaching is described by experts as 'quite valueless,' and 'wholly useless, if not worse[1].'

In January, 1897, a Vice-Regal Commission, with the Earl of Belmore as Chairman, was appointed to inquire how far and in what form manual and practical instruction should be introduced into the National Schools, and they presented their most excellent report in June, 1898. They recommended the extension of Kindergarten to all infants, and of 'Hand and Eye Training' and 'Woodwork' to older children. Drawing should be made compulsory, singing should be brought within the reach of all : drill and physical exercises should be introduced with the least possible delay. Needlework should be continued, and practical agriculture, where feasible, but book-teaching of the latter ought to be replaced by elementary science as part of the ordinary education. Payment by results ought not to be applied to the new subjects : Evening Schools should be released from needless restrictions, and if possible rendered popular and efficient : the Training College courses should be altered so as to provide teachers able to give the new instruction.

If these recommendations seem somewhat numerous, they urge nothing which is not common or actually compulsory in England, and what a measure of the deficiencies of the Irish curriculum they afford !

Elementary Science as a subject is virtually extinct[2], Woodwork and Hand and Eye Training practically unknown[3]. Kindergarten teaching was given in 385 out of

---

[1] P. P., 1898, C. 8,923 ; Final Report of Belmore Commission, p. 40.
[2] Ibid. p. 36.　　　　　　　　　　　　[3] Ibid. pp. 17, 24.

8,631 National Schools in 1897, and physical exercises were very little practised outside the Kindergarten classes. Drawing in 1897 was taught only to 83,913 children, out of 271,568 eligible to learn it. Singing by ear is not recognized, and only 68,977 pupils earned a grant in singing by note out of the 521,141 making an average attendance. Within the last few months only one of the school books supplied by the Board contained any Irish airs at all [1].

The general verdict of the Commission on the education given in the National Schools is that while it fits boys for the Irish Intermediate Schools, it leaves them 'not fit to enter a Technical School, even if they had such a school at their doors [2].'

To turn to the most elementary parts of education, has the policy of the Board been successful? Has a system been created which provides for the whole of the poorer classes in Ireland an efficient rudimentary education?

The numbers have risen from 107,042 children on the rolls in 1833 to 816,001 [3] in 1897, and from 280,005 in average daily attendance in 1852 to 521,141 in 1897, although the population has fallen from 8,175,124 in 1841 to 4,704,750 in 1891. On the other hand, if one-sixth of the population ought to have been present in elementary schools in 1897, the attendance should have been 758,605, whereas, on the average, it was only 68·7 of this number.

The percentage of those who can neither read nor write has fallen to one-third of what it was fifty years ago [4].

There has been no public comparison of the quality of education in Ireland and that given in the rest of the kingdom since the English Assistant-Commissioners took part in the work of the Powis Commission before 1870. The standard in reading, writing, and arithmetic was con-

[1] Cf. Sir C. H. Parry, *The Art of Music*, p. 79. 'Irish folk-music—probably the most human, most varied, most poetical and most imaginative in the world—is particularly rich in tunes which imply considerable sympathetic sensitiveness.' 'As a simple emotional type, this Irish tune (Londonderry Air) is one of the most perfect in existence.'

[2] Belmore Report, p. 6.   [3] Average on rolls.   [4] *Vide* p. 305.

sidered by the late Resident Commissioner to be at least as high as in this country[1].

In 1884 the Royal Commission on Technical Instruction reported that no progress could be effected in Ireland until primary education had been placed on a proper footing, but compulsion was their only suggestion to that end[2].

Although there is no definite judgment on the merits of the schools to-day there can be no doubt that the advance is incalculable on the Pay Schools, where seventy per cent. of the children attending any school went in 1824, or even on the early schools of the National Board with their untrained and incompetent teachers. Even in 1897, however, only 46·2 per cent. of the teachers had been trained.

It is very evident that the improvement has been enormous, but a great deal yet remains to be done. The chief obstacles which have existed from the beginning are still in the path. There is poverty, there is indifference to education, and there is religious exclusiveness.

The poverty of Ireland is a commonplace. The Commission that reported in 1896 on the financial relations between Great Britain and Ireland found that while the former had but eight times as large a population as the latter, it had at least twenty times as much property subject to income-tax, and all circumstances pointed to a similar state of things among the wage-earning classes[3].

Most of the facts which could be cited as evidence of indifference to education are also unfortunately the signs of poverty, and indifference to education is a charge which it is unpleasant to bring against the *Insula Sanctorum et*

---

[1] Childers Report, Q. 927.

[2] Second Report, i. 532. The Director-General of Military Education reported in 1896 that 'the education imparted in the National Schools in Ireland differs so widely from that given in schools in Great Britain that it would be inadvisable to send the children of soldiers to them.' A Committee under Lord Harris had reported to the same effect in 1887 (1896 Report, p. 28). In 1897, for the first time, the English Education Department consented to recognize first-class certificates of Irish teachers who have been trained in a Training College.

[3] P. P., 1896, pp. 2, 19, 26, 39–42.

Doctorum, the Island of St. Patrick and St. Columba. But if the Irish who have not emigrated are not indifferent to education, why has there been no outcry for real reform, why is there so much opposition to compulsory education? Scotland, which for long was quite as poor as Ireland, set her face steadily towards knowledge, and in 1872 was ready before England to undergo compulsion.

As to the religious question, the tendency has been continually towards separate schools.

In 1870 there were 400,000 Catholics and 27,000 Protestants in schools attended by one denomination only. In 1895 there were 455,000 and 125,000 respectively, in spite of the decline in population. In 1870 in schools taught solely by Catholics there were 25,000 Protestant children, in 1895 16,000 [1]. In 1870, in schools in which some or all of the teachers were Protestants, there were 42,000 Catholic children: in 1895 there were but 17,000, although in 1891 75.4 per cent. of the population were Catholics. And yet in all these schools the absence of children during religious teaching of another denomination was enforced as far as the National Board could enforce it.

Mr. Butt in 1865 put it very graphically: 'Walking down King's Inn Street (in Dublin) the passenger may see, divided by a narrow lane, two separate buildings both bearing the inscription of National School. On one side of the lane is a school under the management of the ladies of a convent; on the other side is the school of a Presbyterian Church. Not a single Protestant child attends the one; not a single Roman Catholic child the other. Yet in both religious education is fettered and controlled. . . . In the narrow compass of that lane, about four yards wide, any observer can estimate the reality of the system of united education and the deep practical wisdom of its rules [2].'

In fine it is clear that the Irish, whether Catholics or Protestants, simply will not have combined education.

---

[1] In 1896 a different basis of reckoning was adopted.
[2] Cit. Sadler, *Special Reports*, 1897, p. 227.

2. PRIVY COUNCIL.

The Science and Art Department.

The rules and grants of the Science and Art Department apply to Ireland equally with England; but for elementary drawing and manual training the Department limits its aid to such schools as are not under the National Board. In 1897 eighty-seven schools (of which sixty-seven belonged to the Christian Brothers) earned £1,071 for the drawing of 14,304 children in average attendance[1], but the grant amounted only to 1*s.* 6*d.* per head, against an average of 1*s.* 8*d.* in Scotland and 1*s.* 9*d.* in England and Wales[2]. Only two Irish schools received grants for manual instruction in 1897, both belonging to the Christian Brothers. Apparently the transfer of drawing and manual training to the Education Departments in England and Scotland has not affected the arrangement in Ireland, which is now the only country where the Science and Art Department takes cognizance of elementary teaching in these subjects. The extreme need of Ireland for more instruction in drawing is shown by the fact that in 1897 only 31 per cent. of all the children in the National Schools were taught this subject, and only 24 per cent. passed in it.

Owing to the withdrawal of grants for second class passes by South Kensington, Elementary Science has 'practically disappeared from the primary schools of Ireland[3].'

3. THE COMMISSIONERS OF EDUCATION IN IRELAND.

4. THE COMMISSIONERS OF CHARITABLE DONATIONS AND BEQUESTS.

5. EDUCATIONAL ENDOWMENTS (IRELAND) COMMISSIONERS.

These Commissions have filled relatively so much larger a part in the history of Secondary Education that

---

[1] 1870: about 30 schools.   1880: 12 schools.   1890: 48 schools.
[2] Forty-fifth Report of Science and Art Department, p. xxix; Appendix, p. 643.   [3] Belmore Report, p. 36.

I have placed them under that heading, and they will be found at page 203.

But it must be remembered that they deal also with endowments for elementary education, and that it is only because so much more public money has been granted to the lower branch that its endowments have been of comparatively little importance to it of late years. Thus in 1791 of an income of £30,000 arising from educational endowments, £22,000 sooner or later was applied to elementary foundations[1]; and in 1838 there were 349 elementary endowed schools in Ireland, exclusive of the Erasmus Smith and Royal foundations[2].

6. The Home Secretary for the United Kingdom.

i. *The Factory Acts.*

The English Acts have applied to Ireland from the beginning.

The English Education Act of 1876 did not apply the Factory Act of 1874 to non-textile factories in Ireland, but this was remedied by the Factory Act of 1878.

There are three Inspectors in Ireland who report to the chief office in London. But in 1893 there were only 204 schools attended by factory children, nearly all of them in the North of Ireland[3].

Under 41 Vict. c. 16 a certified efficient school in Ireland is defined as 'any national school or any school recognized by the Lord Lieutenant or Privy Council as affording sufficient means of literary education for purposes of this Act.'

ii. *Mines.*

The first Acts which applied to Ireland were the Coal Mines Regulation Act and the Metalliferous Mines Act in

---

[1] Kildare Report, I. 18.
[2] Wyse Select Committee Report, p. 9.
[3] Report on Child Labour, P. P., 1893, No. 311, p. 27.

1872[1], but since that date the law has been the same throughout the United Kingdom.

7. THE GENERAL PRISONS BOARD.

Prisons in Ireland were regulated after 1826 by 7 Geo. IV, c. 74, and various amending Acts.   There was a Board of Superintendence appointed by the Grand Juries, with whom also the appointment of all officers rested.

In 1843 Gaol Schools were placed on the same footing as Workhouse Schools, and grants of books made on similar terms by the Commissioners of National Education.

In 1853 gratuities were paid to teachers in special cases.

In 1868 thirty-eight masters and twenty-three mistresses were employed in thirty-six gaols. Thirteen of these schools were connected with the National Board, but only four received gratuities[2].

The General Prisons Board was constituted in November, 1877, under 40 and 41 Vict. c. 49[3], and they insisted on the rule for separate confinement being observed. The Commissioners of National Education refused to allow their Inspector to examine prisoners in separate cells, and so the privilege of their inspection was withdrawn[4].

8. THE CHIEF SECRETARY FOR IRELAND.

Reformatories and Industrial Schools.

The Irish system of the Reformatories and Industrial Schools was created by and is administered under different Acts from those in force in Great Britain, but the Irish Acts were modelled on the statutes already passed in this country, and, as far as education is concerned, the differences lie rather in the application of the principles than in the measures themselves. The Chief Secretary for Ireland

---

[1] 35 & 36 Vict. c. 76 and c. 77.   [2] Powis, i. 478.
[3] The appointment of all officers rests with the Lord Lieutenant, subject to the approval of the Treasury (Art. 5).
[4] First Report of Prisons Board for 1879, p. 11.

takes in these Acts the place of the Home Secretary in England.

Reformatories. The first Act for the establishment of Reformatories was passed in 1858[1], and this was repealed and replaced in 1868 by the Irish Reformatory Schools Act[2]. In 1881 44 and 45 Vict. c. 29 gave power to Grand Juries and the Town Councils of Dublin, Limerick, and Cork to contribute to their establishment or maintenance, and to borrow money for building.

Industrial Schools. The Industrial Schools (Ireland) Act[3] was passed in 1868. The Inspector of Reformatories in Ireland was to be identical with the Inspector of Industrial Schools.

43 and 44 Vict. c. 15[4], enabling children found living with prostitutes to be sent to Industrial Schools, applied to Ireland. The chief differences between the English and Irish laws are that in Ireland neither to Reformatories nor Industrial Schools may any child or juvenile offender be sent, except to an institution under the exclusive management of persons of the same religious persuasion as that professed by the parents or guardians of the pupil[5]. With this exception there is but little difference between the Reformatories of the two countries as far as the letter of the law is concerned[6].

With certified Industrial Schools the other chief distinctions are that in Ireland a parent cannot get a refractory child committed to a certified Industrial School, even on payment; nor is a child admitted, one of whose parents has been convicted of a crime or offence punishable with

---

[1] 21 & 22 Vict. c. 103.
[2] 31 & 32 Vict. c. 59.
[3] Ibid. c. 25.
[4] *Vide* p. 57.
[5] This rule led in 1895 to the closing of the only female Protestant Reformatory in Ireland from want of inmates, and Protestant girls eligible for a Reformatory now have to be sent to prison (Report of Inspector of Reformatories and Industrial Schools in Ireland for 1895).
[6] For a list of the variations, *vide* Aberdare Report, i. paragraph 87, and Appendix A. 9.

penal servitude or imprisonment. Guardians of the poor have no power to contribute to these schools [1].

Lord Aberdare's Commission, which inquired into Reformatories and Schools in 1884, has been the only body besides the Powis Commission which included Ireland in its investigations. It recommended that the literary education should be tested in all cases by Inspectors of the National Board of Education [2], and that payment by results should be made to these as to ordinary National Schools, though it would not be necessary to insist on the teachers having certificates.

In Ireland there was more grading of Reformatories and also of Industrial Schools [3] by the age of the children [4]. The certified Industrial Schools in Ireland are regarded as institutions for poor and deserted children rather than for semi-criminals [5], probably because there is no other means of compelling street urchins to attend school [6].

Consequently young children who are criminal in a very slight degree and in England would probably be sent to Industrial Schools, are sent in Ireland to Reformatories [7], and the older and more criminal children do not appear in them at all.

Some twenty years ago the proportion of very young children committed to Reformatories was in this way unduly large, but the percentage of those under twelve has sunk from 32·7 committed in 1880 to 21·7 in 1896, while the children under eight in Industrial Schools have risen from 28·1 to 34·8 in the same year [8]. In 1882 918 out of 1,256 children sent to Industrial Schools were thus committed because they were 'found begging or asking for alms,' and children have been actually sent out to beg with this aim in view [9].

---

[1] Powis, i. 480 ; Aberdare Report, Q. 13,378.
[2] par. 89.
[3] Ibid. Report, par. 88.
[4] Ibid. Q. 1,917.
[5] Ibid. par. 92.
[6] Ibid. p. lxiii.
[7] Ibid. par. 91.
[8] Annual Reports of Inspector.
[9] Aberdare, par. 94. In Scotland a child has been directed to steal for the same purpose (Argyll Report, 1865, p. 255).

In many cases the pupils of the Industrial Schools attend the ordinary National Schools as full-time pupils[1]. If they keep the hundred attendances requisite[2], they are examined as for results fees. But their expenses are paid by the Industrial Schools Department[3], and not in any way by the Commissioners of National Education.

In 1883, out of seventy-one schools of both classes, the pupils of thirty-two were attending National Schools[4]. The schools were usually under the same managers as the National Schools attended, but no objection ever seems to have been made to such attendance. In one case indeed the nuns managing an Industrial School withdrew their children from contamination with the pupils of a National School[5]. The principal object of sending the children to public schools is to obtain the judgment of the Inspectors of the National Board. Even Industrial Schools not in connexion with the Board were voluntarily examined by the National Examiners[6].

Except for such examination there was in 1884 very little literary inspection of Industrial Schools in Ireland[7], and the Inspector naturally did not regard this as a sufficient guarantee in all cases, though the different educational bodies in charge of some of the schools examined them in an efficient manner[8]. The Aberdare Commission reported that the industrial training was better there than in England, and that more children afterwards followed the trades they had been taught[9].

In fact it still seems to be the case, that the only systematic industrial training in the country is to be obtained in these schools[10].

In 1896 there were six Reformatories in Ireland and seventy-one Industrial Schools[11].

---

[1] Aberdare, Q. 13,379.   [2] Ibid. Q. 13,378.   [3] Ibid.
[4] Ibid. Q. 12,414.   [5] Ibid. Q. 13,382.   [6] Ibid. Q. 13,381.
[7] Ibid. Q. 12,414.   [8] Ibid.   [9] i. p. lxii.
[10] *Contemporary Review*, April, 1898, p. 578: 'Irish Elementary Education,' by Edith F. Hogg and A. D. Innes.
[11] Inspector's Report for 1895, p. 1.

	Reformatories.		*Industrial Schools.*	
	R. C.	Prot.	R. C.	Prot.
Male	2	1	17	4
Female	3	0	44	5
Mixed	—	—	1	—

In the end of 1896 there were 553 children in Reformatory Schools, and 7,927 in Industrial Schools.

There was one ship for boys at Belfast, and a fishing school at Baltimore, now recognized by the National Board.

There is no provision for Day Industrial Schools in Ireland, nor are there any Truant Schools.

9. THE LOCAL GOVERNMENT BOARD FOR IRELAND.

The Irish Poor Law was introduced in 1838 by 1 & 2 Vict. c. 56, when regular workhouses were first erected. A Local Government Board was created in 1872 by 35 & 36 Vict. c. 69 to take over the duties of the Poor Law Commissioners [1].

The Commissioners made rules that a schoolmaster and mistress should be appointed by the Board, and that the children should be educated for three hours at least every day [2].

The 49th section of the Act of 1838 was quoted in the Rules and Regulations for that year of the Board of National Education as explanatory of their rules of religious instruction.

It was as follows :—

'No order of the Poor Law Commissioners nor any by-law ... shall authorize the education of any child in any workhouse in any religious creed other than that professed by the parents or surviving parent of such child, and to which such parents or parent shall object, or in the case of an orphan to which the guardian or guardians, godfather or godmother, of such orphan shall object. Provided also that it shall be lawful for any regular minister of the religious persuasion of any inmate of such workhouse at all times in

---

[1] Cf. 10 & 11 Vict. c. 90.   [2] Powis, Q. 10,632.

the day, on the request of such inmate, to visit such work-house for the purpose of affording religious assistance to such inmate, and also for the purpose of instructing his child or children in the principles of his religion.'

In 1843 the Commissioners of National Education received workhouse schools into connexion on condition of their observing this rule and submitting to their inspection. Grants of books only were made to them[1]. In 1850 the Commissioners, with the concurrence of the Poor Law Commissioners, awarded grants to forty male and forty female teachers of these schools on the recommendation of the District Inspectors.

In 1855 it was definitely required that all the rules of the Board applicable to Non-Vested Schools must be observed.

In 1871 the view of the Irish Workhouse School taken by the Irish Poor Law Commissioners was that, 'shut off as it is from all contact with adults other than the teachers, it differs in no respect materially from the boarding school to which parents in a better class of life send their children from home for the purpose of a more systematic course of education and discipline[2].'

The schools are examined on the same plan as the ordinary National Schools, and extracts from the reports of the Inspector are sent to the Local Government Board for the information of the different Boards of Guardians on the plan which was abolished in England in 1863. The salaries of the teachers are fixed by the Poor Law Authorities and paid from the Consolidated Fund. By the National School Teachers (Ireland) Act, 1875[3], power was given to the Guardians of awarding to the teachers of their Poor Law Union National Schools from the rates, the amount of results fees which would have been payable in a National School on the Inspector's Reports, and the National Board in 1877 discontinued their system of gratuities.

---

[1] 1843, viii. 2.   [2] Report for 1870–71, p. 13.
[3] 38 & 39 Vict. c. 96.

In 1848, by 11 and 12 Vict. c. 25, the Poor Law Commissioners were given power to combine Unions into Districts for schools, but it is only within the last ten years that two District schools for eleven Unions have been formed at Trim and Glin.

Most of the workhouse schools are separate for boys and girls. Farms from two to twenty-five acres are attached to all Unions, and some boys acquire practical instruction in agriculture. After April 1, 1863, the Commissioners of National Education, at the request of the Government, discontinued the assistance they had given to the agricultural department of these schools[1]; but in 1897 they consented to allow inspection and examination by their officers[2].

District Inspectors are prepared to examine at the workhouse any boarded-out Pauper Children attending any school not being a National School[3].

For the power of Unions to become contributory to the salaries of National teachers, *vide* p. 108.

By 1876 153 Poor Law Schools were in connexion with the Board, and only five remained outside; in 1897 the number was 154, but the numbers attending these schools have greatly decreased.

	Schools.	Children on the Rolls.	Average daily attendance.
1860	140	13,483	6,654
1870	147	17,250	8,399
1880	158	16,945	8,880
1890	158	9,430	5,221
1897	154	5,334	4,343

10. THE COMMANDER-IN-CHIEF.

Military Schools.

Besides the ordinary Military Schools[4] under the War Office, there is a special institution for the children of

---

[1] 37th Report, Commissioners of National Education, App. p. 30.

[2] 63rd Report, p. 18.   [3] 58th Report: for 1891, p. 98.

[4] In 1895 thirty army schoolmasters and thirty-seven mistresses, besides acting teachers, were serving in Ireland (Director-General's Report, 1896, pp. 19, 23). *Vide* p. 75.

soldiers, the Royal Hibernian School, first opened in 1770, in the Phoenix Park [1]. Charters were granted to it in 1809, 1819, and 1841, and in 1846 [2], when it was assimilated to the Royal Military Asylum at Chelsea.

Half-time was introduced in 1879, and the literary education suffered. The system of education was based on that of the Irish Model Schools, modified to suit the character of the school and the probable career of the pupils, most of whom pass into the Army. Owing to the example of the Royal Military Asylum at Chelsea, full school time was restored in 1890, and the system of standards in force in the Army Schools was introduced. All the Masters now belong to the Army School Department, and the School is examined annually by Inspectors of Army Schools [3].

The establishment consists of 410 boys [4].

11. THE LORDS OF THE ADMIRALTY.

The educational regulations apply to Ireland as far as occasion arises, but there are no special establishments in that country.

[1] P. P., 1810, x. p. 253.
[2] Bartley, *Schools for the People*, p. 233.
[3] Director-General's Report, 1893, p. 27.   [4] Ibid. 1896, p. 26.

I. ELEMENTARY EDUCATION.

C. Scotland.

1. PRIVY COUNCIL.

i. *The Scotch Education Department.*

THE beginning of this century, which found in England only a sprinkling of voluntary schools, and in Ireland only unsuccessful State-aided proselytising societies, and hedge-schools but recently legalized, discovered in Scotland a long-established system of public schools aided by the rates.

The reason is not far to seek. The Scotch had always been zealous for education, and had made several attempts to provide an organized system of schools, which failed chiefly from want of funds. But in 1696 an Act was passed 'for Settling of Schools[1],' which ordained that 'there shall be a school settled and established and a schoolmaster appointed in every paroch not already provided by the advice of the heritors[2] and minister of the paroch.' Under this Act the heritors are bound to provide a commodious school house, and a 'sallary.' not above 200 merks (£11 2s. 2d.) nor under 100 (£5 11s. 1d.). Each heritor is to be assessed in proportion to his valued rent, and is allowed relief from his tenants to the extent of one-half[3]. Then follows the important clause of the Act

---

[1] Scotch Act, William, 1696, c. 26. A similar statute had been passed during the Rebellion (Charles I, 1646, c. 45), and afterwards repealed.

[2] i. e. landowners.

[3] Argyll Commission : Second Report, 1867, p. xxvii.

K

which provided for default, and saved it from the fate of so many Acts by passing on its administration to the hands of other persons interested in it. 'If the heritors or major part of them shall not conveen, or being conveened shall not agree among themselves, then and in that case the Presbitrie [1] shall apply to the Commissioners of the Supply of the shire [2],' who shall carry out the Act.

Under this statute the parish schools grew and prospered without interference for more than a century, the schoolmasters holding office *ad vitam aut culpam.* The schools were in the main elementary schools, but it must always be remembered that they also supplied a considerable quantity of secondary instruction, and sent pupils direct to the Universities. Schools were not cast in such uniform moulds in those days, and Scotland, being a poor country, had in creating a working system of national education to employ the various elements of that system to supplement one another's deficiencies [3].

In 1803 the first amending Act [4] was passed. The schoolmaster's salary was raised to not less than 300 or more than 400 merks, and the heritors were in addition bound to furnish a suitable dwelling-house and a fenced garden; the schoolmaster was a freeholder, and might enforce the supply of his accommodation by appeal to Quarter Sessions. Only those heritors might attend the meeting and vote who owned lands within the parish of at least £100 Scots of valued rent [5].

In parishes of great extent, and especially in the Islands, where two schools were needed in one parish, the heritors might provide 600 merks salary and no house, and distribute

---

[1] A body consisting of the ministers and a lay elder from each parish in the district.

[2] The body of landholders in each county who assessed the land-tax.

[3] Argyll Commission, Third Report, p. 109.

[4] 43 Geo. III, c. 54.

[5] The pound Scots amounted to 1s. 8d. only; it was legally obsolete, as the coinages of England and Scotland were made uniform by 5 Anne, c. 8, Art. xvi.

the amount between two or more teachers.   The additional schools so created were known as Side Schools.

The schoolmaster was to be elected by the heritors and minister acting as one body; he was then examined and approved by the Presbytery, and was required to sign the Confession of Faith[1] and the Formula of the Church of Scotland.

The superintendence of the schools was continued with the ministers of the Established Church.   The hours of teaching and the vacations were regulated by the Presbytery, who also might censure, suspend or deprive a schoolmaster for neglect, immorality or cruelty, without right of appeal.

The system was excellent as far as it extended, but it practically did not affect the large towns[2], and it fell especially short in the Highlands and Islands[3].   The country parishes were very large, for in Scotland there were less than a thousand parishes in all on an area of twenty million acres, whereas the thirty-seven million acres in England and Wales comprised fifteen thousand parishes[4]. The towns, on the other hand, relied chiefly on burgh schools and academies, which were to a great extent secondary[5], and on voluntary effort[6], which proved inadequate.   Even in 1873 thirty thousand elementary school places were wanted in Glasgow, and over four thousand in Edinburgh[7].

In May, 1818[8], Brougham's Select Committee of the House of Commons, investigating the Education of the Poor of the Metropolis[9], were directed to inquire into the state of the education of the poor in Scotland.   The chief result was a collection of returns from the officiating

---

[1] Cf. p. 289.

[2] Cumin, *Report of Select Committee of the House of Commons, 1866*, Q. 1,113.

[3] Craik, *The State in its Relation to Education*, p. 140.

[4] Report of Endowed Institutions (Scotland) Commission on distribution of Grant for Higher Education, P. P., 1881, C. 2,768, p. vii.

[5] *Vide* p. 220.

[6] Chiefly Church (Sessional) and small private schools.

[7] Board of Education, Third Report, 1876, p. viii.

[8] Hansard, First Series, xxxviii. 616.   [9] *Vide* p. 1.

ministers in Scotland of the schools within their parishes, printed in 1819[1].

The recommendations of the Committee were made in June, 1818[2], and in them no distinction was made between Scotland and England, except that for the latter the adoption was recommended of 'the Parish School system, so usefully established in the Northern part of our island.' They noticed that the Scotch sects, differing only 'in certain opinions of a political rather than a religious nature,' could conscientiously use Parish Schools connected with the Establishment and employing the same Catechism.

In 1825 the General Assembly of the Church of Scotland established an Education Committee to supplement the Society for the Propagation of Christian Knowledge in Scotland, which had been founded in 1709 chiefly to promote religious teaching in the Highlands, and was by law connected with the Established Church of Scotland[3].

In 1833, as we have seen, the House of Commons voted £20,000 'for the purposes of Education,' and the Appropriation Act of the same year[4] assigned it to 'the erection of school houses in Great Britain,' but none of the money went to Scotland. For four out of the next five years, however, Scotland received an annual vote of £10,000 for her schools[5].

---

[1] P. P., 1819, ix (c.) p. 1450*. End of 1818 :—

	Schools.	*Children.*	*Revenue.*
Parochial Schools	942	54,161	£20,611
Endowed Schools	212	10,177	£13,679
Dames' Schools	257	5,560	—
Ordinary Schools	2,222	106,627	—
	3,633	176,525	£34,290

[2] P. P., 1818, iv. pp. 57–61.   [3] Argyll Second Report, xxxv.

[4] 3 & 4 Will. IV, c. 96.

[5] The following are the items of the successive Appropriation Acts :—

1834 (4 & 5 Will. IV, c. 84). For erecting school houses in Scotland and Model Schools in England. (This all went to Scotland.)

1835 (5 & 6 Will. IV, c. 80). For erecting Model Schools. (This sum was reserved for England, and spent in 1842: Newcastle Report, i. 643, 645.)

1836 (6 & 7 Will. IV, c. 98) and 1837 (7 Will. IV, c. 79). For the erection of school houses and Model Schools in Scotland.

1838 (1 & 2 Vict. c. 111). For the erection of school houses in Scotland.

The English conditions of 1833[1] were imposed on Scotland in 1834[2], except that the recommendation of the two societies was dispensed with. Help was given also only to large towns[3].

In 1838 an Act[4] was passed authorizing the Treasury, in the case of moneys voted by Parliament, to set aside a fund for the endowment of schools in the Highlands, for which the heritors were to provide school house, residence, and garden. These were afterwards known as 'Parliamentary Schools.'

In April, 1837, and January, 1839, the Treasury appropriated two sums of £6,000 and £4,000 for these purposes out of the annual votes of £10,000.

In 1839 the votes for England and Scotland were re-united, after a severance of six years, in £30,000 'for Public Education in Great Britain[5],' and this time Scotland received her share.

In 1839 the Committee of Council for Education was established at Whitehall, and, as far as State recognition was concerned, the histories of Scotch and of English Schools are almost identical for the next thirty years[6]. But it must be remembered that in Scotland this was only one-half of the story, and that the old rate-aided parish schools steadily continued the second century of their public existence, merely drawing increased revenue from Whitehall if they chose to submit to the conditions of the Committee of Council, and acquiring additional efficiency from inspection and from the training of their teachers. Many of the best schools remained content with their parochial income[7], and pursued their way undisturbed by any one but their

---

[1] *Vide* p. 4.

[2] Minute, October 21, 1834; P. P., 1839, xli. 386, 408.

[3] Ibid. pp. 386, 403, 408.   [4] 1 & 2 Vict. c. 87.

[5] 2 & 3 Vict. c. 89.

[6] A Concordat as to the appointment of Inspectors was concluded between the General Assembly of the Church of Scotland and the Committee of Council early in 1840, several months before the English arrangement (p. 8). Kay-Shuttleworth, *Four Periods of Public Education*, p. 464.   [7] *Vide* p. 137, note 3.

own minister and Presbytery[1]. The heritors took a liberal view of the case, assented to this arrangement[2], and in many instances contributed more to the schools than was required of them by law[3].

Mr. Horace Mann, the Secretary of the Massachusetts Board of Education, gives the picture of a Scotch elementary school at this period, which is a fitting pendant to Mr. Fearon's later description of the burgh schools[4]. He especially admires the 'mental activity' and 'incredible rapidity' displayed. 'I do not exaggerate when I say that the most active and lively schools I have ever seen in the United States must be regarded almost as dormitories compared with the fervid life of the Scotch schools[5].'

The Free Church. In 1843 came the Disruption, when 470 ministers left the Established and formed the Free Church, and this movement was not unnaturally accompanied by great sectarian bitterness. As parish schoolmasters still had to sign the Formula of the Established Church, about 80 of them, accompanied by nearly 300 other teachers, 'went out'; it became necessary to provide for these, and it was determined to aim at providing 500 new schools; consequently a new one, often much needed, was built in connexion with nearly every Free Church[6].

No religious difficulty. But with all this the religious difficulty has been almost unknown in Scotch education[7], and little worse ever resulted than the creation of competing schools in districts where they were not wanted at the expense of those regions where there was no rivalry to fear[8].

[1] Lord Sandford; Evidence before the Commission on Endowed Institutions, Scotland: Report on distribution of Grants for Higher Education, P. P., 1881, C. 2,768, p. 21; Argyll Second Report, App., p. 248.
[2] Ibid.   [3] Ibid. p. 235; Powis Report, ii. 326.
[4] Taunton Report, vi. 51.
[5] Report of an Educational Tour, 1846, p. 61.
[6] Argyll First Report, 1865, p. 95.
[7] General Report of the Assistant Commissioners, 1867, p. 329, xxxv; *Nineteenth Century*, January, 1897: 'The Educational Peace of Scotland,' by T. Shaw, Q.C.
[8] Craik, pp. 143, 152.

In 1829 the Education Committee of the General Assembly of the Church of Scotland stated that their schools were open freely to Roman Catholics, and that the teachers were directed not to press on them any instruction to which their parents or priests might object [1]. The Established and Free Churches and the Roman Catholics all insisted on a Parliamentary Conscience Clause in any Education Act for Scotland [2]. Consequently when the Act came, it was possible to leave the School Boards full discretion to provide what religious education they thought fit, subject only to the time-table and the conscience clause.

No Capitation Grant. Almost the only distinction between Scotland and England made by the Education Department was that the capitation grants of 1853 and 1856 were confined to England and Wales.

The Revised Code. When the days of the Revised Code arrived, the disadvantage of centralization at Whitehall was seen. Scotland bitterly resented her more or less mixed schools being bribed to confine themselves to the merest rudiments of education, and receiving grants for those only out of all the pupils in her public schools whose parents were engaged in manual labour. In consequence of her protests the Revised Code was suspended in Scotland in June, 1864, in respect of payments, although it continued to enforce individual examination [3]; and it is only fair to add that in the opinion of the Education Department this test revealed that there was at least as much reason to attend to the elementary instruction of the children in Scotland as in England [4]. Accordingly in Scotland until 1872, besides grants for maintaining Normal Schools and building grants for elementary schools, Government help was devoted to augmenting the salaries of certificated teachers, and paying

---

[1] 1866, House of Commons Select Committee Report, Q. 1,033.
[2] Ibid. Q. 1,034.　　　　　　　　　[3] Report for 1864, p. lxxvi.
[4] Lord Sandford, Report of Commission on Endowed Institutions, P. P., 1881, C. 2,768, p. 24.

the stipends of assistant and pupil teachers or apprentices, and the gratuities to teachers for instructing them [1].

In 1861 a fresh Act [2] brought the Parish School system up to date. Teachers' salaries were raised to not less than £35 or more than £70, and the minimum of house accommodation in future was increased. Female teachers might now be appointed for elementary education or industrial training at not more than £30 a year [3].

The examination of parish schoolmasters before appointment was transferred to the Scotch Universities from the Presbyteries [4], and the jurisdiction of the Presbyteries as to dismissal for cruelty or immorality was transferred to the Sheriffs. The heritors and ministers might permit or require a schoolmaster to resign for neglect of duty; but if it were through no wilful fault of his, they were bound to grant a retiring allowance of at least two-thirds of his actual salary. Schoolmasters were no longer required to sign anything further than an undertaking not to teach opinions opposed to the Divine Authority of the Scriptures or to the Doctrine of the Shorter Catechism.

The Newcastle Commission in England was followed in 1864 by the appointment of a similar body, presided over by the Duke of Argyll, to inquire into the schools in Scotland. It was not restricted to elementary education, but extended also to all secondary schools, and thus corresponds to the Newcastle, Clarendon, and Taunton Commissions rolled into one.

In their final report, which was presented in 1867, the Commissioners came to much the same general conclusions as the Newcastle Commission.

---

[1] Argyll Second Report, 1867, xci.　　　　[2] 24 & 25 Vict. c. 107.

[3] Mr. Alexander draws attention to the fact that Government had already been paying grants for training schoolmistresses in Scotland for twelve years (Bremner, p. 234).

[4] Scotland was divided into four districts, each of which was allotted to one of the Universities. Each University Court was to appoint six examiners, three being Professors in the Faculty of Divinity and three in the Faculty of Arts; examiners and secretary were paid by the Treasury.

While taking an optimistic view of school attendance[1], which they still had to declare inadequate, they found the existing system of schools 'in a large measure defective.' In the rural districts there were only 1,133 Parish Schools out of a total of 4,451 schools, and many of the subscription, proprietary and private adventure establishments were very inefficient and gave no real education[2]. As to the course to be pursued they were unanimous. In every parish in Scotland there were rate-aided schools; voluntary schools were numerous, many already subsidised by the State, and there was also a Government Department ready to develop all schools in Great Britain. But the systems were not co-extensive[3], and neither separately nor in conjunction were they adequate. It was necessary to extend them, and for this purpose it was recommended to combine them; to compel every parish school to submit to the Education Department, and also as in England to welcome all voluntary schools which accepted the necessary terms, and then compulsorily to fill up the deficiencies remaining. A 2*d.* rate in the country, and 2½*d.* in the Hebrides, Glasgow, and the largest towns, would, it was thought, do all that was necessary[4].

First Education Act, 1872. It was not, however, until 1872, two years after Mr. Forster's Act, that the first Education Act for Scotland was passed[5]. As the State-aided elementary schools in England and Scotland had been governed by the same regulations for upwards of thirty years, the two Statutes were naturally on the same general lines, but the Scotch measure was distinctly in advance of its forerunner, even, in some respects, in advance of the law in England to-day.

The chief points of difference were these: Scotland was

---

[1] They found 418,000 out of 510,000 children on the roll of some school or other (1867, see Report, pp. clxxiii, clxxvi).

[2] Ibid. p. xxxvii.

[3] Of 1,008 Parochial and Side Schools which were returned only 334 were in receipt of grants from Whitehall (ibid. App., p. 48).

[4] Ibid. clxxii.　　　　　　　　　　[5] 35 & 36 Vict. c 62.

ready for a uniform system of School Boards, for universal compulsory education, for freedom in religious instruction, and (although this does not concern us here) for a measure dealing also with her burgh schools and secondary education.

EDUCATION ACT, 1872.

School Boards were created in every parish and burgh, elected triennially by a cumulative vote by owners and occupiers of £4 annual value. 'Parish and Burgh Schools and all other schools established under previous Acts of Parliament were at once transferred to the Boards, which received the powers and obligations of the heritors and minister, the authority of the Presbyteries being likewise abolished so far as concerned public schools. Only seven Boards in Scotland have no schools, and this is owing to their districts being supplied by the schools of an adjoining Board, generally a burgh Board in the same parish. The School Boards were authorized to accept transference of other schools, and within a few years practically all the State-aided Schools in Scotland, with the exception of those connected with the Roman Catholic and Episcopalian Churches and the Practising Schools of the Training Colleges, were under the Boards '.' Even private schools have been absorbed in considerable numbers, though the rule is the same as in England against Board Schools being conducted for private profit or farmed out. It was the School Boards, and not as in England the voluntary agencies, who had the benefit of the last grant from the State in aid of building schools. An interval of grace was allowed till the end of 1873, during which only School Boards might send in applications, and after that date schools could only be built, as in England, by local rates or voluntary efforts.

Compulsion. As for the principle of compulsion, it was

---

¹ Mr. G. W. Alexander in Miss Bremner's *Education of Girls and Women in Great Britain*, p. 241 : Swan Sonnenschein & Co., 1897. In 1897 there were 2,738 public schools, 184 Roman Catholic schools, 197 schools connected with other Churches and undenominational.

declared to be the duty of every parent to provide elementary education for his children between the ages of five and thirteen, and in case of inability from poverty to pay the school fees, he might apply to the parochial board, who were to pay them out of the poor fund. Even blind children were not exempt. The penalty against the parent or employer for disobedience might be as high as 20*s.* with costs, or imprisonment not exceeding fourteen days. If any School Board did not choose to use their powers of compulsion, the Education Department possessed no authority to enforce the exercise of these powers[1].

Total exemption from attendance depended on the certificate of H. M. Inspector, and the requirements for this were fixed for the whole of Scotland by the Scotch Education Department in February, 1874, at the Fifth Standard[2]. The Act was held not to override the Factory Acts[3], and no regulations were imposed as to half-time.

No grants were made for Religious Instruction, but it was given at the discretion of each School Board, subject to no other restrictions than the time-table conscience clause. The Boards, with only two or three exceptions, resolved to make the Bible and the Shorter Catechism the basis of their instruction[4].

Teachers were to be engaged by the School Boards, and to hold office during their pleasure; but the rights of existing teachers under the old system were carefully safeguarded.

Grants might be made under the Act to any School Board for public schools under their management, and also to the managers of any school which is, in the opinion of the Scotch Education . Department, efficiently contributing to the secular education of the parish or burgh in which it is situated.

A separate Committee of the Privy Council for Education was appointed for Scotland, but the Lord President

[1] Craik, p. 164.   [2] First Report, lxxiv.   [3] Ibid. p. lxxviii.
[4] Board of Education, First Report, 1874, xv.

and Vice-President continued to preside over both the Scotch and English Committees, until in 1885 the Vice-President was succeeded in the former by the Secretary for Scotland, whose office was created in that year by 48 & 49 Vict. c. 61 [1]. Scotch Education Bills are as a rule introduced in the House of Lords by the Secretary for Scotland (formerly by the Lord President) and in the Commons by the Lord Advocate [2].

Besides this permanent Department, a special Board of Education for Scotland was created for three or five years to set the new system in motion. It was finally continued till 1878, and then handed over its remaining powers to the permanent Committee.

By the first Scotch Code, issued in 1874, the long-deferred method of payment by results was at last enforced in order to ensure the efficiency of the new and wide-spreading system of education, but it was in a form amended by experience, and more like that introduced into Ireland in 1872. In the six standards (which already existed in Scotland for examination) a certain gradation of payments was observed, an extra 2s. being paid according to the annual average attendance, if scholars present on the day of examination in the classes from which children were examined in Standards II and III, showed an intelligent and grammatical knowledge of the passages read, and a further sum of 2s. if the classes examined in Standards IV, V, and VI passed creditably in history and geography. All children present might be examined, whether they had made 250 attendances or not, and the graduated grants were made on the total annual average attendance [3]. A graded bonus of 1s. 6d. or 1s. was given for organization

---

[1] The headquarters of the Scotch Education Department are at Dover House, Whitehall. There was no separate Secretary for the Scotch Education Department before Sir Henry Craik's appointment in 1885. The inspection is performed by three Chief Inspectors, twenty-two Inspectors, and twenty-eight Sub-Inspectors.

[2] The Duke of Argyll in 1872 and Mr. Mundella in 1883 were exceptions to this practice : the Secretary moreover may be a Commoner.

[3] Board of Education, 1874, xvii; Code 1874, Article 19, c. 4.

and discipline, which was not adopted in England till 1875, nor graduated till 1882.

The restriction of day school grants to persons not above eighteen, which began in 1872, has been maintained until the present day, and there is no other limit.

In 1876 the fourth English Elementary Education Act[1] extended to Scotland its provisions in respect of the conditions required to obtain the annual parliamentary grant, the chief of which were the 17s. 6d. limit[2] and the terms of the grant of £10 or £15 to schools in thinly populated districts.

In 1878 and 1883 further Scotch Education Acts were passed[3], chiefly for the purpose of improving school attendance and smoothing away unforeseen difficulties in working the original Act.

In 1878 the new Act supplemented the effects of the Factory and Workshop Act of the same year, by applying to children in private employment and imposing on them a test of proficiency even for half-time. No child was to be employed at all under ten years of age, no child between ten and fourteen was to be employed except under the Factory Acts, even for half-time, without having passed a Standard, subsequently fixed by a Minute of the Department at the Third. Full-time employment was to be open to children between ten and fourteen only on the certificate granted by H. M. Inspector under the Act of 1872[4], and now granted for the Fifth Standard[5]. Casual employment in the streets after nine p.m. in the summer and seven in the winter was also forbidden to children between ten and fourteen without certificate[6].

The age of unrestricted employment was thus raised to fourteen, but the limits of compulsory attendance at school remained, as in 1872, at thirteen.

School Boards received by this Act the powers of com-

---

[1] 39 & 40 Vict. c. 79.
[2] *Vide* p. 29.
[3] 41 & 42 Vict. c. 78; 46 & 47 Vict. c. 56.
[4] Craik, p. 166.
[5] Minute, February 16, 1874.
[6] School Boards can grant leave for occasional employment.

pulsory purchase of school sites, which had been granted in England in 1870, but this concession has been of little use.

In 1883 the Attendance Order was introduced into Scotland [1], but the child himself could not be committed to an Industrial School, as in England, if unmanageable; the punishment of the parents might, as in 1872, amount to a fine of 20*s.* or a fortnight's imprisonment. The Third Standard was definitely imposed by the new Statute as a requirement of all half-time labour under the Factory Acts, as well as in private employment, and attendance at school was now made compulsory (except in cases of exemption) between thirteen and fourteen, as well as abstinence from employment. Children between thirteen and fourteen can only obtain exemption on a certificate of proficiency, and not, as in England, by a certificate of previous attendance; but, on the other hand, the English Elementary Education Act of 1893 [2] did not apply to Scotland, so that children between ten and eleven can still obtain exemption from school.

In 1887 a Departmental Committee under Mr. C. S. Parker, M.P., reported on Training Colleges and Compulsory Attendance. For the latter the existing powers, used with vigour and firmness, were considered sufficient. For training teachers the existing training colleges were approved, combined as far as possible with University teaching for those who were fit for it. The cost to the State was moderate, and it was not held desirable that it should be reduced [3].

In 1890 an Act for the provision of schools for blind and deaf-mute children [4] was passed, which corresponds in most points with the Act passed in England in 1893. But in Scotland the Act was not to be enforced by the interposition of the Education Department, but any person interested might apply to the sheriff, who might make an order as to the expenses of such education, which was to be

[1] *Vide* p. 28.
[2] 56 & 57 Vict. c. 51.
[3] Report, P. P., 1888, xli. 661.
[4] 53 & 54 Vict. c. 43.

final.   Particular attention has been paid to afflicted children
in Scotland ; in the first Education Act in 1872 parents
were declared to be responsible for the education of their
blind children, and since the Code of 1892 grants of two or
three guineas for progress of blind or deaf-mute pupils in
elementary education or manual instruction are paid in any
school or institution approved by the Department [1].

Free Education.   In 1889 the first step towards free
public education in the United Kingdom was taken by
Scotland.   In the previous year the Probate and Licence
Duties were surrendered by the Treasury in aid of local
taxation [2].   The Scotch share, being eleven-hundredths of
the whole, was dealt with by the Local Government (Scotland) Act, 1889 [3], and in response to the unanimous feeling
of the Scotch members, a proportion estimated at £247,000
was assigned towards the relief of school fees [4].   The
Scotch Education Department, in whose discretion the
management was left, applied the money in remission of
all fees below Standard IV, and partial remission of fees in
Standards IV and V [5].

In 1890 a further sum not exceeding £40,000, granted
by the Local Taxation (Customs and Excise) Act [6], was
applied by the Department to free the Fourth and Fifth
Standard entirely [7]; in 1891 all children between five and
fourteen were freed, irrespective of standard [8]; and in
1893 all children between three and fifteen, as in England [9].

Certain School Boards were permitted, with the sanction
of the Department, after making due provision for free

---

[1] In 1897 there were twelve special schools and twenty-four ordinary
schools with special accommodation for these children (Ed. Dep.
Report, published 1898).

[2] 51 & 52 Vict. c.60. Probate Duties (Scotland and Ireland) Act, 1888.

[3] 52 & 53 Vict. c. 50.

[4] Craik, p. 177; Hansard, T. S., cccxxxiv, p. 1831.

[5] Minute, Aug. 26, 1889.   [6] 53 & 54 Vict. c. 60.

[7] Minute, Aug. 18, 1890.   [8] Minute, June 11.

[9] Art. 133: Code 1894. In 1895-96 there were about 19,000 pupils
in respect of whom full fees were paid (Ed. Dep. Report, pub. 1897).

education, to retain fees in a small number of their schools.

By the Education and Local Taxation Account (Scotland) Act, 1892 [1], the twenty-second section of the Scotch Local Government Act was repealed, and there was paid annually to Scotland from the Treasury in relief of fees a sum of £265,000, or of such other amount as Parliament might determine having regard to the amount of the fee grant under the English Education Act, 1891. Scotland was thus relieved from the consequences of her self-denial in the cause of free education in 1889. Out of the money then set free, however, £90,000 was assigned forthwith to secondary and higher education [2].

Out of her savings from 1889 to 1892 Scotland was able to make up the fee grant to 12*s.* per child until 1897, and in that year the Chancellor of the Exchequer undertook that it should continue at the same amount [3].

As in Ireland so in the Highlands and Islands of Scotland, poverty, a sparse population, and remoteness have been the great obstacles to efficient education. The long sea-lochs on the north and west coasts and the numerous islands have imposed conditions unknown in the most barren districts of the south, and from the first foundation of the Scotch Committee special favour was shown to Inverness, Argyll, Ross, Caithness, Sutherland, Orkney, and Shetland; and since 1888, in these counties the Education Department has been able to associate itself with the local authorities in management of schools and provide extra financial assistance. Fortunately by March, 1895, it proved possible to restrict this arrangement definitely to Ross and Inverness, beyond which counties indeed it had never really extended.

There was no serious mitigation of Payment by Results in the Scotch Codes until 1886, when the two lowest

---

[1] 55 & 56 Vict. c. 51.   [2] *Vide* p. 228.
[3] Hansard, F. S., vol. 1. pp. 462, 906.

standards were excluded from individual examination and received graduated grants ; class subjects were introduced, and thus instruction in Scotland as well as in England was divided into the three sections of elementary, class, and specific subjects.

In 1889, at the request of a number of School Boards, Drawing was removed from class subjects and handed over entirely to the Science and Art Department, as yielding them better financial results.

In 1890 the same change was made as in England, individual examination disappeared as the basis of payment for the ordinary standard work of the school. A fixed grant of 10*s.* was made on the average attendance, supplemented by a grant of 1*s.*, 2*s.*, or 3*s.*, in proportion to the merit of the teaching [1].

In the Code of 1892 a ' merit certificate ' was introduced, which was granted as a distinction to any child over thirteen [2] who attained a standard of thorough efficiency in the three elementary subjects as well as in the class subjects (at least two) professed in the school, and passed an examination embracing all the stages of one specific subject. By March, 1898, 13,373 of these certificates had been granted.

In 1894 Inspectors were allowed at their discretion to omit their annual visits to Infant Schools if two visits without notice had been paid, but in the case of the older children this was not introduced until 1898.

In 1897 an Education Act was passed in aid of the poorer Board and voluntary schools in Scotland, corresponding to the two measures passed for England earlier in the same session. Schools under School Boards received the same treatment as in England, in cases where a 3*d.* rate produced less than 7*s.* 6*d.* per child [3] ; for voluntary schools a grant was made of 3*s.* a head on the total average attendance. The distribution is to be regulated by the annual Code, and no reference was made to voluntary associations. Voluntary

---

[1] 6*d.* more above Standard III. [2] Now, over twelve.
[3] *Vide* p. 34.

schools are also, as in England, to be exempt from rates; but the 17*s.* 6*d.* limit is untouched [1]. In Scotland, out of 3,120 public elementary schools only 390 were voluntary; and the grant to them was only 3*s.* a head per child instead of 5*s.* as in England, because the fee grant in Scotland has been and will be 12*s.* in place of the English 10*s.* [2]

In this year the proportion of eleven to eighty between the Scotch and English grants was definitely abandoned as unworkable, and the grants are paid irrespective of this relation [3]. The arrangement has, at any rate, this disadvantage, that few Scotchmen are able to see that it is consonant with justice.

It is proposed [4] to allow individual School Boards, as in England, with the consent of the Department, to make by-laws raising the standard or age of exemption above those laid down by the Education Acts for the whole country.

Training of Teachers. For the training of teachers a system of denominational colleges was already beginning in Scotland before 1839 [5], and two grants of £5,000 were made in 1841 for the Normal Schools of the Church of Scotland in Edinburgh and Glasgow.

It was recognized by the Department as the national custom in Scotland to live in lodgings out of college [6], and consequently no special creation of Day Training Colleges [7] has ever been necessary. In 1897 there were eight colleges with accommodation for 963 students. In two of these, for female students, residence was compulsory, in four it was optional, and the remaining two made no provision for it.

The system has prospered *pari passu* with the English Training Colleges. It was especially in Scotland that these institutions were utilized for the purposes of general education in the days before the Revised Code, and the Govern-

---

[1] *Vide* p. 34. 60 & 61 Vict. c. 62. [2] Hansard, F. S., 1. pp. 460, 889.
[3] Ibid. pp. 459, 464. [4] House of Lords Bill, 1898.
[5] Alexander, p. 235 of Miss Bremner's *Education of Girls and Women.*
[6] First Revised Code, Art. 99; P. P., 1862, xli. p. 139.
[7] *Vide* p. 40.

ment contributions had to be limited to three-quarters of the actual expenditure in order to restrict the colleges to persons actually intending to become teachers.

In 1890 76 per cent. of the whole body of male teachers and 64 per cent. of the women had studied in these institutions. In 1897 78·9 per cent. of the men and 65·6 per cent. of the women teachers had been trained in them. For a long time in Scotland Queen's Scholars have been allowed to count attendance at one or two University Classes in the winter session as part of their training lectures, and special facilities have been given to enable Graduates after a short period of practical probation to become certificated teachers.

Since 1873 the University fees of certain Queen's Scholars may be reckoned as part of their training college expenses, three-quarters of which may be paid by the Education Department [1].

In 1895 a system was established by which University Students might be admitted as 'Queen's Students' under supervision of a local committee in any of the Scotch Universities or University College, students and committee both receiving a grant : they are examined by a joint board of University Professors and one or more Chief Inspectors.

Teachers' certificates in Scotland are still divided into three classes. The 'woman not less than eighteen, approved by the Inspector,' has received less recognition than in England : not more than one is allowed in each school, and only as an equivalent to a pupil teacher.

Pensions. There was a fund for the relief of widows and children of Burgh and Parochial Schoolmasters in Scotland, started in 1807 [2], to which all masters were bound to contribute. By the Act of 1861 present contributors remained liable to obligations and benefit, but no future teachers need join.

Scotland shared in the limited Pension scheme of 1846,

---

[1] Report for 1896–97, p. xxii.   [2] 47 Geo. III, c. lxxxv.

(suspended in 1862, and revived for the benefit of survivors in 1875,) and also in the Superannuation Act of 1898.

Evening Continuation Schools. These schools have had almost the same history as in England. In 1876 the age limit was raised from eighteen to twenty-one, and in 1886 they received the increased grants made to England in 1882. In 1893 a special Code was issued almost identical with the English Code of the same year. Children of twelve (as against fourteen in England) are allowed to attend, if already exempt from attending day schools; the upper limit of age was removed, and also the obligation to take elementary subjects, and these changes have naturally made the instruction to a great extent secondary [1].

ii. *Science and Art Department.*

Scotland has always shared the grants of this Department under the same conditions as England and Wales.

In 1889 Drawing, which had been introduced as a class subject into Scotch public schools in 1886, was withdrawn from the Education Department and (as in England in 1887) placed entirely under South Kensington. The change was educationally of small importance, as the local superintendent of the Science and Art Department already examined in this class subject, being deemed for this purpose an Inspector of the Scotch Education Department.

By a Minute of July 29, 1897, the administration of Science and Art grants was transferred to the Scotch Education Department [2], but the Science and Art Department continued to account for grants till the following April.

The Scotch Code for 1898 carried on the grants for elementary drawing and manual training upon the same

---

[1]
	Evening Continuation Schools.		*Average attendance.*
1872	. . .	68	3,653
1880	. . .	277	14,297
1890	. . .	191	11,636
1897	. . .	1019	51,967

[2] For the new Higher Grade Science Schools *v. Times*, Aug. 23, Sept. 5, 1898.

general lines, and required that the manual training should be 'progressive in character, educational in aim, and properly allied to instruction in drawing,' and that more advanced instruction should be provided for second and third year pupils in this subject.

2. THE HOME OFFICE.

i. *Factory and Mines Acts.*

Scotland has always been under the same Factory and Mines Acts as England[1], but, as with Ireland, the Factory Act of 1874 was not applied to non-textile factories in Scotland by the English Education Act of 1876, and textile and non-textile factories remained on different footings until 1878.

Under the Factory Act of 1878 a certified efficient school in Scotland was defined as 'any public or other elementary school under Government inspection.'

As the Elementary Education Act of 1893 did not apply to Scotland, the Factory Act of 1891[2] is consequently of more importance in that country, as it raises the minimum age of employment in factories to eleven, although attendance at school is only compulsory under all circumstances until the child has passed the Fifth Standard.

ii. *Reformatories and Industrial Schools.*

Both these classes of schools remain under the Home Secretary, although the Inspector has advised that they should be placed under the Secretary for Scotland, and the English and Scotch Departmental Committees have made similar recommendations[3].

Reformatories. The first Acts of 1854–56 and the Consolidating Act of 1866[4] applied to Scotland as well as England, but the power given in 1857 to English Quarter Sessions or Town Councils to contribute to

---

[1] *Vide* p. 43.
[3] Lushington Report, 1896, i. 104, 253, 322.
[2] 54 & 55 Vict. c. 75.
[4] *Vide* p. 54.

Reformatories was only extended to Scotland in 1866. Lord Leigh's Act of 1893 also applies to Scotland[1].

Industrial Schools. The first statute in these islands, relating to schools of this class and known as Dunlop's Act, was passed in 1854[2] for Scotland only. The Act and its amending Acts passed in the two following years[3] were intended 'to render Reformatory and Industrial Schools more available for the benefit of Vagrant Children.' They did not in fact deal with Reformatories in the modern sense at all, but with Industrial Schools only, for the nomenclature had not yet become fixed. The schools 'were to receive aid out of the Education Vote, administered by the Committee of Council, and to be open to the inspection of Her Majesty's Inspector of Schools or any other inspector specially appointed for the purpose[4].'

Under these Acts the schools were frankly Ragged Schools to take outcast children[5].

In 1860 Industrial Schools were transferred from the Committee of Council to the Home Secretary[6].

'In 1861 the Scotch Acts were consolidated by a temporary Act[7], the provisions of which substantially correspond with those of the English Consolidating Act of the same year, also a temporary measure; and in 1866 the law both for English and Scotch industrial schools was consolidated in the Act now in force[8].' In Scotland the parochial authority was made liable to pay 5*s.* a week to the Treasury for any child sent to an Industrial School who had been chargeable to the parish within the three months preceding[9].

From this point the law in the two countries has been

---

[1] This Act was passed earlier in 1893 as the Reformatory Schools (Scotland) Act, 56 & 57 Vict. c. 15, and was repealed and re-enacted for Great Britain by c. 48.

[2] 17 & 18 Vict. c. 74.

[3] 18 & 19 Vict. c. 86; 19 & 20 Vict. c. 28.

[4] Lushington Report, i. 11.   [5] Ibid. Q. 31,962.

[6] 23 & 24 Vict. c. 108.

[7] 24 & 25 Vict. c. 132, renewed 25 & 26 Vict. c. 10.

[8] *Vide* p. 56; Lushington, i. p. 12.   [9] 29 & 30 Vict. c. 118, s. 38.

the same, except so far as it has been laid down by their different Education Acts and by local Acts of Parliament.

By the Scotch Education Act, 1872, power was given to School Boards to establish and maintain certified Industrial Schools, but they received no power to contribute to these institutions till 1893[1], and the former power they never exercised[2]. On the other hand, School Boards in Scotland were never placed under any obligation to work the Industrial Schools Act, 1866, a result obtained in England by the Education Act, 1876[3].

By the Prisons (Scotland) Act, 1877[4], the Commissioners of Supply of any county or the magistrates of any borough may contribute to any certified Reformatory or Industrial School subject to the approval of the Home Secretary, but they have no power to establish one.

Day Industrial Schools. In Glasgow a Board of Commissioners was constituted by a local Act in 1841[5] for Repressing Juvenile Delinquency, and by an amending Act in 1878[6] they received power to establish Day Industrial Schools, three of which have been established.

In 1893 the Day Industrial Schools (Scotland) Act[7] was passed for the certification of these schools, which may be established and maintained by voluntary agencies or by a School Board; it repealed the liability of the Poor Law authorities in Glasgow to contribute. Its only material result as yet has been the opening of one Day Industrial School in Edinburgh in 1898.

There are no Truant Schools in Scotland.

Lord Aberdare's Commission in 1884, and the Departmental Committee presided over by Sir Godfrey Lushington in 1896, included Scotland in their investigations, and

---

[1] 56 & 57 Vict. c. 48.
[2] Lushington, Q. 28,297.
[3] *Vide* p. 57. The same is true of Day Industrial Schools. Lushington Report, Q. 28,296.
[4] 40 & 41 Vict. c. 53, s. 67.   [5] 4 & 5 Vict. c. xxxvi.
[6] 41 & 42 Vict. c. cxxi.
[7] 56 Vict. c. 12.

a Scotch Departmental Committee reported on Habitual Offenders in 1895[1].

The differences between Scotland and England are due much more to the working of the Acts, as in Ireland, than to the measures themselves. That the Acts were differently worked was due chiefly in the first instance to the absence of Poor Law Schools in Scotland, which caused Industrial Schools to be used to a great extent for destitute children who would have gone to District Schools in England[2]. This tendency, however, was to some extent checked in regard to Reformatories in Scotland by the dislike in that country to put children in prison, and until 1893 imprisonment was an indispensable preliminary to their admission to a Reformatory[3].

In Scotland by the Act of 1866[4] the Parochial Authority is bound to pay the Treasury 5s. a week for any child in an Industrial School chargeable to the Parish within the three months preceding. The local authorities have hitherto contributed a far smaller proportion in relation to the Government Grant than in England[5], and there is said to have been greater laxity in committal[6]. In Scotland these schools all have agents who look out for likely cases, and enable the establishment to be run at its full strength, and as economically as possible[7].

In Scotland in 1896 there were nine Reformatories with 727 juvenile offenders, and thirty-five Industrial Schools with 4,560 children actually in the schools[8].

---

[1] Lushington Report, i. Appendix No. x, p. 250.

[2] Aberdare, Q. 1,569 sqq.

[3] Lushington, p. 131. But in 1882 the proportions of children and young offenders in Industrial Schools and Reformatories to the whole population were in the three countries as follows :—

		Reformatories.	*Industrial Schools.*
Scotland .	.	1 to 3,573	1 to 840
Ireland .	.	„ 4,492	„ 897
England .	.	„ 5,657	„ 2,384

Aberdare Report, Q. 12,460.

[4] s. 38.   [5] Lushington, p. 133.   [6] Ibid. p. 137.

[7] Ibid. p. 144.   [8] Inspector's Report, P. P., 1897, C. 8,566, p. 403.

3. THE SECRETARY FOR SCOTLAND.

A General Board of Directors of Prisons was established in Scotland in 1839[1], each prison being placed under a County Board. By 23 & 24 Vict. c. 105 these Boards were established in every county, and the appointment of teachers as well as other officers was explicitly placed in their hands[2]. In 1887[3] all prisons in Scotland were vested in the Secretary for Scotland, and all local obligations ceased. Three Prison Commissioners might be appointed, but the number of officers and servants is determined by the Secretary of State, subject to the sanction of the Treasury as to their number, and they are appointed by the Commissioners subject to his approval.

4. THE LOCAL GOVERNMENT BOARD FOR SCOTLAND.

This Board was established in 1894 by 57 & 58 Vict. c. 58 to take over the powers and duties of the Board of Supervision, which was created to administer the new Poor Law in 1845[4]. Under the latter Act the Parochial Boards had power to make provisions for the education of children[5], but in Scotland the practice is to board out all such children, who thus attend the ordinary public elementary schools. On May 15, 1897, of 5,862 children chargeable, 4,993 were actually boarded out[6].

Consequently no workhouse or district schools exist in Scotland[6].

5. WAR OFFICE AND ADMIRALTY.

The War Office and Admiralty Regulations apply to Scotland as to England. Instruction is provided for soldiers and their children, and for seamen and boys wherever serving; but they bring their instructors and rules with them, except in the possible case of soldiers' children attending civil schools.

---

[1] 2 & 3 Vict. c. 42.   [2] Ibid. sec. xv.   [3] 40 & 41 Vict. c. 53.
[4] 8 & 9 Vict. c. 83.   [5] Ibid. sec. lxix.
[6] Local Government Board Report for 1896–97, p. xiii.

II. SECONDARY EDUCATION.

A. England.

1. THE CHARITY COMMISSION.

The General Course of Secondary Education [1].

MUCH of what has been said about elementary education in England at the beginning of the nineteenth century applies equally to secondary education at the same date. There were many foundations in various degrees of efficiency; there were many abuses known to exist and few means of correcting them; there was no external control of secondary schools, no responsibility, no general organization. In most cases the only method of rectifying abuses was by long and costly proceedings [2] in the Court of Chancery, which had jurisdiction in the case of all charities, but the power of the Court to interfere or to modify existing regulations was very insufficient and very uncertain.

In the course of the century there have been numerous reforms: procedure has been improved: probably no scandals now exist, but secondary schools are still waiting to be organized into a system.

[1] English elementary education has already been systematized by the State, and therefore the history of the Education Department and its origin includes a complete account of public elementary schools. No Department yet exists in England which controls the whole of secondary education, but that which has affected it most is the Charity Commission, although the Commissioners' authority has been imperfect and has extended only to a part of the Endowed Secondary Schools. Under the heading of the Charity Commission I have consequently included a number of facts relating to general progress, though not strictly belonging to the history of the Commission itself.

[2] Suits by the Attorney-General (1818–37) lasted from five to ten years on the average. In the case of many charities a large part of the funds was swallowed up by costs. Report of Select Committee on Charitable Trusts Acts, P. P., 1884, ix. p. 3; Taunton Commission Report, i. 464.

In 1812 Sir Samuel Romilly's Act [1] had aimed at simplifying Chancery procedure for the reform of charities, but the chief result seems to have been an increase of vexatious suits [2].

Brougham's Commission of 1818 [3] extended to many Grammar Schools and other secondary educational endowments, although charities with special visitors, governors, or overseers were not included within its scope until 1831 [4]; and there were other exceptions, including the Universities and their colleges, and the six large Public Schools.

In 1819 the range of the Commission was extended to charitable endowments in general, and its labours did not come to an end before 1837 [5]. In 1835 a Select Committee of the House of Commons considered their reports, and recommended the appointment of a permanent Board of Commissioners to superintend Charities, to suggest schemes of administration, and to control the institution of proceedings in Equity.

In 1840 the Grammar Schools Act [6] was passed to give the Chancery Courts larger powers in dealing with the regulations of these schools when brought before them. It specially provided that where the classics were retained, the standard of admission was not to be lowered.

Another Royal Commission was appointed under Lord Chichester in 1849, which reported that 'the evils and abuses are still in existence to a very wide extent, and no sufficient remedy has yet been provided for this correction [7],' and they too urged the creation of a permanent public authority.

It was not, however, until 1853 that an Act [8] was passed

---

[1] 52 Geo. III, c. 101.

[2] R. E. Mitcheson, *Charitable Trusts*, p. 4 : Maxwell, 1887.

[3] *Vide* p. 1.

[4] 58 Geo. III, c. 91 ; 59 Geo. III, c. 81 ; 1 & 2 Will. IV, c. 34; 5 & 6 Will. IV, c. 71.

[5] The total number of endowments finally reported on by these Commissioners was 28,840, estimated at the time of the aggregate value of £1,209,395 (Chichester First Report, P. P., 1850, xx. p. 17).

[6] 3 & 4 Vict. c. 77.   [7] First Report, p. 18.

[8] 16 & 17 Vict. c. 137.

which constituted the Charity Commission.   A board of
four members was appointed, three of whom were paid,
while the fourth has always been a member of the House
of Commons, without salary.   Powers were granted to
them for conducting inquiries into the conditions and
management of charities; dealings with the corpus of
charitable property were put under their control, and
their sanction was necessary to the institution of judicial
proceedings[1].   In certain cases, especially those relating
to the appointment and removal of trustees, and the sale,
leasing or improvement of the property of charities, relief
might be given in Chancery by a Judge in Chambers, or, in
cases where the income was less than £30, by the District
Bankruptcy Courts (since abolished), or by the County
Courts.   The Board was empowered to frame schemes for
the appropriation of charitable property to new trusts on
the application of trustees or persons interested, but each
scheme had to be confirmed by Act of Parliament[2].

Practice soon showed that Chancery was too costly and
dilatory, and that the slightest opposition in Parliament was
fatal to any new scheme[3].

In 1860, by 23 & 24 Vict. c. 136, judicial powers were
given to the Charity Commissioners themselves, similar to
those conferred by the Act of 1853 on the Court of
Chancery and the County Courts.   Application, however,
had first to be made to them by some person authorized
under the Act of 1853, the case must not be contentious,
and—most important limitation of all—in charities where
the income exceeded £50, the jurisdiction of the Commissioners only arose upon an application made by a
majority of the trustees of the charity concerned.   This
last restriction is said to apply to eighty-five per cent. in
value of the charities of the country, although in point of

---

[1] Mitcheson, *Charitable Trusts*, p. 11.
[2] Eton and Winchester were exempted from this and the amending
Act, 18 & 19 Vict. c. 124, s. 49.
[3] P. P., 1884, ix. p. iv, Q. 149.

numbers it affected only ten per cent.[1], but the result of the measure in general has been to transfer to the Charity Commission practically all such applications as are made[2].

But in the meantime more direct interference with intermediate education had been taking place. In 1861 a Royal Commission under Lord Clarendon had been appointed to inquire into nine specified leading Public Schools of the order which, receiving the sons of the higher and wealthier classes of the country, has sent the largest proportion of pupils to the Universities, and adhered most exclusively to a classical education[3]. Seven of the schools—Eton, Winchester[4], Westminster, Charterhouse, Harrow, Rugby, and Shrewsbury—were boarding schools; St. Paul's and Merchant Taylors' were day schools: the youngest of them, Charterhouse, had been in existence since the beginning of the seventeenth century; the oldest, Winchester, since 1387. In 1861 they were educating 2,696 boys[5]. In addition to these the Commissioners obtained full returns from Marlborough, Cheltenham, and Wellington, three schools founded within the preceding twenty years, which had rapidly risen to the first rank; and also from the City of London and King's College Schools, two of the leading London secondary day schools.

The report was presented in 1864. As the schools had been selected for their importance and popularity, it was a foregone conclusion that no abuses, which according to the ideas of the time were monstrous, would be found, and the Commissioners had no wish to deal hardly with the

---

[1] Mitcheson, p. 13; Charitable Trusts Acts First Report, 1884, Q. 189.

[2] Mitcheson, p. 14.

[3] Taunton, i. 128; Bryce Report, ix. 426.

[4] Winchester had received new statutes under the University of Oxford Act, 1854, 17 & 18 Vict. c. 81.

[5] Report, i. p. 11. The Taunton Commission returned them as 2,956, apparently in 1866, and the net aggregate income, including exhibitions, above £65,000 a year (Taunton, i. (150)). In 1897 they had nearly 5,000 boys; and the whole of the schools of about the same calibre in England (admitted to the Headmasters' Conference, about ninety in number) had about 24,000 pupils, including these 5,000 (*Public Schools Year Book*, Swan Sonnenschein & Co., 1898, and private information).

schools or to obliterate their individuality. It was desirable to remove a number of restrictions, and considerably to widen their curriculum and bring it up to date, and this they were to be given an opportunity of doing for themselves.

In 1868 the Public Schools Act [1] was passed, dealing with the seven boarding schools specified, requiring them to make new statutes (freed from specified existing restrictions) for the appointment of new governing bodies, which were then to make new statutes for the regulation of their respective schools. A body of seven Special Commissioners was appointed, which had to approve of all the new sets of statutes and regulations before they were submitted to the Privy Council and published. If no objections were made, received, or entertained, the statutes might then be approved by H. M. in Council.

The Special Commissioners were to hold office for one year, or, if necessary, for two, and, in default of the action of the Governing Body of any school within a given time, might make new statutes, regulations, or schemes, which were then to go through the ordinary course directed. Any statute or scheme made by the Commissioners, however, had to lie before both Houses of Parliament for forty days before receiving the Royal Approval.

Meanwhile, at the end of 1864, a Commission had been appointed under Lord Taunton to inquire into the education given in secondary schools included neither in the preceding Commission nor in the Newcastle (Elementary Schools) Commission of 1859. The Commissioners presented their report in 1867, and a most able and thorough report it was [2]. They found there were 572 endowed secondary Grammar Schools at work with a net income of £183,066 and exhibitions to the annual value of £13,897 [3].

---

[1] 31 & 32 Vict. c. 118.

[2] It was for this Commission that Matthew Arnold reported on the corresponding systems in France, Germany, Switzerland, and Italy, and to it he returned with the demand, 'Organize your secondary and your superior instruction' (vi. 640).

[3] Vol. i. App., p. (151): not including elementary schools.

Secondary Schools, public or private, which were thoroughly satisfactory, were few in proportion to the need [1]. The secondary boarding schools were chiefly for the upper classes; the supply of the grades of day schools was described respectively as 'very small,' 'very insufficient,' 'very poor'; and there was an almost total absence of any education in science or studies other than classical [2]. Few endowments applicable to secondary education were put to the best use, and very many were working to little or bad effect [3]; while a hundred towns of five thousand or more inhabitants had no endowed grammar school at all [4].

The Commissioners recommended the appointment of a central administrative authority, which they suggested should be the Charity Commission, with the addition of some specially qualified members [5]. In addition to this there should be local provincial boards in order to deal with the schools in local groups [6]. And, thirdly, examination of the schools was to be the pivot of all improvement, and there ought to be a Council of Examinations [7] 'to decide on the results' of the instruction given, half the members being nominated by the Universities. Private and proprietary schools might be registered and admitted to the examinations [8]. An official Commissioner should be appointed to each district by the Central Body and act as Inspector [9]. Towns or parishes might be allowed to rate themselves for building new and enlarging old schools, and educating meritorious pupils free of charge [10].

In their report the Commission divided secondary schools into first, second, and third grade, according as the age of leaving was eighteen or more, sixteen or fourteen [11]. The Commissioners took evidence from ladies and others on secondary education for girls, and devoted a separate chapter of their report to the subject. There were only twelve

---

[1] Vol. i. p. 104.   [2] pp. 102, 103.   [3] p. 106.
[4] p. 652.   [5] p. 633.   [6] p. 637.   [7] p. 649.
[8] p. 653.   [9] p. 639.   [10] p. 656.   [11] pp. 15, 577.

endowed secondary schools for girls in England and two in Wales[1] besides a few elementary schools[2].

This was followed by the passing of the Endowed Schools Act, 1869[3], but only the first of the preceding recommendations was adopted. By this measure Commissioners, not more than three in number, were to be appointed for a limited period, which was ultimately extended to August. 1874. They received power, in the case of endowed schools, to *initiate* what schemes they thought fitting without waiting for applications, and elaborate regulations were laid down for the submission of these proposals to the parties concerned, to the Committee of Council on Education, to the Queen in Council, and to the Houses of Parliament. The procedure as to schemes is complicated; roughly, it is this— that when the Charity Commission has, after due inquiry, formed a scheme, the Education Department must approve it before it is sent to the Queen in Council. A petition against it is heard by the Judicial Committee[4] of Privy Council, or the scheme may, on petition, be brought before Parliament. Either House may present an address against the whole or part of a scheme, in which case it is dropped or altered. Every scheme must finally be approved by the Queen in Council, when it acquires the force of an Act of Parliament[5].

In practice it has been found that a scheme, however

---

[1] i. p. 565.

[2] The effect, however, produced by the revelation of girls' needs and capacities for education was so great and gave so much impetus and so much support to those who were devoting themselves to this work, that within ten years' time endowments had been provided for 45 new schools for girls, containing from 50 to 400 pupils each (*Frances Mary Buss*, by A. E. Ridley: Longmans, 1896, p. 11). The Girls' Public Day School Company, founded in 1873 on a business basis, had 34 schools in 1897 with 7,150 pupils (*Victorian Exhibition Handbook*, 1897, p. 110). Cheltenham Ladies' College had been already founded in 1854; in 1858 Miss Beale became Principal, and in 1897 it numbered nearly 1,000 pupils (ibid. p. 90). The North London Collegiate School was founded by Miss Buss in 1850 (ibid. p. 101).

[3] 32 & 33 Vict. c. 56. A section of the bill providing for registration of teachers and obligatory examination of endowed schools was dropped.

[4] Since 1873: formerly to a special committee of the Privy Council.

[5] The steps are detailed with clearness in the Report on Secondary Education, 1895, vol. i. p. 21.

non-contentious, is hardly ever passed under a year, and sometimes takes several years to get through [1].

The great Public Schools and public elementary schools in receipt of grants from Government were excluded from their control; endowments less than fifty years old were not to be interfered with unless the governing body concerned assented to the proposed scheme. Endowments for giving doles, marriage portions, or apprenticeship fees, and for any purposes which might have failed altogether or become insignificant in comparison with the magnitude of the endowment, might (if founded before 1800), with the consent of the governing body, be applied for the advancement of education [2]. Existing rights were safeguarded and measures taken to secure freedom of conscience in day and boarding schools. It is to be noticed that, in accordance with the spirit of the Taunton Commission, it was explicitly declared that in all schemes provision was to be made for extending to girls the benefits of endowments 'as far as conveniently may be.'

The chief advances made upon the powers of the Charity Commissioners were that the new Commissioners might originate schemes on their own initiative, and that no distinction was made between endowments with greater or less revenues.

In 1873 there was an amending Act, and the next year, the Commission coming to an end, its functions were, by the Endowed Schools Act, 1874 [3], transferred to the Charity Commissioners, whose powers over endowed schools had been suspended since 1869. The new Act was only to last for five years, but has been renewed until the present time as to the power of making schemes and to paying the salaries of the two additional Commissioners sanctioned by the Act [4]. In 1894 it was estimated that at the then rate

---

[1] Report on the Charity Commission, P. P., 1894, xi. Q. 2,121.

[2] Schemes for schools founded since 1819 could only be made with consent of their governors.

[3] 37 & 38 Vict. c. 87.

[4] 42 & 43 Vict. c. 66; since 1882 by the annual Expiring Laws Continuance Acts.

of progress, without providing for any amendments, nine more years would be required to make schemes for the remaining endowments known to be subject to the Acts[1].

During the existence of the Endowed Schools Commission 235 schemes were passed, dealing with an annual income of £93,635, and proposals submitted dealing with £85,000 more[2].

'If the Endowed Schools Acts were repealed and nothing was substituted for them, the only consequence would be that a particular mode of reorganizing certain endowments would cease to exist. But if the Charitable Trusts Acts were repealed and nothing was substituted for them, the consequence would be a revival of the lengthy and expensive process of the jurisdiction of the Chancery Division of the High Court, in all the above-mentioned respects, over these educational endowments[3].'

In 1876 a full digest was completed of all Endowed Charities in England and Wales then known to the Commissioners. The total gross income was £2,198,464, of which £646,882 was assigned to education, and £87,865 to apprenticing and advancement[4].

In 1873 the University of Cambridge took up the system of Extension lectures, which are to a great extent secondary in their scope and introductory to university teaching, and this example was followed by the other universities[5].

In 1884 the Select Committee under Mr. Childers on Education, Science, and Art (Administration) recommended that the proposed Education Minister should have power to call on the Public Schools for reports merely, but that in the case of all other endowed schools he might require reports and further direct inquiry to be made. But nothing came of it.

Both the Charity Commission and the Endowed Schools Commission excited a good deal of hostility at first, especi-

---

[1] Bryce Report, i. 25, Q. 10,840.
[2] P. P., 1875, xxviii. p. 5.
[3] Bryce Report, i. 21.
[4] P. P., 1877, lxvi. p. 32.
[5] *Vide* p. 252.

ally by the abolition of interests vested but abused, and by the substitution of greater, though perhaps more remote, benefits, such as improved cheap teaching in place of gratuitous inferior instruction. Investigations have been held at various times, and have resulted in a vindication of the Commissioners.

In 1884 a Select Committee of the House of Commons inquired into the working of the Charitable Trust Acts, 1853 to 1869, and found that the Commissioners had exercised their powers with discretion and sound policy, and recommended the abolition of the £50 limit in the Act of 1860 [1].

In 1886 and 1887 there was a similar inquiry into the working of the Endowed Schools Acts, which found that the principles laid down were, on the whole, sound and just, and that the Commissioners had faithfully attempted to carry them out. The Select Committee recommended examination and inspection of the schools, and supported the (Childers) Select Committee of 1884 on Education, Science, and Art (Administration) in desiring a Minister of Education [2]. They pointed out the increase in importance of technical and industrial education since the Endowed Schools Acts had been passed, and the need of giving effect to it in schemes.

A Treasury Departmental Committee in 1893 recommended that the Charity Commission should not be placed under a Minister, but that the number of Commissioners should be reduced as soon as possible. In 1894 a Select Committee of the House of Commons approved the past action of the Charity Commission, especially of recent years, but considered reconstitution necessary, and advised that the control of educational endowments should be added to the functions of a Minister of Education. All draft schemes should be invariably (as they were usually) submitted to District and Parish Councils for comment and advice [3].

[1] P. P., 1884, ix. p. xi.   [2] P. P., 1887, ix. p. viii.
[3] P P., 1894, xi. p. vii.

In 1892 a detailed return[1] was made to the House of Commons by the Charity Commissioners, containing the income of the Educational Endowments in England only[2], known at the end of 1891, available for secondary education. The total amount, exclusive of 'property of an incalculable value in the form of sites and buildings for schools,' was £697,132 a year. Of 1,262 distinct endowments, 668 were then worked under schemes approved by the Commission[3]. A comparison with the results of the Taunton Commission shows that new foundations and discoveries have nearly doubled the schools and enormously increased the revenues since 1868.

London received a separate Commission under the Duke of Northumberland (1878–80) for the Parochial Charities of the City, and a consequent Act[4], which added two special members and gave special powers to the Charity Commission. The ordinary powers had been found 'insufficient for the control of charities so ancient, numerous, and obscure as the City Parochial Charities[5],' and the special body did not complete its work until 1892.

In 1894 a Royal Commission was appointed 'to consider what are the best methods of establishing a well-organized system of Secondary Education in England, taking into account existing deficiencies, and having regard to such local sources of revenue from endowment or otherwise as are available or may be made available for this purpose.' The Right Hon. J. Bryce was chairman, and three out of the seventeen members were ladies, the first of their sex ever appointed Royal Commissioners. The Report in nine volumes was presented in August, 1895, and was not unworthy of the importance of the subject.

They reported in favour of the creation of a General Education Department under a responsible Minister of

---

[1] 1892, Paper 99.   [2] Exclusive of Monmouthshire.
[3] Fortieth Report, 1893, p. 32. E. M. Hance, *The Organization of Secondary Education*: Liverpool, 1896.
[4] 46 & 47 Vict. c. 36.   [5] Mitcheson, p. 18.

Education with a permanent secretary, and a consultative Education Council, of which one-third should be appointed by the Crown, one-third by the Universities, and one-third co-opted. Into this were to be absorbed the Charity Commission (as far as educational endowments are concerned), the Science and Art Department, and the existing Education Department [1].

There were to be local authorities in every county and every county borough (i.e. in boroughs of more than 50,000), appointed as to a majority by the Councils or existing local authorities, partly by the Education Minister and partly co-opted [2]. These local authorities should be bound to provide sufficient secondary [3] education, and the Central Office should see that the duty is fulfilled. They were to have power to initiate schemes for local [4] endowments and to supervise all local secondary [5] schools.

Inspectors of the schools were to be appointed by the local authority and approved by the Central Office, and inspection should be chiefly administrative rather than educational [6]. Examinations were to be regulated by the Central Office [7], but conducted by university or other competent external bodies selected by the governing bodies [8].

Departmental grants, so far as they were secondary [9], and the grants to county and borough councils under the Customs and Excise Act, 1890 [10], were to be applied to the new system, while a local rate, not exceeding 2*d.* in the pound, was recommended [11].

Schools having their pupils as boarders from a distance were to be classed as non-local, and to be exempt from the power of the local authority [12]; registration of teachers was gradually to be adopted [13]; professional training was recommended to the consideration of the Universities [14]. No systematic grading or classifying of schools was to be imposed, but this was to be left to time [15].

[1] Vol. i. pp. 256 sqq., 103.   [2] p. 266 sqq.   [3] p. 273.
[4] p. 275.   [5] p. 277.   [6] pp. 59, 163, 305.   [7] p. 304.
[8] Ibid.   [9] p. 313.   [10] p. 309.   [11] p. 310.
[12] p. 262.   [13] p. 320.   [14] p. 323.   [15] p. 325.

2. THE PRIVY COUNCIL.

i. *The Education Department.*

Although by the Elementary Education Act of 1870 elementary public schools are defined as those in which 'elementary education is the principal part of the education given[1],' the Education Code (1890) Act, 1890, dispensed with this condition in Evening Continuation Schools[2], and the Codes of 1890, and more especially of 1893, carried this permission into effect, and encouraged the study of secondary subjects in these schools.

A number of public elementary day schools, receiving grants from the Department, also carry the instruction in their higher classes well into the domain of secondary education, into the region which the Taunton Commissioners proposed to fill by what they called 'secondary schools of the third grade[3].'   In 1894 there were in England (exclusive of London and Monmouthshire) sixty Higher Grade Public Schools giving genuine secondary instruction[4].

The grants which foster secondary education in day schools are those given for specific subjects, and are of course payable only for scholars under the age of fourteen, or those who have not passed in the three elementary subjects of the Seventh Standard; in Evening Continuation Schools there is no longer any limit of age, but students earning grants must conform to all existing regulations.

This development of elementary schools was due, in the first instance, to the absence or inferiority of secondary instruction, but it has led in many instances to direct competition with secondary schools, endowed and private, and great jealousy has resulted. The Incorporated Association of Headmasters and the Association of Higher Grade Schools and Schools of Science arrived in the beginning of 1898 at a compromise based on the principle of differentia-

[1] s. 3.　　　　　[2] *Vide* p. 37; 53 & 54 Vict. c. 22.
[3] Bryce Commission Report, vol. i. pp. 10, 30.　　　[4] Ibid. p. 53.

tion rather than delimitation ; and the points of difference are to be 'the aim of the school, and economic and school-age conditions.'

In the meantime there is no central authority able or ready to enforce the observance of this concordat, while conditions are further complicated by competition between the new foundations of local authorities and existing secondary establishments[1]. Any scheme under the Endowed Schools Acts, however, must be submitted to the Education Department, and receive its approval, before it is referred to the Privy Council.

No attempt at any complete enumeration of secondary schools was made by the Commission, but the Education Department has since undertaken a voluntary census of all schools in England (excluding Monmouthshire) between the public elementary schools and the universities and university colleges. In the absence of any recognized classification[2] the report[3] is necessarily general and lacking in definition, but it far surpasses in precision and value any information previously in the possession of the public. However, it must be said at the outset that it contains a large number of small private schools which may not be public elementary schools, but certainly have no claim to be called secondary. No less than 1,423 of the schools in the return had *no* pupils over the age of fourteen, and there is no means of knowing how many of these were merely preparatory for the 4,786 higher schools. At any rate the mixed schools, the largest proportion of which (65 per cent.) contained less than 31 pupils, also had the largest proportion of non-graduate teachers.

On June 1, 1897, there were 6,209 'Secondary' Schools, of which 1,958 were for boys, 3,173 for girls, and 1,078

---

[1] Cf. Charity Commission, 45th Report, 1898, p. 29.

[2] One headmaster of a school preparatory to the Public Schools replied that his school did not give 'secondary' education. Many persons who ought to know better confuse secondary schools with second-grade schools (Taunton, i. 15 ; Bryce, i. 41).

[3] P. P., 1898, C. 8,634, price 11*d.*

were definitely 'Mixed' Schools; the totals of pupils were 158,502 boys and 133,042 girls, being 5·4 and 4·5 per thousand respectively of the estimated total population. Of these children, two-thirds were under fourteen, 24 and 21 per cent. of the boys and girls respectively were between fourteen and sixteen, and only 9·3 per cent. of the boys and 11·4 per cent. of the girls were over sixteen.

Of the boys' schools, 1,311 (67 per cent.) were private enterprise schools, and of the girls' schools 2,886 (90 per cent.). 502 boys' schools (25 per cent.) were 'endowed,' and only 86 (2·7 per cent.) of the schools for girls; but 'endowment' need amount to no more than a few shillings. Of all the schools, 51 per cent. had under 31 pupils, 91 per cent. had less than 101. Of the staff exclusively attached to the schools, 55·9 per cent. of the boys' masters were graduates, 29·2 of girls' masters, and 25·8 of the masters at mixed schools. Of the mistresses exclusively attached to schools, those who had qualified by examination for degrees were only 12 per cent. of the total. The average number of pupils for each exclusively attached teacher was just under twenty. A similar return is being prepared in 1898.

An Act was introduced in 1896 and dropped, but legislation is promised. Information has been collected, certain points have been defined, various compromises have been adjusted, and all the usual precedents to educational legislation in this country have been fulfilled.

ii. *The Science and Art Department*[1].

The Science and Art Department is the second great Government department which is directly concerned with education, and offers grants of public money to those managers, teachers, and students who fulfil the conditions it lays down.

There is no necessary connexion between Science and

---

[1] Calendar and History, and General Summary of Proceedings of the Science and Art Department; also the Report and the Directory. All published annually.

Art, and, as we shall see immediately, they owe their combination in this country to a merely administrative device. But this at least they have in common, that before this century they entered into none of the curricula of endowed schools, and when their advantages were realized, the study of them had to be encouraged by direct grants from the current income of the State.

The early history of the Department has a close analogy to that of the Education Department proper.

In 1786 an Order in Council created a Committee of the Privy Council in Trade, which has developed into a department of the Civil Service and is now known as the Board of Trade[1].

The first step towards the creation of the Department was taken in the interests of commerce. Just fifty years after its establishment, the Committee of Trade, acting on the report of a Select Committee of the House of Commons[2], made application to the Treasury, and a sum of £1,500 was voted by the House of Commons for a Normal School of Design. A council was appointed, a central school opened, and in 1841 provincial schools of design were started in the provinces with the aid of grants from Government.

In 1852 the arrangements were remodelled, and a Department of Practical Art established, a Science Division being added in the following year, when the present title of the Department of Science and Art was first bestowed.

By the Order in Council of Feb. 25, 1856, this Establishment was removed from the Board of Trade to the new Education Department under the Lord President of the Council, with whom a Vice-President was associated by the Statute of the same year[3].

Thus both branches of the Department were originally created and worked by Special Committees of the Privy Council administering annual grants voted by the House of

[1] Traill, *Central Government*, p. 125: Macmillan, 1881.
[2] Reports, P. P., 1835, v.; 1836, ix.   [3] *Vide* p. 15.

Commons; both Departments appeared for the first time in the Statute book after a long period of activity upon the appointment of the Vice-President, who was to be their official representative in the House of Commons; and both from very small beginnings on a merely provisional basis have grown into large educational departments, which, whatever their future modifications, have become permanent in themselves. The chief differences in their common elements are that while the Committee of Council on Education is still consulted on important steps in the Education Department proper, the Science and Art Department is controlled only by the President and Vice-President without reference to the Committee [1]. Moreover, the Codes of the Education Department must be submitted to both Houses of Parliament, whereas the regulations of South Kensington need no further sanction.

The Education Department proper is now limited to England and Wales, while the Science and Art Department extends its grants to Scotland and Ireland.

The duties of the former are restricted almost entirely to the inspection and direction of education, while the latter department, in addition to this class of work, not only itself carries on the two Royal Colleges of Science and of Art, but is responsible for several large Museums, and includes in its reports and finance the Geological Survey and Solar Physics Committee. It claims to have inaugurated payment by results in the Science Department in 1859 [2], and in 1863 this system was fully introduced in respect of Art grants.

The Department was originally accommodated in Somerset House, in the old rooms of the Royal Academy, but after a few years at Marlborough House it was removed in 1857 to South Kensington, with the name of which its work is always closely identified.

The organization of the Department has been tentative and very frequently changed, but in 1884 it received a

---

[1] Traill, *Central Government*, p. 148; Cross Report, Q. 507.
[2] Science and Art Calendar, 1898, p. xii.

Secretary and Permanent Head of its own, and was thus rendered more independent of the joint establishment at Whitehall, although it remains directly under the control of the Lord President of Council and the Vice-President [1].

Besides earlier reports on the Schools of Design, Select Committees of the House of Commons reported in 1864 on the Schools of Art, and in 1868 on Scientific Instruction for the Industrial Classes. The latter report especially emphasized the necessity of placing within the reach of every child elementary instruction, in which drawing, physical geography, and instruction in natural phenomena should be included. The reorganization of secondary instruction was urgently recommended, and the introduction of the teaching of science into secondary schools.

In 1870 a Royal Commission on Scientific Instruction was appointed, with the seventh Duke of Devonshire as chairman, and issued a report in ten parts, beginning in 1871 and ending in 1875. This careful investigation dealt with the whole of the scientific instruction given in the United Kingdom from the elementary schools to the Universities, and included the Museums and scientific work recognized by Government. The report contains much general information on educational bodies at the time, which is not to be found elsewhere.

Science Grants.　From 1853, when the Science Division was first created, until 1859, isolated experiments were tried in aiding the establishment of local Science Schools in selected localities, but at the end of the period only four such schools survived, and a new method was adopted.

Minutes were published in accordance with which any place establishing science classes for itself might obtain subsidies from South Kensington on the results it could show in written examinations held on the spot by the Department.

Teachers must have passed the special Examination of the Department and obtained a certificate of competency

[1] Bryce Report, i. 26.

to teach. On these certificates payments were made to them proportionate to the number of pupils they passed, up to a certain maximum, and additional payments were made for pupils gaining prizes. The students themselves could gain prizes and medals, and scholarships and exhibitions were afterwards established. Grants were made to the schools towards apparatus and books. Only six subjects were recognized at first, but the list grew until it now includes twenty-five.

The first examination for teachers was held in 1859, and the first general examination for pupils in May, 1861. In the early sixties, when payment by results became the rule everywhere, many elementary school teachers, seeing their salaries threatened or actually diminished, cast about for some means of restoring their fortunes, and found it at South Kensington. They managed to qualify themselves and give scientific instruction in the evening[1]: the education might be very narrow, but it went beyond the three R.'s of the day, and its pecuniary results were very welcome.

In 1867 the special examination for teachers was abolished, and permission to teach depended henceforth on passing a sufficiently good general examination. In 1868 building grants were extended to Science Schools, and continued until 1897. In 1870 part of the payment of the special local Secretaries appointed by the local authorities was undertaken by the Central Department.

In November, 1872, the first relaxation of payment by results appeared in the creation of a special order of classes known as *Organized Science Schools*. In that year the need for a continuous and systematic course of scientific training to follow the ordinary Elementary Education led the Department to offer special payments for attendance in the case of schools or classes which complied with its regulations for organizing a course of scientific instruction which

---

[1] First Report of Royal Commission on Scientific Instruction, 1872, p. xx.

should occupy three years '.   The school might be held by day or night, but must be properly organized as a ' Science School,' and consequently have a properly constituted and approved Local Committee.   A grant of 10s. a head was offered for each pupil who made 250 day attendances in the year ', and passed in one specific subject in addition to the ordinary payments on results.   The growth of these schools was slow : in 1885 only three were in existence, but by 1895 they numbered 112, and by 1897 there were 169.

In 1892 the attendance grants were doubled, but in 1895 a sweeping reorganization was effected in the system of grants and of the education given in these schools.   Payments on the results of the May examinations were diminished and restricted to the compulsory subjects of the advanced and higher courses, a grant was made for practical work, and a variable grant was introduced, depending on the report of the Inspector upon the work of the school as a whole, both in literary and scientific subjects.

The most remarkable change was the introduction of compulsory literary subjects into all Organized Science Day Schools, while the minimum of scientific instruction was reduced from fifteen to thirteen hours a week.   An Organized Science Day School must provide a thorough and progressive course of education in Science, combined with literary or commercial instruction adapted to students whose education is such as to fit them to enter Standard VII of the English Code for a Public Elementary School '.   The course was no longer specified as consisting of three years, but the regulations provided for its occupying three or four years, and the grant might be discontinued if the number of those attending dwindled beyond a certain point.   No pupil was allowed to earn the attendance and variable grants in a day school for more than four, or in a night school than three, years.   From 1897 manual training was to be compulsory in all Organized Science Day Schools.

' Science and Art Department Report for 1872, App. p. 8.
' 5s. for 75 attendances at night.   ' Directory, 1895, p. 33.

In 1896 there was a complete revision of the grants for ordinary Science Schools. An attendance grant was introduced, varying with the subject and the stage of it, and depending on the efficiency of the class as reported by the Inspector and as shown by its success in the annual examinations. The payments for results were discontinued for everything but Honours. An Inspector of the Department will now, when necessary, visit the Training Colleges and report on the premises and the instruction given.

The Charity Commissioners now co-operate as far as possible with the Department, in order to secure the recognition of Endowed Secondary Schools as Science Schools, and to ensure the representation of local authorities [1].

In the ordinary Science Examinations grants for the most rudimentary science results were abolished in 1892, one elementary division only being recognized; and the principal effect of this was to transfer the support of such elementary instruction to the local authorities. In 1897, in consequence of the recommendations of a Departmental Committee, building grants were discontinued and a fixed minimum salary required for teachers. Organized Science Schools are henceforth to be known as Schools of Science. But more important was the following paragraph, which, in spite of many apprehensions, has been eagerly welcomed by the local authorities affected :—

'VII. In Counties and County Boroughs in England which possess an organization for the promotion of secondary education, such organization, if recognized by the Department, may notify its willingness to be responsible to the Department for the Science and Art instruction within its area. In such cases grants will in general be made to the Managers of new Schools and Classes, only if they are acting in unison with such organization. (The rights of the Managers of existing Schools and Classes will not be interfered with, and Town Councils and School Boards who are managers of Schools receiving Science and Art Grants will not be debarred from establishing in their districts additional Schools where necessary.) In Wales the Intermediate Education

---

[1] Forty-fifth Charity Commission Report, 1898, p. 29.

Authority is for this purpose regarded as the Authority for the promotion of Science and Art[1].'

Students reported by the Inspector as unqualified to derive benefit may be excluded from the Schools of Science and disqualified from receiving the attendance grant in other Science Classes[2].

By July, 1898, twenty-eight Councils had been recognized by the Department as responsible for the Science and Art teaching in their districts. Examination and inspection in these cases are retained by the Department: the grants earned by all the schools in any one area are handed over to the local organization which settles matters relating to the managers and their duties[3]. The Department considers the experiment very successful[4], so far as it has gone.

The Government Bill for 1899[5] proposes to amalgamate South Kensington with the Education Department, but makes no provision for local authorities.

Art Grants. From 1841 to 1852 the Board of Trade appointed and paid masters in the provincial schools of design subject to the locality paying half of the cost of the schools, which it frequently failed to do. It was also found difficult to carry out the prescribed course ' on account of the great need of elementary teaching which existed among the students[6].'

In 1852 the new Department of Practical Art withdrew from direct management and support of the provincial schools, but made grants to them on different terms. A certain amount of instruction in drawing must be provided for, and evening classes for artisans and elementary schools ; payment was made according to the certificates of the Department held by the teacher ; pupil teachers were paid, and medals and prizes were given to pupils. The teacher

---

[1] Directory, 1897, C. 8,635, p. 3.   [2] Ibid., sections lvii, xli.
[3] *The Record of Technical and Secondary Education*, 1893, p. 270.
[4] Sir John Gorst in the House of Commons: *Times*, Aug. 5, 1898.
[5] *Vide* p. xxvii.
[6] House of Commons Select Committee on Schools of Art, Report, 1864, p. iv.

no longer drew a salary from the Board of Trade, but made his own terms with the Committee [1].

In 1857 inspection of all Art schools earning grants was organized, the Inspectors awarded local medals, and sent up a few selected drawings for competition at headquarters.

In 1856 building grants were commenced and continued till 1897.

In 1863 payment by results was substituted for payment on certificates, and from the next year all drawings have been sent direct to South Kensington and there examined for grants and prizes.

In 1865 provision was made for the establishment of Night Classes for instruction in drawing as distinguished from Schools of Art, and the restriction of grants to classes held after 6 p.m. was removed in 1876.

a. Science and Art.

Local Management. In all cases there must be a Local Committee of at least five members. It may be (*a*) the Local Authority under the Technical Instruction Act, or the Committee to which it has delegated its power; (*b*) a School Board, or (*c*) the governing body of a school (other than public elementary) with a scheme under the Endowed Schools Act or the City of London Parochial Charities Act; or (*d*) a Committee formed for the purpose according to the regulations of the Department.

Inspection and Examination. The Inspection of the Department was formerly very inadequate owing to want of Inspectors, of whom in 1870 there were only two, and afterwards only four. Officers of the Royal Engineers were utilized to a considerable extent, but only to see that the regulations of the Department were observed, and not to report on the state of instruction in the schools [2].

In 1893 thirteen more Inspectors were appointed to carry out the new regulations as to Organized Science Schools,

[1] House of Commons Select Committee on Schools of Art, Report, 1864, p. iv.

[2] Report for 1872, pp. x, 41; Bryce Report, i. p. 60; Royal Commission on Scientific Instruction, 1872, Q. 7.

to inspect Training Colleges if necessary, to supervise the temporary Art Inspectors in the elementary schools ; generally to act as advisers in Art and Science in districts where local authorities administered grants for technical education, and to co-operate with the officers of these authorities in securing the efficient and economical administration of science instruction [1].

Restriction of Grants.   The old School of Design tried to exclude from its benefits all persons who were not designers [2].   After 1852 [3], although the instruction was declared to be for the operative classes, the principle adopted was that the schools should be open to the whole community, different classes paying fees according to the instruction received and to their status.   As soon as payment by results began, the State refused to pay for those who were able to pay for themselves, and the Science Grants from 1859 and the Art Grants from 1863 were limited to payments for the results achieved by the industrial classes.   The grant at first included only artisans, children of the labouring poor, scholars, and persons in training as Art teachers or employed as designers for manufacturers [4], but payment rose gradually to coincide [5] with partial exemption from the income tax, which was granted to incomes under £500 a year.

Scholarships and Exhibitions.   There are numerous scholarships and exhibitions derived from public and private sources for both Science and Art.   Some are given absolutely, some in response to local contributions, some to enable students to attend the Royal Colleges ; others enable pupils of an elementary or organized science day school to pursue their studies at approved day schools.   Grants are given to masters and students in Schools of Art to visit South Kensington and to study there ; also to science teachers to attend sessional courses at the Royal College or a summer course in July.

[1] Forty-first Report, 1894, lxvi.
[2] 1864, Select Committee, Q. 26 and Q. 299.
[3] Ibid.
[4] Ibid. p. 279; Minute, Feb. 24, 1863.   [5] In 1895.

N

Public Libraries Acts.

Statutory powers of building and maintaining Schools for Science and Art have been given to local authorities throughout the United Kingdom by a series of Acts relating to the provision of Public Libraries and Museums. The first Act was in 1845, but the first reference to schools was in two Acts of 1855 [1], by which a rate not exceeding one penny in the pound might be raised for the purpose, if the borough or parish decide to adopt the Act, and might be expended on a public library or museum or school for Science and Art.

In 1884 [2] it was expressly declared that any authority acting under these Acts might accept a grant from the public funds made by the Committee of Council on Education on the conditions prescribed by that body, and that where any museum, library, school, or other institution has been established under the Acts, another may be added in connexion without taking further proceedings.

England, Ireland, and Scotland all possess these powers, but under different Acts; the educational clauses, however, present little difference [3].

In 1895–6 the sum of £7,466 was expended by local authorities under these Acts in England.

B. Technical Education.

It is very difficult to give a clear and yet adequate account of the movement which in this country has been comprehended under the name of Technical Education. For one thing, circumstances have caused the term to be applied to a great deal of secondary instruction which has not the slightest claim to be considered technical, either in

---

[1] 18 & 19 Vict. c. 40 (Ireland), c. 70 (Great Britain).

[2] 47 & 48 Vict. c. 37 (Great Britain and Ireland).

[3] England and Wales, 55 & 56 Vict. c. 53 (this Act definitely specifies the Department of Science and Art as the source of grants), 56 & 57 Vict. c. 11; Scotland, 50 & 51 Vict. c. 42; Ireland, 18 & 19 Vict. c. 40, 47 & 48 Vict. c. 37, &c.

its content or its treatment; in the next place, the grants made in its name have been either handed to local authorities with free powers of applying the money, or else provided by independent local associations of various kinds. There has been no recognized *central* authority except the Department of Science and Art, which began its career with no definite recognition of a difference between technical instruction in particular and secondary education in general, and has in consequence only made confusion worse confounded. Technical education has never been dealt with as a whole in England either by statesmen or educational authorities, as may be seen by a consideration of its history.

In the first two decades of this century there was a great craving for knowledge among the intelligent workmen who had been trained by the industrial revolution, and their zeal and desires were naturally for mechanical and scientific knowledge.

Dr. Birkbeck, Professor of Natural Philosophy at Anderson's Institution in Glasgow, established courses of lectures for working men in 1800, and these were continued and developed until in 1823 the Glasgow Mechanics' Institution was founded. In 1824 a similar association was established in London, under the auspices and with the financial help of Dr. Birkbeck, who had left Glasgow in 1804, and the example was followed in a great many towns throughout the country.

But the result showed the truth of the judgment passed so many years later by the Commission on Technical Education—that a good secondary education is the best possible preliminary to all good technical instruction [1]. Dr. Birkbeck himself had found that the want of preliminary teaching prevented many of his hearers from following the simplest explanations, and this absence of solid foundation rendered many of the institutes very unstable. Numbers of them died out, but in some cases they lingered on, often as little more than working men's clubs, until they were utilized as

[1] Report, vol. i. p. 516.

a nucleus for endowments or till the spread of education developed a fresh need for them[1].

The first International Exhibition of 1851 in Hyde Park drew attention to the great want of taste and training in the British manufacturers, but we organized the Department of Science and Art, and said that all was well. The Exhibition of 1862 followed, and we were examining everything that was learned, and engrossed in seeing that we only paid for what we got. Time went on, and Germany, united and reinvigorated after the war, became with her education a formidable rival in trade. The French Exposition Universelle of 1878, which, in the words of M. Leclerc[2], 'annonçait brillamment la rentrée en scène de la France, acheva d'inquiéter les Anglais.' The usual remedy of a Royal Commission was applied in 1880, and Mr. (afterwards Right Hon. Sir) Bernhard Samuelson was Chairman. The Commissioners did their work well, visited most of the important centres on the Continent, and reported finally in 1884. They pointed out the need of a number of good secondary schools of the modern type, and declared that legislation was necessary to enable localities to found and support technical and secondary schools; they recommended that the teaching of the Science and Art Department should be more practical and its inspection more effective, and reported in favour of a general extension of manual, technical, and scientific instruction in elementary and secondary schools.

In 1887 an Act for Technical Schools in Scotland was passed[3]; the next year the Local Government Act, 1888[4], created County Councils in England and Wales, and gave them an income out of the Probate and Licence Duties; in the following year the Technical Instruction Act, 1889[5], became law for England, Wales, and Ireland.

---

[1] J. G. Godard, *Life of Birkbeck*: London, 1884, 8vo.
[2] *L'Education des Classes moyennes et dirigeantes en Angleterre*, p. 230: Armand Colin et Cie, Paris, 1894.
[3] *Vide* p. 227.   [4] 51 & 52 Vict. c. 41.   [5] 52 & 53 Vict. c. 76.

As far as England and Wales were concerned, this last
measure allowed the council of any county or borough, or
any urban sanitary authority (under the Public Health Acts),
to supply or aid in supplying technical or manual instruction,
and to delegate its authority to a committee appointed for
the purpose wholly or partly from its members.   The chief
restrictions were that public elementary schools were not to
be helped [1], a conscience clause was imposed, the principle
was laid down that the body granting supplies must be
represented in the management of the institution subsidised,
and the rate was limited to a penny in the pound.

Under this Act [2] the Department of Science and Art is the
central authority which decides in the case of schools and
institutions, or between schools and local authorities, on
questions of distribution of grants, sufficiency of provision,
and representation on governing bodies.

Technical instruction is defined as 'instruction in the
principles of science and art applicable to industries, and
in the application of special branches of science and art
to specific industries or employments.   It shall not include
teaching the practice of any trade or industry or employment, but, save as aforesaid, shall include instruction in
the branches of science and art with respect to which
grants are for the time being made by the Department
of Science and Art, and any other forms of instruction
(including modern languages and commercial and agricultural subjects) which may for the time being be sanctioned [2]
by that Department by a Minute laid before Parliament,
and made on the representation of a local authority that
such a form of instruction is required by the circumstances
of its district.'

Manual instruction is defined as 'instruction in the use
of tools, processes of agriculture, and modelling in clay,

---

[1] *Vide* p. 39.   [2] Sec. 1 (f).
[3] By 1897, 128 subjects had been recognized, ranging from Modern
Languages, Music, and Electric Engineering to Boot-clicking, Brick-
laying, and Plasterers' work (Report, Appendix A, p. 1).

wood, or other material.' An Amending Act[1] was passed in 1891, removing one or two practical difficulties in administration.

Almost before rates had been levied, the Local Taxation (Customs and Excise) Act, 1890[2], allotted to England and Wales a large sum annually out of the Customs and Excise duties, handed over to local authorities in place of being paid as compensation to publicans, the purpose for which it had originally been raised[3]. £300,000 was to be devoted to police superannuation, and the residue was distributed between the funds of counties and county boroughs, who might, if they chose, contribute it or any part of it for the purpose of technical education over and above any rates. It is this residue which has been the main fund for the local support of technical education in England.

The local authorities all over the kingdom at once responded to the invitation, and in many cases, at first without educational knowledge or expert advice, proceeded to make grants to lecturers and vote money to institutions. The lecturers were often unprocurable or extremely unsatisfactory, but the demand improved the supply, wisdom came with experience : the better counties set a good example to the less fortunate, and education was greatly benefited. South Kensington took a very generous view of the scope of technical instruction, and, fortunately it may be for education in general, but unfortunately for any prospect of delimitation, it has sanctioned under the head of technical instruction almost every subject except the Classics which can well be included under Secondary Education. It has neither restricted the subjects, nor has it endeavoured to secure their treatment from a technical point of view, and thus a great part of the grant has gone to Secondary Education, although many of the better secondary schools have either been unable to profit by it or have had to sacrifice their educational ideals to specialisation.

---

[1] 54 & 55 Vict. c. 4.   [2] 53 & 54 Vict. c. 60.
[3] Popularly known as the ' Whiskey money.'

The Science and Art Department assigned £5,000 to technical instruction in 1890[1], but next year the splendid grant of the Customs and Excise money took its place. The amount of residue assigned to technical education by English local authorities[2] rose from £472,560 in 1892–3 to £654,463 (out of a total of £775,944) in 1895–6. The sum raised by rates in this country under the Technical Instruction Acts has grown from £12,762 in the former year to £45,700 in the latter, exclusive of £7,466 due to the Public Libraries Acts[3].

Tests of Secondary Education.

Examination.

Even as late as the middle of the century, when the Committee of Council was sending out its Inspectors to examine and report upon all elementary schools which earned or desired its grants, there was no external test of merit available for secondary schools. A school might become famous by winning some of the few scholarships open for general competition at the Universities, or, by an arrangement private and purely individual, persons of high standing might be invited to adjudge for school prizes or examine the upper classes of a school. But there was no general test of work which applied to the whole of a school, and was open to any number of schools that chose to apply. The public service[4] at home and abroad was still supplied by nomination, and good and bad were indiscriminately nominated. Examination, however, was on its way: it had revived in the old Universities, it had arisen in the elementary schools, and its adoption in secondary education was only a matter of time.

---

[1] *Vide* p. 231.   [2] Excluding Monmouthshire.   [3] *Vide* p. 178.
[4] The Indian Civil Service was opened for competition in 1854 (16 & 17 Vict. c. 95); for Macaulay's speech on competitive examination, (' The moment you say to an examiner, not " Shall A or B go to India?" but " Here is A; is he fit to go to India?" the question becomes

It began with private agencies. The College of Preceptors, an association of schoolmasters, chiefly of private
schools, had been formed in 1846 for the organization and
improvement of the profession, and had received a charter
in 1849. It sent examiners to schools, and in December,
1853, held its first examination of pupils at headquarters[1].
The subjects included Latin, French, English History,
Geography, Mathematics, and for the higher classes
Drawing, or some branch of physical science, and Greek.
It is difficult to realize how advanced a programme this
was ten years before the report of the Public Schools
Commission, when the classical curriculum was most
strictly observed[2].

The examinations were not restricted to the schools of
members; they were open to girls as well as to boys, and
have been successfully continued to the present time.

In 1852 the Society of Arts had formed a union of
Mechanics' Institutes, which was joined in the course of the
next two years by 362 of these associations[3]. For the
members of these they proposed to hold examinations in
1855, but only one candidate—a chimney-sweep—presented

altogether a different one,') *vide* Hansard, T. S., cxxviii. p. 739. The
first public competitive examination for the Royal Military Academy,
Woolwich, was held in August, 1855 (P. P., Eng., 1857, vi. 519). *The
Civil Service Commissioners* were appointed in May, 1855, 'to make
provision for testing, according to fixed rules, the qualifications of the
young men who may from time to time be proposed to be appointed
to the junior situations in any of Her Majesty's Civil Establishments.'
For some time the examinations were merely qualifying; from 1859
about three candidates were generally nominated for each vacancy, and
it was only in 1870 that the competition was thrown open to all. In
1895–96, £16,666 was spent on salaries, wages, and allowances of the
Commission, and £13,476 on assistant examiners (Appropriation Account,
p. 160). (Chambers, *Encyclopaedia*, 1889: Art. "Civil Service";
Practical Essays, by A. Bain, LL.D., p. 71 : Longmans, Green, & Co.,
1884. For the Universities, *vide* pp. 242, 251, &c.)

[1] *Educational Times*, January, 1854, p. 87.

[2] In 1864 there was little systematic teaching of either History or
Geography at any of the nine Public Schools (Clarendon Report, p. 17);
Natural Science was practically excluded (p. 32). In 1862 French was
not compulsory at Eton, and before 1851 Mathematics also had been
voluntary (Eton Evidence, Q. 6,933, Q. 6,264).

[3] *Journal of the Society of Arts*, 1852, p. 2 ; 1854, p. 823.

himself, and he was not examined[1]. In 1856 there were 52 candidates who were examined in London; in 1857, 220 in London and Huddersfield. In 1858 local Boards were formed and the examinations held at forty centres; there were 1,107 candidates, of whom only 197 ultimately received certificates.

These examinations, however, were by express arrangement[2] confined strictly to persons over fifteen who had left or were leaving school; they were intended at most to test the final result of a school education, and not to ascertain the progress schoolboys were making[3]. The syllabus of examination was very liberal, but aimed rather at special subjects for adults than at a prescribed course[4]. It included Mathematics, Mechanics, Chemistry, Physiology, Botany, Geography, English History, English Literature and Composition, Latin, French, and German. The examiners were men of very high calibre.

The next step led directly to the intervention of the Universities. A local committee of persons interested in education was formed in the West of England and included Mr. (afterwards Sir Thomas) Acland, a double first at Oxford in 1831, Lord Ebrington, who in 1854 had been greatly interested in the scheme of the Society of Arts[5], and the present Archbishop of Canterbury, who had examined for that Society in 1856. An examination was held at Exeter[6] in June, 1857, the Education Department granting the services of two of H. M. Inspectors, one of whom was the 'Rev. F. Temple.' The range of papers was very wide, and included Music, Art, Practical Science, Horti-

---

[1] *Journal of the Society of Arts*, 1859, p. 194.   [2] 1857, p. 461.
[3] *Oxford University Extension Gazette*, 1895, p. 75.
[4] Cf. Acland, p. 78.
[5] *Journal*, 1854, p. 555.
[6] 'Mr. Acland told us that the secret of his success in originating, jointly with Dr. Temple, these examinations, was that they had, as a preliminary step, held an examination similar to that which they desired to see established by the University—"We showed at Exeter that our ideas would march"' (Miss E. Davies, *Women in the Universities of England and Scotland*, p. 9: Macmillan, 1896).

culture, Commerce; both sexes were admitted to the examination. Similar examinations were immediately held in five other counties, and so great was the success of the movement that the University of Oxford acceded in the same year to an application to place the system on a permanent footing[1], and entrusted the working of it to a body of Delegates. The Society of Arts hailed the scheme and offered prizes for Seniors obtaining three first classes[2]. Cambridge followed suit the next year, and in July and December, 1858, respectively, the first examinations of the two Universities were held. A proposal for united action was rejected, as Cambridge was not prepared to grant the title of Associate[3]. For some time they were known as the Middle Class Examinations, a designation which was not social but intellectual[4], but which hindered their extension[5].

The syllabus was in advance of the times, though not so elaborate as in the Exeter experiment. Senior and junior certificates were awarded, and honour lists published. Oxford further granted the title of Associate in Arts to those candidates who passed in the Senior Division.

The examinations were at first open only to boys, but in 1863 the Cambridge Syndicate allowed girls the use of their papers, and in 1865 admitted them fully on the same terms as boys[6]. Examination of schools either in connexion with or separately from the examination for certificates, and a preliminary division for candidates under fourteen, are the chief developments resulting from experience[7]. Commercial

---

[1] *Some Account of the Original Objects of the New Oxford Examinations for the Title of Associate in Arts and Certificates in the year* 1858. By T. D. Acland, 2nd ed.: Ridgway, London, 1858, p. 81.

[2] *Journal,* 1858; Acland, p. xxxi.

[3] *Students' Guide to the University of Cambridge Local Examinations,* by Rev. Canon Brown, D.D., 5th edition, 1893, p. 33.

[4] Acland, p. vii.

[5] The heading of Lord Ebrington's letter in the *Journal of the Society of Arts,* whether due to him or to the editor, was 'Middle Class Education and Public Local Examinations' (*Journal,* 1854, p. 555). On p. 583 there is reference to 'the amount of education befitting an Englishman of the middle classes.'

[6] Oxford followed in 1870.

[7] For Women's Examinations, &c., *v.* pp. 254, 256.

subjects have been tried, abandoned, and resumed by both Universities, but no separate commercial certificate is now given.

The examinations for certificates are in writing only, and are held annually at a number of centres throughout the country, and even in the Colonies, Oxford having chosen July and Cambridge December. The examinations are open to any one, regardless of age, unless in the case of honours. Special papers in religious knowledge are set for Catholics and Jews, but these subjects are not in any case compulsory for candidates where objections are made on conscientious grounds.

Durham also conducts Local Examinations, and since 1895 arranges for the examination and inspection of Grammar, Private, Organized Science, and other Secondary Schools[1]. Victoria University likewise examines and inspects schools. Fifteen schools were examined by it in 1896, but in 1897, in consequence of the progress of the Central Welsh Board, the number fell to eight.

Local Examinations.

OXFORD.

| | Centres.* | Candidates* | | Per cent. | Schools examined.* |
		Examined.	Passed.		
1860	13	864	498	57·6	—
1870	23	1,605	1,009	62·9	—
1880	33	2,119	1,322	62·4	—
1890	62	2,890	1,983	68·6	45
1897	155	8,172	4,959	60·7	80

CAMBRIDGE.

| | Centres.* | Candidates* | | Per cent. | Schools examined.* |
		Examined.	Passed.		
1860	10	355	256	72·1	—
1870	31	2,482	1,501	60·5	13
1880	118	6,429	4,122	64·1	67
1890	190	8,476	6,302	74·4	95
1897	397	13,858	10,499	75·8	108

* Not including colonial candidates, centres, or schools.

[1] Calendar, 1897–98, p. 55.

For the College of Preceptors in 1860 and in 1870, 821 and 1,517 candidates were entered.   In 1880, 11,208, and in 1890, 16,269 were examined.   In 1897, 9,428 passed out of 14,140 examined (66·7 per cent.). · The returns of passes for the earlier years include those candidates who only passed in a lower class than that for which they were entered, and even the later figures include colonial entries.

The Oxford and Cambridge Schools Examination Board, commonly known as The Joint Board[1].

When the Public Schools Bill went into Committee in the Commons in 1868, Mr. Lowe moved that these Schools should be examined in elementary subjects by H. M. Inspectors. This was not pressed to a division, but the principle of inspection was freely discussed. Regular examination was the basis of the recommendations of the Taunton Report in 1867[2], and accordingly the Endowed Schools Bill, as introduced by Mr. Forster in 1869, contained provisions for the compulsory examination of all endowed schools. These clauses were found to be too heavy, and were transhipped into a separate Bill which never came to port. The Endowed Schools and Charity Commissioners, however, made and make a point of providing for annual examination in their schemes.

The Headmasters of the Public Schools, when they met for their second Conference at Sherborne in the end of 1870[3], passed a resolution to urge the Universities to institute a Matriculation examination, and directed their Committee to confer with Oxford and Cambridge as to the best form of it. The Committee were also instructed to press upon Government the importance of instituting a system of leaving-examinations[4]. The Committee, how-

---

[1] *Essays on Secondary Education*, Clarendon Press, 1898, p. 262, P. E. Matheson.   [2] *Vide* pp. 158, 160.

[3] The first conference was held at Uppingham, at the invitation of Mr. Thring, in December, 1869, and was preliminary and informal (*A Memoir of Hugo Daniel Harper, D.D.*, by L. V. Lester: Longmans & Co., 1896).

[4] Report of Meeting, p. 6: James Ellis, Sherborne, 1871.

ever, seem to have disregarded the latter instruction and obtained the sanction of the next Conference to their action [1]. They entered into negotiations with Oxford and Cambridge for providing an efficient examination for schools and individuals.

A Syndicate appointed by the latter University and a Delegacy of the former, after some discussion, formed in 1873 a Joint Board; the Universities consented to recognize its certificates as exempting undergraduates from their earliest examinations, and the first examinations of the Board were held in 1874. In 1878 girls were admitted, and in 1883 a lower class of certificates was instituted, the standard of the higher being still maintained. Commercial certificates as in the Local Examinations were tried and abandoned. To each school examiners are sent; candidates are examined; for certificate purposes all papers are submitted to examiners, assembled in alternate years at Oxford and Cambridge. 'Inspection' denotes that the examiner inspects and reports on sets of papers first marked by masters of the school [2].

	Candidates.	Certificates. Higher.	Lower.	Total.	Percentage.
1880	700	475	—	475	·65
1890	2,087	941	398	1,339	·64
1897	3,073	1,157	499	1,656	·53

In 1874 London University made overtures for joining in the work, but their scheme was too large and not adaptable to the conditions desirable at Oxford and Cambridge. The Matriculation examination of London is now used largely as a leaving-examination, even by pupils who have no intention of exercising the right of entering the University [3].

---

[1] *The Proposed Control of the Public Schools by the Universities,* E. E. Bowen : Rivingtons, 1872. *A Letter to Edward Bowen, M.A.,* by Rev. G. Ridding : Wells, Winchester, 1872.

[2] Bryce Commission Report, v. pp. 277, 288.

[3] Thus in 1890 2,762 persons matriculated, while only 2,222 of all the senior years submitted to any other examination. For statistics

Inspection[1].—The word 'inspection' may mean anything from the visit of an examiner who spends all his time in looking over papers, and at most questioning a class viva voce, to a rigorous scrutiny of the organization, the methods and results of teaching, and the sanitary condition of a school. The Joint Board, the Oxford and Cambridge Local Examinations authorities and the College of Preceptors, undertake the task in senses which vary infinitely and somewhat indefinitely in their approximation to the latter meaning. Since 1887 the Charity Commissioners have employed some of their Assistant-Commissioners to make a systematic inspection of the secondary schools worked by schemes under the Endowed Schools Acts. The work is performed very gradually, and its nature is defined as 'official or administrative rather than educational[2].'

The Board of Agriculture has power to inspect and report on any school giving technical instruction in agriculture[3].

The Education Department inspects the buildings of higher grade Board Schools, and scholars in them in the Standards or under fifteen years of age.

It is probable that, in the future, inspection in its best sense will play a very much greater, and examination a very much less, part in secondary education ; but in the meantime the difficulty is for inspecting bodies to secure the services of men who are competent to carry out a thorough inspection, and whose report would command entire confidence.

TRAINING AND REGISTRATION OF TEACHERS.

i. *Training of Secondary Teachers.*

Little or no separate provision for the training of secondary teachers was made in this kingdom till within the last quarter

vide p. 261; also *Essays on Secondary Education*, Clarendon Press, 1898, p. 232 ; Bryce Report, i. p. 58.

[1] Bryce Report, i. 59.
[2] Ibid.
[3] *Vide* p. 267.

of the century and even yet the need for it has not obtained general recognition.

Mistresses, being less fettered by tradition and more dependent on engagements for diplomas than men, have shown more ardour in making provision, and also in availing themselves of it when made. On the other hand, their secondary training, like much of their other work in education, has suffered greatly from want of funds, and they have been in many cases merely admitted to derive what benefit they could from the institutions for training elementary teachers.

The Home and Colonial Society had for many years a non-Government department which was opened to secondary as well as elementary mistresses, and since 1895 this has become a separate branch establishment at Highbury, with a secondary practising school attached[1].

The Girls' Public Day School Company[2], after its formation in 1873, saw the need of developing the views of its teachers, and organized several short courses of lectures which they were encouraged to attend[3].

In 1878 the Maria Grey Training College was opened by the Teachers' Training and Registration Society as a non-residential secondary training school for women ; it has since been moved to Brondesbury, and a hostel for residence has just[4] been opened. Its work is divided into three departments, lower, higher, and kindergarten ; but all with a view to training secondary teachers. There is accommodation for fifty or more students, and in May, 1898, there were forty-two.

In 1885 the Cambridge Training College for Women[5] was founded, which requires a year's residence, and St. Hilda's

---

[1] *Education of Girls and Women in Great Britain*, C. S. Bremner : Swan Sonnenschein & Co., 1897, p. 171.

[2] *Vide* p. 160.

[3] For this information and for much other kind help I am indebted to Miss A. J. Cooper.

[4] 1898.

[5] Limited to fifty-two students (*Handbook Victorian Era*, p. 132).

hostel was opened as a training department of the Ladies' College at Cheltenham in the same year[1].

For men an institution was opened in Finsbury in February, 1883[2], but it did not meet with sufficient support, and in October, 1886, the experiment was declared to be over[3]. A Secondary Day Training College was opened by the College of Preceptors in October, 1895, but there has been a great want of candidates, and a reduction of expenditure has been found necessary[4]. A Holiday Course of a general nature for teachers was held under the auspices of the College in January, 1898, and met with great success.

The most valuable and successful developments are, however, those which either commenced for the benefit of both sexes, or beginning on behalf of men subsequently included women in their scope.

In 1871 the College of Preceptors (founded in 1846) instituted systematic courses of lectures on teaching, open to both sexes[5], and made their examination for teachers, which had begun in 1847, far more searching than before in the theory and practice of education, which had been a distinctive feature of the examination from the beginning[6].

The Headmasters' Conference of 1872 represented to the Universities the importance of promoting the professional education of teachers, and has continued at intervals with a rising, though tempered, enthusiasm to press the point.

In 1879 a Teachers' Training Syndicate was accordingly appointed by the Senate at Cambridge. Courses of lectures have been delivered, and certificates of theoretical knowledge and practical efficiency granted on examination since 1880. The examinations are now held in London, Cam-

---

[1] Bremner, p. 173.   [2] *The Educational Times*, 1883, p. 120.
[3] Select Committee on Registration, Q. 2,887.
[4] *Educational Times*, February, 1898, p. 63.
[5] Bryce Report, vol. ii, Supplement, p. 3.
[6] *Educational Times*, 1872, p. 258; *Fifty Years of Progress in Education: a review of the work of the College of Preceptors, 1846–96*, pp. 7, 22.

bridge, Cheltenham, Edinburgh, and Aberystwyth[1]. A similar proposal was made at Oxford in the end of 1878, but was lost by a narrow majority, and nothing was done until 1896.

In 1883 the University of London first held an examination in the Art, Theory and History of Education, coupled with a practical examination in teaching and the management of a class[2]. This Diploma is reserved for graduates, and the practical test is indispensable.

The Secondary Commission reported in 1895 that a course for special preparation was generally desirable for persons intending to be teachers, that it should have both a theoretical and a practical side, and the requisite freedom and variety would best be secured if the Universities undertook the task[3].

In 1895 the University of Durham established a Certificate for Secondary Teachers, the instruction for which is given at Newcastle in connexion with the Training of Elementary Teachers[4].

Provision for secondary teachers is also made in some of the university colleges, chiefly in connexion with the Elementary Day Training Colleges already attached to them.

The University of Oxford in November, 1896, instituted an examination to be held twice a year in subjects bearing on the Theory, History, and Practice of Education for the purpose of granting Diplomas in Education. All arrangements were placed in the charge of the Delegates of Local Examinations, who have further to satisfy themselves of the proficiency of candidates in the Practice of Education. No member of the University may be admitted to examination who has not kept residence for at least seven terms, and the Delegates have imposed conditions on other candidates which ensure an adequate previous education of University standard. Lectures in Method are provided and

---

[1] Calendar, 1898.

[2] By 1898 sixty-seven Teachers' Diplomas had been awarded, of which only fifteen belonged to the first seven years.

[3] i. 200, 322.

[4] Newcastle College Calendar, 1896–97, p. 182.

systematic supervision of practice, while shorter holiday courses on the same lines are held for teachers already following their profession. Satisfactory experience in a secondary school approved by the Delegacy is a necessary condition for a Diploma. The Statute[1] only remains in force until November, 1900, but the success of the measure seems likely to ensure its permanency.

Great care has been taken to require as much practical training as possible, while the standard of theory has not been in any way lowered, and Oxford as yet comes nearest to fulfilling the conditions agreed upon by the Joint Committee representing the chief bodies of Secondary Teachers which made its report in December, 1897[2].

In 1897 Cambridge revised its scheme and developed it in connexion with the Elementary Day Training College.

ii. *Registration of Secondary Teachers.*

Some qualification is presupposed in any official register of teachers, and the establishment of registration has been regarded by many as the best means of raising the standard of this profession.

The College of Preceptors first began to examine teachers in 1847, and assigns the grades of Licentiate, Associate, and Fellow to masters and mistresses alike, the theory and practice of teaching[3] being compulsory subjects in each grade[4]. The College likewise began to agitate for registration of teachers about 1860[5], and has shown great energy and persistence in advocating this course.

The original Endowed Schools Bill[6] contained a provision for the examination and registration of the teachers

---

[1] Tit. VI. iii; Tit. VIII. i. § 5. These must not be confused with the Statute for the Training of Teachers, which relates to the Day Training College for Elementary Teachers.

[2] Published by the Incorporated Association of Headmasters, 37, Norfolk Street, Strand, price 3*d.*

[3] p. 192.   [4] Bryce Report, vol. ii, Supplement, p. 7.

[5] *Fifty Years of Progress*, p. 15.   [6] *Vide* p. 160.

in all such schools, but this was in the second part of the measure which finally was abandoned.

The Select Committee of the House of Commons under Sir W. Hart Dyke, appointed to consider a Teachers' Registration and Organization Bill in 1891 [1], reported that the registration of secondary teachers was in principle desirable; that existing teachers should not be registered as such, but should not be under any legal disability; that existing and future teachers should be admitted to the register on evidence of acquirements and teaching ability. Registration might hereafter be made compulsory on all persons in the event of their appointment to endowed (and ultimately to other secondary) schools. Teachers certified by the Education Department should be placed on the register, but in all cases the nature of the certificate should be therein indicated. Any Council for registration should be composed of nominees of the State, representatives of the Universities, and members elected by the teaching profession.

The Royal Commission on Secondary Education reported that upon no subject was there more general agreement than as to the necessity of some measure for the registration of teachers [2]. They recommended that it should be one of the duties of the proposed Educational Council to keep an alphabetical register of teachers, showing their qualifications and experience. Admission should only be granted on a certificate of general attainments, coupled with a special knowledge of the theory and practice of education. After a certain lapse of time no unregistered person should be appointed to any public or recognized secondary school [3].

A Bill on these lines was introduced in 1896, providing for a Register to be kept by a Council appointed for this purpose: the Crown, the Universities, and all registered teachers appointing six members each. The measure was dropped, but is to be brought forward again by Government in 1899.

[1] P. P., 1891, No. 335, p. iv.　　　　[2] Bryce Report, i. 192.
[3] Ibid. p. 318.

II. SECONDARY EDUCATION.

B. Wales.

EVER since elementary education first received recognition from the State, Wales has always been identified with England in the benefits offered and the obligations imposed. Educational endowments of any sort were few, and unduly favoured the Established Church in a country where the mass of the people were Dissenters. Even the scanty foundations that existed were neglected or abused[1]. But enthusiasm for learning and readiness for self-denial[2] have been very great in Wales, and the limited size of the country has perhaps rendered patriotism more effectual and the development of secondary education more practicable than in England. At all events, Wales obtained in 1889 an Intermediate Education Act, which this country must still regard with envious eyes[3].

The Taunton Commission[4] in 1865 and 1866 found that in Wales there were but thirty-six endowed Grammar Schools with a net annual income of £7,576, educating 1,136 boys, of whom 706 were in classical schools, and only two endowed schools for girls with a gross annual income of £5,435[5]. One hundred and twenty-three other endowments were estimated to apply £2,800 annually to education,

---

[1] Report of Commissioners on the State of Education in Wales, P. P., 1847, xxvii. vol. i. p. 45; ii. pp. 21, 393. *Vide* p. 13.

[2] Lord Aberdare's Departmental Committee Report, 1881, i. p. xxvii.

[3] 'The Working of the Intermediate Act in Wales,' by the Right Hon. A. H. D. Acland, M.P., being chapter iii, part ii, of *Studies in Secondary Education*: Percival and Co., 1892.

[4] *Vide* p. 158.   [5] Taunton Report, vol. xxi. pp. 1, 2.

chiefly primary. Twenty towns, averaging 11,000 inhabitants each, had no grammar school endowments at all [1].

Although a University College was established [2], nothing
was done for secondary schools, until in 1881 a Committee
of the Education Department under Lord Aberdare was
appointed by Government to inquire into the conditions of
intermediate and higher education in Wales, and to make
recommendations. They found that whereas secondary
school accommodation should be provided for 15,700 boys
in Wales [3], the Grammar Schools provided only 2,846 places,
and the actual attendance was only 1,540, while seventy-nine
private schools for boys had only 2,287 in attendance [4]. Only
one-third of the boys were being taught any natural science,
and none were receiving any trade or technical instruction.
Girls had three endowed and 73 private schools, attended
by 265 and 1,871 pupils respectively [5]. The aggregate
income of the endowed schools amounted to £19,588.

The Committee recommended that a local rate or Parliamentary Grant, or both, should be applied; that the
schools receiving help should be undenominational in
character, and the governing bodies popularly chosen. They
insisted on the need of provision for girls, and of exhibitions
for enabling scholars to pass to the higher schools, and also
upon the importance of some organized machinery for the
periodical inspection and supervision of these schools.

But the Legislature was as leisurely as usual, and it was
not before 1889 that the Government's hand was forced
and a private Bill, amended by the Government, was
carried [6].

In the new organization there were two chief factors,
the County Councils, established the year before, and the
Charity Commissioners, acting more especially under the
Endowed Schools Acts. Moreover, the Technical Educa-

---

[1] Taunton Report, vol. i. p. 423.   [2] *Vide* p. 270.
[3] At ten instead of the usual sixteen per 1,000 of the population
(Aberdare Report, i. p. xvi).
[4] Ibid. p. xv.   [5] Ibid. pp. xv, xxv, lx, lxi.
[6] 52 & 53 Vict. c. 40. The Welsh Intermediate Education Act, 1889.

tion Act, with its power for levying a local rate, was passed
in the same year, and the Local Taxation (Customs and
Excise) Act, granting money from the Treasury, followed
the year after[1].

The purpose of the Welsh Act was declared to be to
make provision for the intermediate and technical education
of the inhabitants of Wales and the county of Monmouth[2].

Intermediate education is defined by the Act as 'A
course of education which does not consist chiefly of elementary instruction in reading, writing, and arithmetic, but
which includes instruction in Latin, Greek, the Welsh, and
English language and literature, modern languages, mathematics, natural and applied science, or in some of such
studies, and generally in the higher branches of knowledge.'

In every county and county borough in Wales and in
Monmouthshire a Joint Education Committee was constituted, three members being nominated by the county or
borough council and two by the Lord President of the
Privy Council: any of the Assistant Charity Commissioners
had a right to attend the meetings but not to vote. Each
Committee was required to report to its council, but was not
otherwise subject to its control, except in limitation of rate.

The original powers of the Charity Commission were
suspended, except with the consent of the Education Department; the powers of the Education Committees were
given to them originally for three years, but have been continued by the Expiring Laws Continuance Acts. Their
function is to prepare a scheme or schemes for their own
county, alone or in conjunction with their neighbours,
specifying the local educational endowments which ought to
be employed and recommending, if they chose, to their
council a payment out of the county rate, not exceeding
$\frac{1}{2}d$. in the pound. The scheme is to be submitted to the
Charity Commission, has always been drafted by them, and,

---

[1] *Vide* p. 182.

[2] Monmouthshire is largely Welsh-speaking, and it is claimed as
practically a Welsh county.

if approved, goes forward as if it had been an original scheme under the Endowed Schools Acts. If there is any difference of opinion, the local scheme and that of the Charity Commissioners are both submitted to the Education Department for selection.

The Treasury makes a grant to meet all local contributions, the amount for each county not exceeding in the aggregate the sum payable in pursuance of the Act out of the county rate. The Imperial contribution depends on the efficiency of the schools, as testified by such annual inspection and report as the Treasury may require.

Except in the case of cathedral schools or others excepted from the Endowed Schools Act, 1869, every scheme must provide that no catechism or denominational formulary shall be taught to any day scholars in schools receiving aid, and that times for prayer or religious worship or lesson shall be arranged conveniently for the withdrawal of a day scholar therefrom.

Administration of Schemes. 'The duty of the Joint Education Committee is confined to the framing of schemes; it has no administrative functions. The funds and schools are administered by governing bodies constituted by the several schemes. The only requirement of the Welsh Act, besides those contained in the Endowed Schools Acts with regard to the religious opinions of governors, is to the effect that the County Council is to be " adequately " represented on the governing body of any school receiving aid from it.'

Constitution of Governing Bodies. ' In the county boroughs the scheme is administered by a single governing body. In the counties there is a division of administrative functions between a county governing body and local governing bodies for particular districts or schools. In every county the County Council nominates at least a bare majority of the county governing body, which also contains in every case representatives of some one of the three Welsh University Colleges. The remainder of the body is composed of representatives of the local governing bodies and of co-opted members. The size of the county governing body varies, but is seldom more than thirty or less than twenty members. The local governing body ranges in size from eleven to sixteen members, and generally contains representatives of the County Council, the county governing body, the local government authority, and the elementary schools.'

'On both the county and the local body women are eligible, and in many cases provision is made for ensuring their presence.'

Technical Instruction Acts in Wales [1]. 'In many counties the Joint Education Committee was nominated by the County Council to act also as its committee under the Technical Instruction Acts, with a view to avoid friction, or conflict, or overlapping of schemes. Power is taken in every scheme under the Welsh Act to add to local governing bodies any number of governors required, in order to allow of aid under the Technical Instruction Acts being given to a school [2].'

The harmonious working of the Joint Education Committees was secured in the first instance by the attendance at them all of the same Assistant Charity Commissioner, who thus acted as an informal channel of communication and means of comparison between them [3]. It was found expedient also to organize Conferences of the several Committees, which in turn led to the preparation of a scheme for the establishment of a Central Welsh Board for Intermediate Education ; to provide, along with some minor matters, for the examination and inspection of all intermediate schools regulated by schemes under the Act [4].

The work of schools and instruction given to adults, even when it is of a secondary nature, are regarded as different [5] in

---

[1] The Technical Instruction Acts apply to Wales and Monmouthshire as well as to England, and have been put into force side by side with the Welsh Intermediate Education Act.

[2] Bryce Report, v. pp. 50–51.

[3] Report of Elgin Committee, Scotland : P. P., 1892, xli, Q. 692, Q. 704, Q. 706.

[4] Bryce Report, v. 51.   [5] *Education*, July 9, 1898, p. 16.

kind, and superintended generally by different county committees.

In 1892 the Lords of the Treasury published regulations as to the inspection and examination of these schools, sanctioning the conduct of them by such a Board, which, however, could not enter upon its functions before 1897.

Inspection in the meantime was conducted by Assistant Charity Commissioners, and examinations were held by various persons and bodies selected by the governors and approved by the Charity Commission.

	Schools inspected and examined.	Number of boys.	of girls.
1895	30	1,164	644
1896	47	1,913	1,484

In 1897 the Central Welsh Board for the Inspection and Examination of County Schools examined eighty schools, containing 6,427 children [1], employing one Chief and one temporary Inspector for the purpose. The examination of pupils for certificates has been deferred till 1899.

'There are now in Wales ninety-five secondary public schools, of which nine only are not regulated by schemes under an Act ; while of the other eighty-six, sixty-nine are altogether newly founded under the Welsh Act of 1889.' Of these eighty-six county schools, nineteen are for boys only and nineteen for girls only, forty-two are dual, and six are mixed schools [2].'

Fifty-nine of these schools had in 1897 an attendance of about 5,000 pupils, who paid about £22,000 in fees, in addition to the general income of £43,019 [3].

The whole public income of the Principality for secondary and technical education amounted in 1897 to about £92,000, £38,000 being Customs and Excise money under the Act of 1890, £20,000 was raised by rates under the

---

[1] As against 3,367 in 1896.

[2] *The Record of Technical and Secondary Education*, 1898, pp. 77, 159 ; Charity Commission, Forty-fifth Report, p. 24.

[3] *The Record*, ibid. p. 77.

Technical Instruction Acts, and the remaining £34,000 was produced in equal moieties by rates under the Welsh Act of 1889 and by the corresponding contribution from the Central Government[1].

The Science and Art Department offers its grants to Wales on the same terms as to England.

Training of Secondary Teachers. Wales has not failed to pay attention to this important point. The three University Colleges all make provision for training secondary teachers, in addition to normal Departments for elementary teachers. Bangor and Cardiff require them to be graduates, or at any rate to possess a really high qualification. At Bangor the practice is in the County Council Schools.

[1] *The Record*, ibid. p. 70.

II. SECONDARY EDUCATION.

C. Ireland.

1. THE COMMISSIONERS OF CHARITABLE DONATIONS AND BEQUESTS.

2. THE COMMISSIONERS OF EDUCATION IN IRELAND.

3. THE EDUCATIONAL ENDOWMENTS COMMISSIONERS.

THE history of Irish Secondary Education is a record of poverty, of abused endowments, and of numerous inquiries preceding tardy reform. There was very much less proselytism than in the elementary schools, but the chief benefits of the endowments were secured to the Protestants, who, after all, had founded them.

There is no doubt but that the present provision is very inadequate ; but Ireland is so poor a country that less secondary education is possible for it at present than would appear from a superficial comparison with its neighbours. The religious question has been avoided rather than settled ; and beyond a rectification of endowments little has been done as yet except the establishment of an independent Government Examination Board, which applies its tests to all or any persons applying to it, and remunerates the teachers in accordance with the results.

Diocesan Free Schools. In 1570 an Irish Act of Parliament[1] was passed for the foundation of a free school in every diocese in Ireland at the cost of each diocese, with an income to be provided—one-third by the ordinaries, and two-thirds by the other ecclesiastical persons in the diocese.

[1] 12 Eliz. (first session), c. 1.

Royal Free Schools. In 1608 James I ordered a Royal Free School to be founded in each of six of the counties of Ulster, and he and his successor assigned lands for the support of these and several other schools founded by them [1].

The Act of William III, prohibiting Catholic education in Ireland [2], contained a provision for enforcing the Act of Elizabeth, describing her foundations as 'publick Latin free schools'; but neither the original nor the supplementary Act was ever carried out to the full extent.

Such of the Diocesan and Royal Free Schools as were established were [3] of the class known in England as Grammar Schools. There was no intention of excluding Catholics from the benefits offered [4], and some of the scholars at any rate were to be admitted free of charge [5], but the latter provision was much neglected, and in practice almost all the pupils seem to have been Protestants [6].

During the seventeenth and eighteenth centuries there were various grammar schools founded in Ireland by private benefactors [7], the best known being the three Erasmus Smith Schools [8]; but the total provision for secondary education was very inadequate, and the majority of the existing schools were reported by the successive Commissions to be in a very inefficient state.

The Commissioners of 1791 [9] found that there was a sum of £7,600 [10] spent upon forty-six grammar schools of public or private foundation, educating in all 1,214 pupils. They reported, however, that neither the Diocesan nor the Royal Free Schools had answered the intentions of the founders [11],

---

[1] Kildare Report, i. pp. 7–10.

[2] Irish Act, 7 Will. III, c. 4, s. x; *vide* p. 80.

[3] Carysfort has become since 1812 an 'English' primary school, and admits girls (Kildare Report, i. pp. 9, 121).

[4] Ibid. pp. 30, 53.   [5] Ibid. pp. 30, 52.

[6] Ibid. pp. 30, 56, 59, 61.   [7] Ibid. p. 14.

[8] Ennis, the fourth, was founded 1773 (ibid. pp. 10, 11, 65).

[9] *Vide* p. 81.

[10] Kildare, iii. pp. 370–378. Allotting £850 of the Erasmus Smith endowment to secondary education.   [11] Kildare, iii. p. 364.

and recommended that an unpaid Board of Control should be established for all endowed schools, with a summary jurisdiction for their improvement [1].

In 1806 there were seven Royal Free Schools and only thirteen Diocesan Schools in existence [2].

Commissioners of Charitable Donations and Bequests. There was a sort of standing Charity Commission in Ireland in the last century, being a Select Committee of the Irish House of Lords appointed annually from 1763 to take into consideration the several charities and charitable donations in this kingdom, and to prevent their concealment or misapplication. In the year of the Union, 1800, their duties were by an Irish Act [3] entrusted to a new corporate body entitled the Commissioners of Charitable Donations and Bequests, and consisting of the prelates of the Irish Church, the Irish judges, the Provost of Trinity, the incumbents of the Dublin parishes and two other clergymen, and these Commissioners received power to sue for the recovery of charitable donations, and to apply property *cy près* [4].

The composition of the Board does not look well for its efficiency, and cases of gross neglect and mismanagement occurred [5], though I cannot find that it was ever the subject of an inquiry. It lasted, however, nearly half a century, and when it was reformed, sectarian difficulties rather than its past inactivity seem to have caused most concern to the House of Commons [6].

In 1844, by 7 & 8 Vict. c. 97, this Board was reconstituted and composed of three judges and ten members nominated by the Crown, of whom five were to be Catholics; the power of *cy près* application was withdrawn, and power given to hold lands in trust for Catholic priests in Ireland. In 1858 the endowments in their hands produced an income

---

[1] Kildare Report, iii. p. 365. One of their conclusions was that large salaries to schoolmasters are generally ruinous to schools (p. 347).

[2] First and Fourth Reports.　　　[3] 40 Geo. III, c. 75.

[4] Kildare Report, i. p. 104; *cy près* = to kindred purposes.

[5] Ibid. i. p. 105.　　　[6] Hansard, T. S., lxxvi. 1,538, &c.

of £2,461 mainly applicable to education, primary or secondary[1].

Board of Commissioners of Education in Ireland. In 1813 the Board of Commissioners of Education in Ireland was created by 53 Geo. III, c. 107, a measure introduced by the elder Sir Robert Peel. It consisted of two Judges, three Protestant Archbishops, four Bishops, the Provost of Trinity, and four members nominated by the Lord-Lieutenant. All the members were unpaid, and there was no religious restriction as to the nominated members. All endowed schools in Ireland were placed under their charge, except the Erasmus Smith Schools, the Charter Schools, the Parish Schools, and schools with visitors appointed by Charter or Statute, or schools of private foundation intended for the education of persons not belonging to the Church of Ireland. It was declared lawful to form several dioceses into one district for the purpose of consolidating the diocesan schools.

The Royal School estates were vested in them, and the Court of Chancery might transfer to them the funds of other schools in their charge; they were empowered by themselves or deputy to visit all these schools and make orders for their management, and they had stringent statutable powers of inquiry; but their right to incur expenditure under these heads was very ill defined.

In 1822[2] two nominated and four *ex-officio* members were added to the Board, and the power of the Commissioners was extended over schools of private foundation endowed after 1813.

In 1824 the Commissioners exercised their powers and consolidated twenty-nine dioceses into thirteen districts for Diocesan schools, five dioceses only remaining separate[3].

In 1828 and 1834 they founded exhibitions at Trinity

---

[1] Kildare Report, i. p. 105. Their powers have been extended by 30 & 31 Vict. c. 54, and 34 & 35 Vict. c. 102, but remain more limited than those of the English Charity Commissioners.

[2] 3 Geo. IV, c. 79.　　　　　　　　　[3] Kildare Report, i. p. 28.

College, Dublin, for four of the Royal Free Schools out of their surplus funds [1], and with that the activity of the Board seems to have ended.

It was hardly to be expected that a large body of Commissioners, some of them members *ex officio*, some non-resident in Ireland, most of them with important public duties, and none of them paid for their services, should have spent much time or trouble over matters in which their duties and powers were seriously questioned [2]. At any rate, during the first three quarters of their eighty years of unreformed existence they seem to have given an average attendance of three or four members at their infrequent meetings [3], to have managed the estates rather than the schools [4], to have done that badly [5], to have acted with great want of uniformity [6], and not even to have taken care of the deeds relating to the endowments under their care [7].

The Commissions of 1806–12 and 1823–27, and the Select Committee of 1828 [8] limited their general recommendations to primary education, although the Commissioners had reported in detail on some or all of the endowed secondary schools.

In 1806 there were thirty-three endowed Classical Schools of public foundation (including the Erasmus Smith grammar schools) educating nearly 1,000 pupils, chiefly boarders, and possessing endowments worth about £9,000 a year [9]; and there seem to have been in 1809–12 eleven grammar schools out of fifteen private foundations educating some 420 boys [10].

Mr. Wyse's Select Committees of 1835–38 [11] reported on the Diocesan and Royal Schools and other schools of public

---

[1] Kildare Report, p. i. 53.   [2] Rosse Report, i. p. 12.
[3] Kildare, i. p. 245; Rosse, i. p. 8.
[4] Wyse, Select Committee, 1838, p. 63.
[5] Kildare, i. 242; Rosse, i. 22.   [6] Ibid.
[7] Kildare, i. 243; Rosse, i. 14.   [8] *Vide* pp. 81, 86.
[9] Fourteenth Report, p. 4. The figures on p 2 give 1,065 pupils (less Carysfort, 12–50) and £7,620 income.
[10] Twelfth Report, 1812; Second Report, 1807.   [11] *Vide* p. 102.

foundation, and drew up a scheme of secondary and higher education not less remarkable or extensive than their proposals for elementary instruction. There were to be in every county an Academy, and a Provincial College and an Agricultural School in each of the four provinces. This system was to utilize the existing secondary endowed schools: these were to be enlarged and made applicable to both commercial and classical education in general and special literary and scientific courses, and thus adapted to the needs both of the middle and upper classes[1].

The Board of Commissioners of 1813 was to be amalgamated with the National Board as a central authority, and the Grand Juries (or Town Councils when chosen by election, and afterwards 'County Boards or County Councils') were to be the local authorities for secondary education and levy local rates[2].

A Normal School was to be preferred to a general University training for secondary teachers, but a Chair of Education in the University and a Course of the Science of Education were recommended[3].

Reform of Endowments. In 1854 a Royal Commission was appointed under the Marquis of Kildare to inquire into the Endowed Schools in Ireland, and their report in four volumes was presented in 1858.

They found fifty-two endowed grammar schools with an estimated annual income of £14,954, and two superior English schools with an income of £498; but no less than ninety-one towns, which in the census of 1851 had contained over 2,000 inhabitants apiece, had to rely solely on private enterprise or subscriptions for their secondary education[4].

Of the nineteen Diocesan Free Schools in existence only six were in a satisfactory state, with 196 out of a total of 240 pupils[5]; while four out of the six Royal Free Schools educated 221 pupils out of 277[6].

---

[1] Wyse Report, pp. 64–77.　　[2] Ibid. 70, 76.　　[3] Ibid. p. 41.
[4] Kildare Report, i. Appendix, 55, 56.　　[5] Ibid., Report, p. 45.
[6] Ibid. i. p. 63: allowing fifty boys for Armagh.

The Commissioners found that in many places the National Schools had displaced teachers who had given secondary as well as elementary instruction [1], and that there was great need of more means of intermediate education, which ought, they reported, to be provided by local funds under the management of local trustees in combination with grants of public money [2].

They recommended that in place of the Commissioners of Education a Board should be established to control endowments not exclusively confined to one sect ; that it should consist of persons of different religious persuasions, and include at least one paid Commissioner [3].   Schools earning a grant must give united literary education to persons of all persuasions [4].   This last recommendation lost the Commissioners one signature to the Report, which was only signed by three out of five members.

Nothing was done in furtherance of this Report, but throughout the seventies the Commissioners of Education continued in their annual reports to demand reform in their constitution and an increase of their powers.   The Dis-establishment of the Irish Church gradually deprived them of some of their episcopal members, and as no provision was made for the future support of the Diocesan Schools after the termination of life interests, these gradually became extinct, and their funds fell into the hands of the Church Temporalities Commissioners [5].

Rosse Commission.   In December, 1878, a Vice-Regal Commission was appointed under Lord Rosse to inquire into the Endowed Schools of Ireland, and reported in 1880. They drew more attention to the conservative nature of secondary education in Ireland than to the deficient amount of it, but did not consider themselves instructed to offer any recommendations.

---

[1] Kildare Report, i. p. 222 ; Powis, i. 501.   [2] Kildare Report, i. p. 222.
[2] Ibid. p. 246.   [4] Ibid. p. 223.
[5] *Vide* p. 104.   By 1880 only three schools survived, the masters of the remaining eleven having compounded their life interests (Rosse Report, i. 46, 47).

'The want of more extensive provisions for practical and technical training, and of an education adapted to prepare pupils for commercial life and other pursuits not calling for classical study, has been much felt.'

'The course of discipline and instruction in the larger Grammar Schools in most cases is satisfactory,' but 'many of the smaller local endowments (especially for higher education) have proved inadequate[1].'

The Commissioners criticised 'the marked and most injurious absence of system, vigour, and efficiency in the discharge of the functions committed to the Board of Education[2],' and the inadequacy of their powers.

Difficulties existed in dealing with endowments formerly vested in persons or bodies affected by the Disestablishment of the Irish Church, and in all cases there was a great want of summary powers for the control of educational endowments.

Educational Endowments Act. At last, in 1885, the Educational Endowments (Ireland) Act was passed (48 & 49 Vict. c. 78), corresponding more or less to the English Endowed Schools Act of 1869, and very closely to the Scotch Educational Endowments Act of 1882[3].

Two Judges of the Irish Supreme Court were appointed Judicial Commissioners, and with them were associated three paid Assistant Commissioners, 'persons of experience in education.' The Commission was to last till the end of 1888, but was ultimately continued till April, 1893[4]. Dublin University and Trinity College, all endowments for theological instruction, and all foundations for the exclusive benefit of persons of any particular religious denomination and under exclusive control of such denominations, were not to be dealt with by the Commissioners unless with the consent of the founder or governing body.

The chief duty of the Commissioners was to draft schemes for the future government and management of educational

---

[1] Rosse Report, i. 229.
[2] Ibid. p. 25.
[3] *Vide* p. 236.
[4] 54 & 55 Vict. c. 60.

endowments, and these were submitted to the Lord Lieutenant in Council, and were subject to the same course of publications, petitions, appeals, and submission to Parliament as similar English proposals under the Endowed Schools Act. But the only remedy in case of default by a governing body in carrying out a scheme was by summary compulsion of the High Court on the application of the Attorney-General.

Vested interests were carefully guarded, but in all schemes due regard was to be paid 'to merit as ascertained by examination' or other means; and benefits of endowments were, as far as possible, to be extended to both sexes. Inspection of all endowed schools by an inspector appointed by the Lord Lieutenant and due audit of accounts were to be provided for in all schemes, and due provision might be made for future alterations of schemes from time to time by the Commissioners of Charitable Bequests.

Two hundred and twelve schemes were submitted to the Lord Lieutenant, dealing with an estimated income from endowments of £67,385[1], and most of these were passed, including several made with the consent of the governors: but several others, including a scheme for the Erasmus Smith schools, were abandoned owing to diversity of opinions, and no ready means of dealing with them is in existence since the termination of the Commission[2].

Among the schemes framed by the Commissioners was one for the reform of the Board of Commissioners of Education in Ireland, which was made with the consent of that body, and finally approved by the Viceroy in May, 1891[3].

In future there are to be twenty Commissioners: ten appointed by the Lord Lieutenant and holding office during his pleasure—five being Protestant and five Catholic resident in Ireland—and .ten persons elected by the ten new local Boards of Education.

[1] In addition to private income from fees, subscriptions, &c., of £73,601 (Final Report, 1894, C. 7,517, p. xxiii).

[2] A Bill introduced by Mr. Healy in 1897 fell through.

[3] Annual Report of Educational Endowments Commissioners for 1890–91, p. 234.

The Commissioners are to possess and exercise all the powers possessed by their predecessors, to hold and manage the estates, to pay an inspector appointed by the Lord Lieutenant who must inspect all schools in their charge at least once a year; but nearly all the management of the schools is left to the local Boards.

Of these there are ten, all in Ulster, according to the situation of the principal endowments dealt with, the districts being Armagh, Tyrone, Fermanagh, Cavan, and Donegal [1]. For each of these there are a Protestant and a Roman Catholic Board, consisting of nine members each, but the number may be increased to fifteen by co-optation on the vote of a majority of seven. The first Boards were nominated in the scheme, but after that the Protestant Boards have been elected annually in fixed proportions (varying according to the locality) by the Diocesan (Episcopal) Councils, the General Assembly (Presbyterian), and, in two cases, by the Methodist Conference: in three cases the Boards co-opt a member representing other Protestant denominations [2].

Each Catholic Board consists of a prelate, four ecclesiastics, and four laymen, and upon a vacancy occurring by death, resignation, or failure to attend it is filled by co-optation among the ecclesiastics and laymen respectively.

The Boards establish or maintain such school or schools in their separate districts as they think expedient, administer the endowments, hold property bequeathed to or vested in them, exercise general supervision and control over the schools, and make all necessary regulations for them; the two Boards in each district appoint an Estates Committee from among themselves, to advise and assist the Commissioners. They promote intermediate education in their district generally, and elect annually a Commissioner who need not belong to their Board.

They also administer a special scheme for the Ulster Royal Foundations [3] (for the Royal Free Schools) which have

---

[1] Report for 1890-91, pp. 211-241.　　　[2] Ibid.　　　[3] Ibid. 211.

been divided between the Protestants and Catholics. The income of these schools, however, has been greatly reduced by agricultural depression.

&Superior Schools' in Ireland according to the Census[1].

	Establishments.	Pupils.
1861 . . .	729	21,674
1871 . . .	574	21,225
1881 . . .	488	20,405
1891 . . .	474	24,271

4. THE COMMISSIONERS OF NATIONAL EDUCATION.

The Commissioners of National Education in their fourth Report, published in 1837, announced a future division of their schools into primary and secondary, the latter to afford manual training ; but of course money was never forthcoming to develop this scheme, and it was dropped.

In 1867 a plan was approved by the Board for the introduction of Classics and French into the National Schools, but there was a delay in making pecuniary arrangements[2].

The Powis Commission on Primary Education in 1870 recommended that the course of education in Primary Schools should not be extended to secondary or intermediate subjects, but that Masters of Primary Schools should be freely allowed to teach as extra branches out of school hours any subjects in which they might have qualified themselves. The lessons must be regarded as private tuition, to be paid for by the parents or friends of the pupils who received them[3]. Endowed schools should be revised and provision made for admission of promising pupils by open competition into superior schools without distinction of locality or creed[4].

This last article, however, only obtained the assent of eight of the fourteen Commissioners.

In 1873 the recommendation to introduce higher subjects

---

[1] P. P., 1892, C. 6,780, p. 64.
[2] Powis Report, i. 189.
[3] Ibid. Art. 120, 121.
[4] Ibid. Art. 122.

out of school hours was carried out, and grants were given for three years' courses of Classics, German, French or Irish, and for a number of subjects in Science [1].

The Model Schools of the Board [2] give a definitely higher education than the ordinary National Schools, but, as we have seen [3], there is a strong Catholic feeling against them in spite of their educational merits.

5. THE PRIVY COUNCIL.

The Science and Art Department.

In the matter of grants, Ireland has always shared the bounty of the Science and Art Department on the same terms as Great Britain.

In 1868 the Government proposed to form a separate Department for Ireland analogous to the existing Science and Art Department in London, but a Commission of the Committee of Council for Education reported unanimously in the following year that such a step would be detrimental to the interests of Science and Art in Ireland. The Science schools and classes in that country were declared to be most successful, but the absence of industrial opportunity was a great discouragement to instruction of artisans in drawing or design [4].

The Technical Instruction Act, 1889, applies to Ireland, but the money granted by the Local Taxation (Customs and Excise) Act, 1890 [5], to Ireland is not applicable to technical education [6]. The Science and Art Department, which in the other countries has withdrawn its grants from subjects which can be encouraged out of this fund by the local authorities in Ireland, promised in 1891 £500 for this purpose, and has subsequently given grants equal in amount to the contributions made by local authorities out of the

---

[1] P. P., 1874, xix. p. 120.   [2] *Vide* p. 94.   [3] *Vide* p. 95.
[4] Report of Commission on Science and Art Department in Ireland, 1869. i. pp. xxxi, xxxiv.
[5] *Vide* p. 182.   [6] *Vide* p. 217.

rates under the Technical Instruction Acts. The amount so granted in 1896 was £2,422 [1], and the total expenditure under the Technical Instruction Acts and the Public Libraries Acts was £4,399 [2].

The total amount of results fees earned in Ireland under the Science and Art Department fell from £8,875 in 1890 to £4,870 in 1 97 [3].

TESTS OF SECONDARY INSTRUCTION.

1. *Middle Class Examinations.*

In 1858, after the institution of the Universities' Local Examinations in England, Dublin University considered favourably a similar proposal [4], but nothing came of it; and it was the Queen's University which established 'Middle Class Examinations' in Ireland in January, 1860, with the assent of the Lord Lieutenant [5]. There were senior and junior divisions for persons who were not members of the University, and in the former the title of Associate in Arts was given [6].

They seem never to have attained any importance, but only died with the Queen's University [7].

2. *The Commissioners of Intermediate Education.*

The national system of elementary schools had, as we have seen [8], actually diminished the available amount of secondary instruction in Ireland. In 1878, of every 100,000 persons in Scotland 371 were receiving education in the endowed intermediate schools; of every 100,000 Protestants in Ireland 199 were receiving a similar secondary training; but of every 100,000 Catholics in the same country

---

[1] Science and Art Department Report for 1896, App. p. 4.
[2] Ibid., Calendar for 1898, p. xxxix.
[3] Report of Committee of Royal Dublin Society, 1898; vide *Education*, 1898, p. 19.
[4] T. D. Acland, *Some account*, &c., p. vii.
[5] P. P., 1861, vol. xx. p. 816.
[6] Ibid., 1870, xxvi. 405.   [7] *Vide* p. 283.   [8] *Vide* p. 209.

only two were being educated in the endowed secondary schools[1].   If secondary education needed assistance in Ireland, and concurrent endowment was admitted to be out of the question, the only feasible course was to omit religious instruction from the scheme, provide against proselytism, and subsidise the best secular training.   Accordingly the Intermediate Education (Ireland) Act[2] was passed in 1878, offering public examinations in secondary subjects to any persons presenting themselves who have been educated in Ireland during the twelve months preceding, and— in addition to a number of prizes and scholarships given to the scholars themselves—making payments for the results to the managers of the schools where those pupils were being educated.

An unpaid Board of Commissioners of Intermediate Education was appointed to administer the annual interest of £1,000,000 paid to them from the funds of the disestablished Irish Church.

Examiners are appointed annually from a list prepared by the Board and approved by the Lord Lieutenant; written examinations are held once a year at centres selected by the Board.   The examinations last for two weeks, and include Latin, Greek, modern languages and Celtic, drawing, mathematics, science, and commercial subjects.   There are four classes—Seniors under eighteen, Middle under seventeen, Junior under sixteen, and since 1892 Preparatory between twelve and fourteen.   Since 1890 candidates under twelve have not been admitted.

The Conscience Clause is as follows: 'No payment is made to any school unless the rule is strictly observed that no pupil attending is permitted to remain in attendance during the time of any religious instruction which the parents or guardians of such pupil shall not have sanctioned, and that the time for giving such religious instruction is so fixed that no pupil not remaining in attendance is excluded directly or indirectly from the advantages of the secular education given in the school.'

[1] Hansard, T. S., ccxli. p. 436.   [2] 41 & 42 Vict. c. 66.

The examinations at once became as great a success in point of numbers as could well be expected : difficulties were chiefly financial, as the £1,000,000 originally allotted had been intended for boys only [1].   Nowhere—not even at South Kensington—do grant-earning and competition seem to have been pushed to such extremes.   Not only do the pupils compete for large money prizes, but all the secondary schools are in self-defence compelled to make the best appearance possible in these universal lists [2].

It was originally intended that the two Assistant Commissioners should pay occasional visits of inspection to the Intermediate Schools, but this has not proved feasible [3].

By the Local Taxation (Customs and Excise) Act, 1890 [4], after a sum of £78,000 had been paid to the Commissioners of National Education [5], the residue of the Irish share was assigned to the Commissioners of Intermediate Education for results fees or prizes, exhibitions, and certificates to be distributed according to a scheme which should be settled by the Board with the approval of the Lord Lieutenant and the Treasury.

The money was spent in adding examinations in a commercial course for the middle and lower grades, and in a preparatory grade for students between twelve and fourteen. The new course includes book-keeping, commercial history and geography, foreign weights and currencies, and commercial terms in foreign languages.

The new course and new grade came fully into effect in 1892.

The decline in numbers of candidates taking Physics and Chemistry since 1891 has been the subject of an inquiry by a Committee of the Royal Dublin Society.   The former fell from 1790 to 596, the latter 1095 to 312 [6].

On May 30, 1898, a Vice-Regal Commission of seven

---

[1] Report for 1880, p. 6.
[2] *Westminster Review*, Nov., 1897 ; March, 1898 : Rev. A. Murphy.
[3] Childers Committee Report, 1884, Q. 935.
[4] 53 & 54 Vict. c. 60.   [5] *Vide* p. 111.
[6] *Journal of Education*, 1898, p. 378.

members was appointed, Chief Baron Palles being Chairman, to inquire into and report on the system of Intermediate Education in Ireland and its practical working; as to whether any reforms or alterations are desirable, and, if so, whether further legislation is necessary. The Commission should be familiar with its subject and prompt in its judgment, for it consists exclusively of the seven members of the Board whose work it is reviewing.

Intermediate Examinations.

	Boys.			Girls.					
	Examined.	*Passed.*	*Percentage of Passes.*	*Examined.*	*Passed.*	*Percentage of Passes.*	*Centres.*	*Localities.*	*Amount paid in results fees.*
1880	4,114	2,899	70·4	1,447	1,111	76·7	128	52	£9,681
1890[1]	3,943	2,333	59·1	1,293	767	59·3	150	65	£8,875
1897	6,661	4,134	62·1	2,216	1,404	63·3	263	99	£48,870

TRAINING OF SECONDARY TEACHERS.

The first provision to secure this end in Ireland was an examination in the University of Dublin in the History and Theory of Education, and also an examination in the Practice of Teaching. It is open only to graduates, who must pass the former of these tests, for which a certificate is awarded, before they can be admitted to the latter. For those who have passed both there is a diploma. No provision for lectures or a course of instruction seems to have been made. The first examination was held in January, 1898, when three candidates, all English teachers, presented themselves.

A statute of the Royal University creating a Diploma in Teaching for graduates of the University was approved in March, 1898[2].

---

[1] More stringent rules came into force, and children under twelve were excluded.

[2] P. P., C. 8,846.

II. SECONDARY EDUCATION.

D. Scotland.

1. THE PRIVY COUNCIL.

i. *The Scotch Education Department.*

WE have seen already in dealing with Scotland that the lines of division in Public Education were laid rather according to localities than to grades of instruction: that so far as systematic provision had been made, the town children, young and old, had been taught in the burgh schools or Academies [1], and the country children in the schools of the parishes.

When the Assistant Commissioners of the Argyll Commission came in 1866 to investigate the Scotch secondary schools they found eighty-two public schools of all sorts existing within seventy-six burghs, three burghs only having no public schools.

> Of these 32 were Burgh Schools,
> 23   „   Academies,
> 9   „   Mixed Burgh and Parochial Schools,
> 18   „   Parochial Schools [2].

And there were four public secondary schools outside the limits of burghs, one of which, Glenalmond, was a reproduction of an English 'Public School [3].' Of these eighty-six schools there were, besides Glenalmond, only five in all Scotland, two in Edinburgh, and three in Aberdeen to which the designation of secondary school was strictly applicable [4], for all the others presented 'a con-

---

[1] *Vide* p. 131 : and in Sessional (Church) and small private schools.
[2] Third Report, i. p. lxxvii.   [3] Ibid. i. 258; ii. 241.   [4] Ibid. i. 110.

fusion of Infant, Primary, and Elementary Schools combined in one [1].'

Less than half of the preparation for the Universities, however, was in the hands of the Burgh Schools and Academies. The figures obtained for the Argyll Commission from the Universities showed that at Edinburgh, Glasgow, St. Andrews, and Aberdeen only 35, 46, 47, and 47 per cent. respectively of the students had been educated at Burgh and Middle Class Schools, the remainder coming from parochial schools (about 15 per cent.) or Free Church Schools, or having been educated either out of Scotland or by private means [2].

Burgh Schools. On the whole, however, although mixed instruction was given in both cases, as elementary education was represented by the parish schools, so the burgh schools and academies stood for secondary education in Scotland.

The characteristic marks of a burgh school were that although it might be supported either out of burgh funds or by endowment, it was subject to regulation by the authorities of the burgh as such, and under that regulation it was open to the community [2].

The Presbyteries claimed and generally exercised a jurisdiction over the Burgh Schools until 1861, when it was abolished by 24 & 25 Vict. c. 107, just after it had been established before the Court of Session [3].

Burgh schools dated back to periods before the Reformation, but it is interesting to note that although recognized in Statute, they were never endowed or organized by any enactment [4]. So far as a nation wants schools, it will have them, and the means matter but little.

Academies. The chief elements, rival or complementary, to Burgh Schools in Scotch secondary education were supplied by the Academies and the Universities.

---

[1] Third Report, i. 146.   [2] Opinion of Counsel, ibid. p. 229.
[3] *History of the Burgh Schools of Scotland*, p. 93, by James Grant, M.A.: W. Collins, Sons, & Co., London and Glasgow, 1876.
[4] Ibid. 462.

'About the middle of last century there arose a cry for a more liberal and more practical course of education than that supplied by the old burgh schools, where the neglect or omission of the commercial branches was felt to be a great evil—an evil which the burgesses and others interested in education endeavoured to remove by introducing science classes into the schools. At first in some academies this branch alone was taught, but in a short time they lost their original characteristics, became in fact grammar schools with this difference, that the new schools, designated academies, had a more practical course of studies, more commodious buildings, better staff of teachers, better organization, and generally a new body of patrons. Though at first the academies were intended merely to supplement the grammar schools, in a short time they superseded or absorbed them ; and, in a few instances, instead of amalgamating with them became their rivals[1].'

The academies in most instances were ultimately under the combined management of proprietors and the Town Councils[2].

When we come to the Universities we find that the task of preparation for them had been imperfectly accomplished, and that they were compelled to undertake a large measure of education which did not rise above secondary. Statistics collected in 1866 show that of 862 students in senior and junior classes in the four Universities,

7 per cent. were	15 years of age or less		
15 ,,	,, 16	,,	,,
16 ,,	,, 17	,,	,,
13 ,,	,, 18	,,	,,

whereas the usual age of matriculation at Oxford was between eighteen and nineteen[3]. Youth does not necessarily disqualify well-taught boys from attaining to higher education : but the Junior Greek Class at the Universities used to begin with the Greek alphabet, while in Mathematics

---

[1] J. Grant, p. 114.   [2] Ibid. p. 127.

[3] Argyll Third Report, i. pp. 246, 157.

it was but little better [1]; and as long as there was no entrance examination for students proceeding to degrees, there is no doubt but that there was a good deal of overlapping of university and school teaching [2].

It must also be noted that very many of the children of the upper classes are, as in the case of Ireland, sent to English schools for their education.

The Scotch secondary schools differed among themselves and also differed from the English schools generally in their relation to a standard curriculum and the advancement of classes.

In some cases there was no settled curriculum : different masters taught kindred subjects, and competition arose between the teachers [3].

In other cases there was a course, but it was not imperative : some subjects were optional and were taught at extra charge [4].

In the third class of schools there was a regular course, which lasted four years, through which all boys who entered in the same year were conducted by the same master. At the end of each year, the whole class was promoted, and the master went up along with them. At the end of the fourth year the class was handed over to the Rector, or Headmaster (who might have little or no control over the other teachers), and the master began another four years' course with the new boys [5].

The hours were usually very long. In 1866 a boy at a Scotch Day School had 1980 hours of lessons during the year, as against the 1110 hours of Rugby, a normal English Public School [6].

The system went on without interference or investigation of any sort until 1866, when both Scotland and England were at work inquiring into their secondary schools.

[1] Report of first Scotch Universities Commission, 1830, pp. 28, 31.
[2] Argyll Third Report, p. 150; Fearon, Taunton Report, vi. p. 31.
[3] Argyll Third Report, p. 99.					[4] Ibid. p. 101.
[5] Ibid. p. 102; Fearon, p. 24.		[6] Argyll Third Report, p. 87.

The Assistant Commissioners of the Argyll Commission [1] found 15,946 pupils in 70 secondary schools, and estimated that these numbers represented the children of about two-thirds of the middle-class population of Scotland [2]. They also reported as to the quality of 210 Departments of secondary schools which they had examined.

	Good and Fair.	Indifferent.	Bad.
Classics . .	54 per cent.	31 per cent.	15 per cent.
English . .	58 ,,	33 ,,	9 ,,
Mathematics .	56 ,,	33 ,,	11 ,,
Modern Languages	37 ,,	41 ,,	22 [3] ,,

On the whole they considered secondary education in Scotland to be in a satisfactory condition, though requiring and capable of amendment [4]. They saw that if the Parochial schools were to be subject to the Revised Code and were bribed to devote all their energies to the barest rudimentary teaching, secondary education would need increased support, and they recommended the foundation of efficient District or Supplementary schools and the establishment of bursaries or scholarships to these schools and to the Universities [5]. 'The number of distinguished men who have risen up in Scotland through these schools and our Universities has long been the glory of this country and the wonder and envy of other countries, and it would be a matter of infinite regret if this national feature were to be obliterated [6].'

The Commissioners, however, did not think it necessary to adopt this recommendation, but contented themselves with advising grants for the buildings and repairs of Burgh schools, and special grants to Parochial schools which were discharging the functions of secondary schools [7]. They also reported in favour of an annual inspection of the teaching and buildings of all Burgh schools by one of H. M. Inspectors of Schools [8].

[1] *Vide* p. 136.   [2] Third Argyll Report, p. vii.   [3] Ibid. p. lxxiv.
[4] Ibid. p. xviii.   [5] Ibid. p. 146.   [6] Ibid.
[7] Ibid. p. xxvi.   [8] Ibid.

In 1866 the Taunton Commission sent Mr. Fearon as Assistant Commissioner to institute a comparison between the Middle Class Schools in England and Scotland. He was immensely struck with the educational zeal and sympathy of the public and the good attendance at the burgh schools [1].

He found, for example, 390 children attending as day scholars at the burgh school of Ayr, 'a town with less than the population of Reading or Canterbury [2].' 'Where in England could we produce such an example of interest and confidence in a public school among the middle classes of our rural population [3] ? '

He dwells on the ardour of the Scotch teacher, 'with the dignity of a ruler in his gestures and the fire of an enthusiast in his eye,' and draws a lively contrast between an endowed English grammar school at its afternoon lessons and a Scotch burgh school [4].

He notes, however, that few of the schools would rank in respect to the age of the pupils as more than second grade secondary schools [5], and that superior education had been almost extinguished in Scotland for the sake of elementary and secondary instruction. The blending of the middle and lower classes in the burgh schools was complete, but the upper classes resorted almost entirely to English schools and universities [6].

The Scotch secondary schools were almost entirely day schools, although by 1866 private boarding schools were becoming of more importance [7]. There are now four Scotch schools admitted to the Headmasters' Conference [8], but these in all educate less than a thousand boys, and not all of these are boarders. Yet when the proportion of wealthy people in Scotland and England and the number of Scotch boys at the English public schools are taken into account

---

[1] Taunton Report, vi. p. 60.
[2] 18,573. Ibid. p. 9.
[3] Ibid. p. 60.
[4] Ibid. p. 51.
[5] Ibid. pp. 6, 8.
[6] Ibid. pp. 21, 22.
[7] Ibid. p. 11.
[8] *Public Schools Year Book*, 1898.

the difference in the upper classes is not so great as would at first appear. It is in the class just below this that the distinction must be made.

Though girls were admitted to many of the burgh schools, and did well there, yet the majority of them went to schools partly of a proprietary and partly of a private character [1].

The first Statute affecting burgh schools was the Act of 1861 (24 & 25 Vict. c. 107) [2], which besides abolishing the jurisdiction of Presbyteries over these schools [3], also absolved the Masters from signing the Confession of Faith or the Formula of the Church of Scotland, and did not, as in the case of the Parish Schoolmaster, impose any subscription in place of it.

After several attempts the first Education (Scotland) Act [4] was passed in 1872. It was not, as in England, an Act for Elementary Education only, but dealt with burgh schools, in which it included all schools to which the term was legally applicable, by whatever name they might be called, and all schools established or managed by School Boards in burghs and vested in them by this Act.

School Boards, as we have seen, were established in every parish and burgh, and superseded the Town Councils in the management of burgh schools.

The existing burgh schools in which the education given did not consist chiefly of elementary instruction, but included classics, modern languages, mathematics, natural science, and generally the higher branches of knowledge, were to be deemed higher class public schools and managed accordingly, to promote the higher education of the country. Eleven such schools were specified as higher class public schools, and any School Board might resolve that any burgh school should be so deemed, or any parish school which could not reasonably be considered as chiefly elementary [5].

As far as practicable, and subject to the approval of the

---

[1] Taunton Report, vi. p. 58. [2] *Vide* p. 136.
[3] Sec. 22. [4] 35 & 36 Vict. c. 62; *vide* p. 138.
[5] Thirty-one in June, 1898 (Ed. Dep. Report, pub. 1898, p. 25).

Board of Education, School Boards were to relieve these schools of the necessity of giving elementary instruction[1]. These schools were to be annually examined in the higher branches of knowledge by examiners appointed and employed by the School Boards. The school fees were to be fixed at intervals of not less than three years by the principal teachers and the ordinary teachers of the school, subject to the determination of the Board of Education. Their funds were to be kept entirely separate from the school fund, from which they were to receive nothing. The contributions payable to them from the 'common good' of the burgh were confirmed to them by law. The endowment of each school for general purposes was assigned to it, and also any endowments for instruction in particular subjects or for teachers in particular branches. The full amount of fees was to be divided among the teachers as each School Board should determine.

The School Board might fix for its masters in any higher class school such qualifications as it thought fit, and might appoint as examiners professors of any Scotch university or teachers of distinction in a higher class public school.

The Education Act of 1878 (41 & 42 Vict. c. 78)[2] allowed the expenses of higher class public school buildings, or the expenses of maintaining them, or such other expenses for the promotion of efficient education as were not provided for by other revenues[3], to be paid for out of the school fund, with consent of the Education Department, and expressly authorized School Boards to maintain the buildings.

Provision was also made for the examination of any higher class schools by H. M. Inspectors or other persons appointed by the Department on the application of the authority of such school, whether a public school or not, on their undertaking to pay such expenses as the Education Department might fix.

---

[1] Practically a dead letter. *School Board Chronicle*, lix. p. 633.

[2] *Vide* p. 141.

[3] The Education Department interpreted this as not applicable to masters' salaries.

In 1887 Scotland obtained the first Act passed by Parliament for Technical Education [1].

It gave power to any School Board to provide a technical school for its district and pay the expenses out of the school fund. A School Board had the same powers as in the case of a higher class public school under the Act of 1878, and the Technical School was to be deemed a public school, except for attendance to earn grants under the Education Acts.

Hardly any use has been made of the Act, and only one School Board has availed itself of it in erecting a Technical School [2].

In 1890 the Local Taxation (Customs and Excise) Act allowed Burgh and County Councils, as in England, to apply the residue of their new funds to technical education, but there was a doubt as to whether grants could be made except to School Boards. The money was appropriated before this was settled, and less has been done than in England [3].

It must, however, be remembered that the powers of the School Boards for definite secondary education are considerably greater than in England, and it is chiefly by means of its Education Acts that Scotland has fostered that secondary education which, in the South, is often described as ' technical [4].'

In 1888 a Committee appointed by the Education Department under Mr. Charles Parker, M.P.[5], reported on Secondary Education in Scotland, and recommended that the country should look mainly to schools especially appropriated to it. They found that in the large cities the School Boards dealt satisfactorily with the schools, but that in the small burghs secondary education was starved for the sake of elementary grants, and that consequently it was expedient that it should receive a State grant.   In each country parish

---

[1] 50 & 51 Vict. c. 64, amended by 55 & 56 Vict. c. 63.

[2] Alexander: Bremner's *Education*, p. 262.   [3] Ibid. p. 262.

[4] In 1896–97, out of £39,000 available under the Act, £28,000 was devoted by local authorities to education (*The Record of the Association for Technical and Secondary Education*, 1898, p. 10).

[5] *Vide* p. 142.

a school capable of preparing its best pupils for the Universities should be maintained, the staff of such schools should be recognized, evening schools should be encouraged, and leaving examinations at secondary schools should be instituted [1].

In 1892 Scotland received her share of the money which England and Ireland, following her example, now spent on freeing education [2].

Education Act, 1892. By the Education and Local Taxation Account (Scotland) Act, 1892 [3], of the sums so assigned £60,000 were given annually—

(*a*) to defray the cost of the inspection of higher class schools in Scotland, and of the holding of examinations for and granting the leaving-certificates of the Scotch Education Department.

(*b*) To make provision for secondary education, under Minutes of the Department submitted to Parliament, in urban and rural districts in Scotland, but only to schools under the same management as a State-aided or higher class public school, or school managed under an Act, scheme, or provisional Order. Subject to vested interests, the control of fees was transferred from teachers to managers in schools receiving the new grant.

A Committee under Lord Elgin was at once appointed by the Scotch Education Department to inquire into the best means of distributing the latter of these two grants, for which it was estimated that £57,000 would be available; the cost of inspection of Higher Class Schools and of the examinations for Leaving-Certificates being £3,300 [4]. The Committee took evidence [5] and, in accordance with their report, Committees on Secondary Education were elected for each county and for the burghs of Edinburgh, Glasgow, Aberdeen, Leith, and Dundee, and for Govan parish.

These Committees were elected for three years on the principle of equal representation of the county or burgh

---

[1] P. P., 1888, xli. p. 643; cf. P. P., 1892, lxii. p. 158.
[2] *Vide* p. 144.   [3] 55 & 56 Vict. c. 51.
[4] P. P. Eng., 1892, lxii. p. 67.   [5] Ibid. p. 71.

council and of the School Boards. In counties the chairmen
of all the School Boards elected their members, in the five
burghs they were chosen by the burgh School Board. To
these was added in each case one of H. M. Inspectors,
nominated by the Department, and in the burghs representatives of specified local endowments.

The Committees were to report on the existing provision
for higher education and any deficiencies in their district,
and make recommendations to the Department.

'Under the original Minute' the money available was to
be distributed on the principle that the amount earned by
each school should be determined mainly by the work done
in that school, the schools entitled to share being selected
by the Burgh or County Committee.'

'After Parliamentary discussion, however, the plan was
changed, and a new Minute was issued on May 1, 1893, in
accordance with which a proportionate amount was allotted
to each Burgh or County, to be distributed according to
a scheme drawn up for the approval of the Department
by each Committee[2].'

Due regard must be paid in such schemes both to educational efficiency and to the extension of the benefits of
secondary education to the largest possible number of
scholars[3].

The Committees were elected for a second time in 1896,
and while the original elements were retained, a provision
was inserted that if the local authority under the Local
Taxation (Customs and Excise) Act, 1890, or the Education and Local Taxation Account (Scotland) Act, 1892,
entrusted any Secondary Education Committee with the
administration of funds available for secondary or technical
education, the local authorities were to be represented on
such Committee by additional members not exceeding one-
third of the whole Committee in number[4].

[1] August 11, 1892, modified January 31, 1893.
[2] Report of Ed. Dep. for 1892–93, pp. 141–156; for 1895–96, p. 142.
[3] Ibid. 1892–93, p. 155.   [4] Ibid. 1895–96, p. 143; one-half, 1897.

In 1893 the new Code for Evening Continuation Schools was issued [1], which greatly increased the amount of secondary education given by them.

In 1898 a further annual grant of a residue of about £35,000 was assigned to Scotch secondary and technical education by the Local Taxation Account (Scotland) Act, on conditions to be set forth by Minutes of the Department.

Since the Education Department appeared on the scene as an inspecting and examining Board for secondary schools, the public and endowed schools have submitted to it, and it has naturally drawn to itself many of the private institutions.

Schools inspected.

	Higher Class Public Schools.	*Endowed Schools.*	*Voluntary.*	*Total.*
1887	22	10	6	38
1890	22	22	8	52
1897	31	25	20	76

The Leaving-Certificate Examination is held at the Higher Class Schools, and at a certain number of the State-aided schools, but candidates from the latter are also examined at other centres [2].

	Total Number of Schools.	*State-aided Schools.*	*Candidates.*
1888	29	—	972
1889	41	—	2,066
1890	43	—	2,528
1891	50	—	3,120
1892	115	63 [3]	5,175
1893	152	97	7,148
1894	212	148	9,833
1895	270	202	13,173
1896	329	259	15,735
1897	362	289	16,378

[1] *Vide* p. 148.
[2] State-aided schools were first admitted to the examination in 1892.
[3] For the obverse vide *Journal of Education*, 1898, p. 25.

ii. *Science and Art Department.*

The grants of this Department have always been given
to Scotland on the same terms as to England, and though
Scotland obtained her Technical Schools Act in 1887, no
help was offered in support of it from South Kensington
until 1890, the year after the English Technical Instruction
Act was passed. In that year [1], £5,000 was allotted by
the Department to Great Britain and Ireland, but the grant
was withdrawn from Great Britain the following year in
consequence of the Customs and Excise money given in 1890.

In June, 1897, the Education Department was entrusted
with the administration of all Science and Art Grants in
Scotland.

The Department maintains no Science or Art College
of its own in Scotland, which consequently has to send her
students to South Kensington or elsewhere.

Local Examinations.

Local Examinations were introduced into Scotland in
1865, when the Universities of Edinburgh and St. Andrews
both held them. But there seemed to be little demand;
in 1867 St. Andrews had not candidates enough for an
examination [2], and the system never prospered as in England.

It was chiefly of service in testing the education of girls [3].
In 1883 Edinburgh had 47 centres where 891 candidates
were examined, and of these 746 were girls [4].

Glasgow took up the Examinations in 1877 and Aberdeen
in 1880, but the University Preliminary Examinations and
the Education Department Leaving-Certificate Examinations have reduced their importance, and Glasgow and
St. Andrews have discontinued them. The Senior and
Junior Examinations of Edinburgh are still held, and all
three classes of Aberdeen [5].

---

[1] For Technical Instruction, *v.* p. 227; Public Libraries Acts, p. 178.
[2] Argyll Third Report, p. 133. [3] Taunton Report, vi. p. 35.
[4] Sir A. Grant, *University of Edinburgh*, ii. 157.
[5] Miss Galloway, p. 265 of Miss Bremner's *Education of Girls and*

TRAINING OF SECONDARY TEACHERS.

The Argyll Commission found in 1867 that while over 70 per cent. of the teachers in Burgh and Middle Class Schools had studied at some University and about half of these had taken a degree, 10 per cent. had been trained in the Training Colleges, and that the teachers in private schools were largely drawn from these training institutions [1].

In 1876 the trustees of the will of Dr. Andrew Bell [2] (who died in 1832) founded professorial chairs at Edinburgh and St. Andrews for teaching the Theory, History, and Practice of Education [3], this being the first endowment of the sort in any University in these islands.

A Lectureship was founded in Aberdeen University in October, 1893, and a year later the University of Glasgow made a similar provision [4].

In all these Universities a hundred lectures are delivered each session, and attendance now qualifies towards graduation in Arts.

At Edinburgh arrangements are made for securing sufficient practice to qualify for the University Schoolmasters' diploma recognized by the Education Department.

Formerly the Edinburgh diploma was open only to Graduates of that University [5].

St. George's Training College, Edinburgh, was opened in 1886 for women only, and two years later started a High School in connexion with it.[6]. The students attend the lectures of the University; but very few of them graduate.

The greater part of the Scotch training is directed to those who will be masters in the ordinary public schools, and I can only repeat once more that the lines between

Women; *School Calendar*, 1897–98: Whitaker & Co. For Higher Locals, L.L.A., &c., *vide* p. 303.

[1] Argyll Third Report, pp. 78, 173.　　　　　　　　[2] *Vide* p. 3.

[3] The endowment at St. Andrews produced £223 in 1897 towards the salary of £400, Edinburgh drawing £361.

[4] *The Scottish Educational Year Book*, 1898, p. 171: The Free Press Office, Aberdeen, 1s. 6d.

[5] Registration Select Committee Report, 1891, p. 335.

[6] *Handbook Victorian Exhibition*, 1897, p. 132.

elementary and secondary schools are less marked in Scotland than in other parts of the kingdom [1].

THE REFORM OF EDUCATIONAL ENDOWMENTS.

The Scotch endowments for education seem in comparison with England and Ireland to have suffered little from neglect or misappropriation: the national thrift and zeal for education rendered great abuses impossible.

In the matter of endowments the secondary schools had fared badly in Scotland. If John Knox had been able to carry out his scheme [2], a grammar school would have been founded in every town and endowed out of the patrimony of the Church. But the barons who had got possession of the said patrimony successfully resisted all such endeavours on the part of the Reformed Church, and in 1867 only ten burgh schools had any endowments, and these only amounted to £1,400 a year, while six of the Academies had an income of £870 [3]. This does not include the endowed 'Hospitals,' which spent £44,182 in giving 1,064 free boarders 'what may in the majority of cases be termed a liberal education, including Latin, Greek, and Mathematics [4],' and also supporting a number of elementary day schools.

Of the endowments for schools nearly half of the total amount belonged to the ' Hospitals,' which derived their name from Christ's Hospital in London, in imitation of which the first of them was founded by George Heriot in 1624 for the maintenance, clothing, and education of orphan or destitute children [5]. The instruction was almost always both elementary and secondary, following the precedent of the Parochial and Burgh Schools.

But though there were no crying scandals, the administration of these trusts became in many cases unsuited to

---

[1] Report of Select Committee on Registration, Prof. Laurie, App. 5.
[2] *First Book of Discipline*, Laing's ed., ii. 210, 221 ; J. Grant, pp. 76–78.
[3] Argyll Third Report, p. 60.　　　　　[4] Ibid. pp. xix, xx.
[5] Colebrooke Commission, Third Report, p. 19.

the ideas or deficiencies of modern days, and even when reforms were desired by the trustees it was not always easy to effect them. Heriot's Hospital, for example, contrary to the intentions of the founder, had gradually come to educate all its foundationers within its own walls instead of sending the children to the grammar school [1]. In 1836 the Governors obtained a private Act [2], which enabled them to devote their surplus funds to establishing elementary free schools in the most crowded parts of Edinburgh, and from the control over the attendance these day schools produced exceptionally good results. But it was fifty years more before the other funds of the Hospital were employed to the best advantage.

The Argyll Commission [3] drew attention to the Hospitals, and recommended that, subject, where necessary, to the approval of Parliament, the General Board of Education should amend the statutes of these institutions with a view to the extension of education [4].

In 1869 an Endowed Institutions (Scotland) Act [5] was passed, enabling governors, trustees, or managers of institutions or endowments for educational or charitable purposes to apply to the Home Secretary for Provisional Orders to provide for their better government and administration. These Orders were to be laid before Parliament, and then, if not opposed, to come into operation. But after a few such Orders had been issued, the law officers of the Crown advised that the powers granted by the Act were inadequate, and no more action was taken.

In 1872 a Royal Commission was appointed, with Sir T. E. Colebrooke as Chairman, to inquire into all Educational Endowments in Scotland (except those founded in the Universities before 1808 and reported on by the Commission of 1858), and into the hospitals and schools supported by them.

---

[1] Colebrooke Commission, Third Report, p. 21.
[2] 6 & 7 Will. IV, c. 25.   [3] *Vide* pp. 136, 223.
[4] Argyll Third Report, p. xxvii.   [5] 32 & 33 Vict. c. 39.

They reported the annual income of Educational Charities
to be as follows :—

		£
Hospitals	. . . .	79,245
Schools—Elementary	. . . . . .	42,979
,, Secondary	. . . . . .	16,550
General Endowments[1]	. . . . . .	17,118
Mixed Endowments—proportion for Education	.	18,640
		£174,532 [2]

They advised opening the Hospital Schools and reducing
the foundationers as far as possible. Endowments for
education were to be devoted to improving education, sub-
sidising higher instruction, and establishing exhibitions and
bursaries. Examination by qualified independent inspectors
and audit of accounts were recommended and the appointment of a temporary Executive Commission.

Accordingly, in 1878, a Commission of seven members,
Lord Moncrieff being Chairman, was appointed[3] with the
powers which had been wanting in 1869. Governing Bodies
might apply as before for Provisional Orders to the Home
Secretary, who now could remit the application to the
Commissioners for inquiry. The Order must be consistent
with the general principles of the petition and must still be
laid before Parliament.

The Commissioners being also directed to report to the
Education Department on the best means of promoting
higher education in public and State-aided schools, recommended that in every parish there should be at least one
teacher qualified to give instruction in the higher subjects,
and declared its opinion that it was not only possible to

---

[1] Under this head was included the celebrated Dick Bequest, dating
from 1828, an endowment, both in itself and its administration, far in
advance of its times, increasing the salaries of parish schoolmasters in
Aberdeen, Banff, and Moray as a reward of merit, and in encouragement
of higher instruction (Bryce Report, v. 506; Report to the Trustees of
the Dick Bequest, by Professor Laurie: Edinburgh, 1890).

[2] Third Report, 1875, p. 239. Excluding £22,020 of University
Endowments given since 1808.

[3] 41 & 42 Vict. c. 48. Endowed Institutions (Scotland) Act.

combine thorough elementary teaching with instruction in the higher branches, but that any separation of these subjects was detrimental to the tone of the school and dispiriting to the master. Secondary schools might be serviceable in crowded centres, but they were impracticable in country parishes [1].

The Commissioners reported on thirty-one Endowments, but, on the same principle as the Charity Commission in England, had no power to take action except at the request of the Governing Bodies themselves.

To remedy this want of initiative the Educational Endowments (Scotland) Act [2], 1882, provided for the appointment of a new Commission of seven members under Lord Balfour of Burleigh, with power to prepare draft schemes for the future government and management of educational endowments only. They were directed to have special regard to making provision for secondary or higher or technical education in public schools or otherwise in the respective districts [3].

Any endowment of a State-aided school, or school coming under the Education Acts, being of less annual value than fifty pounds, might be reformed by a scheme approved by the Education Department.

On the termination of the Commission (which ended in 1890) the revision of schemes might be dealt with by the Court of Session and by consent of the Education Department.

The Commissioners adopted as their principle that relief to the poor through an educational endowment must be given in the form of educational opportunities for the children of the poor, and not in the form of a payment in aid of general rates in which many besides the poor would participate [4].

[1] Final Report, p. vii.   [2] 45 & 46 Vict. c. 59.
[3] The Act applied to all endowments created before 1872, and was the original of the Irish Educational Endowments Act of 1885, q. v., which, *mutatis mutandis*, was almost identical with it.
[4] Seventh Report, P. P., 1890, C. 5,957, p. xx.

The interests of girls, 'merit as ascertained by examination,' inspection of schools and audit of accounts received the same recognition as in the Irish Endowments Act [1].

The Commissioners' schemes had to be approved by the Scotch Education Department, and ultimately sanctioned by an Order in Council. If any petition were presented to the Department against a scheme, such scheme must be laid before both Houses of Parliament, and then unless either House presented an address against it, it might be approved by an Order in Council. A 'special case' might be submitted to the Court of Sessions on any point of law.

The Commissioners submitted 379 schemes dealing with 821 endowments, and a revenue of nearly £200,000 [2], which they assigned to the following purposes :—

	£
Free Education	11,387
Clothing and Maintenance	29,055
Elementary School Bursaries	13,386
Bursaries for Higher Class and Technical Schools and Universities	11,954
Grants to School Boards for Higher Education .	18,176
Grants to Higher Class Schools	32,189
Grants to Technical Schools	33,300
Evening Classes	4,305
Girls' Education (besides what they share with boys)	14,259
Rural School Boards	534
Miscellaneous Educational Purposes . . .	9,600
Sum to be apportioned by Governing Bodies . .	27,455
	£199,500

[1] *Vide* p. 211.   [2] Seventh Report, P. P., 1890, xxxi. p. 771.

III. HIGHER EDUCATION.

A. England.

1. Oxford and Cambridge.

In the year 1800 the form of higher education in
England and Wales was confined almost exclusively to the
two ancient universities of Oxford and Cambridge, and
even their direct influence extended little beyond the
Church of England. At Oxford a Dissenter was not suffered
to matriculate at all or to enjoy the instruction or any other
privilege either of University, College or Hall[1]. At Cambridge
he might become a student, but could obtain no degree,
hold no office, receive no emolument, and take no part in
the government of the University or of any foundation [2].

In spite of the penal laws against Nonconformist and
Catholic schoolmasters and tutors[3], they seem to have given

[1] Report of Royal Commission on Oxford, 1852, p. 54.

[2] Report of Royal Commission on Cambridge, 1852, pp. 38, 43.

[3] The clauses of the Act of Uniformity against Nonconforming schoolmasters and tutors (13 & 14 Car. II, c. 4, ss. 8, 11), though mitigated
by the Toleration Act (1 W. & M. c. 18) and by 19 Geo. III, c. 44,
were not definitely removed from the Statute-book till 1865 (28 & 29
Vict. c. 122, s. 15), but George II expressed his disapproval of the
attack on Dr. Philip Doddridge in 1734 (*Dictionary of National Biography*), and no more prosecutions seem to have taken place. The
Schism Act, passed in 1714 (12 Anne, stat. 2, c. 7), was repealed five
years later (5 Geo. I, c. 4). The Five Mile Act and the Conventicle
Act were only formally repealed in 1812.

Numerous small Nonconformist Academies, for laymen as well as for
ministry students, existed during the course of the eighteenth century,
though Homerton and Hoxton were exceptional in having any long
continuous life (D. Bogue and J. Bennett, *History of Dissenters*:
London, 1808–12, 4 vols., ii. 34, iii. 282, iv. 261, 262; Hansard, T. S.,
xxv. 643). Manchester College was founded at Manchester in 1786.
Having no endowments, most of them rose and fell with individual
teachers.

In the case of the *Catholics*, an Act of 1699 (11 & 12 Will. III, c. 4)

instruction in England and Wales without much interruption during the greater part of the eighteenth century, but their schools, being only on sufferance, never attained any great importance, and except in principle counted for little in the intellectual history of the time.

The advantages offered by Oxford and Cambridge were, however, disproportionate to the favours they had received. The curriculum at either university was narrow, and was neglected with impunity, and distinctions were awarded under the most arbitrary rules, when they were not a matter of pure favouritism. Residence for four academic years was the one real qualification for a degree [1]. Cambridge held an honour examination in mathematics only, and until 1797 the proctors exercised the privilege of inserting names into the honour list at will [2]. Oxford, until 1802, granted its degrees on the formal report of three unpaid examiners, Masters of Arts appointed for three days without regard to their qualifications [3].

Fellowships and scholarships were in most cases restricted to certain localities, certain families, or certain schools [4]. There was no power in most cases to vary these restrictions, and the utmost to be hoped was that there might be an

inflicted perpetual imprisonment on papist schoolmasters or tutors. Relief was granted in 1791 (31 Geo. III, c. 32), and in 1795 Stonyhurst was founded. But Catholics seem to have had no difficulty in obtaining education in England during the eighteenth century (Lecky, *History of England*, i. 309). Even after the abolition of Tests in 1871, a Catholic embargo remained on the English Universities, and was only removed by a decision of the Pope in 1895 (*Tablet*, April 27, 1895).

The proposal to recognize St. Edmund's House (an establishment for Roman Catholics at Cambridge) as a public hostel was rejected on May 12, 1898, by 462 votes to 218. A private Hall for Catholics was opened at Oxford in 1896, under the usual regulations, without remark, and probably no opposition would be raised to a similar course at Cambridge.

[1] This minimum had dwindled at Cambridge to three years and a term, and in 1858 was reduced to three years. In 1859 the Oxford necessary residence was changed from four academical years to three.

[2] J. B. Mullinger, 'History of the University of Cambridge,' *Epochs of Church History*, p. 178: Longmans, 1888.

[3] 1852 Report of Royal Commission in Oxford, p. 60.

[4] Oxford Report, 1852, pp. 149, 174; Cambridge Report, pp. 157, 185.

honest selection of the best capacity within the required
limits, instead of a nomination which each fellow exercised
in turn, and regarded as his right and his private property[1].
Fellows in nearly all cases were obliged to take Orders in
the Church of England, and were in all cases forbidden to
marry[2]. Every student for centuries past, before he could
become a member of either University, had been obliged to
attach himself to some College or Hall, and in the case of
Oxford must take up his residence within its walls. The
Colleges had eight or nine times as much property as their
University, and most of the University professorships were
but poorly paid in comparison with College offices. It is
not surprising that the Colleges had overshadowed the
Universities, and the professorial system had been almost
entirely superseded in the instruction of undergraduates
by the College tutors[3]; but these in turn, especially at
Cambridge, had been largely supplemented by private
' coaches[4].'

The constitution of both Universities seemed to have
been devised to prevent any attempts at change. All
initiative in Cambridge rested with the *Caput Senatus*, consisting of the Vice-Chancellor and of five members elected
from fifteen persons nominated by the Vice-Chancellor and
Proctors : the veto of one member of this body was sufficient
to put a stop to any measure[5]. At Oxford the analogous
Hebdomadal Board consisted solely of the Heads of
Houses[6] and the two Proctors ; and the Vice-Chancellor
singly and the Proctors jointly had a similar power of veto.
Convocation, the general body of Oxford graduates, corre-

---

[1] Oxford Report, p. 168.

[2] Oxford Report, pp. 163, 164; Cambridge Report, p. 171.

[3] Oxford Report, p. 93 ; Cambridge Report, p. 70.

[4] ' The cessation of professorial teaching is designated by the Hebdomadal Board as a "temporary interruption," but it is an interruption
which, so far as we can ascertain, has been the rule and not the exception
for at least a century and a half' (1852 Oxford Report, p. 93).

[5] Cambridge Report, p. 13.

[6] The Vice-Chancellor is appointed from among the Heads of Houses
only, and was thus already a member of the Board.

sponding to the Cambridge Senate, could only accept or reject without amendment any proposal sent to them, and their debates were still conducted in Latin. Congregation, the intermediate body of regent masters, had lost all but its formal existence [1]. Oxford was governed by the Laudian Statutes accepted in 1636, which had been so little modified that in 1850 it was contended that only the Crown and University in conjunction could alter them [2]. The Cambridge Code had been given by Queen Elizabeth in 1570 [3]. The Colleges at both Universities were governed nominally by the original founders' statutes or revised and adapted versions of these, for which at Cambridge, in two or three instances, the sanction of the Crown had been obtained, but which in most cases were quite without legal authority [4]. Modification was thus for the most part impossible without the intervention of Parliament, and neither the Crown nor the Houses of Parliament interfered before the middle of the century.

In the meantime such reforms as were practicable had already begun from within, and there was in either University a considerable party which ardently desired improvement. At Oxford, in the end of the eighteenth century, Dr. Cyril Jackson, the Dean of Christ Church, had instituted examinations within his own College [5]. In 1795 Oriel had begun to elect to its fellowships from outside solely on the results of its own examinations [6]: in 1829 the Master and Fellows of Balliol began to elect scholars after examination, and in 1834 obtained such sanction as the Visitor could give to this change in their statutes [7]. The most

[1] Oxford Report, pp. 10, 11.

[2] Ibid. pp. 3-5. Some of the Statutes, of course, were of much more remote date. Every one taking his M.A. degree had until 1827 to swear that he would neither give nor attend lectures at Stamford—*non leges nec audies Stanfordiae*—a relic of the secession to that town in 1334—five centuries before (A. Clark, *The Colleges of Oxford*, p. 254: Methuen, 1891).

[3] Cambridge Correspondence, 1852, p. 2.

[4] Oxford Report, p. 148; Cambridge Report, p. 150.

[5] A. Clark, *The Colleges of Oxford*, p. 316: Methuen, 1891.

[6] Ibid. p. 122.   [7] Ibid. p. 56; 1852 Report, pp. 152, 189, 190.

brilliant success attended these reforms, and encouraged similar measures elsewhere.

Cambridge, it must be said once for all, had not sunk into so deep a lethargy as Oxford: there were fewer restrictions in fellowships and scholarships, and fewer abuses in filling them [1]. Its defect was narrowness rather than indifference. In 1772 the Master of St. John's established examinations in his college [2]. In 1838 Dr. Whewell, the Master of Trinity, revived the lectures of Moral Philosophy [3]; in 1844 Trinity obtained new Statutes, and was followed by St. John's in 1849 [4].

Nevertheless, in spite of the higher intellectual life, and the great names which Cambridge could show: in spite of the greater openness of the endowments, and the tolerance to Dissenters, there was no great increase in the numbers resorting to the Whig University. In 1800 matriculations were twice as numerous at Oxford, and the nation at large seems to have been quite indifferent to the apparent intellectual superiority of her rival.

Even the absence of examinations will not account for this preference, for after 1800, when the requirements of Oxford had become at least as severe as those of Cambridge, the majority in matriculations remained with the elder University until two-thirds of the century were passed.

In 1800 a University Statute was passed at Oxford by which a genuine examination for the B.A. degree [5] was established in 1802, and a small honours list published with names in order of merit. In 1807 Literae Humaniores and Mathematics were separated, and two classes of honours in alphabetical order were created for either 'school.' Improvements were continually made, until in 1830 Honour Schools were separated from Pass Schools, and leave was given to illustrate ancient by modern authors [6].

---

[1] Report, p. 156; Oxford Evidence, p. 36.
[2] Mullinger, p. 182.   [3] Ibid. p. 194.   [4] Ibid. p. 198.
[5] An examination for the M.A. degree was also instituted, but never became more than formal, and was discontinued in 1807 (1852 Report, p. 83).   [6] Ibid. p. 61.

In 1824 the Classical Tripos was first held at Cambridge, but until 1850 it was open only to those who had taken honours in Mathematics [1]. In 1849 Cambridge revised such of its ordinances as, having been made by the University alone, were open to alteration [2], and the Moral Science and Natural Science Triposes were recommended for adoption [3]. In the next year Oxford further reorganized its examinations, and introduced Moderations as a test of pure scholarship in the middle of the University course [4].

It may be as well to point out here that Oxford, Cambridge, and Durham (apart from Newcastle) are national institutions only by virtue of their influence and position, and the importance of the various privileges they have received. Queen Elizabeth granted them a Charter of Incorporation in 1570 [5], which confirmed to them the patents they already enjoyed.

The power of Parliament to interfere with the Universities and Colleges is only that right which it possesses to deal with any private institution or property in the interest of the nation [6]. The endowments of these Universities proceed solely from private benefactions and bequests. Among other persons, different sovereigns have exercised their liberality in endowing certain professorships and readerships, which were at first supported out of the Privy Purse or Civil List, regarded at that time as private property. On the accession of William IV the hereditary revenues of the Crown were surrendered to the people, who in return undertook to make suitable provision for the Throne. Consequently two sums of about £100 are still paid annually by the Commissioners of Woods and Forests. Two sums of about £1,000 each, which were voted annually by the House of Commons to Oxford and Cambridge till after the

---

[1] Mullinger, p. 189.
[2] Ibid. p. 199.
[3] In 1848, ibid. p. 196.
[4] Report, 1852, p. 65.
[5] 13 Eliz. c. 29.
[6] Oxford 1852 Report, p. 155. Cf. M. Pattison, *Suggestions on Academical Organisation*, p. 10: Edmonston and Douglas, Edinburgh, 1868. Oxford Correspondence, p. 32.

passing of the first University Acts, were surrendered in return for the abolition of the stamp duties on matriculations and degrees[1], which brought in at least twice the total amount to Government.   But these grants were due to the pledge given to the representatives of the original donor, and Oxford, Cambridge, and Durham differ as yet from all other Universities in the kingdom in that they draw no annual subsidy and have received no building grants from the national Treasury.

At last came the interference of the State.   In 1834 a Bill to admit Dissenters to Oxford and Cambridge had passed the House of Commons, but had been thrown out by the Lords and disappeared for a generation.   But in August, 1850, the Queen under her Sign Manual appointed two Commissions to inquire into the state, discipline, studies, and revenues of Oxford and Cambridge respectively : power was given to call for information and documents, but when these were refused, no means of compulsion were afforded.

Obstruction in Parliament was for the present rendered impossible, but recalcitrance in high places was soon manifested.   The Vice-Chancellor of Cambridge in 1850 refused to answer any questions[2].   At Oxford the Governing Body withheld all information and disputed the legality of the Commission[3].   The Dean of Christ Church did not even acknowledge the letters addressed to him[4].   Dr. Routh, who had already been sixty years President of Magdalen College, 'declined giving information concerning property which he was not conscious of having misused or misapplied, or surrendering statutes . . . which he had sworn to observe[5].'   Dr. Phillpotts, Bishop of Exeter and Visitor of Exeter College, wrote to the chairman that there was 'absolutely no parallel to the Commission since the fatal attempt of King James II to subject these venerable bodies

---

[1] Imposed by 55 Geo. III, c. 184.
[2] Cambridge Correspondence, p. 2.   [3] Report, p. 1.
[4] Oxford Correspondence, p. 20.   [5] Oxford Evidence, p. 334.

to his unhallowed control[1].' Six Colleges at Oxford and two at Cambridge gave no evidence whatever to the Commissioners.

The Chairman of the Oxford Commission was Dr. Hinds, Bishop of Norwich, an enthusiast for education, and its Secretary was the Rev. A. P. Stanley, already author of *The Life of Thomas Arnold*, and afterwards Dean of Westminster. They had a fertile subject, an intimate knowledge, and no particular desire to spare anybody; and further, the Secretary was a master of English. The result was a classic among Blue Books, far superior to the Report of the Cambridge Commissioners, over which Dr. Graham, Bishop of Chester, presided, and which had at once a smaller opportunity and a general amiable desire to make things pleasant.

Both reports appeared in 1852, and change could be no longer averted. In 1854 Oxford received an Act of Parliament embodying some of the chief recommendations made[2]; a Cambridge Act followed in 1856[3].

The constitutions were reformed; the Hebdomadal Council and the Council of the Senate were to be elected in certain proportions from Heads of Houses, Professors and other Doctors and Masters of Arts. The Cambridge veto was abolished; Oxford Congregation, the body of resident Doctors and Masters, was constituted[4]. Convocation and the Senate were reformed.

Oaths and Declarations were abolished for all degrees at Cambridge except in Divinity, but no graduate could become a member of the Senate without declaring himself a member of the Established Church. At Oxford these tests were removed from Matriculation and the Bachelors' Degrees; for all Doctors' and Masters' degrees, and for the B.D., they were retained.

---

[1] Oxford Correspondence, p. 7.   [2] 17 & 18 Vict. c. 81.

[3] 19 & 20 Vict. c. 88.

[4] The Ancient House of Congregation, which grants degrees and appoints examiners, was, perhaps accidentally, left in existence (*The Historical Register of the University of Oxford*, p. 13: Clarendon Press, 1888).

The Act provided for the abolition of the stamp duties[1] on degrees and matriculations, which in 1853 had drawn £5,279 from Oxford and Cambridge[2]. They, on the other hand, had to give up the £2,000 a year of royal grants which the House of Commons had undertaken to pay since 1831[3]. The arrangement was carried into effect by two separate Acts, for Oxford in 1854[4], and for Cambridge in 1858[5].

An executive Commission was appointed in either case with power to require the production of documents and the giving of information; 'all oaths not to disclose such information being declared illegal.

The Universities and Colleges were allowed to amend their Statutes, which were then to be submitted to the Commissioners, and in the event of their omitting to do this, the Commissioners might frame Ordinances and Regulations. The Statutes must be laid before both Houses of Parliament, and receive the sanction of the Queen in Council. Petitions might be presented by parties interested and referred to a special Committee of the Privy Council. After the expiration of the Commission, Statutes might be altered by University or Colleges, subject to their obtaining similar sanction.

The chief changes introduced by the Statutes as passed were the removal of a great number of restrictions in electing to fellowships and scholarships, and the resuscitation of the professoriate.

The reform as yet was rather permissive than accomplished. The Oxford Commission had recommended that fellows should no longer of necessity be ordained[6], and that a University matriculation examination should be established[7]. A few restrictions were removed, but in the case of tutors and most fellows ordination was still required, and the conditions of entrance were still left in the hands of

---

[1] Imposed by 55 Geo. III, c. 184.   [2] P. P., 1854, vol. l, 435.
[3] *Vide* p. 244.   [4] 18 & 19 Vict. c. 36.   [5] 21 & 22 Vict. c. 11.
[6] Report, p. 163.   [7] p. 68.

the Colleges. At Cambridge the Colleges refused to throw
open their fellowships, and the Statutes merely granted them
a permission of which they need not avail themselves [1].
The reorganization of professors' lectures left much for
future reformers; at Cambridge the Colleges refused the
invitation to contribute five per cent. of their income for
this purpose [2]. Nevertheless, the minute restrictions, devised two hundred years before for entirely different conditions, were now removed, and the Universities were set free
to develop themselves, according to the ideas of their leaders,
to meet the wants of the present day.

Statutes were passed at Oxford in 1868 and at Cambridge
in 1869 allowing persons to become members of the Universities without joining any College, as long as they lived
in licensed lodgings and were subject to a special Board.
In 1853 many people had thought such a step opened the
way to 'demoralization and irreligion of which no man can
see the end [3].' It has resulted at either University in the
creation of a large unendowed and consequently rather
understaffed [4] society without hall, chapel, or dwelling-rooms,
which has opened a University career to a number of men
who could not otherwise afford it [5].

Undergraduates at Cambridge had been allowed to live
out of College in licensed lodgings, at any rate, since the
end of the eighteenth century [6]; by the Statute of 1868 this
privilege was granted at Oxford, the new Delegacy taking

---

[1] Final Report, 1861, p. 16.   [2] Ibid. p. 7: with three exceptions.
[3] *Report and Evidence upon the Recommendations of H. M. Commissioners presented to the Board of Heads of Houses and Proctors,*
p. 387: Oxford, 1853.
[4] Bryce Commission Report, v. 134.
[5] Number of Non-Collegiate undergraduates:—

				Oxford.	*Cambridge.*
1870	.	.	.	96	18
1880	.	.	.	308	185
1890	.	.	.	247	143
1897	.	.	.	224	129

Oxford and Cambridge Calendars.

[6] J. W. Clark, *Cambridge: Historical and Picturesque Notes,* p. 291:
Seeley, 1890.

charge for the first two years both of lodging-houses and of Non-Collegiate Students [1].

The Colleges are thus no longer restricted in numbers by the size of their buildings, and the larger and wealthier bodies threaten to become unwieldy at some expense to the prosperity of the smaller foundations.

In 1871, after many struggles, the Universities Tests Act [2] was passed, abolishing all oaths and affirmations at Oxford, Cambridge, and Durham except in Divinity. It applied to professorships, fellowships, scholarships, and emoluments of all kinds as well as matriculation and degrees, and included Universities, Colleges, and Halls alike.

The opposition in 1850 had at the time rendered any complete statement of revenue impossible, but in 1872 a Royal Commission under the Duke of Cleveland was appointed to inquire into the property [3] and income of the two Universities, the Colleges and Halls, but without power to do more than report facts. They found the annual gross incomes from all sources, at the end of 1871, to be as follows :—

	External. Rents, Dividends, &c.	*Internal. Fees, &c.*	*Subject to Trusts.*	*Total.*
	£	£	£	£
University of Oxford .	13,605 [4]	18,546 [6]	15,438	47,589
Colleges and Halls .	271,953	58,884	35,417	366,254
University of Cambridge	2,930 [5]	20,133 [7]	10,408	33,471
Colleges . . .	229,621	42,255	27,541	306,512 [8]

[1] An executive Committee appointed by the University is called a Delegacy at Oxford, and a Syndicate at Cambridge.

[2] 34 Vict. c. 26.

[3] The Cambridge Commission had only been able to reckon the gross income of the seventeen Colleges as 'not less than £185,000' (p. 197). At Oxford the College endowments, exclusive of fees, were said to be £150,000 a year (1852 Report, p. 151), whereas in 1871 they were £271,952 (i. p. 200, Cleveland Report).

[4] 1897: £16,568.　　　　[5] 1897: £2,051.　　　　[6] 1897: £30,174.

[7] 1897: £40,182 (*Oxford University Gazette, Cambridge University Reporter*).　　　　[8] Including Sidney Sussex College.

The total income from all sources [1] was £753,826.

Thus out of the revenue of three-quarters of a million the Universities possessed little more than £80,000, while the Colleges received more than eight-ninths of the total [2]. The College incomes varied at Cambridge from Trinity with £59,735 and St. John's with £45,704 to nine Colleges with less than £10,000; and at Oxford from Christ Church with £39,291 to five Colleges with less than £10,000 a year each of internal and external revenue [3].

In 1877 an Act [4] was passed for Oxford and Cambridge appointing executive Commissions for either University. The chief purpose was to make further provision out of College revenues for University purposes, and to remove any still remaining unnecessary restrictions. The Universities and Colleges were to pass new Statutes with the aid of the Commission; each College might name three Commissioners to act with the representatives of Government in making its own ordinances. The draft Statutes were to be laid before the Queen in Council and both Houses of Parliament, much as in the case of Public School and Charity Commission schemes, but there was a special Universities Committee permanently appointed to hear petitions. Future alterations made by either University or any College must be submitted to the Crown and Parliament and go through the usual course.

The Commissioners could not make regulations for endowments founded within the last fifty years, but with this exception [5] the Universities and all Colleges subject to the commission have received new Statutes under these conditions.

---

[1] Including £7,095 for Sidney Sussex College, Cambridge, not subdivided, but not any capital sold out (Report, i. pp. 29, 197, 204).

[2] Ibid. pp. 197, 200, 207, 208.

[3] Ibid. pp. 200, 204. Agricultural depression has subsequently altered most of these figures to a serious extent. The total divisible revenue of the Cambridge Colleges fell off by 34 per cent. between 1881 and 1898 (*Times*, April 23, 1897). Cf. *Statistical Society Journal*, 1895, p. 39.

[4] 40 & 41 Vict. c. 48.   [5] And that of Lincoln College, Oxford.

Fellowships have been remodelled, and are mostly attached to College offices or University appointments. In Oxford a sum of more than £20,000 per annum was thus assigned to endow professorships and readerships, and about 100 sinecure prize fellowships were created [1].

Ordination and celibacy were only retained as far as was rendered necessary by the maintenance of chapel services and of college life ; but the tenure of fellowships was in all cases for specified periods only, though subject to renewal. College scholarships were made more uniform in conditions and value.

No University Matriculation Examination was imposed, but the matter was left, as before, to the tests which each [2] College found it desirable to apply.

Studies were grouped under Boards of Faculties, the nomination and appointment of University examiners were regulated, and provision was made for the publication of accounts.

More important in practice at Oxford than the restoration of the Professors has been the gradual opening of College lectures to members of other Colleges. Under the existing system all honours lectures are open to any member of the University, similar arrangements in the case of pass lectures being determined by the tutors and the lecturers themselves. The same practice has been introduced at Cambridge, but to a less extent.

The gradual enlargement of the curriculum cannot be better shown in a brief space than by a list of the various new Honours Examinations which have been from time to time created, with the years in which they were first held.

---

[1] Hon. G. Brodrick, *History of the University of Oxford*, p. 201 : 1886.

[2] In 1873 only two Colleges in Cambridge had an entrance examination, or required more than a certificate of fitness from any M.A. of Cambridge or Oxford (P. P., 1873, xxviii. p. 644).

Oxford.		*Cambridge.*	
Natural Science	1853	Moral Science	1851
Jurisprudence and Modern History	1853	Natural Science	1851
Theology (as an Honour School)	1870	Law	1858
		Law and History	1870
Jurisprudence and History separated	1872	Theology	1874
Literae Indicae	1887	Law and History separated	1875
Literae Semiticae	1891	Semitic Languages	1878
Literae Orientales	1896	Indian Languages	1879
Literae Anglicae	1897	Medieval and Modern Languages	1886

Oxford in 1880, and Cambridge in 1886, passed Statutes for affiliating to themselves Colleges in the United Kingdom (or subsequently in the Colonies).

Students from these institutions receive certain privileges as to admission to examinations and length of residence. At Cambridge, Extension Students who have taken a three years' course are excused a year of residence.

	Matriculations.		*Undergraduates on the books.*	
	Oxford.	*Cambridge.*	*Oxford.*	*Cambridge.*
1800	247	129	—	—
1840	396	345	—	—
1850	409	360	—	—
1862	433	407	—	1,526
1872	632	—	2,392	2,102
1882	757	892	3,013	2,818
1892	799	934	3,197	2,909
1897	852	887	3,408	2,929

The number of men gaining honours in the final schools (not including the Second Part of any Tripos at Cambridge) now averages slightly more than 400 each year in either University.

University Extension.

We have already seen how in 1858 Oxford and Cambridge assumed an indirect control over the education of persons who were not members of either University [1], but besides establishing external examinations and inspection of schools,

---

[1] p. 186.

they have subsequently taken steps for extending their actual teaching to students who are unable to matriculate or reside [1].

In 1867 the North of England Council for Promoting the Higher Education of Women was formed, and in the same year Professor Stuart of Cambridge had delivered some lectures before several schoolmistresses' associations in Yorkshire and Lancashire, and also before working men at Crewe, Rochdale, and elsewhere. The new Council took up the arrangements for lectures and developed them with such good result that in 1873 the University of Cambridge allowed a Syndicate, which they had appointed to consider the question, to undertake the organization of these courses. Two years later the Syndicate was made permanent, and in 1878 was amalgamated with the Syndicate which already had charge of the Local Examinations.

In 1876 the London Society for the Extension of University Teaching was formed.

In 1878 Oxford made a premature attempt to undertake the work, which was entrusted to a Committee of the Delegacy for Local Examinations, but it almost died out until it was reorganized in 1885, and a special Delegacy for the purpose was not appointed before 1892.

. The movement has to a greater or less extent been taken up also by the University of Durham (in co-operation with Cambridge) and the Victoria University, as well as most of the University Colleges. A great deal of the instruction given is merely secondary, as is shown by the fact that an estimate given to the Bryce Commission [2] showed that of the 60,000 persons attending Extension Courses in 1893–94,

---

[1] *University Extension, Past, Present, and Future*, by H. J. Mackinder and M. E. Sadler: Cassell & Co., 1891. *Eighteen Years of University Education*, by R. D. Roberts: Cambridge, 1891. *L'éducation en Angleterre*, &c., Leclerc, chap. xviii. *L'extension universitaire par l'enseignement*: Armand Colin, Paris, 1894. Report of Royal Commission as to New University for London. *The Nineteenth Century*, 1894, vol. xxxvi, pp. 203, 371, 598: by C. Whibley and M. E. Sadler.

[2] Report, i. p. 55.

ten to twelve per cent. were actually at the time pupils in secondary schools. But for some time to come this agency will perhaps do the work most needed by being introductory as well as supplementary to the Universities themselves.

In 1888 the first Summer Meeting was held at Oxford and attended by 900 Students. In 1890 Cambridge held its first Summer Course on a more restricted scale; and meetings have subsequently been held each Summer and have been well attended.

In 1886 Cambridge granted curtailment of one year of residence to undergraduates who had already taken a recognized three years' course of Extension lectures.

The recommendation of the Local Examinations and Lectures Syndicate at Cambridge to grant a diploma in Arts to external students without residence was rejected by the Senate on May 26, 1898, by 122 votes to 70.

The method pursued is that, as in the case of Local Examinations, a centre is formed, a certain sum is guaranteed, and all arrangements on the spot are made by a local committee. The University or Society sends the lecturer who delivers a course on a subject selected originally by the committee, an hour's class follows each lecture, essays are invited and corrected, books are lent, finally an examination is held and certificates are granted. Women have been throughout on an equal footing.

	Cambridge.			Oxford.			London.		
	Centres.	*Courses.*	*Average Attendance.*	*Centres.*	*Courses.*	*Average Attendance.*	*Centres.*	*Courses.*	*Average Attendance.*
1873-74	7	29	3,200	—	—	—	—	—	—
1879-80	20	47	5,009	—	—	—	—	44	2,237
1889-90	37	89	9,295	109	148	17,904	—	130	12,923
1896-97	57	86	8,496	104	146	18,263	64	160	14,150

Women's Colleges, Cambridge and Oxford.

The most conspicuous advance in the establishment of higher education for women was made at Cambridge, and was the result of two distinct movements along similar but not identical lines.

In 1869 a college 'designed to hold in relation to girls' schools and home teaching a position analogous to that occupied by the Universities towards the public schools for boys' was established at Hitchin by a Committee. In 1870 by a private arrangement some of its scholars were examined in the subjects of the Previous Examination of the University of Cambridge. The institution throve, became incorporated as Girton College in 1872, and in 1873 removed to a building of its own within two miles of Cambridge. The College now accommodates 106 students and 9 resident officials, and it is proposed to double this accommodation as soon as possible[1].

The supporters of Girton have consistently demanded a common standard of education for both sexes, and have believed that any separate scheme of examination for women only tended to keep down the level of female acquirements.

The other champions of feminine education held that instruction and examinations alike should be specially adapted to women, different, though not necessarily less difficult. In 1869 the Syndicate for Local Examinations at Cambridge instituted an Examination for Women over Eighteen[2], in response to a petition presented to the University to that effect in the preceding year.

A Lectures Committee was formed to prepare girls to meet this special test, and also generally to improve and extend the education of women, and with 1870 courses of lectures began. In October, 1871, a house of residence for

---

[1] *Women in the Universities of England and Scotland*, Miss Emily Davies: Macmillan, 1896, price 6*d.*; Girton College Report, 1897.
[2] Opened to men in 1874, and known as the Higher Local Examination.

students attending lectures was opened in Cambridge, and this developed into Newnham Hall, opened in 1875. which in turn became Newnham College in 1880[1].   It also has prospered and grown, until now it provides for 158 students in addition to the staff[2].

Thus the two Colleges have worked side by side in the same University town, the one desiring special education for women, the other demanding the same tests as men ; both using the same examination and working harmoniously together, and presenting a united front to a yet uncon-vinced University.

The expedient of allowing University examiners to examine women unofficially was continued till 1881, and was utilized by students belonging to Girton or Newnham. Pass as well as honours examinations were taken ; and no requirement was made of first passing the Previous Exami-nation or as to length of residence.

In 1881 women were admitted to all the Honours Exami-nations of the University for the degree of B.A., received a University Certificate of their classes, and had their names published in a separate section of each Tripos ; but these privileges are granted to those only who belong to either Girton or Newnham, or reside within the precincts of the University under their regulations[3], and who have fulfilled the conditions of residence imposed on members of the University, and have passed the Previous Examination or some recognized substitute for it.   All Triposes are open to women on these terms, and examiners may certify that a woman has reached a standard equivalent to that re-quired for an ordinary degree, though insufficient for honours.

In 1897 a proposal to confer on women by diploma the

---

[1] The Lectures Committee became the Association for Promoting the Higher Education of Women in Cambridge in 1873, was dissolved, and was replaced by Newnham College Association when it came into existence in 1880.

[2] *Life of Miss A. J. Clough*, especially chapter v, by Miss B. A. Clough: Arnold, 1897.

[3] There is no class of Home Students as at Oxford.

title of B.A., without admitting them to membership of the University, was submitted to the Senate and rejected by 1713 to 662 votes[1].

	Girton.		*Newnham.*	
	Students.	*Degree Certificates.*	*Students.*	*Degree Certificates.*
1869–70	6	—	—	—
1879–80	52	16	80	—
1889–90	103	24	135	26[2]
1896–97	116	26	162	43[3]

Oxford. Before 1879 various lectures had been delivered to women in Oxford, but in that year several more or less independent schemes matured simultaneously, and the arrangements for teaching women began to assume their present form. The Higher Local Examinations of the University, open to women only, authorized in 1875, were first held in 1877. The Association for Promoting the Education of Women in Oxford was founded in 1878 to establish and maintain a system of instruction. In 1878 Lady Margaret Hall was founded on Church of England principles (with a conscience clause), and Somerville Hall, strictly undenominational, followed in the next year. In October, 1879, the two Halls were opened, and the Association began its first course of lectures.

The Association has not been absorbed as at Cambridge, but has in practice proved a sort of general deliberative Council on which each corporate body is represented[4]; it has always supervised resident students who belonged to no Hall; in 1893 it recognized them officially as Home Students, and placed them under a special committee.

St. Hugh's Hall was founded in 1886; St. Hilda's Hall, founded in 1893 as an offshoot from Cheltenham, was constituted a Hall in 1896. In 1894 Somerville assumed the title of College.

In 1884 Honour Moderations and the Final Honour

---

[1] *Times*, May 22, 1897.　　　　[2] 1890.　　　　[3] 1897.
[4] Each Hall has its own Council.

Schools of Mathematics, Science, and Modern History were opened to women by the University, all arrangements and payments being made through the Delegates of Local Examinations. Every couple of years a fresh school was conceded to women, until finally in 1894 the remaining examinations for the degree of B.A., including all Pass Schools, were opened. The Delegates still conduct the First Examination for Women (corresponding generally with Responsions, but including Modern Languages), the Higher Local Examinations (a sort of blend of Moderations and Pass Final Schools, first held in December, 1894). and an Honour Examination in Modern Languages, in which the University has as yet no Final Honour School.

In 1896 Congregation rejected a proposal to admit women to University degrees[1], or even to grant them diplomas recording their achievements[2]. The Association consequently grants two classes of diplomas, the one to students who have 'resided' for three years and taken a full B.A. course in due order, the other to those who have passed an alternative course; certificates are awarded for a distinguished but less complete career[3].

The main difference between Oxford and Cambridge in this connexion is that at Oxford women are admitted to Pass as well as Honour Schools, and for such admission, as far as the University is concerned, they need not have studied in Oxford, nor have fulfilled any conditions of residence or previous training, nor belong to any organization or society.

	Number of Registered Students.		*Honours.*	
	1890.	1897.	1890.	1897.
Lady Margaret Hall	34	53	8	5
Somerville College	32	75	6	8
St. Hugh's Hall	13	24	—	5
St. Hilda's Hall	—	14	2	1
Home Students	17	36	—	3
	96	202	16	22

[1] By 215 to 140, March 3, 1896.   [2] By 178 to 111, March 10, 1896.
[3] For exact details see the Calendar of the A. E. W., 1897–98, p. 16: Oxford, price 6*d*.

In 1897 twenty-two students obtained honours in Final Schools of the University, but only two qualified for full B.A. diplomas.

2. DURHAM [1].

In the seventeenth century the foundation of a University for the North of England was often proposed, and in 1657 Cromwell granted his assent to such a foundation at Durham. On the Restoration this scheme came to an end, and it was not until 1832 that the present University of Durham was established by means of some £3,000 a year and certain preferments, ceded by the Dean and Chapter of the Cathedral [2]. Colleges were founded, as at Oxford and Cambridge, to be constituent parts of the University [3]; but the funds had to come from the University itself, and Durham has always been at a disadvantage from the smallness of its resources. In 1841 some further provision was made by the Ecclesiastical Commissioners under an Order in Council. An executive Commission was appointed in 1861 [4], with the usual powers of making schemes to be submitted to the Queen in Council and the Houses in Parliament, but very little resulted from it.

The College of Medicine at Newcastle, founded in 1851, was admitted into connexion with the University in 1852, and more closely associated in 1870. In 1865 a School of Physical Science was established, but it was in 1871 that the most important step in the history of the University was taken. A College of Physical Science was established at Newcastle, partly by the Corporation of that city, partly by the leading landowners in the neighbourhood. It received the hearty support of the University of Durham, to which it was affiliated, and which devoted £1,000 a year to its purposes [5].

---

[1] Report of Commission, P. P. Eng., 1863, vol. xvi; University Calendars; Devonshire Commission on Scientific Instruction, vol. v. P. P., 1874, xxii. p. 78.

[2] 2 & 3 Will. IV, Private Act, c. 19.

[3] University College in 1837, Bishop Hatfield's Hall 1846, and Bishop Cosin's Hall 1851, closed in 1854.

[4] 24 & 25 Vict. c. 82.   [5] P. P., 1874, xxii. p. 78.

Durham has always provided special opportunities and training for theological students. In other respects it has always, to the best of its abilities, taken up the movements initiated by the older Universities. Like them, it has always required residence, although in 1865, the numbers having fallen very low, the Arts course, unfortunately, was reduced to two years. Thus in 1870 unattached students were admitted, in 1871 (but this was by the same Act of Parliament) theological tests were abolished. Colonial colleges are admitted to affiliation. Local examinations, examination and inspection of schools, and, in collaboration with Cambridge, extension lectures have been adopted. In 1895 —and this was giving a lead which has not been followed— all degrees except those in divinity were opened to women. There is an elementary matriculation examination, and in 1896 certificates were given for Proficiency in General Education, which, under certain conditions, dispense with the necessity of passing the former test.

In 1853–54 the average number of students in residence was 120 ; in 1862, the impulse of the North countrymen towards Durham having died out[1], the number had fallen to 44[2].

In 1897 there were 432 undergraduates on the books of the University, exclusive of musical and medical students and of the 184 students of the College of Science[3].

The receipts of the University from all sources in 1859–61 averaged £9,000 a year[4].

3. University Colleges and Modern Universities.

Thus much of Oxford and Cambridge, and of Durham, which, apart from Newcastle, has not differed greatly from the two older Universities. The most important change in English higher education has been the creation throughout the country of University Colleges, which in some instances have become constituent parts of a new university, but in

[1] P.P., 1872, xxv, Q. 8,757.   [2] P.P., 1863, xvi. p. 7.
[3] Calendar, 1897–98.   [4] P.P., 1863, xlvi, Evidence, pp. 4, 7.

all cases have extended higher teaching to towns and to individuals it had never reached before, at low charges and in numerous subjects for which a demand has come into existence.

The movement began in 1826 by the foundation of an institution, which was an undenominational teaching college, and was also intended to be a university for London. It was opened in 1828. King's College, a Church of England establishment, was founded by Royal Charter in the same year and was opened in 1831. It is unnecessary here to detail even the first of the many controversies which the very name of London University seems to evoke. The earlier foundation received its first charter in 1836 as University College, London, and in the same year there was also incorporated the University of London, an examining body which for fourteen years granted degrees to none but qualified members of University and King's Colleges. In 1850 the University received a new charter, and admitted candidates from additional affiliated colleges, over which it had no visitatorial power or effectual control. The new qualifications varied so much that in 1858 they were all swept away, and all matriculated candidates were admitted to the examinations without any requirements as to residence or previous courses of study [1].

In 1860 the Faculty in Science was created, and the degrees of Bachelor and Doctor of Science were introduced into England.

In respect to the success of the University of London, as Fyffe has well said, 'When a University has but one function to fulfil, the only question that can be asked about it is whether it fulfils this function well. It can no more suffer from the peculiar infirmities of Oxford and Cambridge than a skeleton can suffer from gout [2].' The standard of its examinations has always been well maintained, and it has insisted on Bachelors of Arts proving their fitness for

---

[1] Calendar, 1898–99, pp. xx–xxii.
[2] C. A. Fyffe, T. H. Ward's *Reign of Queen Victoria*, ii. 313.

the higher degree of M.A. Yet when that question is satisfactorily answered, 'there is something chilly and forlorn in the spectacle of a University which gathers to it no glad troops of youth, which is the home of no one learned man, which ceases even to have any concrete existence between the recurring throes of examination[1].'

In 1889 a Royal Commission under the Duke of Northumberland reported on the requirements of London in respect of a University. Another Commission, with Earl Cowper as Chairman, was appointed in 1892 to report on the Bill for constituting a teaching University in London, to be known as the Gresham University; they took much evidence and reported in January, 1894.

At last, in 1898, the London University Commission Act was passed, appointing seven executive Commissioners to frame new statutes for the University. A distinction is to be established between Internal and External Students, who are to have separate examinations, which nevertheless shall test as far as possible the same standards of knowledge and attainments. All certificates and diplomas shall be marked Internal or External, but Internal Students shall, if they prefer, be admitted to the External examinations, and graduate accordingly.

The Internal Students are those pursuing approved courses of study at the Schools of the University, which are to include University, King's and Bedford Colleges, the Royal College of Science, the City and Guilds Institute, ten medical schools, six theological colleges, four colleges of music, and in some degree the four Inns of Court and the Incorporated Law Society. Besides teachers directly appointed by the University, members of the teaching staffs of public educational institutions within thirty miles of London[2] will also be recognized as Teachers of the University by the Senate, after consulting with the Academic Council (the Committee for Internal Students). There is

---

[1] C. A. Fyffe, T. H. Ward's *Reign of Queen Victoria*, ii. 314.
[2] Also Wye Agricultural College, Kent.

to be a widely representative Senate of fifty-six members, with standing committees for the Internal and External Students, and for the extension of University teaching.

In 1867 a supplemental charter was granted enabling the University to hold examinations for women, and in 1880 they were admitted to all degrees.

UNIVERSITY OF LONDON.

| | Matriculations. | | Total Candidates for all Examinations. |
	Candidates.	Percentage passed.	
1840 . .	77	89·6	186
1850 . .	206	50·5	355
1860 . .	428	68·0	788
1870 . .	845	50·8	1,459
1880 . .	1,400	58·6	2,572
1890 . .	2,762	46·3	4,984
1897 . .	3,508	49·4	6,294

Queen's College, London, was founded for women in 1848 on Church of England lines[1], but its best work as yet has been done in secondary education.

Bedford College was founded in 1849 for the higher teaching of women, and has been the first woman's institution to receive a share of the grant to University Colleges[2].

In 1846 Mr. John Owens left nearly £100,000 to found an institution at Manchester for 'providing or aiding the means of instructing and improving young persons of the male sex (and being of an age not less than 14 years) in such branches of learning and science as are now, and may be hereafter, usually taught in the English Universities, but subject nevertheless to the fundamental and immutable rule' that no religious tests whatever should be applied. It was to be open to all without respect to place of birth, and without distinction of rank or condition in society. The College was opened in 1851, incorporated in 1871, and lodged in its present buildings in 1874. Women were admitted to its classes in 1875; a separate College for them, founded in 1877, was incorporated in Owens College in 1883[3].

In 1871, as we have seen, Newcastle College was estab-

---

[1] Bremner, p. 128.   [2] £700, 1894; £1,200, 1897.
[3] *The Owen's College*, by Joseph Thompson: Manchester, 1886.

lished in connexion with Durham.   In 1874 the Yorkshire
College was founded at Leeds, and then for some time
came almost one a year:—1876, Bristol ; 1879, Sheffield[1];
1880, Birmingham—Mason College ; 1881, Nottingham ;
1882, Liverpool.

In 1892 and 1893 the success of Oxford and Cambridge
Extension work resulted respectively in the establishment
of the Reading University Extension College and of the
Technical and University Extension College, Exeter : two
combinations of diverse forms of local effort with University
teaching which have hardly yet had time to secure their
position or establish their claim to a State subsidy.   In 1896
a similar college was founded at Colchester.

The characters of these institutions differ so much
according to the needs of their cities and the means at
their disposal, that it is not easy to give a description in
general terms which shall be applicable to them all, while
their numbers render it impracticable to detail their differences.   They all possess constitutions, professorial staffs,
and buildings, but, except at Bedford College, there is no
official provision made for lodging the students, although
recognized residential halls exist in most places for the
women.   The work of a University standard is carried on
principally in the day classes, but there is abundant opportunity provided in the evening classes for those unable to
attend during the day.   Many of the colleges spread their
influence by extension lectures and otherwise in smaller
towns in the neighbourhood.   In many instances they have
drawn around them the Denominational Colleges and
Seminaries of the districts, the students of which receive
instruction and associate freely with the other students.   In
almost all cases women are received on exactly the same
terms as men, the chief exceptions being in medical studies.

Having been created in and for their present environment,
it is in many respects easier for them than for the older
Universities to meet existing needs and deal with existing

[1] Firth College, Sheffield, became in 1897 Sheffield University College.

arrangements, especially in connexion with lower, secondary, and technical education. Thus they have solved for themselves numerous difficulties and reduced to practice many theories which elsewhere have not yet been adjusted to the old traditions, and they have developed studies which it may not always be desirable for the more strictly classical Universities to direct.

In respect of endowments over a million and a half has been expended on the University Colleges from all sources, partly from magnificent donations or bequests, and partly from local subscriptions. In 1889 the House of Commons decided to recognize them as a national institution by voting £15,000 for distribution among them [1]. This grant, which was recommended for the London Colleges and Manchester by the Devonshire Commission in 1874 [2], has been renewed annually, and in 1897 was increased to £25,000, a fresh apportionment being made on the report of the President of Magdalen College, Oxford, and Professor Liveing of Cambridge, who made a careful inspection of them all at the request of the Chancellor of the Exchequer.

The Inspectors say that 'the Colleges are, to speak generally, doing good work, fulfilling their function and realizing the purpose for which they were established, namely, of bringing education of an advanced and University kind to those who cannot go to the Universities to seek it, of forming a link between the Universities and the great commercial communities of the country, and of establishing in the minds of these communities centres of intellectual enlightenment and culture [3].'

A report was also issued by Mr. Chalmers, who made a financial inspection at the same time. An annual report and statement of accounts is sent to the Education Department by each College in receipt of a grant.

[1] The Colleges receiving this grant report, under a Treasury Minute of July 1, 1889, each year to the Education Department, which is thus— in addition to its hold upon the Training Colleges—an authority on higher education (Bryce Report, i. p. 30).

[2] *Vide* p. 171.   [3] Report, p. 3; P. P., 1897, No. 245.

	Number[1] of Day Students, 1895–96.	Total Capital Expenditure. £	Annual Income, 1895–96. £	Annual Grant[2], 1897. £
Owens College, Manchester	670	348,702	36,295	3,500
University College, London	747	400,000	18,333	3,000
Liverpool	433	152,745	16,385	3,000
Leeds	501	190,000	12,871	2,200
King's College, London .	599	220,970	13,286	2,200
Birmingham . . .	500	106,000	13,284	2,700
Newcastle . . .	499	72,365	10,381	2,200
Bristol	213	34,449	5,707	1,200
Nottingham . . .	456	90,257	8,132	1,500
Sheffield	183	28,966	5,435	1,300
Bedford College, London .	176	23,137	6,589	1,200
	4,976	£1,667,591	£146,688	£24,000[3]
University Extension College, Reading	40	11,602	2,388	—
University Extension College, Exeter	—	10,000	620	—
	5,016	£1,689,193	£149,696[4]	

In this list *Holloway College* finds no place, as it has
not yet had time to outgrow its endowments; its importance, however, entitles it to mention. It was founded at
Mount Lee, Egham Hill, by Mr. Holloway, who died in
1883, but it was not opened for students until October,
1887. The intention of the founder was that it should
'afford the best education suitable for women of the middle
and upper middle classes,' and it was intended to be mainly
self-supporting. With this view he spent some £400,000
on land and buildings, and then added another £300,000
for endowment[5].

The founder desired that the College should ultimately
obtain power to confer degrees, and that in the meantime
the students should qualify themselves for degrees at
London and other Universities. In the end of 1897 an

---

[1] Excluding medical students; including Training College students.

[2] These grants are not in any case to exceed one-fourth of the local
income of each institution, and depend further on the performance of
'an appreciable amount of advanced University work' (P. P., 1897,
No. 245, p. 74).

[3] Also £1,000 to Dundee.		[4] P. P., 1897, No. 245, pp. 64, 66, 75.

[5] *Dictionary of National Biography.*

important meeting was held to consider the advisability of constituting Holloway the University for women, but the plan was favoured by none but those who were opposed to the acceptance of women elsewhere, and it seems definitely settled that this scheme will never be carried out.

The buildings contain ample lodging for two hundred and fifty students ; the number of students in March, 1898, was 107.

In 1880 a charter was granted to *Victoria University*, of which Owens College, Manchester, was the only original member ; University College, Liverpool, was admitted in 1884, and three years later it was followed by the Yorkshire College, Leeds. All persons matriculating must be members of one of these Colleges, and all candidates for degree examinations must furnish certificates of having passed through a recognized three years' course in one of the Colleges. The University receives an annual grant of £2,000 from Government, and may, besides examination fees, receive contributions from the Colleges. Bachelors of Arts or of Science must, unless they have taken honours, pass a further examination for higher degrees. All the degrees are open to women, except in the case of medicine, the regular courses for which are not opened to them by the Colleges. There are no University lectures apart from the Colleges, but certain Berkeley fellowships have been founded for research.

The foundation of a University at Birmingham is probably near at hand, and depends only upon the necessary money ; and in time to come the dream of a southern University may be realized.

4. The Board of Agriculture.

Among the many miscellaneous tasks which were given at various times to Committees of the Privy Council was the supervision of the Contagious Diseases (Animals) Acts and of the Destructive Insects Act, 1877. To this Agricultural Committee was assigned in 1888 a Parliamentary grant of £5,000 for the promotion of agricultural education[1]. In the following year a Board of Agriculture was created[2] to take over the functions of this Committee and of the Land Commissioners, and to supervise the working of various Acts connected with the land ; and it was composed of several Ministers of State with a specially appointed President.

By the terms of the Act they may 'undertake the inspection of and reporting on any schools which are not public elementary schools, and in which technical instruction, practical or scientific, is given in any manner connected with agriculture or forestry ; and the aiding of any school which admits such inspection, and in the judgment of the Board is qualified to receive such aid ; and the aiding of any system of lectures or instruction connected with agriculture or forestry, and the inspection of and reporting on any examination in agriculture or forestry.'

At first in order to preserve and develop the few existing institutions, the Government grants were given partly to schools and courses of a local character, but afterwards the chief aim of the Department has been to establish and maintain collegiate centres for agricultural instruction for the benefit of groups of County Councils, and to furnish inspection for such agricultural instruction as these Councils provide[3].

In 1896–97, £6,950 of the grant was given to fourteen institutions, eight of which were of a collegiate character, and received £5,500 between them. Twenty County Councils were acting in close association with the Board. Of the money devoted by local authorities to technical education it was reckoned that £78,000 was spent on agricultural teaching in this year[4].

[1] Hansard, T. S., cccxxv, p. 1,819.
[2] 52 & 53 Vict. c. 30.
[3] 1894, C. 7,495.
[4] Report of Board on Grant, 1898, p. vii.

5. The Privy Council.

i. *The Education Department.*

Besides its control over the Elementary Training Colleges, the Education Department is the authority to whom the University Colleges in receipt of grants have annually to report.

ii. *The Science and Art Department.*

The Science and Art Department provides higher instruction in both ranges of its subjects at its two Colleges at South Kensington.

Royal College of Science. In 1851 a 'Government School of Mines and of Science applied to the Arts' was opened, and two years later a 'Royal College of Chemistry,' a private institution, amalgamated with it. In 1862 Royal exhibitions and scholarships were bestowed on it. During the seventies the various sections of the school migrated one after another to South Kensington. In 1868 Summer courses were started for teachers who received allowances for maintenance during their attendance. These proved so successful, and the need for science teachers had so greatly increased, that, after some delay, the whole school was[1] reorganized in 1881 as the 'Normal School of Science and Royal School of Mines,' and in 1890 it received the title of 'The Royal College of Science, London.'

'It is primarily intended for the instruction of teachers in the various branches of Physical Science, and of students of the industrial classes selected by competition in the examination of the Department of Science and Art, but other students are admitted so far as there may be accommodation for them on the payment of fees[2].' The College confers the title of Associate.

Short Summer courses are given to country teachers, who receive their fares and a bonus, while evening courses are given to working men[3].

---

[1] As recommended by the Board of Trade in 1852 (Calendar, 1898, pp. xxx and xxxv).
[2] Ibid. p. xxxvi.
[3] Ibid. p. xxxvii.

The Royal School of Mines continues to exist as an affiliated institution, but its students obtain their general scientific training in the Royal College.

Royal College of Art. In 1837 a central Government School of Design was established.

In 1852 the Department of Practical Art was founded, and greatly improved the Central School, making it a National Training School of Art, which in 1896 received the title of Royal College of Art. 'The special object of the school is the training of Art Teachers of both sexes, of designers, and of Art workmen, to whom facilities and assistance are offered in the shape of Studentships, in Training Royal Exhibitions and National Scholarships with maintenance allowances. Free Studentships with complete or partial remission of fees are also granted [1].'

6. City and Guilds of London Institute.

The Livery Companies of London formed a Committee in 1877 to prepare a scheme for a national system of technical education; in 1879 schools were opened, and in 1880 the City and Guilds of London Institute was registered as a Company, its objects being to provide and encourage education adapted to the requirements of all classes of persons engaged, or preparing to engage, in manufacturing and other industries. A large Central Technical College was opened at South Kensington in 1884, where most of the higher education is given, the instruction being more specialized than that of the Science and Art Department. Technological Examinations are held throughout the country to encourage the formation of technical classes, but payments are made only to persons actually engaged in industries [2]. The headquarters of the Institute are at Gresham College in the City, a sixteenth-century foundation, which has endowments for lectures [3], and should long ago have formed part of a teaching University for London.

[1] Calendar, p. xxxviii.
[2] Second Report, Samuelson Commission, i. 527; *Hazell's Annual*, 1891, 1898.   [3] P. P., 1892, lix. p. 401.

III. HIGHER EDUCATION [1].

B. Wales.

University Colleges and the University of Wales.

As in secondary so in higher education, the Welsh people have shown great ardour and great public spirit.

As early as 1854 it was proposed to raise funds for a University College in Wales, but the scheme had to be postponed to the creation of a Training College [2], and it was not until 1872 that the University College of Wales was opened at Aberystwyth [3]. The foundation was unsectarian, and the fees very low, less than one-fifth of the cost of the students being met by their fees.

The Committee on Intermediate Education [4] reported in 1881 in favour of a Parliamentary grant, which should be given to one University College in South Wales and another in North Wales. Accordingly, in 1883, the former was opened at Cardiff [5], and the latter at Bangor in 1884, and each of these received £4,000 a year. The claims of Aberystwyth were also pressed, and it received in 1884 £2,500, increased in 1886 to £4,000 a year [6]. In 1895 and 1896 Aberystwyth and Bangor each received special grants of £10,000 for building purposes.

In 1893 the three Colleges were incorporated by Royal Charter in the University of Wales, which receives an annual grant from Government [7]. When the petition for this Charter [8]

---

[1] *Studies in Secondary Education*, pp. 109 seqq.
[2] Opened at Bangor, 1862.
[3] Aberdare Report, i. p. xvi.   [4] *Vide* p. 197.
[5] The University College of South Wales and Monmouthshire.
[6] In 1882 and 1883 it had received £2,000 and £4,000 (Appropriation Acts).
[7] 1894, £3,000; 1898–9, £3,900.
[8] Undated. Between 1889 and 1893.

was drawn up there were 650 students attending the three Colleges, and one-eighth of the Bachelor's Degrees in Art and Science granted at the London University during the preceding year were taken by Welsh students[1].

The Charter created a University Court, containing the Chancellor, nominees of the Lord President, representatives of local authorities, of the various sections of each College and of the Graduates of the whole University, representatives of Welsh secondary and elementary teachers and of the Intermediate Education Board—a hundred members in all. It also created a Senate, composed of the Principals and Professors, and also a Guild of Graduates, consisting of all Graduates and the teaching staff of the Colleges. Statutes were to be made by the Court, but schemes of studies or of examinations must first be recommended by the Senate. In all examinations for degrees at least one examiner in each subject must be appointed, who is not a teacher in any of the constituent Colleges.

A University examination is held at each of the three Colleges for matriculation, open only to persons not under sixteen. The first was held in 1895. No candidate is admitted for any examination to an initial degree unless he or she has pursued a recognized course in one of the Colleges for three years, part of which may, however, under certain conditions be spent at a theological college. Candidates for Doctor's or Master's degrees must give further proof of knowledge or skill.

Nine theological colleges (including Lampeter[2]) have been recognized as giving education for degrees in theology. All degrees, and every office and the membership of every authority, are, by the Charter, open to women equally with

[1] Petition.

[2] St. David's College, Lampeter, is a theological college, opened in March, 1827; it has however an Arts course, and power to grant the degrees of B.A. and B.D. In 1880 it was affiliated to the University of Oxford, and in 1886 to Cambridge.

Before 1827 some of the Welsh Grammar Schools had apparently been licensed as institutions from which clergymen might be ordained (Report on Welsh Education, P. P., 1847, xxvii A, p. 45).

men, and there is a recognized hostel or hall of residence for them in each of the three towns.

Day Training Colleges exist at Aberystwyth, Bangor, and Cardiff, and great efforts have been made to extend these benefits of training to secondary teachers. University Extension is also promoted by means of lecturers.

Number of Students.

	Aberystwyth.	Bangor.	Cardiff.
1884–85	—	58	—
1890	165	97	—
1897–98	407	267	—

Jesus College, Oxford, has always been specially connected with Wales, and even after the changes made by Commissioners, half its fellowships and half its scholarships are still reserved for Welshmen.

III. HIGHER EDUCATION.

C. Ireland.

1. The University of Dublin and Trinity College.

Irish higher education before the grant to Maynooth[1] closely resembled its English original. There was but one University, and that was open only to members of the Established Church.

In March, 1591–92, Queen Elizabeth granted 'a Charter or Letters Patent[2],' incorporating Trinity College, Dublin, 'unum Collegium Mater Universitatis[3],' the commencement of a University similar to those of Oxford and Cambridge[4], and nominating the Provost, three Fellows *nomine plurium*[5], and three Scholars, and also the Chancellor and Visitors. The Provost and Fellows received power to make statutes for the College, to appoint acts and exercises for degrees, and to elect University Officers[6]. The Crown

---

[1] Vide p. 280.

[2] *The Dublin University Calendar*, 1877, vol. ii. p. 1; *The History of the University of Dublin*, p. 8, by Rev. J. W. Stubbs, D.D.: Dublin, 1889; *The Book of Trinity College*: Belfast, 1891; *The Constitutional History of the University of Dublin*, p. 14, by D. C. Heron (Catholic): Dublin, 1847; Report of the Royal Commission (Archbishop Whately, Chairman) on the University of Dublin and Trinity College, 1853, p. 2.

[3] Heron, p. 15; Calendar, ii. p. 1.

[4] 'We license the Provost and Fellows of the said College that they may establish amongst themselves whatever well-constituted laws they may perceive in either of our Universities of Cambridge or Oxford, provided that they shall consider them proper and suitable for themselves' (Translation of the Charter, *vide* Heron, p. 19). The first four Provosts were all Cambridge men (Stubbs, pp. 4, 18, 19, 27), and the influence of Cambridge was naturally great.

[5] The distinction between Senior and Junior Fellows was not made until early in the seventeenth century (Stubbs, p. 29).

[6] Heron, p. 15; Calendar, ii. p. 1.

granted certain confiscated lands in the North for an endowment, and about £2,000 was collected in money [1].

No provision was made for admitting any other Colleges, if founded, to a share in the University. In fact, none of the later subsidiary foundations ever became Colleges or attained any importance [2], and no division of aim or interest has arisen between Trinity College and the University [3].

In 1637 Charles I granted a new Charter, resuming for the Crown the exclusive right of making Statutes, and in exercise of this right he issued therewith a new code of Royal Statutes which, with modifications by Royal Letters and Statutes, lasted till the days of modern reform [4].

The endowments of the College and University, which at first had been very inadequate, gradually increased; professorships were founded, and between 1752 and 1763 £45,000 were granted by Government for building [5].

Catholics in the eighteenth century might neither learn from Catholics at home nor go abroad [6], yet in Dublin the College Statutes exacted from all students an oath denying the temporal supremacy of the Pope in these dominions [7], and required attendance at religious services in the College Chapel; and it was further necessary to take the Oath of Supremacy and the declaration against transubstantiation before proceeding to a University degree [8]. Subscription of the Thirty-nine Articles, however, was not required as in England, and in practice Catholic and Nonconformist Students had been from time to time excused from attendance at Chapel [9].

In 1793 the Roman Catholic Relief Act [10] provided that any persons might graduate in the University without oath

---

[1] Heron, p. 24.   [2] Hansard, T. S., ccxiv. 398.
[3] Such as occurred at Glasgow (Scotch Universities Commission Report, 1863, p. xiv).
[4] Calendar, ii. p. 3.   [5] *The Book*, p. 192.
[6] *Vide* p. 80.   [7] Heron, p. 46.
[8] Stubbs, p. 283; Heron, p. 82.
[9] Ibid.; Lecky, *History of Ireland in the Eighteenth Century*, ii. 280, 514.
[10] Irish Act, 33 Geo. III, c. 21.

or declaration save of allegiance and abjuration, if the laws of the University were altered to admit of it. In 1794, accordingly, a Royal Letter made the necessary changes, and consonantly with the spirit of the law the College authorities admitted Dissenters on the same terms with Catholics to all privileges of study and graduation and to sizarships[1]. But no relaxation was made in the case of Scholars, who had to attend Chapel and take the Communion, or of Fellows, who must all belong to the Established Church, and nearly all take its Orders[2].

The University and College were practically indivisible, and were ruled by the Provost and Senior Fellows. The University was, fortunately for its efficiency, not too independent to admit changes in its Statutes effected by the means of Royal Letters. There had long been a matriculation examination[3]; the exercises for degrees were a formality, but the examinations were genuine[4]. For graduation in all Faculties except Music, it was and is necessary first to take the B.A. degree. But Classics did not reign supreme, for besides the Faculties of Law, Medicine, and Divinity, in 1776 two Royal Chairs of Modern Languages were founded[5]. In 1841 the first School of Engineering in the kingdom was established[6].

In 1840 a Royal Letter removed the condition of celibacy attaching to the fellowships, which had been continually violated before it was stringently re-enacted in 1811[7].

This further increased the value of these endowments to Dublin, which has always been a home of learning, and numbered among its Fellows many distinguished men[8].

The great defect of Dublin is that residence is not necessary for the Arts degree. Provided that a man passes an examination each term, he never need reside at all,

---

[1] Whately Commission Report, pp. 4, 53; Heron, p. 49.
[2] Report, pp. 10, 54.
[3] Stubbs, p. 204; Report, p. 64.
[4] Report, p. 57.
[5] Ibid. p. 44.
[6] Ibid. p. 41.
[7] *The Book*, p. 93; Report, p. 5.
[8] *The Book*, p. 123, and passim.

whether in College or out of it. Many Students do reside, and attendance on the Professors' lectures is necessary for taking a degree in Divinity, Law, Medicine, or Engineering[1]; but a man may become Bachelor of Arts without ever having spent more than a few days at any one time in Dublin, or setting eyes on his fellow students except in the examination room.

In 1851 the tide of University reforms, which had reached England the year before, brought a Royal Commission under Archbishop Whately to inquire into the State, Discipline, Studies, and Revenues of the University of Dublin and of Trinity College.

They found the College income for 1852 amounted to £35,994 from external, and £26,816 from internal sources[2], while the University fees for degrees had been in 1850 £3,143[3]. There were 1,217 undergraduates on the books; of these only 118 were living in College[4], and 518 residing in the city and suburbs[5]. A public registry of addresses was kept, but the out-college residents were under very little control, and the Commission recommended that they should be required to live in licensed Halls or Lodging Houses.

The desirability of enforcing residence seems not to have been raised, though it was necessary for the only other University in Ireland at that time, and all the other Universities in the kingdom.

The Commission reported in 1853 'that numerous improvements of an important character have been from time to time introduced by the authorities of the College, and that the general state of the University is satisfactory. There is great activity and efficiency in the different departments, and the spirit of improvement has been especially

---

[1] Dublin University Calendar.

[2] In 1888 the net college income was returned at £55,987 (P. P., 1889, No. 334), of which £12,960 was received from students.

[3] Evidence, pp. 12, 267.

[4] There is accommodation in College for 230 men, but most sets of rooms are for two occupants (Report, p. 56; Calendar, 1898–99, p. 20).

[5] Report, p. 63.

shown in the changes which have been introduced in the course of education to adapt it to the requirements of the age '.'

In 1855 certain alterations were made in accordance with these recommendations with regard to fellowships, professorships, fees, and other minor matters; the number of lay fellows was increased from three to five; forty exhibitions, open without distinction of creed, were founded [2]; the formal exercises for degrees were abolished, and all the higher degrees, except the M.A., were made tests of merit [3]. The constitution itself, however, was not dealt with until 1857. In that year by Letters Patent power [4] was again given to the Provost and Senior Fellows (known as The Board) to make or alter rules, but such rules must be sanctioned by the Senate or Congregation of the University, now for the first time incorporated, and consisting of Doctors and Masters on the books of the University. The Chancellor or Vice-Chancellor was bound to convene this body on the requisition of the Board, and had power to adjourn or dissolve the meeting. The Caput of the Senate consisted of the Chancellor of the University and the Provost of the College or their substitutes, and the Senior Master, who was elected by the Senate, and any one of these three could veto a grace. In the Senate the Chancellor or Vice-Chancellor had an absolute veto; no 'grace' for any purpose might be proposed which had not been previously adopted by the Provost and Senior Fellows [5].

In 1867 Mr. Fawcett introduced a Bill to remove all religious disabilities, but they were removed only from certain Chairs [6]. In 1873 [7] all tests were abolished in University and College for all offices and emoluments whatsoever, except for any Professor of, or Lecturer in, Divinity.

---

[1] Report, p. 92.
[2] Fourteen open studentships were founded in 1858.
[3] *The Book*, p. 95.   [4] Calendar, ii. p. 6.
[5] *The Book*, p. 97; Calendar, 1877, ii. p. 9.
[6] 30 & 31 Vict. c. 9.
[7] 36 Vict. c. 21, University of Dublin Tests Act.

Early in 1873 Mr. Gladstone made a heroic attempt to settle the Irish University question. He brought in a Bill to emancipate the University of Dublin from the control of Trinity College, which henceforth was to be only one among several Colleges. The Catholic University, Magee (Presbyterian) College [1], and the Queen's Colleges of Belfast and Cork were to share in its government and privileges. The theological faculty was to be disestablished and handed over to the representative body of the disestablished Church of Ireland [2]. To remove further grounds of controversy the new University was to take no cognizance of metaphysical or moral philosophy or of modern history [3].

The Protestants did not like the measure, because it deprived them of power ; the Catholics did not like it, because it failed to provide them with endowments; and on the second reading it was rejected by three votes [4]. The Letter of 1857 was a measure of reform, but Mr. Gladstone in 1873 could with accuracy describe the University of Dublin as being in servitude to a single College [5]. 'It means servitude to eight gentlemen who elect the other Fellows, who elect also themselves, and who govern both the University and the College.' To secure a more real representation for the University, a Council of the University was instituted in 1874 for co-operating in regulation of studies, lectures, and exercises in the College, and in appointment and regulation of the tenure of office of Professors. It consists of the Provost and four groups elected from the Senate by Senior and Junior Fellows, Professors, and the rest of the Senate respectively [6]. It can, however, only be said to 'interfere a little' with 'the small and perfectly homogeneous governing body [7].'

In 1878 a Royal Commission reported that the College had received £140,661 as compensation for the loss of

---

[1] Opened 1865. [2] Hansard, T. S., ccxiv. p. 408.
[3] Ibid. p. 416. [4] Ibid. p. 1,863. [5] Ibid. p. 392.
[6] Calendar, 1877, p. 11.
[7] Royal Commission, Gresham University, Professor Mahaffy, Q. 24,682.

advowsons on the Disestablishment of the Irish Church [1], and recommended that the income of this sum should be devoted to increasing the number of Senior Fellows. They also thought that the Divinity School should be transferred to the Representative Body of the Church of Ireland, together with a liberal provision for its support [2]. None of these recommendations were, however, carried into effect.

In 1870 special examinations for women were first held, but it was not until 1896 that women were admitted to any of the ordinary University examinations, and then only to certain Honours examinations, in separate rooms from the men, and as an experiment to be tried for three years. In the matter of matriculation and degrees, Dublin has proved no less unyielding than Oxford and Cambridge. The first examinations in the History and Theory of Education and the Practice of Teaching were held in January, 1898 [3].

The maximum and minimum of students (including Bachelors) on the College books within the last forty years were 1,308 in 1886 and 1,063 in 1894 [4]. In the end of 1897 there were 1,084, of whom 798 were undergraduates.

As for the religious question, the following Census returns show to how small an extent the Catholics avail themselves of the leading University :—

		Students on books, including Roman Catholics.	
1871	. .	991	74
1881	. .	1,338	115
1891	. .	1,162	76 [5]

It was estimated that of the 1,200 students who matriculated between 1891 and 1895, only about six per cent. were Catholics [6].

In the matter of residence, in 1866 there were 568 resident undergraduates; 488 were non-resident, or had failed to attend a quarter of their lectures; the total number, how-

---

[1] Report, p. 3.		[2] Ibid. p. 11.
[3] *Vide* p. 218.		[4] Calendar, 1898, p. 524.
[5] Census, P. P., 1892, C. 6,780, p. 64; cf. also P. P., 1889, lix. p. 393.
[6] *Edinburgh Review*, January, 1898, p. 119.

ever, of those who had kept terms during the preceding year
was 1,218 [1].

In 1891 Professor Mahaffy stated that less than twenty
per cent. thus got degrees by examination only [2].

2. THEOLOGICAL ENDOWMENTS.

i. *Maynooth.*

The French Revolution broke up many of the Colleges
on the Continent at which the Irish Catholic priesthood was
trained [3], and in 1795 the Irish Parliament passed an Act
appointing trustees for endowing an academy for the education
of Catholics only [4].   The Duke of Leinster let a house and
grounds on favourable terms [5] at Maynooth, 15 miles north-
west of Dublin.   The seminary was opened in 1795, and
the next year the Lord Lieutenant laid the foundation-stone
of new buildings.   The Irish House of Commons voted
£8,000, and this became an annual grant, varying slightly
in amount.   By the Act of Union it was provided that the
sum granted *inter alia* for maintaining institutions for pious
and charitable purposes in Ireland should not be reduced
for twenty years [6].   A separate 'lay College' was started in
1800 for boys admitted under fifteen [7], but was discontinued
in 1817.   Since that year Maynooth has been a clerical
seminary pure and simple.   The grant, after one or two
fluctuations, was fixed at £8,928 [8], and was voted annually
by the House of Commons till 1845, a constant cause of
exasperation to ultra-Protestant members.   In 1845 an Act
of incorporation was passed [9], and the annual grant raised to

---

[1] P. P., 1867, lv. p. 774.
[2] Gresham University Commission, Q. 24,688.
[3] *Maynooth College: the Centenary History*, p. 95, by Rev. John
Healy, D.D., Bishop of Macra: Dublin, 1895.   Of 478 Irish students
who were abroad at the time of the Revolution, 348 were in France
itself (Lecky, *History of Ireland in the Eighteenth Century*, iii. 348).
[4] 35 Geo. III, c. 21.   [5] Healy, p. 127.
[6] 40 Geo. III, c. 38, Article 7.   [7] Healy, pp. 312, 319, 692.
[8] Appropriation Acts.   Bishop Healy states it as £9,673, p. 263.
[9] 8 & 9 Vict. c. 25.

£26,360, provision being made for 520 students; a sum of £30,000 was also given for buildings. There were two Royal Commissions of inquiry, which reported in 1827 and 1855.

On the disestablishment of the Irish Protestant Church in 1869 [1], all denominational endowment ceased and existing interests were compensated. Maynooth received a sum of £369,040 [2], being fourteen times the annual grant, and the Acts of 1800 and 1845 were repealed.

When the Royal University of Ireland was established, the Senate were disposed to give three of their fellowships for lecturing to the students at Maynooth, but the Catholic bishops declined the offer, and students are not now expressly prepared for the examinations of the University [3]. Maynooth is a College of the Catholic University, but apparently co-operation is, or was, imperfectly organized [4].

ii. *The Belfast Academical Institution.*

Another educational grant to a denomination was made in the case of the Belfast Academical Institution, which, opened in 1814 as an undenominational establishment for affording youth a classical and mercantile education [5], soon became a college for the education of the Presbyterian clergy of Ireland. It received from Parliament after 1828 an annual subsidy [6], which began at £1,500 and amounted to £2,500 in 1849, when the Institution was merged in the General Assembly's Theological College, Belfast. The grant was still continued for the retiring allowances of Theological Professors, and at the Disestablishment was commuted for £43,976 [7].

---

[1] *Vide* p. 104.   [2] Healy, p. 481.   [3] Ibid. p. 527.
[4] Ibid.   [5] 1824 Commissioners' Fourth Report.
[6] Besides an annual grant, 1816-18.
[7] Being fourteen times the grant, which then amounted to £2,050, and £15,000 for the College buildings (Appropriation Acts; Hansard, T. S., clv. 428; Ellis, *Irish Education Directory*, 1887, p. 89).

3. THE QUEEN'S COLLEGES.

4. THE QUEEN'S UNIVERSITY.

5. THE ROYAL UNIVERSITY.

In 1845, Sir Robert Peel being in office, an Act[1] was passed providing for the establishment of three 'Queen's Colleges' 'in order to supply the want, which had long been felt in Ireland, of an improved academical education equally accessible to all classes of the community without religious distinction[2].'

A sum of £100,000 was granted for sites and buildings for three colleges at Belfast, Cork, and Galway, and each college received £7,000 a year. Three Faculties were established in each, viz. Arts, Law, and Physic. The colleges were strictly undenominational, and professors were forbidden by the Statutes to make any statement disrespectful to the religious convictions of their classes, or to introduce political or polemical subjects[3].

They were opened in the end of 1849, and in 1850 the Queen's University was founded, as a part of the original design, to examine for degrees students who had qualified by attending courses at these colleges.

In August, 1850, as we have seen[4], the Synod of Thurles assembled, and the Roman Catholic clergy were prohibited, under penalty of suspension, from taking part in the administration of the colleges, on the ground that they were dangerous to faith and morals[5]. There were eight Catholic students that year at the Queen's Colleges, and twenty-one the next, but the scheme failed—the Catholics as a body would none of it, and though the colleges have done and continue to do good work, the problem of

---

[1] 8 & 9 Vict. c. 66.

[2] Report of Royal Commission, 1858, p. 1. The scheme was suggested in the report of the Select Committee on Foundation Schools and Education in Ireland, 1838, under Mr. Wyse, *vide* p. 208.

[3] Ibid. p. 7.   [4] *Vide* p. 104.

[5] Powis Report, Q. 3,690; *The Catholic Case*, pp. 401–404, Archbishop Walsh.

providing a generally acceptable teaching University still awaits solution.

In 1870 a declaration, signed by most of the leading Catholic laymen in Ireland, was presented to the Lord Lieutenant, demanding such a change in the system of collegiate and university education in Ireland as would admit those persons at present debarred by conscientious scruples to a full enjoyment of the honours and emoluments and examinations already possessed by others of their fellow-countrymen [1].

In 1879 an Act was passed for the abolition of the Queen's University and the establishment of the Royal University of Ireland in its place. The old annual grants of about £5,000 continued until 1882, and in 1883 the new University first received its full income of £20,000 a year from the Church Temporalities Commissioners, who administered the funds of the disestablished Church [2].

Its Charter was granted in April, 1880 ; power was given to confer degrees in all Faculties except Theology, but the distinctive change was that no residence in any College was required, nor attendance at any lectures, except in the case of medical students. Thus the new foundation was only an examining University, but the religious difficulty was shelved, and the Catholics have readily availed themselves of its examinations and accepted its offices and fellowships.

The corporation consists of a Chancellor, Senate, and Graduates, the Senators being to the maximum number of thirty nominated by the Queen, while six are appointed by the Convocation of the University.

A scheme was prepared by the Senate, submitted to the Lord Lieutenant, and laid before Parliament. It provided for the creation of fellowships, scholarships, and prizes, and for the holding of public examinations for matriculation and degrees. There are thirty-five fellowships of £400 a year,

[1] This was again signed and presented in 1897 (P. P., 1897, No. 80).
[2] 44 & 45 Vict. c. 52.

and nineteen of these are at present filled by Catholics[1]. Women have always been admitted to the University on equal terms with men.

The Matriculation Examination and the First University Examination are held at seven or eight different local centres; the other examinations at Dublin only.

QUEEN'S COLLEGES.

Number of Students entered in each year.

	Belfast.			Cork.			Galway.		
	Matriculated.	*Non-Matriculated.*	*Total Catholics.*	*Matriculated.*	*Non-Matriculated.*	*Total Catholics.*	*Matriculated.*	*Non-Matriculated.*	*Total Catholics.*
1849–50	90	105	5	70	45	62	64	4	38
1859–60	66	24	6	144	27	85	35	5	25
1869–70	83	15	8	228	24	94	49	5	25
1879–80	127	23	10	271	29	152	96	3	39
1889–90	142	28	6	228	10	155	118	4	51
1896–97	87	21	4	202	4	116	101	4	46

QUEEN'S UNIVERSITY.

		Entered for Examinations.	*Passed.*
1860	. .	—	—
1870	. .	302	—
1880	. .	748	—

ROYAL UNIVERSITY.

1884	. .	2,364	1,458
1890	. .	2,845	1,803
1896	. .	2,743	1,754[2]

6. THE CATHOLIC UNIVERSITY.

The Catholic University in Ireland was opened in 1854 in accordance with the resolutions of the Synod of Thurles.

[1] *The Quarterly Review*, April, 1898, p. 579.
[2] P. P., 1880, vol. xxiii. 269; 1890–91, vol. xxviii.

John Henry Newman, afterwards Cardinal, was sent over to Dublin as its first Rector[1], and there delivered those lectures which expressed in such perfect language his 'Idea of a University.'

Between 1851 and 1865 £125,000 were collected for the new institution in voluntary subscriptions, and £59,000 more by 1874. Five out of the six thousand pounds of its annual cost were spent on salaries, as the fees were almost nominal[2].

It was modelled on the University of Louvain, but was sorely hampered for want of funds, and negotiations for its endowment, entered into with Lord Derby's Government in 1867, came to nothing. The Bill of 1873[3] proposed to recognize but not to endow it. The Royal Commission on Scientific Instruction were, in 1874, owing to its restrictions and provisional character, unable to recommend it for a grant[4].

In 1879 the O'Conor Don brought forward a measure for the endowment of an examining and grant-giving University[5]; but the Royal University was established instead.

In October, 1882, the Establishment at St. Stephen's Green, hitherto known as 'The Catholic University,' became 'University College, Dublin,' one of the six constituent Colleges of the Catholic University, another being Maynooth[6].

In 1896–97, with only 130 pupils, St. Stephen's Green obtained forty-nine first class distinctions at the Royal University, against thirty-three obtained by the Queen's Colleges[7].

In 1873–74 there were only 116 students in the University,

---

[1] He resigned in 1858 (*Quarterly Review*, April, 1898: 'The Irish University Question').

[2] Devonshire Fifth Report, P. P., 1874, xxii. p. 92.

[3] *Vide* p. 278. [4] Fifth Report.

[5] Hansard, T. S., ccxlvi. 475.

[6] *The Irish University Question; The Catholic Case, selected from the speeches and writings of the Archbishop of Dublin* (*Dr. W. J. Walsh*), *with an historical sketch*, p. 46: Dublin, 1897.

[7] Right Hon. John Morley in the House of Commons, Feb. 17, 1898.

of whom some were resident in Dublin, either as Intern students in its buildings, or Extern either in licensed lodging-houses or living with their families. Others were Non-resident or Affiliated, in kindred institutions throughout the country, while others, again, non-matriculated and not necessarily Catholics, were known as Auditors [1].

The University gives degrees in Theology and Philosophy only, and in other faculties sends its students to the examinations of the Royal University [2]. The Catholic University is a purely private body, and has never received any recognition or support from Government. Its governing body consists of the Roman Catholic Archbishops and Bishops of Ireland.

The Irish Catholics have long made up their mind to be content with nothing less than a Catholic University. Dr. Walsh, the Archbishop of Dublin, declared in 1890, 'To us Catholics it comes as a fixed principle that every institution such as Trinity College, embodying that which is known as the " mixed " system, is from the nature of that system a source of danger to Catholic students, if they frequent it ; a source of danger to the vigour and even to the integrity of their faith ; a source of danger also to their constancy in the full and faithful observance of the practical duties by which they are bound as Catholics [3].'

They may be right or they may be wrong ; but the principle has been conceded by leading statesmen of both English parties in Parliament [4], and the official recognition and endowment of this or some other Catholic University seem near at hand.

---

[1] Devonshire Commission on Scientific Instruction, i. 83.
[2] Ellis, *Irish Education Directory*, 1887, p. 43.
[3] *The Irish University Question ; an Address*: Dublin, Gill & Son, 1890.
[4] *Edinburgh Review*, January, 1898, p. 106.

7. SCIENCE AND ART DEPARTMENT.

The Royal Hibernian College of Science.

In 1845 the Royal Dublin Society founded a Museum of Economic Geology, which two years later resulted in a School of Science applied to Mining and the Arts, and in 1853 this was transferred to the Department of Science and Art. The course of events throughout was the same as in England, but rather more rapid, for in 1867 the Royal Hibernian College of Science was opened. At the time it was in advance of any institution of the sort which England possessed [1], but it is now sorely in need of new buildings and appliances [2].

This absorbed the School of Science, and supplies as far as practicable a complete course of instruction in Science applicable to the Industrial Arts, especially those which may be classed broadly under the heads of Mining, Engineering, and Manufactures ; it is intended also to aid the instruction of Teachers for the local schools of Science.

The Royal Exhibitions and National Scholarships are tenable either in Dublin or in London. There is a three years' curriculum for ' Associated Students ' who can obtain the Diploma, but it is not compulsory to become associated and follow this course.

In the Session of 1896–97 there were twenty-seven Associated and eighty Non-associated Students.

HIGHER EDUCATION OF WOMEN.

In 1866 Alexandra College, Dublin, was founded for the higher education of women, and a residence house was opened for their reception [3].

In 1870 the University of Dublin held its first exami-

---

[1] Report of Commission on Science and Art Department in Ireland, 1869, i. xxxiii.

[2] *Journal of Education*, 1898, p. 293.

[3] Ellis, *Irish Education Directory*, 1887, p. 226.

nation for women ; as we have seen [1], it was not until 1896 that the other sex were admitted by the University to do any papers which were set for men.

Not only does the University refuse degrees, but the College, unlike English and Scotch Colleges, refuses instruction to women. Some of the University lectures are open to the general public, of which women are admitted to form part, but Trinity College reserves its teaching for men alone [2].

The first Statutes of the Royal University of Ireland declared all degrees, honours, exhibitions, prizes, and scholarships open to students of either sex.

In 1882 Queen's College, Belfast, opened its honour lectures to matriculated women students [3], and the example has been followed by the two other Colleges.

St. Mary's University College and the Loretto High School for Girls are in connexion with the Catholic University [4].

Alexandra College, Victoria College, Belfast, and the Rochelle Seminary, Cork, are, with St. Mary's, the chief institutions which prepare their pupils for the examinations of the Royal University.

---

[1] *Vide* p. 279.

[2] Statement of the Proceedings from 1892 to 1895 in connexion with the Movement for the Admission of Women to Trinity College, Dublin, by W. G. Brooke : Dublin University Press, 1895. 48 pp.

[3] Ellis, *Irish Education Directory*, 1887, p. 223.

[4] Sadler, Special Reports, 1897, p. 698.

III. HIGHER EDUCATION.

D. Scotland.

1. The Universities of St. Andrews, Glasgow, Aberdeen, and Edinburgh.

The University system of Scotland differs from that of England at almost every point, but it has adapted its growth to the wants of the people, and, if limited in some respects, it has served the nation well, and has needed but few alterations in order to meet modern requirements.

On the one hand, the Scotch Universities are more numerous, better distributed, less expensive than Oxford and Cambridge, and except in the case of the teaching body they have scarcely been limited at all by sectarian restrictions[1]. Consequently they have received many more students, and thus represented more completely the various elements of which the nation is composed. Sessions can be kept only by actual attendance at specified lectures, and not by mere residence within the precincts of the University.

On the other hand, being inadequately endowed, the Universities have practically abolished the College system, there has been little corporate life among the younger students, and few men have been enabled to devote themselves to the pursuit of learning for its own sake. Too

---

[1] 'Professors, Principals, Regents, Masters, or others bearing office' had to subscribe the Westminster Confession of Faith (Scotch Acts, 1690, Will. III, c. 25; 1707, Anne, c. 6), but this was accepted (with more or less reservation) by all or most of the Protestant denominations; the rule was, in any case, not regularly observed (Rosebery Report, p. 33). Only the Principals and Divinity Professors had to be ordained. Celibacy of course found no place in the regulations.

much of the teaching has been merely secondary, but one most important point Scotland and England (except London) have retained in common—no student has been able to obtain a university degree without spending several years among his fellows in attendance at the University.

At the beginning of the century there were four cities in Scotland which contained Universities, and two of these had received more than one foundation.

In 1411 St. Andrews had been founded, and two years later had obtained a Papal Bull from Benedict XIII[1]. In 1455 the foundation of the College of St. Salvator had been confirmed, in 1512 the College of St. Leonard had been founded, and these had been united in 1747 by an Act of Parliament[2]. In 1537 St. Mary's College had been founded[3], and at the Reformation in 1579 had been appropriated exclusively to Theology.

In 1450 Glasgow had received a Bull from Nicolas V[4].

In 1494 the University and King's College of Aberdeen was erected by a Bull of Alexander VI[5]. In 1593 the Marischal College was founded by the Earl Marischal under Royal authority[6]. The two Colleges were temporarily united in the seventeenth century[7], but the amalgamation was incomplete, and they again became distinct foundations with separate constitutions and distinct staffs.

Edinburgh differed from the others in its constitution, and in its subordination to the Municipality. In 1582 King James VI or I granted a Charter to the Provost, Bailies, and Council of Edinburgh for building a 'College,' granting them the right of electing and dismissing the professors; and in 1621 an Act was passed granting to the Provost, Bailies, Council, and Community of Edinburgh, on behalf of the College, all privileges granted to any other College in the realm[8].

[1] Rosebery Report, p. 387.
[2] Ibid. p. 390.
[3] Ibid. p. 388.
[4] Ibid. p. 213.
[5] Report, 1830, p. 305.
[6] Ibid. p. 343.
[7] 163--1670 (ibid. p. 308).
[8] Ibid. p. 99.

On the whole this government by the local authorities worked well : 'they succeeded where they might have been expected to fail, and failed where they might have been expected to be particularly successful. In the intellectual development of the University their success was brilliant; they took good advice and did the right thing at the right moment, and in their appointments they rarely made a mistake. On the other hand, the material interests of the University did not flourish in their hands[1].'

Thus Scotland, which a hundred years ago had only a fifth of the population of England and Wales, had twice as many University towns, and though the distance between each of these and its nearest neighbours was even less than the seventy miles between Oxford and Cambridge, or the journey between either of them and London, three out of these four were also three of the four largest towns in Scotland[2].

The contrast with England is most marked in respect of denominational exclusion. In 1830 the Commissioners reported, ' The Universities of Scotland are not now of an ecclesiastical character, or in the ordinary acceptation of the term, ecclesiastical Bodies. They are connected, it is true, with the Established Church of Scotland, the standards of which the Professors must acknowledge. Like other seminaries of education, they may be subject to the inspection of the Church on account of any religious opinions which may be taught in them. The Professors of Divinity, whose instructions are intended for the members of the Established Church, are in their character of Professors members of the Presbytery of the Bounds, and each University returns a representative to the General Assembly of the Church of Scotland. But in other respects the Universities of Scotland are not Ecclesiastical Institutions, not

---

[1] Sir A. Grant, *The Story of the University of Edinburgh*, ii. 229.

[2] The Rosebery Commissioners in 1830 recommended the establishment of a University at Dumfries out of the Crichton funds, which were then available (Report, p. 85), but the money went to a lunatic asylum (*Encyclopaedia Britannica*: Art. ' Dumfries ').

being more connected with the Church than with any other profession [1].

'They are intended for the general education of the country, and in truth possess scarcely any Ecclesiastical feature except that they have a certain number of Professors for the purposes of teaching Theology in the same manner as other Sciences are taught. . . . Neither their constitutions, endowments, nor provisions for public instruction are founded on the principle that the Universities are appendages of the Church. All the classes may be taught by laymen, with the exception of the classes of Divinity [2].'

It was generally provided that the students should attend public worship in a body, but the rules appear to have been greatly relaxed, and there seems to have been no difficulty in obtaining a dispensation [3].

Such apartments as had ever been provided for the residence of students within the college buildings had long been forsaken [4] for private lodgings. No doubt one great motive for this had been economy, and in Scotland the expenses of a university education had been reduced to the lowest possible amount.

The present Archbishop of Canterbury found, apparently by personal experience, that at Balliol in his time [5] a careful man could, without withdrawing himself from the society of the place, live for £86 a year, with a preliminary outlay of £36 [6] exclusive of recoverable payments.

In 1851 the late Master of Balliol considered that economy could not bring the whole expenses of a year at Oxford to less than £100 or £120, and he put the average allowance at £200 to £300 [7]. At Cambridge, £150 to

---

[1] Cf. Professor Halford Vaughan's evidence before the Oxford Commission : 'A man who can take a degree is already, in point of attainments, three-fourths of a Clerk in Orders, but he is not one-fourth of any other profession' (1852, Evidence, p. 86).

[2] Rosebery Report, p. 8.

[3] Ibid., Appendix, pp. 163, 265, 328, 359, 409.

[4] Ibid. pp. 180, 283, 329, 359, 409.

[5] 1839-41.   [6] 1852 Oxford Evidence, p. 123.

[7] Ibid. p. 32.

£250 was an average estimate at the same period[1]. It is
reckoned nowadays that, apart from vacations, it is within
the bounds of possibility for an unattached student at
Oxford to spend no more than £50 a year on his education,
lodging, and board. Few men can live in College under
£80, and £150 is estimated as the normal amount[2].

But these figures stand out as spendthrift extravagance in
comparison with the minimum possible in Scotland. Dr.
Lee, in evidence before the Rosebery Commission[3], mentioned an Aberdeen student whose total expenses for his
first session were only £16, more than a quarter of this
being fees. At Edinburgh, lodging and maintenance for
the whole twenty-four weeks amounted in another case to
no more than £8 2s.[4], or yet again even to £6[5]. As in
England, the academic year included only six months' term,
but this was broken by a vacation of a very few days, and
so it has been easier for poor students to make provision
for their winter course by doing other work in the summer[6].
The bursaries, or exhibitions as they would be called in
England, though small, were numerous, and seemed to reach
the poorest students of any real ability.

In consequence of all this, the attendance at the Universities was far greater than in England. In 1800 there must
have been about 1,000 undergraduates at Oxford and
Cambridge[7]. In 1801 there were 993 students at Edinburgh alone[8].

In 1830 the English Universities had under 3,000
undergraduates[9]. In any of the years 1825-6-7 Scotland

---

[1] Cambridge Report, p. 148.

[2] J. Wells, *Oxford and Oxford Life*, pp. 52, 54: Methuen, 1892.

[3] Edinburgh Evidence, printed 1837, p. 598.

[4] The annual fees for an Arts Course nowadays amount at the most to
about ten guineas (Edinburgh Calendar, 1894-95, p. 118).

[5] Edinburgh Evidence, p. 599.

[6] Rosebery Report, p. 34; Inglis Report, 1863, p. xxx; Argyll Third
Report, iii. 156.

[7] The matriculations at both Universities in 1800 were 366 (p. 251).

[8] Rosebery Appendix, p. 161.

[9] Oxford 1852 Report, App. p. 55, 1481 undergraduates on the books;

had about 4,400 students[1]. A certain number of these came from outside Scotland especially to attend the Medical Classes at Edinburgh. But in 1830 England and Wales had six times as many inhabitants as Scotland[2].

The mixture of classes was great. It is true that English pupils like Lord John Russell and private tutors like Sydney Smith soon ceased to frequent Edinburgh, and as time went on it became the custom for the sons of Scotchmen of good position to resort to the reformed English Universities[3]. But the fusion of professional and lower classes on the benches of the lecture-rooms was complete. The Argyll Commission reported that of a number of students in the Professors' classes 16 per cent. were sons of skilled labourers and artisans[4].

The profession of teaching naturally benefited largely by this diffusion of knowledge. The Argyll Commission found in 1866 that in 69 secondary schools, out of 286 masters 72 per cent. had studied at a University, and more than half of these had taken a degree[5]. In 1897–98 796 of the masters in public elementary schools in Scotland, being 19 per cent. of the whole, were university graduates[6].

The chief drawback to this large attendance was that many of the students still required not higher but secondary instruction. There was no test whatever at matriculation, and boys matriculated as early as possible to secure the material benefits of a university course without prolonging the expenses of their education[7]. The Rosebery Commission reported in 1830 that the average age at which the students of the Marischal College, Aberdeen, commenced their course was twelve, some of them being as young as

Cambridge matriculations (1830), 424, i.e. probably 1,400 undergraduates in residence.

[1] Rosebery Appendix, pp. 161, 263, 327, 357, 409; Edinburgh, 1825, 2,236; Glasgow, 1826–27, 1,257; Aberdeen, 1826–27, 610; St. Andrews, 1825–26, 312.

[2] *Vide* p. 305.   [3] Taunton Report, vi. p. 20.

[4] Third Report, i. p. 154.   [5] Ibid. i. p. 77.

[6] Annual Report of Scotch Education Department, p. 18.

[7] Taunton Report, vi. p. 30.

eleven[1], and fourteen and a half was then an average age
to enter the Humanity Classes at Edinburgh[2].   Hence it is
not wonderful that the professors found it necessary to have
a junior class, or that these junior classes in Greek and
Mathematics had often to begin at the very beginning[3].

In point of examinations and definite tests of knowledge
the Scotch Universities in the early part of the century seem
not to have been much better than England.   The Rosebery
Commission reported that 'in all the Universities in Scotland till very recently, and in some of them even at the
present time (1830), the degree of Master of Arts (that of
Bachelor having fallen into disuse) has been conferred almost
as a matter of form. . . . In general there was no examination or a very slight one.' 'The degrees ceased to be objects
of solicitude, and in general have been viewed with so little
respect that at Edinburgh and Glasgow comparatively few
individuals have of late applied for them'.'   In Glasgow only
the students attending gown classes continued to matriculate[4],
and generally discipline was left to the Professors, who did
not always test the acquirements of their classes[5].

The absence of graduation, however, was partly due to
its being an unremunerative expense : even in 1895–96 only
230 students graduated in Arts at the four Universities,
while there were 2,057 matriculations in Arts in the same
year.

Universities which were competing with High Schools
could scarcely satisfy aspirations for the highest learning.
The one beneficial result of the enormous classes was the
provision of adequate salaries for the professors from their
fees, and thus it was not difficult to secure the services of
teachers even of a European reputation[7].

---

[1] Report, Appendix, p. 357.
[2] Ibid. p. 119.   For average ages in 1866 *vide* p. 221.
[3] Taunton Report, vi. pp. 30, 622 ; Rosebery Report, pp. 28, 31.
[4] Rosebery Report, p. 39.   [5] Ibid. App. p. 263.
[6] Ibid. p. 34.   Graduation remained more in favour at Aberdeen than
elsewhere (Rosebery Report, pp. 329, 359 ; P. P., 1863, xvi. p. xxx).
[7] Taunton Report, vi. p. 30.

Despite the want of fellowships, Scotland has produced many distinguished men, eminent in philosophy and scientific discovery rather than in the exact scholarship and classical research which found its reward with facility elsewhere.

Nevertheless Lord Jeffrey admitted to the Rosebery Commissioners the justice of the reproach which had been levelled against the general national instruction—that though there was a greater number of all ranks who possessed considerable information, there were fewer who were completely learned: their knowledge, in short, though more general, was more superficial than with their neighbours in England [1].

The Commission reported: 'There are no endowments or fellowships for the maintenance of a number of literary men . . . in order that they may have further opportunities for literary or scientific pursuits. . . . There is no encouragement to prosecute to any great extent those branches of literature which do not directly tend to useful objects in life [2].'

Mr. Matthew Arnold in his report to the Taunton Commission compares the Scotch and Swiss, and declares that 'so far as intellectual culture has an industrial value, makes a man's business work better, and helps him to get on in the world, so the Scotch middle class has thoroughly appreciated it and sedulously employed it, both for itself and those whose labour it uses'; but 'instead of guarding, like the Germans, the "wissenschaftlicher Geist" of their Universities, they turn them into mere school classes [3].'

And the number of Universities had its bad side as well as the number of students, for Lord Lingen was able to say in 1866, 'You have four Universities competing as to which shall make a graduate on the cheapest and lowest terms [4].'

[1] Edinburgh Evidence, 1837, p. 393.
[2] Report, 1830, p. 10.
[3] Report, vi. 622.
[4] Taunton Commission, Q. 13,123.

In 1826 a Royal Commission under Sign Manual was issued to view and report upon the Scotch Universities, the fourth Earl of Rosebery being Chairman. The preamble stated that it was 'His Majesty's undoubted right and prerogative to name Visitors and Commissioners to inquire into irregularities and disputes in the Universities, and to remedy the same,' and no objection appears to have been raised. Government was just completing a grant of £120,000 for the Edinburgh buildings[1], and the Marischal College, Aberdeen, at this·time received £20,000 for the same purpose[3]; so the Universities may have felt they had something to lose as well as to gain, even if the king's authority had ever been questioned. The Committee reported in 1830, but for nearly thirty years no result followed.

A Bill introduced in 1837 to appoint Visitors (as Executive Commissioners) to the Universities fell through[2], but the Evidence of the former Commission was then printed, and fresh Commissions were then and subsequently appointed to inquire separately into the affairs of Aberdeen, Glasgow, and St. Andrews, and reported respectively in 1837, 1839, and 1845.

The tests for lay professors were relaxed in 1853[4], practically for the benefit of the Free Church, but it was not until 1858 that the Universities (Scotland) Act[5] was passed. Provision was made for the amalgamation of the two Aberdeen foundations (for which a fresh Commission had issued the year before) as the University of Aberdeen, and the constitutions of all four Universities were revised and assimilated. The ordinary administration of the affairs of each remained vested (as in practice it had been previously in all cases except that of Edinburgh) in the hands of the Senatus Academicus, a body consisting of the Principal (who might henceforth be a layman) and the Professors. The acts of the Senatus were now 'made, "subject to the

---

[1] Grant, ii. 208.
[3] Grant, ii. 52.
[5] 21 & 22 Vict. c. 83.
[2] P. P., 1857-58, xx. p. 41.
[4] 16 & 17 Vict. c. 89.

control and review of the University Court," a new governing body introduced by the Act,' consisting in each case of
the Rector, the Principal, and four or five assessors elected
or nominated by various sections of the University[1]. There
was also established a General Council of each University,
composed practically of the registered graduates in all
faculties. Edinburgh was now assimilated to its sister
Universities, and the war which it had been waging with
the Town for the past thirty years was stopped. It received
a Chancellor and a Senatus Academicus, neither of which
it had possessed before; but the Lord Provost and an
assessor nominated by the magistrates and Council of the
City were made members of the new University Court, to
which most of the powers formerly exercised by the Town
were transferred, including that of appointing the professors.

An Executive Commission was appointed to carry out
the Act by making the necessary ordinances, and the
Right Hon. John Inglis of Glencorse, the Lord Justice
Clerk (afterwards Lord President), was elected Chairman.
The draft proposals were to be laid before Parliament for
approval; any petitions to the Crown might be referred
to the Commissioners themselves to report upon, and the
ordinances must finally be sanctioned by the Queen in
Council before they became valid.

Up to this date, with the exception of some large grants
for building[2], the Scotch Universities received from Parliament little more than those royal grants which, before the
accession of William IV, were defrayed from the hereditary
revenues of the Crown[3], and in 1832 amounted to £5,496.
In 1860 the grant was only £7,630, but the Commissioners
freely exercised their discretionary powers in founding
several chairs, supplying additional teaching, and providing
for superannuation, and by 1862 the grant had increased to
£20,161[4]. They had been empowered, on the motion of

---

[1] Report, 1878, p. 3.   [2] Cf. p. 297.
[3] P. P., Eng., 1833, xxiv. p. 570.
[4] *Vide* Appropriation Acts; cf. P. P., 1875, xxviii. p. 346.

Mr. Gladstone, to found a National University of which the existing Universities might be the colleges, but this scheme they found neither practical nor expedient, nor was it favoured by any of the bodies whom they consulted [1].

By the ordinances also the curriculum was widened, and though no matriculation examination was imposed, the Arts course was shortened by a year for those students who qualified at once for the senior classes by passing a 'First Examination [2].'

The Commissioners refused to make a Summer Session in any way compulsory, even at the urgent solicitation of Glasgow. Instruction in Science was already given between May and August, and courses in other faculties gradually sprang up, but they were purely voluntary at first, and attendance at them did not count towards graduation until 1892 [3].

In 1864 the old buildings of the University of Glasgow, which were dilapidated, inadequate, and badly placed, were sold for £100,000, and the University prepared to remove to a new site. Government gave £120,000, public subscriptions and bequests brought £261,429, and the total amounted to £520,329 [4].

Edinburgh also made large additions to her buildings in 1884, no less than £170,000 being collected from private sources, while Government contributed £80,000 [5].

It may be mentioned that in 1876 the trustees of the will of Dr. Andrew Bell, of Madras and monitorial fame, founded at Edinburgh and St. Andrews professorial chairs of the Theory, History, and Practice of Education.

In 1876 there was another Universities Commission, with the Lord President Inglis again as Chairman, and they reported in 1878 [6]. They advised the increase of the popular element in the University Courts, and the creation of a

---

[1] Report, p. xlvi.   [2] Ibid. p. xxvii.   [3] Ordinance 11.
[4] Calendar, 1897–98, p. 28.
[5] *The Quarterly Review*, July, 1898: 'The Scottish Universities'; *Edinburgh University Calendar*, 1889–99, p. 38.   [6] P.P., 1878.

General Universities Court to sanction new ordinances; specialization in five different lines was recommended for the latter part of the Arts course, but attendance was not to count towards graduations until a preliminary examination had been passed. The foundations at St. Andrews were to be amalgamated, and a college affiliated to St. Andrews was to be established at Dundee. Nothing, however, came of these proposals, until in 1889 another Universities (Scotland) Act was passed[1]. An executive Commission was appointed with Lord Kinnear as Chairman, and also a permanent Scottish Universities Committee of the Privy Council, to which petitions from the Universities or persons directly affected might be referred.

In each University Court the numbers of the assessors elected by the Senatus Academicus, and of those elected by the General Council, were in nearly every case increased from one to four, and the management of the University and College funds was transferred to each University Court from the Senatus. Provision was also made for the extension of the Universities in the future by affiliation of new Colleges.

All ordinances made by the Commissioners were to be laid before Parliament, and if no address from either House were lodged against them, they might then be sanctioned by the Queen in Council. Among the various subjects specified for regulation, ordinances have been passed for all the Universities which make the preliminary examination necessary for graduation[2], prescribe the same fees for matriculation, entrance, and graduation in all four Universities[3], and enable each University to admit women to graduation in one or more faculties, and to provide for their instruction[4]. After the expiration of the Commission (which finally took place at the end of 1897) each University Court might make ordinances, subject to the approval of the Queen in Council, and, if necessary, to a reference to the Universities Committee.

---

[1] 52 & 53 Vict. c. 55.   [2] No. 11.   [3] No. 50.   [4] No. 18.

Each University Court has by the Act to make an annual statistical and financial report, and the first of these was made in 1892.

For the purposes of the Act £42,000 was given as an annual grant to the Universities in place of the £17,000 they were receiving in 1889 [1].

By the Education and Local Taxation Account (Scotland) Act, 1892 [2], £30,000 a year of the money which Scotland had been voluntarily spending in freeing her elementary education [3] was transferred to the Universities, and the distribution of these grants has been settled by the Commissioners in the following proportions [4]:—

		£42,000	£30,000
Edinburgh	. .	£15,120	£10,800
Glasgow	. .	£12,180	£8,700
Aberdeen	. .	£8,400	£6,000
St. Andrews	. .	£6,300	£4,500

In 1895 the Government stamp duty on taking the M.D. degree ' at either of the Scotch Universities ' was abolished, the last of the duties on degrees [5].

Aberdeen received £40,000 from Government for the enlargement of its buildings, the grant being completed in 1895-96, and has raised £100,000 from private sources [6].

Income of Scotch Universities, 1896-97.

	Edinburgh.	Glasgow.	Aberdeen.	St. Andrews
	£	£	£	£
Fees, &c. . . .	36,364	22,015	10,500	2,666
Parliamentary Grant .	25,870	20,880	14,400	7,425
Endowments, &c. . .	11,429	16,602	5,761	29,094
Income for bursaries, &c.	11,264	7,423	8,900	3,586
	84,927	66,920	39.561 [7]	42,771

[1] 52 & 53 Vict. c. 70.
[2] p. 144.
[3] 58 Vict. c. 16, s. 10.
[4] *Journal of Education,* April, 1898, p. 228.
[2'] 55 & 56 Vict. c. 51, s. 2 (2).
[4'] Ordinances 25, 26, 27, 46.
[7] Presumably it was intended that the annual returns should make-

Number of Students attending the Scotch Universities[1].

	1861–62.	1871–72.	1881–82.	1891–92.	1896–97.
Edinburgh	1,462	1,854	3,269	3,368	2,833
Glasgow	1,140	1,349	2,320	2,113	1,871
Aberdeen	634	605	813	914	798
St. Andrews[2]	163	176	193	189	236
	3,399	3,984	6,595	6,584	5,738

University Extension[3].

University Extension has found very little to do in
Scotland. It was inaugurated by the Queen Margaret
Guild in 1885, an association of old students of the ladies'
college at Glasgow, who handed over the work three years
later to the Glasgow University Extension Board; but in
1895 there were only twelve centres with an attendance of
about a thousand persons. Edinburgh and St. Andrews
took up the work in 1888, but in four years' time both gave
up the attempt to form centres. The fact is that University
influence needs little extension, and there are very few
possible centres outside the large towns, the chief of which
possess Universities.

The Summer School at Edinburgh, which in some respects corresponds to a summer meeting, commenced in
1887.

The Higher Education of Women[4].

Educational associations for women were formed in the
four University towns of Scotland—at St. Andrews in 1868,

a comparison between the finances of the four Universities possible,
but the form in which some of the statements are drawn defied my
analysis. Not the least of my obligations to Mr. Alexander is for his
help and that which he obtained : without it I should have been quite
unable to present any table. The Parliamentary grant for St. Andrews
should amount to nearly £4,000 more, withheld pending the settlement
with Dundee, and subsequently paid.

[1] P. P., 1888, Commons Paper, No. 365, Annual Statistical Reports.
[2] Excluding Dundee.
[3] Article by Dr. Wenley, of the Glasgow University Extension Board,
reprinted in the *Oxford University Extension Gazette*, June, 1895, p. 95.
[4] Chiefly derived from Miss Galloway's account in Miss Bremner's
Education of Girls and Women, pp. 264–273.

at Edinburgh in 1869, and at Glasgow and Aberdeen in 1877. In several instances courses of lectures had previously been delivered to women, but in St. Andrews and Aberdeen, some years after the establishment of the associations, the lectures were discontinued for want of support.

As for examination and recognition of merit, in 1874 the University of Edinburgh granted a diploma in Arts to women who attended courses and passed examinations which would have entitled men to degrees. In 1876 St. Andrews instituted a higher examination for women only, and have continued to grant on this the Diploma of Lady Literate in Arts, while Glasgow in 1874 created a Higher Local Examination for Women.

At Glasgow in 1883 the Association was transformed into Queen Margaret College, on the council of which the University was represented by two members.

In 1892, when the Commissioners' Ordinance was passed, empowering each University to admit women to graduation and to provide for their separate or joint instruction, Glasgow adopted the separate method, and Queen Margaret College was amalgamated with the University and became the women's department. The three other Universities at the same time opened their ordinary classes in Science and Art to women, who receive their instruction in common with the men.

Halls of residence exist in Edinburgh, Glasgow, and St. Andrews, but women students are as free to live in lodgings as men.

2. DUNDEE UNIVERSITY COLLEGE.

Glasgow, Edinburgh, Dundee, and Aberdeen are the four largest towns in Scotland, and of these the third alone is without a University. Various schemes were proposed to remedy this lack, but the plan favoured by the Universities Commission of 1876 was carried out in 1881 by the foundation of a University College, which should be in close connexion with the University of St. Andrews, only a dozen miles distant. In 1885 the Science degree of St. Andrews was thrown open to Dundee. In 1890 the University Commissioners issued an affiliating order instituting a closer connexion, and all classes at Dundee were recognized as qualifying for the degrees of St. Andrews. Unfortunately a flaw was discovered in the instrument of affiliation, and it was declared null in 1895.

An Ordinance was made by the Commission, which constituted Dundee 'part of' St. Andrews University. The Principal is a member of the University Court, the Professors are members of the Senatus, and the students of Dundee College who matriculate as University students are in the same position as students at the Colleges in St. Andrews. A clause conferring on the Council of the College representation in the University Court was however struck out by the Privy Council.

Dundee has been included among the English Colleges by the Treasury, and received £500 a year from 1889, but in 1897 this grant was doubled. Its total capital expenditure by 1896 had been £66,799. In 1892–93 there were 200 day students, and in 1895–96 there were eighty-four [1].

3. THE PRIVY COUNCIL.

i. *The Scotch Education Department.*

Besides controlling Training Colleges, the Department has since 1896 administered an annual vote of £2,000 for agricultural education.

ii. *The Science and Art Department.*

The higher teaching of the Science and Art Department is of course open to the Scotch, but no local institutions are maintained by it.

The Glasgow and West of Scotland Technical College and the Heriot Watt College, Edinburgh, are the chief local endowments for higher scientific teaching.

[1] P. P., 1897, No. 245, p. 52.
[2] Report of Inspectors, P. P., 1897, No. 245.

APPENDIX A.

Population of the British Isles, according to the Census Returns.

	1	2	3	4
	England and Wales.	*Ireland.*	*Scotland.*	Wales and Monmouth (included in Column 1).
1801	8,892,536	...	1,608,420	587,653
1811	10,164,256	...	1,805,864	673,952
1821	12,000,236	6,801,827	2,091,521	794,694
1831	13,896,797	7,767,401	2,364,386	906,217
1841	15,914,148	8,175,124	2,620,184	1,049,915
1851	17,927,609	6,552,385	2,888,742	1,170,858
1861	20,066,244	5,798,564	3,062,294	1,296,001
1871	22,712,266	5,412,377	3,360,018	1,421,670
1881	25,974,439	5,174,836	3,735,573	1,571,269
1891	29,002,525	4,704,750	4,025,647	1,776,405

Percentage of Persons married who signed the Register by mark[1].

	England and Wales.		*Ireland.*		*Scotland.*	
	Men.	*Women.*	*Men.*	*Women.*	*Men.*	*Women.*
1841	32·7	48·9	...	...	...	...
1851	30·7	45·2	...	...	...	...
1861	24·6	34·7	...	...	10·6	21·3
1871	19·4	26·8	37·5	45·2	10·0	19·6
1881	13·5	17·7	26·1	30·7	7·1	13·9
1891	6·4	7·3	19·4	19·4	3·4	5·3

Ireland: Census.

Persons five years old and upwards.

	Able to read, but unable to write, per cent.	Able neither to read nor to write, per cent.
1841	19	53
1851	20	47
1861	20	39
1871	17	33
1881	16	25
1891	11	18

[1] Registrar-General's Returns.

APPENDIX B.

Public Elementary Day Schools.

	Number of Schools.	Number of Certificated Teachers.	Average Attendance.	Annual Cost per Child.		
England and Wales.				£	s.	d.
1860	6,012	6,433	751,325	1	1	7½ [1]
1870	8,919	12,744	1,168,981	1	5	4
1880 Board . .	3,433	8,920	769,252	2	1	11¾
Voluntary .	14,181	22,502	1,981,664	1	14	7¾
1890 Board . .	4,676	19,527	1,457,358	2	5	11½
Voluntary .	14,743	27,012	2,260,559	1	16	11½
1897 Board . .	5,539	30,371	2,023,850	2	13	2½
Voluntary .	14,418	28,443	2,465,193	2	0	6
Scotland.						
1870	2,030	2,499	203,522	1	6	8½
1880	3,064	5,330	404,618	{ 2	2	4½ B.
				{ 1	17	3¾ V.
1890	3,076	7,745	512,690	{ 2	4	4 B.
				{ 1	9	8¾ V.
1897	3,105	9,893	605,389	{ 2	11	4¼ B.
				{ 2	4	6¼ V.
Ireland.						
1860	5,632	5,068	262,823	...		
1870	6,806	7,626	359,199	...		
1880	7,590	10,674	468,557	...		
1890	8,298	11,119	489,144	2	1	0¾
1897	8,631	11,996	521,141	2	6	6¾

[1] 1864 : Annual Grant Schools only.

APPENDIX C.

PARLIAMENTARY VOTES AND LOCAL RATES.

Parliamentary Votes.

	(A) for Public Education (excluding Universities and Colleges).				(B) for the Science and Art Department (including Museums, &c.).
	Great Britain.	England and Wales.	Scotland.	Ireland.	
	£	£	£	£	£
1833	20,000	...	...	25,000	...
1840	30,000	...	...	50,000	1,300
1850	125,000	...	...	125,000	14,755
1860	798,167	...	...	270,722	94,951
1870	914,721	...	...	381,172	218,336
1880	...	2,536,077	464,203	722,366	336,002
1890	...	3,782,224	611,581	918,316	474,896
1898	...	8,520,175	1,281,867	1,226,734	600,781

Local Rates for Public Education[1].

		£	£	£
1880	...	1,579,752	205,011	8,324
1890	...	2,968,096	559,273	8,192[2]
1897	...	4,858,487[2]	795,963	8,098[2]

Voluntary Subscriptions and Income from Endowments for Public
Elementary Schools in England and Wales, 1871–95, £32,922,173
[Sadler and Edwards : *Special Reports*, 1897, p. 30].

[1] Exclusive of rates under the Technical Instruction Act, Welsh
Intermediate Education Act, &c.
[2] Exclusive of the money repaid to Boards of Guardians under the
Local Taxation (Customs and Excise) Act.
[3] Exclusive of £51,209 paid under the Agricultural Rates Act, 1896.

INDEX

6/10/98

Clarendon Press Series.

The English Language and Literature.

HELPS TO THE STUDY OF THE LANGUAGE.

1. DICTIONARIES.

A NEW ENGLISH DICTIONARY, ON HISTORICAL PRIN-CIPLES: founded mainly on the materials collected by the Philological Society. Imperial 4to.

PRESENT STATE OF THE WORK.

			£ s. d.
Vol. I. {A/B} Edited by Dr. Murray.	. . . .	Half-morocco	2 12 6
Vol II. C Edited by Dr. Murray.	. . . .	Half-morocco	2 12 6
Vol III. {D/E} Edited by Dr. Murray / Edited by Henry Bradley	. .	Half-morocco	2 12 6
Vol. IV. {F/G} Edited by Henry Bradley	F–Field	. . . .	0 7 6
		Field–Frankish	0 12 6
		Franklaw-Fyz—G-Gain-coming .	0 5 0
		Gaincope—Germanizing . .	0 5 0
Vol. V. H-K Edited by Dr. Murray.	H-Haversian	. . .	0 5 0
	Haversine-Heel . . .	0 2 6

Bosworth and Toller. *An Anglo-Saxon Dictionary,* based on the MS. Collections of the late Joseph Bosworth, D.D. Edited and enlarged by Prof. T. N. Toller, M.A. Parts I-III, A-SÁR. . . . [4to, 15s each.
 Part IV, Section I, SÁR—SWÍDRIAN. . . . [4to, 8s. 6d.
 „ „ II, SWÍÞ-SNEL—ÝTMEST . . . [4to, 18s. 6d.
. *A Supplement, which will complete the Work, is in active preparation.*

Mayhew and Skeat. *A Concise Dictionary of Middle English,* from A. D. 1150 to 1580. By A. L. Mayhew, M.A., and W. W. Skeat, Litt.D.
 [Crown 8vo, half-roan, 7s. 6d.

Skeat. *A Concise Etymological Dictionary of the English Language.* By W. W. Skeat, Litt.D. *Sixth Edition.* . . [Crown 8vo, 5s. 6d.

2. GRAMMARS, READING BOOKS, &c.

Earle. *The Philology of the English Tongue.* By J. EARLE, M.A.,
Fifth Edition. . . . . [Extra fcap. 8vo, 8s. 6d.
———— *A Book for the Beginner in Anglo-Saxon.* By J. EARLE, M.A.,
Third Edition. . . . . [Extra fcap. 8vo, 2s. 6d.
Mayhew. *Synopsis of Old-English Phonology.* By A. L. MAYHEW,
M.A. . . . . [Extra fcap. 8vo, bevelled boards, 8s. 6d.
Morris and **Skeat.** *Specimens of Early English—*
 Part I. From Old English Homilies to King Horn (A.D. 1150 to A.D. 1300).
  By R. MORRIS, LL.D. *Third Edition.* . . [Extra fcap. 8vo, 9s.
 Part II. From Robert of Gloucester to Gower (A.D. 1298 to A.D. 1393). By R.
  MORRIS, LL.D., and W. W. SKEAT, Litt.D. *Third Edition.* [7s. 6d.
Skeat. *Specimens of English Literature,* from the 'Ploughmans
Crede' to the 'Shepheardes Calender.' . . [Extra fcap. 8vo, 7s. 6d.
———— *The Principles of English Etymology—*
 First Series. The Native Element. *Second Edition* [Crown 8vo, 10s. 6d.
 Second Series. The Foreign Element. . [Crown 8vo, 10s. 6d.
———— *A Primer of English Etymology.* [Extra fcap. 8vo, *stiff covers,* 1s. 6d.
———— *Twelve Facsimiles of Old-English Manuscripts.* [4to, 7s. 6d.
Sweet. *A New English Grammar, Logical and Historical.* Part I.
Introduction, Phonology, and Accidence. . [Crown 8vo, 10s. 6d.
———— *A Short Historical English Grammar.* [Extra fcap. 8vo, 4s. 6d.
———— *A Primer of Historical English Grammar.* [Extra fcap. 8vo, 2s.
———— *History of English Sounds from the Earliest Period.* With full
Word-Lists. . . . . [8vo, 14s.
———— *First Steps in Anglo-Saxon.* . . [Extra fcap. 8vo, 2s. 6d.
———— *An Anglo-Saxon Primer, with Grammar, Notes, and Glossary.*
Eighth Edition. . . . . [Extra fcap. 8vo, 2s. 6d.
———— *An Anglo-Saxon Reader.* In Prose and Verse. With Gram-
matical Introduction, Notes, and Glossary. *Seventh Edition, Revised and
Enlarged.* . . . . [Crown 8vo, 9s. 6d.
———— *A Second Anglo-Saxon Reader.* . . [Extra fcap. 4s. 6d.
———— *Old English Reading Primers—*
 I. *Selected Homilies of Ælfric.* . . [Extra fcap. 8vo, *stiff covers,* 2s.
 II. *Extracts from Alfred's Orosius.* . [Extra fcap. 8vo, *stiff covers,* 2s.
———— *First Middle English Primer, with Grammar and Glossary.*
Second Edition. . . . . [Extra fcap. 8vo, 2s. 6d.
———— *Second Middle English Primer.* Extracts from Chaucer, with
Grammar and Glossary. . . . . . [Extra fcap. 8vo, 2s. 6d.
———— *A Primer of Spoken English.* . . [Extra fcap. 8vo, 3s. 6d.
———— *A Primer of Phonetics.* . . . [Extra fcap. 8vo, 3s. 6d.
———— *A Manual of Current Shorthand, Orthographic and Phonetic.*
[Crown 8vo, 4s. 6d.
Tancock. *An Elementary English Grammar and Exercise Book.*
By O. W. TANCOCK, M.A. *Third Edition.* . . [Extra fcap. 8vo, 1s. 6d.
———— *An English Grammar and Reading Book,* for Lower Forms
in Classical Schools. By O. W. TANCOCK, M.A. *Fourth Edition.* [3s. 6d.

A SERIES OF ENGLISH CLASSICS.

(CHRONOLOGICALLY ARRANGED.)

Chaucer. I. *The Prologue to the Canterbury Tales.* (*School Edition.*)
Edited by W. W. SKEAT, Litt.D. . . . [Extra fcap. 8vo, *stiff covers*, 1*s.*

—— II. *The Prologue; The Knightes Tale; The Nonne Prestes
Tale.* Edited by R. MORRIS, LL.D. *A New Edition, with Collations and
Additional Notes,* by W. W. SKEAT, Litt.D. . . [Extra fcap. 8vo, 2*s.* 6*d.*

—— III. *The Prioresses Tale; Sir Thopas; The Monkes Tale;
The Clerkes Tale; The Squieres Tale, &c.* Edited by W. W. SKEAT, Litt.D.
Sixth Edition. . . . . [Extra fcap. 8vo, 4*s.* 6*d.*

—— IV. *The Tale of the Man of Lawe; The Pardoneres Tale;
The Second Nonnes Tale; The Chanouns Yemannes Tale.* By the same
Editor. *New Edition, Revised.* . . . [Extra fcap. 8vo, 4*s.* 6*d.*

—— V. *Minor Poems.* By the same Editor. [Crown 8vo, 10*s.* 6*d.*

—— VI. *The Legend of Good Women.* By the same Editor.
[Crown 8vo, 6*s.*

—— VII. *The Hous of Fame.* By the same Editor. [Crown 8vo, 2*s.*

Langland. *The Vision of William concerning Piers the Plowman,*
by WILLIAM LANGLAND. Edited by W. W. SKEAT, Litt.D. *Sixth Edition.*
[Extra fcap. 8vo, 4*s.* 6*d.*

Gamelyn, The Tale of. Edited by W. W. SKEAT, Litt.D.
[Extra fcap. 8vo, *stiff covers*, 1*s.* 6*d.*

Wycliffe. *The New Testament in English,* according to the Version
by JOHN WYCLIFFE, about A.D. 1380, and Revised by JOHN PURVEY, about
A.D. 1388. With Introduction and Glossary by W. W. SKEAT, Litt.D.
[Extra fcap. 8vo, 6*s.*

—— *The Books of Job, Psalms, Proverbs, Ecclesiastes, and the
Song of Solomon:* according to the Wycliffite Version made by NICHOLAS DE
HEREFORD, about A.D. 1381, and Revised by JOHN PURVEY, about A.D. 1388.
With Introduction and Glossary by W. W. SKEAT, Litt.D. [Extra fcap. 8vo, 3*s.* 6*d.*

Minot. *The Poems of Laurence Minot.* Edited, with Introduction
and Notes, by JOSEPH HALL, M.A. *Second Edition.* [Extra fcap. 8vo, 4*s.* 6*d.*

Spenser. *The Faery Queene.* Books I and II. Edited by G. W.
KITCHIN, D.D., with Glossary by A. L. MAYHEW, M.A.
[Extra fcap. 8vo, 2*s.* 6*d.* each.

Hooker. *Ecclesiastical Polity,* Book I. Edited by R. W. CHURCH,
M.A., late Dean of St. Paul's. . . . . . [Extra fcap. 8vo, 2*s.*

Marlowe and Greene. MARLOWE'S *Tragical History of Dr. Faustus,*
and GREENE'S *Honourable History of Friar Bacon and Friar Bungay.*
Edited by A. W. WARD, Litt.D. *New and Enlarged Edition.* [Crown 8vo, 6*s.* 6*d.*

Marlowe. *Edward II.* Edited by O. W. TANCOCK, M.A. *Second
Edition.* . . . . . [Extra fcap. 8vo. *Paper covers,* 2*s.*; *cloth,* 3*s.*

Shakespeare. Select Plays. Edited by W. G. CLARK, M.A., and W. ALDIS WRIGHT, D.C.L. . . . . [Extra fcap. 8vo, *stiff covers*

The Merchant of Venice. 1s. 　　　*Macbeth.* 1s. 6d.
Richard the Second. 1s. 6d. 　　*Hamlet.* 2s.

Edited by W. ALDIS WRIGHT, D.C.L.

The Tempest. 1s. 6d. 　　　　　　*Coriolanus.* 2s. 6d.
As You Like It. 1s. 6d. 　　　　　*Richard the Third.* 2s. 6d.
A Midsummer Night's Dream. 1s. 6d. 　*Henry the Fifth.* 2s.
Twelfth Night. 1s. 6d. 　　　　　　*King John.* 1s. 6d.
Julius Caesar. 2s. 　　　　　　　　*King Lear.* 1s. 6d.
Henry the Eighth. 2s. 　　　　　　*Much Ado About Nothing.* 1s. 6d.
Henry the Fourth, Part I. 2s.

Shakespeare as a Dramatic Artist; *a popular Illustration of the Principles of Scientific Criticism.* By R. G. MOULTON, M.A. [Cr. 8vo, 7s. 6d.

Bacon. *Advancement of Learning.* Edited by W. ALDIS WRIGHT, D.C.L. *Third Edition.* . . . . . [Extra fcap. 8vo, 4s. 6d

—— *The Essays.* Edited, with Introduction and Illustrative Notes, by S. H. REYNOLDS, M.A. . . . . [Demy 8vo, *half-bound*, 12s. 6d.

Milton. I. *Areopagitica.* With Introduction and Notes. By JOHN W. HALES, M.A. *Third Edition.* . . . . [Extra fcap. 8vo, 3s.

—— II. *Poems.* Edited by R. C. BROWNE, M.A. In two Volumes. *New Edition.* . . . . [Extra fcap. 8vo, 6s. 6d.
Sold separately, Vol. I. 4s., Vol. II. 3s.
In paper covers, *Lycidas*, 3d. *Comus*, 6d.

By OLIVER ELTON, B.A.

Lycidas, 6d. 　　*L'Allegro*, 4d. 　　*Il Penseroso.* 4d. 　　*Comus*, 1s.

—— III. *Paradise Lost.* Book I. Edited with Notes, by H. C. BEECHING, M.A. . . [Extra fcap. 8vo, 1s. 6d. *In Parchment*, 3s. 6d.

—— IV. *Paradise Lost.* Book II. Edited by E. K. CHAMBERS, B.A. . . . [Extra fcap. 8vo, 1s. 6d. Books I and II together, 2s. 6d.

—— * V. *Samson Agonistes.* Edited, with Introduction and Notes, by JOHN CHURTON COLLINS, M.A. . . [Extra fcap. 8vo, *stiff covers*, 1s.

Milton's Prosody. By ROBERT BRIDGES. [Extra fcap. 8vo, 1s. 6d.

Bunyan. I. *The Pilgrim's Progress, Grace Abounding, Relation of the Imprisonment of Mr. John Bunyan.* Edited by E. VENABLES, M.A.
[Extra fcap. 8vo, 3s. 6d. *In Parchment*, 4s. 6d.

—— II. *The Holy War, and the Heavenly Footman.* Edited by MABEL PEACOCK. . . . . [Extra fcap. 8vo, 3s. 6d.

Clarendon. I. *History of the Rebellion.* Book VI. Edited, with Introduction and Notes, by T. ARNOLD, M.A. *Second Edition.* [Crown 8vo, 5s

—— II. *Selections.* Edited by G. BOYLE, M.A., Dean of Salisbury
[Crown 8vo, 7s. 6d.

Dryden. *Select Poems.* (*Stanzas on the Death of Oliver Cromwell ; Astræa Redux ; Annus Mirabilis ; Absalom and Achitophel ; Religio Laici ; The Hind and the Panther.*) Edited by W. D. CHRISTIE, M.A. *Fifth Edition.* Revised by C. H. FIRTH, M.A. . . . . [Extra fcap. 8vo, 3s. 6d.

—— *Essay of Dramatic Poesy.* Edited, with Notes, by T. ARNOLD, M.A. *Second Edition.* . . . . . [Extra fcap. 8vo, 3s. 6d.

Locke. *Conduct of the Understanding.* Edited, with Introduction, Notes, &c., by T. FOWLER, D.D. *Third Edition.* . [Extra fcap. 8vo, 2s. 6d.

Addison. *Selections from Papers in the 'Spectator.'* By T. ARNOLD, M.A. *Sixteenth Thousand.* . . . . . . [Extra fcap. 8vo, 4s. 6d.

Steele. *Selections from the Tatler, Spectator, and Guardian.* By AUSTIN DOBSON. *Second Edition* . . . . . [Crown 8vo, 7s. 6d.

Swift. *Selections from his Works.* Edited, with Life, Introductions, and Notes, by Sir HENRY CRAIK, K.C.B. Two Vols.
[Crown 8vo, cloth extra, price 15s.
Each volume may be had separately, price 7s. 6d.

Pope. I. *Essay on Man.* Edited by MARK PATTISON, B.D. *Sixth Edition.* . . . . [Extra fcap. 8vo, 1s. 6d.

———— II. *Satires and Epistles.* By the same Editor. *Fourth Edition.*
[Extra fcap. 8vo, 2s.

Thomson. *The Seasons,* and *The Castle of Indolence.* Edited by J. LOGIE ROBERTSON, M.A. . . . . . [Extra fcap. 8vo, 4s. 6d.

———— *The Castle of Indolence.* By the same Editor. [Extra fcap. 8vo, 1s. 6d.

Berkeley. *Selections.* With Introduction and Notes. By A. C. FRASER, LL.D. *Fourth Edition.* . . . . . . [Crown 8vo, 8s. 6d.

Johnson. I. *Rasselas.* Edited, with Introduction and Notes, by G. BIRKBECK HILL, D.C.L.
[Extra fcap. 8vo, *limp,* 2s.; *Bevelled boards,* 3s. 6d.; *in Parchment,* 4s. 6d.

———— II. *Rasselas; Lives of Dryden and Pope.* Edited by ALFRED MILNES, M.A. . . . . . . [Extra fcap. 8vo, 4s. 6d.

Lives of Dryden and Pope. . . [*Stiff covers,* 2s. 6d.

———— III. *Life of Milton.* Edited, with Notes, &c., by C. H. FIRTH, M.A. . . . [Extra fcap. 8vo, *stiff covers,* 1s. 6d.; *cloth,* 2s. 6d.

———— IV. *Vanity of Human Wishes.* With Notes, by E. J. PAYNE, M.A. . . . . [*Paper covers,* 4d.

Gray. *Selected Poems.* Edited by EDMUND GOSSE, M.A.
[*In Parchment,* 3s.

———— *The same,* together with Supplementary Notes for Schools. By FOSTER WATSON, M.A. . . . . [Extra fcap. 8vo, *stiff covers,* 1s. 6d.

———— *Elegy,* and *Ode on Eton College.* . . . [*Paper covers,* 2d.

Goldsmith. *Selected Poems.* Edited, with Introduction and Notes, by AUSTIN DOBSON. . . [Extra fcap. 8vo, 3s. 6d. *In Parchment,* 4s. 6d.

———— *The Traveller.* Edited by G. B. HILL, D.C.L. [*Stiff covers,* 1s.

———— *The Deserted Village.* . . . . . [*Paper covers,* 2d.

Cowper. I. *The Didactic Poems of* 1782, with Selections from the Minor Pieces, A.D. 1779-1783. Edited by H. T. GRIFFITH, B.A.
[Extra fcap. 8vo, 3s.

———— II. *The Task, with Tirocinium,* and Selections from the Minor Poems, A.D. 1784-1799. By the same Editor. [Extra fcap. 8vo, 3s.

Burke. I. *Thoughts on the Present Discontents; the two Speeches on America.* Edited by E. J. PAYNE, M.A. . . [Extra fcap. 8vo, 4s. 6d.

———— II. *Reflections on the French Revolution.* By the same Editor. *Second Edition.* . . . . . . [Extra fcap. 8vo, 5s.

———— III. *Four Letters on the Proposals for Peace with the Regicide Directory of France.* By the same Editor. [Extra fcap. 8vo, 5s.

Burns. *Selected Poems.* Edited by J. LOGIE ROBERTSON, M.A.
[Crown 8vo, 6*s*.

Keats. *The Odes of Keats.* With Notes and Analyses and a Memoir,
by ARTHUR C. DOWNER, M.A. With Four Illustrations.
[Extra fcap. 8vo, 3*s*. 6*d*. *net*.

——— *Hyperion*, Book I. With Notes, by W. T. ARNOLD, B.A. 4*d*.

Byron. *Childe Harold.* With Introduction and Notes, by H. F. TOZER,
M.A. . . . . . [Extra fcap. 8vo, 3*s*. 6*d*. *In Parchment*, 5*s*.

Shelley. *Adonais.* With Introduction and Notes. By W. M.
ROSSETTI. . . . . Crown 8vo, 5*s*.

Scott. *Lady of the Lake.* Edited, with Preface and Notes, by
W. MINTO, M.A. With Map. . . . . [Extra fcap. 8vo, 3*s*. 6*d*.

——— *Lay of the Last Minstrel.* Edited by W. MINTO, M.A. With
Map. . . . [Extra fcap. 8vo, *stiff covers*, 2*s*. *In Parchment*, 3*s*. 6*d*.

——— *Lay of the Last Minstrel.* Introduction and Canto I, with
Preface and Notes, by W. MINTO, M.A. . . . . [*Paper covers*, 6*d*.

——— *Lord of the Isles.* Edited, with Introduction and Notes, by
THOMAS BAYNE. . . . [Extra fcap. 8vo, *stiff covers*, 2*s*.; *cloth*, 2*s*. 6*d*.

——— *Marmion.* By the same Editor. . [Extra fcap. 8vo, 3*s*. 6*d*.

Campbell. *Gertrude of Wyoming.* Edited, with Introduction and Notes,
by H. MACAULAY FITZGIBBON, M.A. *Second Edition.* [Extra fcap. 8vo, 1*s*.

Wordsworth. *The White Doe of Rylstone.* Edited by WILLIAM
KNIGHT, LL. D., University of St. Andrews. . . [Extra fcap. 8vo, 2*s*. 6*d*.

Typical Selections *from the best English Writers. Second Edition.*
In Two Volumes. . . . . . . [Extra fcap. 8vo, 3*s*. 6*d*. each.

HISTORY AND GEOGRAPHY.

Greswell. *History of the Dominion of Canada.* By W. PARR
GRESWELL, M.A. . . . . [Crown 8vo, 7*s*. 6*d*.

——— *Geography of the Dominion of Canada and Newfoundland.* By
the same Author. . . . . [Crown 8vo, 6*s*.

——— *Geography of Africa South of the Zambesi.* By the same
Author. . . . . [Crown 8vo, 7*s*. 6*d*.

Hughes (Alfred). *Geography for Schools.* Part I, *Practical Geography*.
With Diagrams. . . . . . . [Extra fcap. 8vo, 2*s*. 6*d*.

Lucas. *Historical Geography of the British Colonies.* By C. P. LUCAS,
B.A.

    Introduction. With Eight Maps. . . . . [Crown 8vo, 4*s*. 6*d*.

    Vol. I. *The Mediterranean and Eastern Colonies (exclusive of India).* With
    Eleven Maps. . . . . [5*s*.

    Vol. II. *The West Indian Colonies.* With Twelve Maps. . . [7*s*. 6*d*.

    Vol. III. *West Africa.* With Five Maps. . . . . . . [7*s*. 6*d*.

    Vol. IV. *South and East Africa.* Historical and Geographical. With
    Eleven Maps. . . . . [9*s*. 6*d*.

           Also Vol. IV in two Parts—
   Part I. *Historical.* 6*s*. 6*d*.   Part II. *Geographical.* 3*s*. 6*d*.

MATHEMATICS AND PHYSICAL SCIENCE.

Aldis. *A Text Book of Algebra (with Answers to the Examples).* By W. STEADMAN ALDIS, M.A. . . . . . . [Crown 8vo, 7s. 6d.

Emtage. *An Introduction to the Mathematical Theory of Electricity and Magnetism.* By W. T. A. EMTAGE, M.A. . [Crown 8vo, 7s. 6d.

Fisher. *Class-Book of Chemistry.* By W. W. FISHER, M.A., F.C.S. *Fourth Edition.* . . . . [Crown 8vo, 4s. 6d.

Fock. *An Introduction to Chemical Crystallography.* By ANDREAS FOCK, Ph.D. Translated and Edited by W. J. POPE. With a Preface by N. STORY-MASKELYNE, M.A., F.R.S. . . . . . [Crown 8vo, 5s.

Hamilton and Ball. *Book-keeping.* By Sir R. G. C. HAMILTON, K.C.B., and JOHN BALL. *New and Enlarged Edition.* [Extra fcap. 8vo, 2s.
*** *Ruled Exercise Books adapted to the above may be had,* price 1s. 6d.;
also, *adapted to the Preliminary Course only,* price 4d.

Harcourt and Madan. *Exercises in Practical Chemistry.* By A. G. VERNON HARCOURT, M.A., and H. G. MADAN, M.A. *Fifth Edition.* Revised by H. G. MADAN, M.A. . . . . . . [Crown 8vo, 10s. 6d.

Hensley. *Figures made Easy: a first Arithmetic Book.* By LEWIS HENSLEY, M.A. . . . . . . [Crown 8vo, 6d. *Answers,* 1s.

—— *The Scholar's Arithmetic.* By the same Author.
[Crown 8vo, 2s. 6d. *Answers,* 1s. 6d.

—— *The Scholar's Algebra.* An Introductory work on Algebra. By the same Author. . . . . . [Crown 8vo, 2s. 6d.

Johnston. *An Elementary Treatise on Analytical Geometry.* By W. J. JOHNSTON, M.A. Crown 8vo, 6s.

Minchin. *Geometry for Beginners.* An easy Introduction to Geometry for Young Learners. By GEORGE M. MINCHIN, M.A., F.R.S. Extra fcap. 8vo, 1s. 6d.

Nixon. *Euclid Revised.* Containing the essentials of the Elements of Plane Geometry as given by Euclid in his First Six Books. Edited by R. C. J. NIXON, M.A. *Third Edition.* . . . . . . [Crown 8vo, 6s.
*** May likewise be had in parts as follows—
Book I, 1s. Books I, II, 1s. 6d. Books I–IV, 3s. Books V, VI, 3s. 6d

—— *Geometry in Space.* Containing parts of Euclid's Eleventh and Twelfth Books. By the same Author. . . . [Crown 8vo, 3s. 6d.

—— *Elementary Plane Trigonometry; that is, Plane Trigonometry without Imaginaries.* By the same Author. . . . [Crown 8vo, 7s. 6d.

Russell. *An Elementary Treatise on Pure Geometry.* By J. WELLESLEY RUSSELL, M.A. . . . . [Crown 8vo, 10s. 6d.

Selby. *Elementary Mechanics of Solids and Fluids.* By A. L. SELBY, M.A. . . . . [Crown 8vo, 7s. 6d.

Williamson. *Chemistry for Students.* By A. W. WILLIAMSON, Phil. Doc., F.R.S. . . . . [Extra fcap. 8vo, 8s. 6d.

Woollcombe. *Practical Work in General Physics.* By W. G. WOOLLCOMBE, M.A., B.Sc. . . . . [Crown 8vo, 2s.

—— *Practical Work in Heat.* By the same Author.
[Crown 8vo, 2s.

—— *Practical Work in Light and Sound.* By the same Author.
[Crown 8vo, 2s.

—— *Practical Work in Electricity and Magnetism.* By the same Author. *In the Press.*

MISCELLANEOUS.

Cookson. *Essays on Secondary Education.* By Various Contributors. Edited by CHRISTOPHER COOKSON, M.A.   . [Crown 8vo, *paper boards, 4s. 6d.*

Balfour. *The Educational Systems of Great Britain and Ireland.* By GRAHAM BALFOUR, M.A.   [Crown 8vo, 7s. 6d.

Buckmaster. *Elementary Architecture for Schools, Art Students, and General Readers.* By MARTIN A. BUCKMASTER. With thirty-eight full-page Illustrations.   .   .   .   . [Crown 8vo, 4s. 6d.

Fowler. *The Elements of Deductive and Inductive Logic.* By T. FOWLER, D.D.   .   .   .   . [Extra fcap. 8vo, 7s. 6d.

Also, separately—

The Elements of Deductive Logic, designed mainly for the use of Junior Students in the Universities. With a Collection of Examples.
[Extra fcap. 8vo, 3s. 6d.

The Elements of Inductive Logic, designed mainly for the use of Students in the Universities. *Sixth Edition.*.   .   . [Extra fcap. 8vo, 6s.

Music.—Farmer. *Hymns and Chorales for Schools and Colleges.* Edited by JOHN FARMER, Organist of Balliol College, Oxford   .   . [5s.
☞ *Hymns without the Tunes, 2s.*

Hullah. *The Cultivation of the Speaking Voice.* By JOHN HULLAH.
[Extra fcap. 8vo, 2s. 6d.

Maclaren. *A System of Physical Education: Theoretical and Practical.* By ARCHIBALD MACLAREN. *New Edition*, re-edited and enlarged by WALLACE MACLAREN, M.A., Ph.D.   .   .   .   . [Crown 8vo, 8s. 6d. *net.*

Troutbeck and Dale. *A Music Primer for Schools.* By J. TROUTBECK, D.D., and R. F. DALE, M.A., B.Mus.   .   .   . [Crown 8vo, 1s. 6d.

Tyrwhitt. *Handbook of Pictorial Art.* With Illustrations, and a chapter on Perspective by A. MACDONALD. By R. ST. J. TYRWHITT, M.A. *Second Edition.*   .   .   .   . [8vo, *half-morocco, 18s.*

Upcott. *An Introduction to Greek Sculpture.* By L. E. UPCOTT, M.A.   .   .   .   . [Crown 8vo, 4s. 6d.

Helps to the Study of the Bible, taken from the *Oxford Bible for Teachers.* New, Enlarged and Illustrated Edition. Pearl 16mo, stiff covers, 1s. *net.* Large Paper Edition, Long Primer 8vo, cloth boards, 5s.

Helps to the Study of the Book of Common Prayer. Being a Companion to Church Worship. By W. R. W. STEPHENS. B.D. [Crown 8vo, 2s.

The Parallel Psalter, being the Prayer-Book Version of the Psalms, and a new Version arranged on opposite pages. With an Introduction and Glossaries by the Rev. S. R. DRIVER, D.D., Litt.D. Fcap. 8vo, 6s.

Old Testament History for Schools. By T. H. STOKOE, D.D
Part   I.   From the Creation to the Settlement in Palestine. (*Second Edition.*)
Part II.   From the Settlement to the Disruption of the Kingdom.
Part III.   From the Disruption to the Return from Captivity. *Completing the work.*   [Extra fcap. 8vo, 2s. 6d. each Part.

Notes on the Gospel of St. Luke, for Junior Classes. By E. J. MOORE SMITH, Lady Principal of the Ladies' College, Durban, Natal.
[Extra fcap. 8vo, *stiff covers, 1s. 6d.*

Oxford
AT THE CLARENDON PRESS
London, Edinburgh, and New York
HENRY FROWDE

Clarendon Press Series.

Modern Languages.

FRENCH.

Brachet. *Etymological Dictionary of the French Language,* with a Preface on the Principles of French Etymology. Translated into English by G. W. Kitchin, D.D., Dean of Durham. *Third Edition.* [Crown 8vo, 7s. 6d.

—— *Historical Grammar of the French Language.* Translated into English by G. W. Kitchin, D.D. . . . [Extra fcap. 8vo, 3s. 6d.

Brachet and **Toynbee.** *A Historical Grammar of the French Language.* From the French of Auguste Brachet. Rewritten and Enlarged by Paget Toynbee, M.A. . . . . [Crown 8vo, 7s. 6d.

Saintsbury. *Primer of French Literature.* By George Saintsbury, M.A. *Fourth Edition, Revised.* . . . . [Extra fcap. 8vo, 2s.

—— *Short History of French Literature.* By the same Author. *Fifth Edition, Revised, with the Section on the Nineteenth Century greatly enlarged* . . . . [Crown 8vo, 10s. 6d.

—— *Specimens of French Literature,* from Villon to Hugo. By the same Author. . . . . [Crown 8vo, 9s.

Toynbee. *Specimens of Old French (ix–xv centuries).* With Introduction, Notes, and Glossary. By Paget Toynbee, M.A. [Crown 8vo, 16s.

Beaumarchais. *Le Barbier de Séville.* With Introduction and Notes by Austin Dobson. . . . . [Extra fcap. 8vo, 2s. 6d.

Blouët. *L'Éloquence de la Chaire et de la Tribune Françaises.* Edited by Paul Blouët, B.A. (Univ. Gallic.) Vol. I. *French Sacred Oratory.* [Extra fcap. 8vo, 2s. 6d.

Corneille. *Horace.* With Introduction and Notes by George Saintsbury, M.A. . . . . [Extra fcap. 8vo, 2s. 6d.

—— *Cinna.* With Notes, Glossary, &c. By Gustave Masson, B.A. . . . . . . [Extra fcap. 8vo, *stiff covers,* 1s. 6d.; *cloth,* 2s.

Gautier (Théophile). *Scenes of Travel.* Selected and Edited by G. Saintsbury, M.A. . . . . [Extra fcap. 8vo, 2s.

Masson. *Louis XIV and his Contemporaries;* as described in Extracts from the best Memoirs of the Seventeenth Century. With English Notes, Genealogical Tables, &c. By Gustave Masson, B.A. [Extra fcap. 8vo, 2s. 6d.

Molière. *Les Précieuses Ridicules.* With Introduction and Notes by Andrew Lang, M.A. . . . . . . [Extra fcap. 8vo, 1s. 6d.

—— *Les Femmes Savantes.* With Notes, Glossary, &c. By Gustave Masson, B.A. . [Extra fcap. 8vo, *stiff covers,* 1s. 6d.; *cloth,* 2s.

—— *Le Misanthrope.* Edited by H. W. Gegg Markheim, M.A. [Extra fcap. 8vo, 3s. 6d.

B 3

Molière.　*Les Fourberies de Scapin.*　With Voltaire's Life of Molière.
By Gustave Masson, B.A. .　.　. [Extra fcap. 8vo, *stiff covers*, 1s. 6d.

Musset.　*On ne badine pas avec l'Amour*, and *Fantasio.*　With
Introduction, Notes, &c., by Walter Herries Pollock. [Extra fcap. 8vo, 2s.

NOVELETTES—

Xavier de Maistre.	*Voyage autour de ma Chambre.*	
Madame de Duras.	*Ourika.*	By Gustave
Erckmann-Chatrian.	*Le Vieux Tailleur.*	Masson, B.A., 3rd Edition.
Alfred de Vigny.	*La Veillée de Vincennes.*	Ext. fcap. 8vo,
Edmond About.	*Les Jumeaux de l'Hôtel Corneille.*	2s. 6d.
Rodolphe Töpffer.	*Mésaventures d'un Écolier.*	

Voyage autour de ma Chambre, separately, limp, 1s. 6d.

Quinet.　*Lettres à sa Mère.*　Edited by G. Saintsbury, M.A.
[Extra fcap. 8vo, 2s.

Racine.　*Esther.*　Edited by G. Saintsbury, M.A. [Extra fcap. 8vo, 2s.

Regnard. .　.　. *Le Joueur.* } By Gustave Masson, B.A.
Brueys and Palaprat.　*Le Grondeur.* } [Extra fcap. 8vo, 2s. 6d.

Sainte-Beuve.　*Selections from the Causeries du Lundi.*　Edited by
G. Saintsbury, M.A. .　.　.　.　.　.　. [Extra fcap. 8vo, 2s.

Sévigné.　*Selections from the Correspondence of* **Madame de Sévigné**
and her chief Contemporaries.　By Gustave Masson, B.A. [Extra fcap. 8vo, 3s.

Voltaire.　*Mérope.*　Edited by G. Saintsbury, M.A. [Extra fcap. 8vo, 2s.

ITALIAN AND SPANISH.

Primer of Italian Literature.　By F. J. Snell, B.A.
[Extra fcap. 8vo, 3s. 6d.

Dante.　*Tutte le Opere di Dante Alighieri,* nuovamente rivedute nel
testo dal Dr. E. Moore: Con un Indice dei Nomi Propri e delle Cose
Notevoli contenute nelle Opere di Dante, compilato da Paget Toynbee, M.A.
[Crown 8vo, 7s. 6d.

*** Also, an India Paper edition, cloth extra, 9s. 6d.; and
Miniature edition, 3 vols., in case, 10s. 6d.

———— *Selections from the 'Inferno.'*　With Introduction and Notes,
by H. B. Cotterill, B.A. .　.　.　.　. [Extra fcap. 8vo, 4s. 6d.

Tasso.　*La Gerusalemme Liberata.*　Cantos i, ii.　With Introduction
and Notes by the same Editor. .　.　.　. [Extra fcap. 8vo, 2s. 6d.

Cervantes.　*The Adventure of the Wooden Horse, and Sancho Panza's
Governorship.*　Edited, with Introduction, Life and Notes, by Clovis Bévenot,
M.A. .　.　.　.　.　.　.　.　.　.　.　.　. [Extra fcap. 8vo, 2s. 6d.

GERMAN, &c.

Buchheim. *Modern German Reader.* A Graduated Collection of Extracts in Prose and Poetry from Modern German Writers. Edited by C. A. BUCHHEIM, Phil. Doc.

Part I. With English Notes, a Grammatical Appendix, and a complete Vocabulary. *Seventh Edition.* . . . [Extra fcap. 8vo, 2s. 6d.
Part II. With English Notes and an Index. . [Extra fcap. 8vo, 2s. 6d.

—— *German Poetry for Beginners.* Edited, with Notes and Vocabulary, by EMMA S. BUCHHEIM. . . . . . [Extra fcap. 8vo, 2s.

—— *Short German Plays, for Reading and Acting.* With Notes and a Vocabulary. By the same Editor. . . . [Extra fcap. 8vo, 3s.

—— *Elementary German Prose Composition.* By EMMA S. BUCHHEIM. *Second Edition.* [Extra fcap. 8vo, *cloth*, 2s. ; *stiff covers*, 1s. 6d.

Lange. *The Germans at Home;* a Practical Introduction to German Conversation, with an Appendix containing the Essentials of German Grammar. By HERMANN LANGE. *Third Edition.* . . . . . [8vo, 2s. 6d.

—— *The German Manual;* a German Grammar, a Reading Book, and a Handbook of German Conversation. By the same Author. [7s. 6d.

—— *A Grammar of the German Language,* being a reprint of the Grammar contained in *The German Manual.* By the same Author. [8vo, 3s. 6d.

—— *German Composition;* a Theoretical and Practical Guide to the Art of Translating English Prose into German. By the same Author. *Third Edition.* . . . . [8vo, 4s. 6d.

[*A Key to the above, price* 5s.]

—— *German Spelling:* A Synopsis of the Changes which it has undergone through the Government Regulations of 1880. . [*Paper cover*, 6d,

---

Becker's Friedrich der Grosse. With an Historical Sketch of the Rise of Prussia and of the Times of Frederick the Great. With Map. Edited by C. A. BUCHHEIM, Phil. Doc. . . . [Extra fcap. 8vo, 3s. 6d.

Chamisso. *Peter Schlemihl's Wundersame Geschichte.* With Notes and Vocabulary. By EMMA S. BUCHHEIM. *Fourth Thousand.* [Extra fcap. 8vo, 2s.

Goethe. *Egmont.* With a Life of Goethe, &c. Edited by C. A. BUCHHEIM, Phil. Doc. *Fourth Edition.* . . . [Extra fcap. 8vo, 3s.

—— *Iphigenie auf Tauris.* A Drama. With a Critical Introduction and Notes. Edited by C. A. BUCHHEIM, Phil. Doc. *Fourth Edition.* [Extra fcap. 8vo, 3s.

—— *Dichtung und Wahrheit:* (The First Four Books.) Edited by C. A. BUCHHEIM, Phil. Doc. . . . . . [Extra fcap. 8vo, 4s. 6d.

Halm's *Griseldis.* With English Notes, &c. Edited by C. A. BUCHHEIM, Phil. Doc. . . . . [Extra fcap. 8vo, 3s.

Heine's *Harzreise.* With a Life of Heine, &c. With Map. Edited by C. A. BUCHHEIM, Phil. Doc. *Second Edition.* [Extra fcap. 8vo, *cloth,* 2s. 6d.

—— *Prosa,* being Selections from his Prose Works. Edited, with English Notes, &c., by C. A. BUCHHEIM, Phil. Doc. [Extra fcap. 8vo, 4s. 6d.

Hoffmann's *Heute Mir Morgen Dir.* Edited by J. H. MAUDE, M.A. [Extra fcap. 8vo, 2s,

Lessing. *Laokoon.* With Notes, &c. By A. HAMANN, Phil. Doc., M.A. Revised, with an Introduction, by L. E. UPCOTT, M.A.
[Extra fcap. 8vo, 4s. 6d.

—— *Minna von Barnhelm.* A Comedy. With a Life of Lessing, Critical Analysis, Complete Commentary, &c. Edited by C. A. BUCHHEIM, Phil. Doc. *Seventh Edition.* . . . . [Extra fcap. 8vo, 3s. 6d.

—— *Nathan der Weise.* With English Notes, &c. Edited by C. A. BUCHHEIM, Phil. Doc. *Second Edition.* . [Extra fcap. 8vo, 4s. 6d.

Niebuhr's *Griechische Heroen-Geschichten.* Tales of Greek Heroes. Edited with English Notes and a Vocabulary, by EMMA S. BUCHHEIM.

Edition A. Text in German Type. } [Extra fcap. 8vo, *stiff,* 1s. 6d.;
Edition B. Text in Roman Type. } *cloth,* 2s.

Riehl's *Seines Vaters Sohn* and *Gespensterkampf.* Edited with Notes, by H. T. GERRANS. . . . . [Extra fcap. 8vo, 2s.

Schiller's *Historische Skizzen:—Egmonts Leben und Tod,* and *Belagerung von Antwerpen.* Edited by C. A. BUCHHEIM, Phil. Doc. *Fifth Edition, Revised and Enlarged, with a Map.* . [Extra fcap. 8vo, 2s. 6d.

—— *Wilhelm Tell.* With a Life of Schiller; an Historical and Critical Introduction, Arguments, a Complete Commentary, and Map. Edited by C. A. BUCHHEIM, Phil. Doc. *Seventh Edition.* [Extra fcap. 8vo, 3s. 6d.

—— *Wilhelm Tell.* Edited by C. A. BUCHHEIM, Phil. Doc. *School Edition.* With Map. . . . . . [Extra fcap. 8vo, 2s.

—— *Jungfrau von Orleans.* Edited by C. A. BUCHHEIM, Phil. Doc. *Second Edition.* . . . . . [Extra fcap. 8vo, 4s. 6d.

—— *Maria Stuart.* Edited by C. A. BUCHHEIM, Phil. Doc.
[Extra fcap. 8vo, 3s. 6d.

Scherer. *A History of German Literature.* By W. SCHERER. Translated from the Third German Edition by Mrs. F. C. CONYBEARE. Edited by The Rt. Hon. F. MAX MÜLLER. 2 vols. . . . . [8vo, 21s.
₊ Or, separately, 10s. 6d. each volume.

—— *A History of German Literature from the Accession of Frederick the Great to the Death of Goethe.* Reprinted from the above. [Crown 8vo, 5s.

Max Müller. *The German Classics from the Fourth to the Nineteenth Century.* With Biographical Notices, Translations into Modern German, and Notes, by The Rt. Hon. F. MAX MÜLLER, M.A. A New edition, revised, enlarged, and adapted to WILHELM SCHERER's *History of German Literature,* by F. LICHTENSTEIN. 2 vols. . . . . . . [Crown 8vo, 21s.
₊ Or, separately, 10s. 6d. each volume.

Wright. *An Old High German Primer.* With Grammar, Notes, and Glossary. By JOSEPH WRIGHT, M.A., Ph.D. . [Extra fcap. 8vo, 3s. 6d.

—— *A Middle High German Primer.* With Grammar, Notes, and Glossary. By the same Author. . . . [Extra fcap. 8vo, 3s. 6d.

—— *A Primer of the Gothic Language.* With Grammar, Notes, and Glossary. By the same Author. . . . . [Extra fcap. 8vo, 4s. 6d.

𝕺𝖝𝖋𝖔𝖗𝖉

AT THE CLARENDON PRESS

𝕷𝖔𝖓𝖉𝖔𝖓, 𝕰𝖉𝖎𝖓𝖇𝖚𝖗𝖌𝖍, 𝖆𝖓𝖉 𝕹𝖊𝖜 𝖄𝖔𝖗𝖐
HENRY FROWDE

Clarendon Press Series.

Latin Educational Works.

GRAMMARS, LEXICONS, &c.

Allen. *Rudimenta Latina.* Comprising Accidence, and Exercises of a very Elementary Character, for the use of Beginners. By J. BARROW ALLEN, M.A. . . . . [Extra fcap. 8vo, 2s.

—— *An Elementary Latin Grammar.* By the same Author. *New Edition, Revised and Enlarged.* . . . . [Extra fcap. 8vo, 2s. 6d.

— *A First Latin Exercise Book.* By the same Author. *Eighth Edition.* . . . . [Extra fcap. 8vo, 2s. 6d.

—— *A Second Latin Exercise Book.* By the same Author. *Second Edition.* . . . . [Extra fcap. 8vo, 3s. 6d.

[*A Key to First and Second Latin Exercise Books : for Teachers only, price 5s.*]

Fox and **Bromley.** *Models and Exercises in Unseen Translation.* By H. F. Fox, M.A., and T. M. BROMLEY, M.A. [Extra fcap. 8vo, 5s. 6d.

[*A Key to Passages quoted in the above : for Teachers only, price 6d.*]

Gibson. *An Introduction to Latin Syntax.* By W. S. GIBSON, M.A. [Extra fcap. 8vo, 2s.

Jerram. *Reddenda Minora.* By C. S. JERRAM, M.A. [Extra fcap. 8vo, 1s. 6d.

—— *Anglice Reddenda.* FIRST SERIES. [Extra fcap. 8vo, 2s. 6d.

—- -- *Anglice Reddenda.* SECOND SERIES. [Extra fcap. 8vo, 3s.

—— *Anglice Reddenda.* THIRD SERIES. [Extra fcap. 8vo, 3s.

Lee-Warner. *Hints and Helps for Latin Elegiacs.* By H. LEE-WARNER, M.A. . . . . [Extra fcap. 8vo, 3s. 6d.

[*A Key is provided : for Teachers only, price 4s. 6d.*]

Lewis. *An Elementary Latin Dictionary.* By CHARLTON T. LEWIS, Ph.D. . . . . [Square 8vo, 7s. 6d.

—— *A Latin Dictionary for Schools.* By the same Author. [Small 4to, 18s.

Lindsay. *A Short Historical Latin Grammar.* By W. M. LINDSAY, M.A.. . . . . [Crown 8vo, 5s. 6d.

Nunns. *First Latin Reader.* By T. J. NUNNS, M.A. *Third Edition.* [Extra fcap. 8vo, 2s.

Ramsay. *Latin Prose Composition.* By G. G. RAMSAY, M.A., LL.D. *Fourth Edition.* Extra fcap. 8vo.

Vol. I. *Syntax, Exercises with Notes, &c.,* 4s. 6d.

Or in two Parts, 2s. 6d. each, viz.

Part I. *The Simple Sentence.* Part II. *The Compound Sentence.*

₊ *A Key to the above, price 5s. net. Supplied to Teachers only, on application to the Secretary, Clarendon Press.*

Vol. II. *Passages of Graduated Difficulty for Translation into Latin, together with an Introduction on Continuous Prose,* 4s. 6d.

Ramsay. *Latin Prose Versions.* Contributed by various Scholars. Edited by G. G. RAMSAY, M.A., LL.D. . . . . [Extra fcap. 8vo, 5s.

Owen and **Phillimore**. *Mvsa Clavda.* Translations into Latin Elegiac Verse. By S. G. OWEN and J. S. PHILLIMORE. [Crown 8vo, paper boards, 3s. 6d.

Sargent. *Easy Passages for Translation into Latin.* By J. Y. SARGENT, M.A. *Seventh Edition.* . . . . . . [Extra fcap. 8vo, 2s. 6d.

    [*A Key to this Edition is provided : for Teachers only, price 5s., net.*]

—— *A Latin Prose Primer.* By the same Author. [Ex. fcap. 8vo, 2s. 6d.

King and **Cookson**. *The Principles of Sound and Inflexion, as illustrated in the Greek and Latin Languages.* By J. E. KING, M.A., and CHRISTOPHER COOKSON, M.A. . . . . [8vo, 18s.

—— *An Introduction to the Comparative Grammar of Greek and Latin.* By the same Authors. . . . . . [Crown 8vo, 5s. 6d.

Papillon. *A Manual of Comparative Philology.* By T. L. PAPILLON, M.A. *Third Edition.* . . . . [Crown 8vo, 6s.

Caesar. *The Commentaries* (for Schools). With Notes and Maps. By CHARLES E. MOBERLY, M.A.

    The Gallic War. New Edition. Extra fcap. 8vo—

        Books I and II, 2s. ; I–III, 2s. ; III–V, 2s. 6d. ; VI–VIII, 3s. 6d.

    The Civil War. Second Edition. . . . [Extra fcap. 8vo, 3s. 6d.

Catulli Veronensis *Carmina Selecta*, secundum recognitionem ROBINSON ELLIS, A.M. . . . . . . [Extra fcap. 8vo, 3s. 6d.

Cicero. *Selection of Interesting and Descriptive Passages.* With Notes. By HENRY WALFORD, M.A. In three Parts. *Third Edition.*

                                [Extra fcap. 8vo, 4s. 6d.

    Part I. *Anecdotes from Grecian and Roman History.* . [*limp,* 1s. 6d.
    Part II. *Omens and Dreams; Beauties of Nature.* . . [„ 1s. 6d.
    Part III. *Rome's Rule of her Provinces.* . . . . [„ 1s. 6d.

—— *De Amicitia.* With Introduction and Notes. By ST. GEORGE STOCK, M.A. . . . . [Extra fcap. 8vo, 3s.

—— *De Senectute.* With Introduction and Notes. By LEONARD HUXLEY, B.A. *In one or two Parts.* . . . . [Extra fcap. 8vo, 2s.

—— *Pro Cluentio.* With Introduction and Notes. By W. RAMSAY, M.A. Edited by G. G. RAMSAY, M.A. *Second Edition.* [Extra fcap. 8vo, 3s. 6d.

—— *Pro Marcello, pro Ligario, pro Rege Deiotaro.* With Introduction and Notes. By W. Y. FAUSSET, M.A. .. . . [Extra fcap. 8vo, 2s. 6d.

—— *Pro Milone.* With Notes, &c. By A. B. POYNTON, M.A. [Extra fcap. 8vo, 2s. 6d.

—— *Pro Roscio.* With Introduction and Notes. By ST. GEORGE STOCK, M.A. . . . . [Extra fcap. 8vo, 3s. 6d.

—— *Select Orations* (for Schools). *In Verrem Actio Prima. De Imperio Gn. Pompeii. Pro Archia. Philippica IX.* With Introduction and Notes. By J. R. KING, M.A. *Second Edition.* . [Extra fcap. 8vo, 2s. 6d.

—— *In Q. Caecilium Divinatio* and *In C. Verrem Actio Prima.* With Introduction and Notes. By J. R. KING, M.A. [Extra fcap. 8vo, 1s. 6d.

—— *Speeches against Catilina.* With Introduction and Notes. By E. A. UPCOTT, M.A. *Second Edition.* . . . [Extra fcap. 8vo, 2s. 6d.

Cicero. *Philippic Orations.* With Notes, &c., by J. R. KING, M.A. Second Edition. . . . . [8vo, 10s. 6d.

—— *Selected Letters* (for Schools). With Notes. By C. E. PRICHARD, M.A., and E. R. BERNARD, M.A. *Second Edition.*
[Extra fcap. 8vo, 3s.

—— *Select Letters.* With English Introductions, Notes, and Appendices. By ALBERT WATSON, M.A. *Fourth Edition.* . . [8vo, 18s.

—— *Select Letters.* Text. By the same Editor. *Second Edition.*
[Extra fcap. 8vo, 4s.

Early Roman Poetry. *Selected Fragments.* With Introduction and Notes. By W. W. MERRY, D.D. . . . . . [Crown 8vo, 6s. 6d.

Horace. With a Commentary. Volume I. *The Odes, Carmen Seculare,* and *Epodes.* By EDWARD C. WICKHAM, D.D. *New Edition.*
[Extra fcap. 8vo, 6s.

—— *Odes,* Book I. By the same Editor. . . [Extra fcap. 8vo, 2s.

—— *Selected Odes.* With Notes for the use of a Fifth Form. By the same Editor. . . . . [Extra fcap. 8vo, 2s.

—— *The Complete Works.* By the same Editor.
[On writing-paper, 32mo, 3s. 6d.; on India paper, 5s.

Juvenal. *XIII Satires.* Edited, with Introduction, Notes, &c., by C. H. PEARSON, M.A., and H. A. STRONG, M.A. *Second Edition.* [Crown 8vo, 9s.

Livy. *Selections* (for Schools). With Notes and Maps. By H. LEE-WARNER, M.A. . . . . [Extra fcap. 8vo.
    Part I. *The Caudine Disaster.* . . . . . . [limp, 1s. 6d.
    Part II. *Hannibal's Campaign in Italy.* . . . . [„ 1s. 6d.
    Part III. *The Macedonian War.* . . . . . . [„ 1s. 6d.

—— *Book I.* With Introduction, Historical Examination, and Notes. By J. R. SEELEY, M.A. *Third Edition.* . . . . . [8vo, 6s.

—— *Books V—VII.* With Introduction and Notes. By A. R. CLUER, B.A. *Second Edition.* Revised by P. E. MATHESON, M.A. [Extra fcap. 8vo, 5s.
    Book V, 2s. 6d.; *Book VII,* 2s. By the same Editors.

—— *Books XXI—XXIII.* With Introduction, Notes, and Maps. By M. T. TATHAM, M.A. *Second Edition* . . . [Extra fcap. 8vo, 5s.

—— *Book XXI.* By the same Editor. . . [Extra fcap. 8vo, 2s. 6d.

—— *Book XXII.* By the same Editor. . . [Extra fcap. 8vo, 2s. 6d.

Nepos. With Notes. By OSCAR BROWNING, M.A. *Third Edition.* Revised by W. R. INGE, M.A. . . . [Extra fcap. 8vo, 3s.

—— *Lives from. Miltiades, Themistocles, Pausanias.* With Notes, Maps, Vocabularies, and English Exercises. By JOHN BARROW ALLEN, M.A.
[Extra fcap. 8vo, 1s. 6d.

Ovid. *Selections* (for the use of Schools). With Introductions and Notes, and an Appendix on the Roman Calendar. By W. RAMSAY, M.A. Edited by G. G. RAMSAY, M.A. *Third Edition.* . [Extra fcap. 8vo, 5s. 6d.

—— *Tristia,* Book I. The Text revised, with an Introduction and Notes. By S. G. OWEN, B.A. *Second Edition.* . [Extra fcap. 8vo, 3s. 6d.

—— *Tristia,* Book III. With Introduction and Notes. By the same Editor. . . . . [Extra fcap. 8vo, 2s.

Persius. *The Satires.* With Translation and Commentary by J. CONINGTON, M.A., edited by H. NETTLESHIP, M.A. *Third Edition.* [8vo, 8s. 6d.

Plautus. *Captivi.* With Introduction and Notes. By W. M. LINDSAY, M.A. . . . . [Extra fcap. 8vo, 2s. 6d.

—— *Trinummus.* With Notes and Introductions. By C. E. FREEMAN, M.A., and A. SLOMAN, M.A. . . . . . [Extra fcap. 8vo, 3s.

Pliny. *Selected Letters* (for Schools). By C. E. PRICHARD, M.A., and E. R. BERNARD, M.A. *Third Edition.* . . . [Extra fcap. 8vo, 3s.

Quintilian. *Institutionis Oratoriae Liber X.* Edited by W. PETERSON, M.A. . . . . [Extra fcap. 8vo, 3s. 6d.

Sallust. *Bellum Catilinarium* and *Jugurthinum.* With Introduction and Notes, by W. W. CAPES, M.A. . . [Extra fcap. 8vo, 4s. 6d.

Tacitus. *The Annals.* Books I—IV. Edited, with Introduction and Notes for the use of Schools and Junior Students, by H. FURNEAUX, M.A. [Extra fcap. 8vo, 5s.

—— *The Annals.* Book I. By the same Editor. . . [limp, 2s.

—— *The Annals.* (Text only). . . . . . [Crown 8vo, 6s.

Terence. *Adelphi.* With Notes and Introductions. By A. SLOMAN, M.A. . . . . [Extra fcap. 8vo, 3s.

—— *Andria.* With Notes and Introductions. By C. E. FREEMAN, M.A., and A. SLOMAN, M.A. *Second Edition* . . [Extra fcap. 8vo, 3s.

—— *Phormio.* With Notes and Introductions. By A. SLOMAN, M.A. . . . . [Extra fcap. 8vo, 3s.

Tibullus and **Propertius.** *Selections.* Edited, with Introduction and Notes, by G. G. RAMSAY, M.A. *Second Edition.* . [Extra fcap. 8vo, 6s.

Virgil. With an Introduction and Notes. By T. L. PAPILLON, M.A., and A. E. HAIGH, M.A.
[Crown 8vo, 2 vols., *cloth, price 6s. each, or in stiff covers, 3s. 6d. each.*

—— *The Text, including the Minor Works.*
[On writing-paper, 32mo, 3s. 6d.; on India paper, 5s.

—— *Aeneid.* With Introduction and Notes, by the same Editors. In Four Parts. . . . . [Crown 8vo, 2s. each.

—— *Aeneid I.* With Introduction and Notes, by C. S. JERRAM, M.A. [Extra fcap. 8vo, limp, 1s. 6d.

—— *Aeneid IX.* Edited, with Introduction and Notes, by A. E. HAIGH, M.A. . . . [Extra fcap. 8vo, limp, 1s. 6d. In two Parts, 2s.

—— *Bucolics.* With Introduction and Notes, by C. S. JERRAM, M.A. [Extra fcap. 8vo, 2s. 6d.

—— *Bucolics and Georgics.* By T. L. PAPILLON, M.A., and A. E. HAIGH, M.A. . . . . [Crown 8vo, 2s. 6d.

—— *Georgics.* Books I, II. By C. S. JERRAM, M.A. [Extra fcap. 8vo, 2s. 6d.

—— *Georgics.* Books III, IV. By the same Editor. [Extra fcap. 8vo, 2s. 6d.

𝕺𝖝𝖋𝖔𝖗𝖉

AT THE CLARENDON PRESS

𝕷𝖔𝖓𝖉𝖔𝖓, 𝕰𝖉𝖎𝖓𝖇𝖚𝖗𝖌𝖍, 𝖆𝖓𝖉 𝕹𝖊𝖜 𝖄𝖔𝖗𝖐

HENRY FROWDE

Clarendon Press Series.

Greek Educational Works.

GRAMMARS, LEXICONS, &c.

Chandler. *The Elements of Greek Accentuation* (for Schools). By H. W. CHANDLER, M.A. *Second Edition.* . [Extra fcap. 8vo, 2s. 6d.

Fox and **Bromley.** *Models and Exercises in Unseen Translation.* By H. F. Fox, M.A., and T. M. BROMLEY, M.A. [Extra fcap. 8vo, 5s. 6d.

[*A Key to Passages quoted in the above: for Teachers only, price 6d.*]

Jerram. *Graece Reddenda.* By C. S. JERRAM, M.A. . . [2s 6d.

—— *Reddenda Minora.* . . . . [Extra fcap. 8vo, 1s. 6d.

—— *Anglice Reddenda.* First Series. . [Extra fcap. 8vo, 2s. 6d.

—— —— Second Series. . . . . [Extra fcap. 8vo, 3s.

—— —— Third Series. . . . . . [Extra fcap. 8vo, 3s.

Liddell and **Scott.** *A Greek-English Lexicon.* . . [4to, 36s.

—— *An Intermediate Greek-English Lexicon.* [Small 4to, 12s. 6d.

—— *A Greek-English Lexicon,* abridged. . [Square 12mo, 7s. 6d.

Sargent. *A Primer of Greek Prose Composition.* By J. YOUNG SARGENT, M.A. . . . . [Extra fcap. 8vo, 3s. 6d.

*** A Key to the above, price 5s. Supplied *to Teachers only*, on application to the Secretary, Clarendon Press.

—— *Passages for Translation into Greek Prose.* [Extra fcap. 8vo, 3s.

—— *Exemplaria Graeca*; being Greek Renderings of Selected "Passages for Translation into Greek Prose." . . . [Extra fcap. 8vo, 3s.

—— *Models and Materials for Greek Iambic Verse.* . . [4s. 6d.

Wordsworth. *A Greek Primer.* By the Right Rev. CHARLES WORDSWORTH, D.C.L. *Eighty-third Thousand.* [Extra fcap. 8vo, 1s. 6d.

—— *Graecae Grammaticae Rudimenta in usum Scholarum.* Auctore CAROLO WORDSWORTH, D.C.L. *Nineteenth Edition.* . . . [12mo, 4s.

King and **Cookson.** *An Introduction to the Comparative Grammar of Greek and Latin.* By J. E. KING, M.A., and C. COOKSON, M.A. [Crown 8vo, 5s. 6d.

Papillon. *A Manual of Comparative Philology.* By T. L. PAPILLON, M.A. . . . . [Crown 8vo, 6s.

A COURSE OF GREEK READERS.

Easy Greek Reader. By EVELYN ABBOTT, M.A. [Extra fcap. 8vo, 3s.

First Greek Reader. By W. G. RUSHBROOKE, M.L. *Third Edition.* [Extra fcap. 8vo, 2s. 6d.

Second Greek Reader.   By A. M. BELL, M.A.   [Extra fcap. 8vo, 3*s*.

Specimens of Greek Dialects; being *a Fourth Greek Reader*. With Introductions and Notes. By W. W. MERRY, D.D.   [Extra fcap. 8vo, 4*s*. 6*d*.

Selections from Homer and the Greek Dramatists; being *a Fifth Greek Reader.* By EVELYN ABBOTT, M.A. .   .   [Extra fcap. 8vo, 4*s*. 6*d*.

Wright. *The Golden Treasury of Ancient Greek Poetry.* By Sir R. S. WRIGHT, M.A. *Second Edition, Revised.* .   .   [Extra fcap. 8vo, 10*s*. 6*d*.

Wright and **Shadwell.** *A Golden Treasury of Greek Prose.* By Sir R. S. WRIGHT, M.A., and J. E. L. SHADWELL, M.A. [Extra fcap. 8vo, 4*s*. 6*d*.

THE GREEK TESTAMENT.

A Greek Testament Primer. An Easy Grammar and Reading Book for the use of Students beginning Greek. By E. MILLER, M.A. *Second Edition.*
[Extra fcap. 8vo, *paper covers*, 2*s*.; *cloth*, 3*s*. 6*d*.

Evangelia Sacra Graece.   .   .   [Fcap. 8vo, *limp*, 1*s*. 6*d*.

Novum Testamentum Graece juxta Exemplar Millianum.   [2*s*. 6*d*.

Novum Testamentum Graece. Accedunt parallela S. Scripturae loca, &c. Edidit CAROLUS LLOYD, S.T.P.R.   .   .   .   [18mo, 3*s*.

—— Critical Appendices to the above. By W. SANDAY, M.A. 3*s*. 6*d*.

The Greek Testament, with the Readings adopted by the Revisers of the Authorised Version, and Marginal References.   .   . [Fcap. 8vo, 4*s*. 6*d*.

Outlines of Textual Criticism applied to the New Testament. By C. E. HAMMOND, M.A. *Fifth Edition.* .   .   . [Crown 8vo, 4*s*. 6*d*.

GREEK CLASSICS FOR SCHOOLS.

Aeschylus. *Agamemnon.* With Introduction and Notes, by ARTHUR SIDGWICK, M.A. *Fourth Edition.*   .   .   .   . [Extra fcap. 8vo, 3*s*.

—— *Choephoroi.* By the same Editor. .   . . [Extra fcap. 8vo, 3*s*.

—— *Eumenides.* By the same Editor. .   .   . [Extra fcap. 8vo, 3*s*.

—— *Prometheus Bound.* With Introduction and Notes, by A. O. PRICKARD, M.A. *Second Edition.*   .   .   .   . [Extra fcap. 8vo, 2*s*.

Aristophanes. *The Acharnians.* With Introduction and Notes, by W. W. MERRY, D.D. *Fourth Edition.* .   .   . [Extra fcap. 8vo, 3*s*.

—— *The Birds.* By the same Editor. .   . [Extra fcap. 8vo, 3*s*. 6*d*.

—— *The Clouds.* By the same Editor. *Third Edition.*
[Extra fcap. 8vo, 3*s*.

—— *The Frogs.* By the same Editor .   .   [Extra fcap. 8vo, 3*s*.

—— *The Knights.* By the same Editor.   .   [Extra fcap. 8vo, 3*s*.

—— *The Wasps.* By the same Editor .   . [Extra fcap. 8vo, 3*s*. 6*d*.

Cebes. *Tabula.* With Introduction and Notes, by C. S. JERRAM, M.A.
[Extra fcap. 8vo, 2*s*. 6*d*.

*** Abridged School Edition. Paper boards,* 1*s*. 6*d*.

Demosthenes. *Orations against Philip.* With Introduction and Notes. By EVELYN ABBOTT, M.A., and P. E. MATHESON, M.A.

    Vol. I. *Philippic I* and *Olynthiacs I—III.* . . [Extra fcap. 8vo, 3*s.*

    Vol. II. *De Pace, Philippic II, De Chersoneso, Philippic III.* . [4*s.* 6*d.*

    Philippics only, reprinted from the above, 2*s.* 6*d.*

Euripides. *Alcestis.* By C. S. JERRAM, M.A. [Extra fcap. 8vo, 2*s.* 6*d.*

—— *Bacchae.* By A. H. CRUICKSHANK, M.A. . . [3*s.* 6*d.*

—— *Cyclops.* By W. E. LONG, M.A. . [Extra fcap. 8vo, 2*s.* 6*d.*

—— *Hecuba.* By C. H. RUSSELL, M.A. [Extra fcap. 8vo, 2*s.* 6*d.*

—— *Helena.* By C. S. JERRAM, M.A. . . [Extra fcap. 8vo, 3*s.*

—— *Heracleidae.* By the same Editor. . . [Extra fcap. 8vo, 3*s.*

—— *Ion.* By the same Editor. . . . [Extra fcap. 8vo, 3*s.*

—— *Iphigenia in Tauris.* By the same Editor. [Extra fcap. 8vo, 3*s.*

—— *Medea.* With Introduction, Notes, and Appendices. By C. B. HEBERDEN, M.A. *In one or two Parts.* . . . [Extra fcap. 8vo, 2*s.*

Herodotus. Book IX. Edited, with Notes, by EVELYN ABBOTT, M.A. *In one or two Parts.* . . . . . [Extra fcap. 8vo, 3*s.*

—— *Selections.* Edited, with Introduction, Notes, and a Map, by W. W. MERRY, D.D. . . . . . [Extra fcap. 8vo, 2*s.* 6*d.*

Homer for Beginners. *Iliad,* Book III. By M. T. TATHAM, M.A.
    [Extra fcap. 8vo, 1*s.* 6*d.*

Homer. *Iliad,* Books I–XII. With an Introduction, a brief Homeric Grammar, and Notes. By D. B. MONRO, M.A. . . [Extra fcap. 8vo, 6*s.*

—— *Iliad,* Books XIII–XXIV. By the same Editor. . . [6*s.*

—— *Iliad,* Book I. By the same Editor. . [Extra fcap. 8vo, 1*s.* 6*d.*

—— *Iliad,* Book XXI. By HERBERT HAILSTONE, M.A. [1*s.* 6*d.*

—— *Odyssey,* Books I–XII. By W. W. MERRY, D.D. . . [5*s.*

—— *Odyssey,* Books I and II. By the same Editor. . [Each 1*s.* 6*d.*

—— *Odyssey,* Books VI and VII. By the same Editor. . [1*s.* 6*d.*

—— *Odyssey,* Books VII–XII. By the same Editor. [Extra fcap. 8vo, 3*s.*

—— *Odyssey,* Books XIII–XXIV. By the same Editor. *New Edition.* . . . . [Extra fcap. 8vo, 5*s.*

—— *Odyssey,* Books XIII–XVIII. By the same Editor.
    [Extra fcap. 8vo, 3*s.*

Lucian. *Vera Historia.* By C. S. JERRAM, M.A. [Extra fcap. 8vo, 1*s.* 6*d.*

Lysias. *Epitaphios.* Edited by F. J. SNELL, B.A. [Extra fcap. 8vo, 2*s.*

Plato. *The Apology.* With Introduction and Notes. By ST. GEORGE STOCK, M.A. *Second Edition.* . . . . [Extra fcap. 8vo, 2*s.* 6*d.*

—— *Crito.* With Introduction and Notes. By the same Editor. [2*s.*

—— *Meno.* By the same Editor. . . [Extra fcap. 8vo, 2*s.* 6*d.*

Plato. *Selections.* With Introductions and Notes. By J. PURVES, M.A., and Preface by B. JOWETT, M.A. *Second Edition.* . [Extra fcap. 8vo, 5s.

Plutarch. *Lives of the Gracchi.* Edited, with Introduction, Notes, and Indices, by G. E. UNDERHILL, M.A. . . . . [Crown 8vo, 4s. 6d.

Sophocles. Edited, with Introductions and English Notes, by LEWIS CAMPBELL, M.A., and EVELYN ABBOTT, M.A. New Edition. 2 Vols. 10s. 6d. [or, Vol. I. Text, 4s. 6d. ; Vol. II. Notes, 6s.

☛ *Also in single Plays. Extra fcap. 8vo, limp, 2s. each.*

—— *Oedipus Rex:* Dindorf's Text, with Notes by W. BASIL JONES, D.D., late Bishop of St. David's. . . . [Extra fcap. 8vo, *limp*, 1s. 6d.

Theocritus. Edited, with Notes, by H. KYNASTON, D.D. (late SNOW). *Fifth Edition.* . . . . . [Extra fcap. 8vo, 4s. 6d.

Thucydides. Book I. With Introduction, Notes, and Maps. By W. H. FORBES, M.A. . . . . [8vo, 8s. 6d.

Xenophon. *Easy Selections.* By J. S. PHILLPOTTS, B.C.L., and C. S. JERRAM, M.A. With Map. *Third Edition.* . . . . . [3s. 6d.

—— *Selections* (for Schools). With Notes and Maps. By J. S. PHILLPOTTS, B.C.L. *Fourth Edition.* . . . [Extra fcap. 8vo, 3s. 6d.

A Key to Sections I–III, for Teachers only, price 2s. 6d. net.

—— *Anabasis.* Book I. With Introduction, Notes, and Map. By J. MARSHALL, M.A. . . . . [Extra fcap. 8vo, 2s. 6d.

—— *Anabasis,* Book II. With Notes and Map. By C. S. JERRAM, M.A. . . . . [Extra fcap. 8vo, 2s.

—— *Anabasis,* Book III. With Introduction, Analysis, Notes, &c. By J. MARSHALL, M.A. . . . . . . [Extra fcap. 8vo, 2s. 6d.

—— *Anabasis,* Book IV. With Introduction, Notes, &c. By the same Editor. . . . . [Extra fcap. 8vo, 2s.

—— —— Books III and IV. By the same Editor. [Extra fcap. 8vo, 3s.

—— *Vocabulary to the Anabasis.* By the same Editor. . [1s. 6d.

—— *Cyropaedia,* Book I. With Introduction and Notes. By C. BIGG, D.D. . . . . [Extra fcap. 8vo, 2s.

—— *Cyropaedia,* Books IV, V. With Introduction and Notes. By the same Editor. . . . . [Extra fcap. 8vo, 2s. 6d.

—— *Hellenica,* Books I, II. With Introduction and Notes. By G. E. UNDERHILL, M.A. . . . . [Extra fcap. 8vo, 3s.

—— *Memorabilia.* Edited for the use of Schools, with Introduction and Notes, &c. by J. MARSHALL, M.A. . . . [Extra fcap. 8vo, 4s. 6d.

Oxford

AT THE CLARENDON PRESS

London, Edinburgh, and New York

HENRY FROWDE